THE MOST
TRUSTED NAME
IN **TRAVEL**

BELIZE

2nd Edition

By Ali Wunderman

FROMMER'S STAR RATINGS SYSTEM

Every hotel, restaurant, and attraction listed in this guide has been ranked for quality and value. Here's what the stars mean:

★ Recommended
★★ Highly Recommended
★★★ A must! Don't miss!

AN IMPORTANT NOTE

The world is a dynamic place. Hotels change ownership, restaurants hike their prices, museums alter their opening hours, and buses and trains change their routings. And all of this can occur in the several months after our authors have visited, inspected, and written about these hotels, restaurants, museums, and transportation services. Though we have made valiant efforts to keep all our information fresh and up-to-date, some few changes can inevitably occur in the periods before a revised edition of this guidebook is published. So please bear with us if a tiny number of the details in this book have changed. Please also note that we have no responsibility or liability for any inaccuracy or errors or omissions, or for inconvenience, loss, damage, or expenses suffered by anyone as a result of assertions in this guide.

Some 60% of Belize is jungle, and 80% of that is protected by the government. In this photo, visitors hike through pristine lowlands of Mayflower Bocawin National Park, which is just a few miles from the town of Hopkins (p. 186).

CONTENTS

A LOOK AT BELIZE

When I took my children to Belize on spring break several years back, a miracle occurred: For a full two weeks they didn't argue once. What with tubing on rivers, climbing pyramids, snorkeling with giant turtles, rappelling down cliffs, exploring caves and more, they were too tired—and happy—to quarrel. Belize is *that* exciting, a relatively small country with pristine jungles, intricate cave systems to explore, the world's second longest coral reef, and, perhaps most intriguingly, remnants from what was once the mighty Mayan Empire, the sophisticated, powerful group of nation-states that ruled this part of the planet for centuries. In the pages ahead are photos of some of the adventures you'll have and the sights you'll see. And then following that, is our author Ali Wunderman's detailed, savvy advice on how to make the most of a Belize vacation. Enjoy!

—Pauline Frommer, Editorial Director

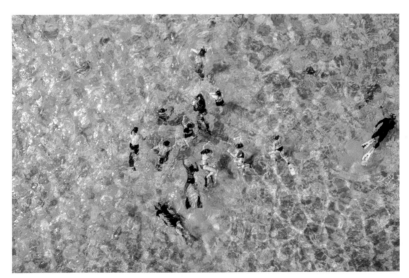

INLAND BELIZE

Mountain Pine Ridge (p. 278) is the oldest and largest protected forest reserve in Belize. It is home to several spectacular waterfalls, including the tallest one in the country.

A detail from the ruins at Lamanai (p. 231). The site was continuously inhabited from 500 B.C. until the Spanish arrived in the 1670s, which means that this is one of Belize's few Mayan sites to still retain its original name. Lamanai is thought to mean "submerged crocodile."

Another photo of Mountain Pine Reserve which, because of its elevation, is a place of pine needles more than palm fronds. The reserve encompasses some 300 square miles of deep ravines, dramatic granite ridges, lazy looping rivers, and lots of wildlife.

Travelers entering the Actun Tunichil Muknal (ATM; p. 251) caves, an important archeological site. After swimming into the cave, visitors climb up to a cathedral-like chamber where they learn how the ancient Mayans altered the cave's structure for religious use, and view museum-worthy artifacts that have been calcified to the floor.

Inside ATM: Known as the "Crystal Maiden," this skeleton of a teenaged girl was likely a victim of human sacrifice.

Vacationers rappel into Actun Loch Tunich, today known as the "Black Hole," another popular caving expedition.

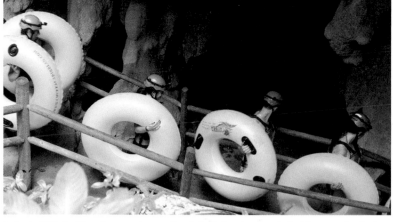

Belize is riddled with underground caves, thanks to its limestone crust. And there are few better ways to explore these systems of (often) water-filled caverns than by tubing.

A Tarzan-style view of Belize's jungles is available at numerous zipline courses across the country.

The Rio On Pools splash over this granite "lawn," creating a series of pools and small waterfalls for visitors to bathe in. See p. 281.

The Belmopan region is renowned for its equestrian centers (p. 246).

Five side-by-side falls, plus a swimmable pool at the bottom, makes Five Sisters Falls a very popular spot (p. 282).

Tikal (p. 290) was the capital of one of the most powerful kingdoms in the ancient Mayan world. Some of its ruins date back to the 4th century B.C.

Xunantunich (p. 264) is another major ancient Mayan site, its name translating as "Sculpture of Lady." Over the past century and a half, locals have claimed that the lady in the name haunts the site. She wears white, her eyes glow red, and she's been seen climbing El Castillo (pictured) before disappearing into its stone facade.

Some 20,000 Mennonites (p. 228) live in Belize, their ancestors having come here in the 19th and 20th centuries from Russia, Canada, and the United States. Many eschew the use of electricity, and dress in traditional clothing.

Visitors to St. Herman's Cave (p. 253) see ancient Mayan artifacts and a wide variety of eye-popping speleothems (stalactites, stalagmites, flowstones, crystals, and more).

The ancient city of Caracol (p. 282) covered an area far bigger than the one occupied by Belize City today. It was a capital city during the Classical Mayan period (A.D. 250–550).

A sculpture found in on-site excavations, on view in Caracol's museum.

A baboon hangs from a tree in Belmopan.

REEF & COAST

Steady trade winds, and more than 400 islands to explore, make Belize one of the world's top sailing destinations.

To celebrate the start of the fishing season, San Pedro holds a yearly lobster festival (p. 146), with concerts, contests, and lots of lobster, prepared every which way.

Which number will the fowl foul? That's the main question as gamblers gather each Thursday night at Ambergris Caye's "Chicken Drop." See p. 24.

Traditional dancers in Orange Walk Town.

Hanging out on the beach in San Pedro.

Taking a lesson at the Lebeha Drumming Center (p. 188) in Hopkins Village.

Snorkelers off the shore of Laughing Bird Caye.

Jacques Cousteau called the Blue Hole (p. 167) one of the top five scuba diving destinations in the world. It's a sinkhole, formed before the oceans covered this area, and it is over 400 feet deep.

The Belize Barrier Reef Reserve System teems with life and is well preserved. The Blue Hole is just one part of the extended system.

Divers who attempt the Blue Hole swim through caves that were formed some 153,000 years ago and still have stalactites and stalagmites from when this sinkhole was above the ocean.

Taking a spa day at Turtle Inn (p. 202), the resort owned by film director Francis Ford Coppola in Placencia, is an international experience. The design of the spa is Balinese, the products used are organic and Belizean, and the specialty is Thai massage.

Biking is the perfect way to get around quiet Hopkins Village (p. 186).

Goods for sale at Hopkins' yearly mango festival.

Nightlife in Caye Caulker is laid back, friendly, and doesn't involve gambling on poultry.

In 1961, Hurricane Hattie caused Caye Caulker to split in two. The waterway that's now between the two sides of the island, called "The Split," is a favorite spot for watersports and socializing.

The private island resort of Cayo Espanto offers over-water bungalows. It is an incredibly luxurious version of the prototypical Belizean resort, many of which feature shiny wood floors and walls, and beds handsomely draped in mosquito netting.

The Pan Yaad Steel band concerts.

People are pelted with paint during the Ambergris Caye Don Juan Festival (p. 139).

Bonefish are prized by fly fishermen and are the most numerous species in Belize. While they are relatively eager to take flies and lures, they put up a challenging fight once hooked.

THE BEST OF BELIZE

Belize proves the cliché that big things come in small packages. This tiny Central American country has the longest continuous barrier reef in the Western Hemisphere; the largest known Classic Mayan city, Caracol; and the highest concentration per square mile of the largest new-world cat, the jaguar. It also has one of the most extensive and easily accessible cave systems for amateur and experienced spelunkers alike, as well as a nearly endless supply of some of the world's best snorkeling and scuba-diving opportunities.

The best part about all these world-class places and experiences is that Belize's compact size makes it easy to sample a wide range of them in a short period of time. The lists below should help you zero in on a few personal bests of your own.

THE best PURELY BELIZEAN EXPERIENCES

o **Sitting on the Dock of a Caye:** One of the most distinctive features of most beachfront hotels in Belize is the private pier jutting out into the sea. Many of these have a thatch-roofed shade structure at the end, often strung with hammocks. This is a great place to read a book, take a siesta, or simply spend an hour or two marveling at the ocean's amazing shades of blue. See chapters 7 and 8.

o **Betting on a Chicken Drop:** A chicken drop is a sort of island version of roulette, and is arguably more fun. Numbers are painted on a grid and bets are placed. Then, a chicken is set loose on the grid, and whichever number it "drops" (poops) on, is the winner. In addition to any monetary winnings, the "winner" often must clean the grid. You'll find a chicken drop held every Thursday night at the Wahoo's Lounge on Ambergris Caye. See chapter 7.

o **Staying with a Maya Family:** It certainly isn't going to be like a night at the Four Seasons, but if you're looking for a real cultural exchange, you should consider staying with a traditional Maya family. **The Maya Village Homestay Network** (demdatsdoin@btl.net; ⓒ **722-2470**) can organize this for you. See "Punta Gorda & the Toledo District" in chapter 8.

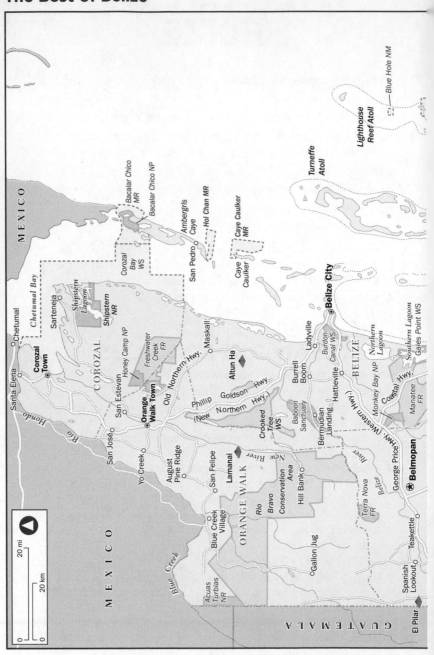

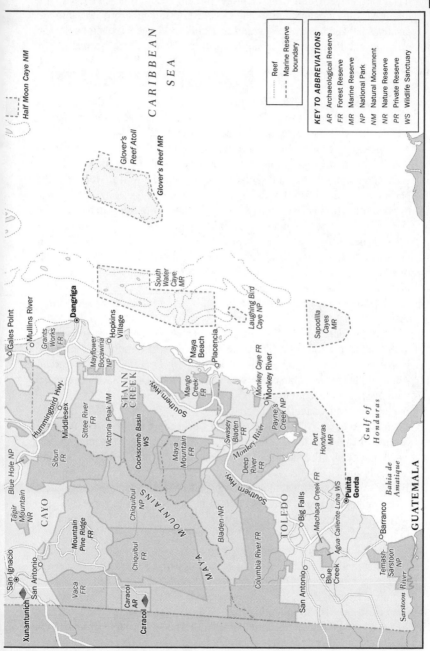

o **Spending the Night in a Maya Ceremonial City:** An intimate and luxurious nature lodge, **Chan Chich Lodge** (p. 235) is built right on the site of a minor Mayan ceremonial city. The hills just outside your private cabin are unexcavated residences and pyramids. Ruins and basic excavations dot the grounds, and the surrounding rainforests are rich in bird and animal life.

THE best OF NATURAL BELIZE

o **The Cayes & Barrier Reef:** Running the entire length of the country's coastline, the Belize Barrier Reef is the second-longest continuous barrier reef in the world. Headlines were made in early 2018 after the Belizean government agreed to ban offshore oil exploration along the reef, meaning it will stay pristine for a long time. Here you will find some of the best snorkeling opportunities and scuba-diving sites in the world. Moreover, the barrier reef is lined with hundreds and hundreds of small islands, or cayes. Most are uninhabited. These cayes range in size from tiny patches of sand or mangrove smaller than a football field to the larger and more developed vacation destination islands of Caye Caulker and Ambergris Caye. Whether you want the hustle and bustle of the latter, the deserted isle feel of a smaller or even private caye, or something in between, your choices are many and uniformly inviting. See chapters 7 and 8.

o **The Atolls:** Belize's three mid-ocean atolls are arguably more spectacular than the barrier reef and its many cayes. Unique formations of small islands and reef surrounding a mid-ocean saltwater lagoon, atolls are an isolated and stunning phenomenon. There are only four in the Caribbean, and Belize has three of them: Turneffe Island, Lighthouse Reef, and Glover's Reef. These atolls are very sparsely developed, and any visit here will be imbued with a sense of adventure, isolation, and romance. See "The Outer Atolls" in chapter 7 and "Dangriga" in chapter 8.

o **Cockscomb Basin Wildlife Sanctuary & Cockscomb Basin Forest Reserve** (Southern Belize): This is a huge protected area composed of rugged, forested mountains. The sanctuary was designed to protect and help researchers study the largest new-world cat, the jaguar. The park is also home to Belize's other four wildcat species, as well as Baird's tapirs, coati-mundi, tayra, kinkajous, deer, peccaries, anteaters, armadillos, and some 300 species of birds. Inside the park you'll also find Victoria Peak, the country's highest mountain. See "Dangriga" in chapter 8.

o **Crooked Tree Wildlife Sanctuary** (Northern Belize): A swampy lowland that is home to more than 250 resident species of birds, Crooked Tree serves as a resting spot for scores of migratory species. It is also the principal nesting site of the endangered jabiru stork, the largest bird in the Americas. The sanctuary is an excellent place to spot other wildlife as well, including crocodiles, iguanas, coati-mundi, and howler monkeys. The best way to explore Crooked Tree is by paddling around the network of lagoons in a dugout canoe. See chapter 9.

o **Río Bravo Conservation Area** (Northern Belize): This massive mixed tract of virgin forest, sustainable-yield managed forest, and recovering reforestation areas is home to nearly 400 bird species and more than 200 species of tropical trees. It also supports a healthy population of most of the new-world cat species, and is one of the best areas in the Americas to try your luck in spotting a jaguar. The Río Bravo Conservation Area is also home to La Milpa, an ongoing excavation of a major Mayan ceremonial city. See "Going West: Río Bravo Conservation Area, La Milpa & Chan Chich" in chapter 9.

o **Caves** (Cayo District and Western Belize): Belize has an extensive network of caves, which were considered by the ancient Maya to be a mystical portal between the world of the living and the underworld of spirits and the dead. They called this mystical realm Xibalba. In almost every explored cave in Belize, some evidence of use by the Mayans has been uncovered. Fire pits, campsites, burial mounds, and ritual altars have all been found. Numerous pieces of pottery and abundant skeletons, bones, and artifacts have also been encountered. These caves are relatively easily accessible and you should not leave Belize without at least one foray into Xibalba. There are lots of great caves to visit, but if you had to choose just one, I'd recommend **Actun Tunichil Muknal** (p. 251).

o **Río On Pools** (Cayo District and Western Belize): This series of flowing falls and pools is somewhat reminiscent of Ocho Ríos in Jamaica. While the views and swimming are fine at the base of the falls, it's worth the hike upstream to even better views and numerous pools flowing between big rocks, which are perfect for sunbathing. It can get crowded on weekends, when locals come for family picnics and getaways. See chapter 10.

THE best DIVING & SNORKELING

Belize is rightly considered one of the top scuba-diving and snorkeling destinations on the planet. The Belize Barrier Reef, second only in size to Australia's Great Barrier Reef, runs the length of its coastline, and the country has three open-ocean atolls. Diving and snorkeling are superb all along the barrier reef; the following are just a few of the truly standout sites and dives.

o **Shark-Ray Alley & Hol Chan Marine Reserve** (Northern Cayes and Atolls): These two very popular snorkeling sites are threatened with overcrowding but still live up to their billing. Shark-Ray Alley guarantees a very close encounter with schools of large stingrays and nurse sharks. The experience provides a substantial adrenaline rush for all but the most nonchalant and veteran divers. Hol Chan Marine Reserve is an excellent snorkeling destination composed of a narrow channel cutting through a rich and well-maintained shallow coral reef. See "Ambergris Caye" in chapter 7.

o **Caye Caulker** (Northern Cayes and Atolls): If you're looking for a relaxed vacation spot to serve as a base for some good snorkeling, you can't do much better than Caye Caulker, which has some excellent and easily accessible snorkeling sites. It's also less developed and less crowded than its more popular neighbor, Ambergris Caye. Many of the dive sites are a very short boat ride from shore. See "Caye Caulker" in chapter 7.

o **Turneffe Island & Lighthouse Reef Atolls** (Northern Cayes and Atolls): For many divers coming to Belize, these spots are the holy grail, and justifiably so. Both of these mid-ocean atoll formations feature nearly endless opportunities for world-class wall, drift, and coral-garden diving. As a cherry to top this cake, this is also where you'll find the Blue Hole. A host of dive operators all across Belize offer day trips to dive these sites, although these usually involve a 90-minute to 3-hour ride each way. Alternatively, you can stay at one of the very few lodges out here, or take a vacation on a live-aboard dive boat. See "The Outer Atolls" in chapter 7.

o **Glover's Reef Atoll** (Southern Belize): Glover's Reef is the third of Belize's mid-ocean atolls. The diving here is spectacular and underexploited. As compared to the Turneffe Island and Lighthouse Reef atolls, far fewer day-trippers visit the dive sites around Glover's Reef Atoll. The best way to really take advantage of the diving and snorkeling is to stay out here, and for this, **Isla Marisol Resort** (p. 183) is your best option.

o **Gladden Spit** (Southern Belize): More or less due east of Placencia, Gladden Spit is a world-renowned spot for diving with massive whale sharks. This mid-ocean site is the natural spawning ground for a variety of marine species. Whale sharks come regularly to feed on the energetically rich and very plentiful reproductive effluence. Whale shark sightings are fairly common here from late March to early July, more so on the days preceding and following the full moon. The sharks tend to feed and cruise close to the surface, so snorkelers can also enjoy the spectacle, but there's no guarantee that this is where they'll be, so diving is your best chance to get close to the gentle giants. See "Placencia" in chapter 8.

THE best NONDIVING ADVENTURES

o **Chartering a Sailboat for Isolated Island Explorations:** The protected waters, steady gentle trade winds, and hundreds of isolated islands and anchorages make Belize an ideal place for bareboat charters. You can charter these as bareboats, or with a skipper and crew. Given the shallow draft, increased interior space, and reduced drag, a multihull is your best bet. **The Moorings** (p. 198) and **TMM** (p. 134) are two large-scale charter companies with operations on Ambergris Caye and in Placencia.

o **Fly-Fishing for Bonefish, Permit & Tarpon on the Outer Atoll Flats:** Belize is a world-class fishing destination, and while offshore fishing for bigger game is possible, the real draw here is fly-fishing for feisty and world-record-size bonefish, permit, and tarpon (actually, the tarpon get as big as most deep-sea game). **Turneffe Flats** (p. 167) is an excellent fishing operation located on Turneffe Island Atoll.

o **Kayaking & Camping Around Glover's Reef Atoll:** The relatively calm protected waters of the atoll and manageable distances between islands make this a perfect place to explore under your own power, paddling a one- or two-person sea kayak. Both **Island Expeditions** (p. 182) and **Slickrock Adventures** (p. 182) run adventurous multiday kayak tours to small camps and lodges on private isolated cayes of Glover's Reef Atoll.

o **Riding an Inner Tube Through the Caves Branch River Cave System** (Cayo District and Western Belize): This is certainly the most popular and probably the easiest way to explore Belize's vast network of caves. You strap on a battery-powered headlamp, climb into the center of an inflated car inner tube, and gently float through a series of limestone caves, your headlamp illuminating the stalactites and the occasional bat. The entire sensation is eerie and slightly claustrophobic, but fun nonetheless—especially if you go with a small group on a day when the caves are not crowded. See "Belmopan" in chapter 10.

o **Canoeing, Kayaking, or Inner Tubing on the Macal or Mopan Rivers** (Western Belize): These two rivers converge around the city of San Ignacio, in the Cayo District. Upstream from town on either river are ample opportunities for paddling or floating. Depending on the water level and the section you choose, this can range from a lazy canoe or inner-tube paddle to a Class III kayak trip over rushing rapids. Any of the hotels in the Cayo District can help you organize one of these adventures. See chapter 10.

o **Horseback Riding Through the Cayo District** (Western Belize): The Cayo District is a perfect area to explore on horseback. Rides can be combined with visits to jungle waterfalls and swimming holes, as well as nearby Mayan ruins. **Mountain Equestrian Trails** (p. 286) has one of the better stables and horse-riding operations in the Cayo District.

THE best DAY HIKES & NATURE WALKS

o **Cockscomb Basin Forest Reserve** (Southern Belize): In addition to being the world's only dedicated reserve designed to protect the endangered jaguar, Cockscomb Basin is also home to an amazing array of tropical flora and fauna. It boasts an excellent network of well-maintained trails. Truly adventurous hikers can arrange to climb Belize's tallest mountain, Victoria Peak, which is found inside this reserve. See "Dangriga" in chapter 8.

o **Guanacaste National Park** (Cayo District and Western Belize): Located right on the side of the George Price (Western) Highway, about 3.2km (2 miles) north of Belmopan, the gentle trails and easy accessibility here make this an excellent choice for an introduction to tropical forests. There are nearly 3.2km (2 miles) of well-marked and well-maintained trails in the park, with several benches for sitting and observing wildlife. The park is named after a giant Guanacaste tree, and is bordered on the west by Roaring Creek and on the north by the Belize River. See "Belmopan" in chapter 10.

o **Blue Hole National Park** (Cayo District and Western Belize): The hike here combines a pleasant 2.4km (1.5-mile) hike through dense primary and secondary tropical forest with the chance to hike farther inside the large and long St. Herman's Cave, while also stopping for a refreshing dip in the park's beautiful namesake swimming hole, or cenote. If you hire a guide, you can actually hike for several miles more inside the stunning **Crystalline Cave.** See "Belmopan" in chapter 10.

o **Tikal National Park** (Tikal, Guatemala): In addition to being one of the best excavated and preserved ancient Mayan cities, Tikal offers an extensive trail network running through dense tropical rainforest. Howler and spider monkeys clamor overhead, and parrots squawk through the canopy. You can see a wealth of tropical fauna here, as you slowly wander from plaza to plaza and pyramid to pyramid. See "Tikal" in chapter 11.

THE best BIRD-WATCHING

Belize is home to some 618 species of resident and migratory birds. With varied ecosystems including coastal mangroves and swamps, isolated barrier-reef cayes, dense tropical rainforest, and clear, open savannahs, Belize is a wonderful destination for avid bird-watchers and amateurs alike.

o **Half Moon Caye National Monument** (Northern Cayes and Atolls): This isolated wildlife and marine reserve is a major nesting site for the red-footed booby. Thousands of these birds can be spotted on the island at any one time; it's an amazing sight. In addition, you can spot a wide range of resident and migratory seabirds here. See "The Outer Atolls" in chapter 7.

o **Man-O-War Caye** (Southern Belize): This small caye is a government-monitored bird sanctuary and major nesting site for the magnificent frigate, or man-o-war. Circling the island in a small boat, you'll see hundreds of these large seabirds roosting on and hovering above the tiny caye. In addition to the frigates, the island is home to a large community of brown boobies. See "Dangriga" in chapter 8.

o **Cockscomb Basin Forest Reserve** (Southern Belize): In addition to its jaguar reserve, the Cockscomb Basin Forest Reserve is home to a large number of tropical forest–dwelling bird species. This is one of the best sites in Belize to spot the large and loud scarlet macaw, as well as several toucan species and the imposing king vulture. See "Dangriga" in chapter 8.

o **Crooked Tree Wildlife Sanctuary** (Northern Belize): This rich wetland is perhaps the top bird-watching site in Belize. Home to hundreds of resident and migrant species, it is one of the best spots to see the giant and rare jabiru stork, especially during the dry season. You can spot various heron and kingfisher species here, as well as the yellow-lored parrot and Yucatán jay. See "En Route North: Crooked Tree Wildlife Sanctuary" in chapter 9.

o **New River Lagoon** (Northern Belize): Reach this wide open lagoon via the winding and narrow New River; it branches off into a network of narrow canals, streams, and marshlands, the perfect and preferred habitat for a wide range of bird species. Common species sighted include the black-collared hawk, northern jacana, and purple gallinule. You can combine a bird-watching trip here with a visit to the Lamanai Mayan ruin, which also has wonderful opportunities for bird-watching all along its trails and from the peaks of its pyramids. See chapter 9.

o **Shipstern Nature Reserve** (Northern Belize): Covering some 8,903 hectares (22,000 acres), including several distinct ecosystems, Shipstern Nature Reserve is home to more than 250 bird species. You can explore the area on foot, as well as in little dugout canoes and flat-bottomed boats. See "Corozal Town" in chapter 9.

o **Caracol** (Cayo District and Western Belize): Also a major Mayan ruin, Caracol and its surrounding forest are prime bird-watching destinations. The area is replete with numerous tropical forest species, including such beauties as the keel-billed motmot, violaceous trogon, ocellated turkey, crested guan, and great curassow. Some visitors have even spotted the harpy eagle here. See "Mountain Pine Ridge & Caracol" in chapter 10.

THE best MAYAN RUINS

o **Altun Ha** (Northern Belize): One of the most easily accessible Mayan ruins from Belize City, Altun Ha is a small yet well-preserved site featuring two large central plazas surrounded by midsized pyramids and mounds. Only a few of the most imposing temples, tombs, and pyramids have been uncovered and rebuilt; hundreds more lie under the jungle foliage. Many jade, pearl, and obsidian artifacts have been discovered here, including the unique jade-head sculpture of **Kinich Ahau** (the Mayan sun god), the largest carved jade piece from the Mayan era. See chapter 9.

o **Lamanai** (Northern Belize): One of the more interesting and picturesque Mayan ruins in Belize, Lamanai features three large pyramids, a couple of residential areas, various restored stelae, and open plazas, as well as a small and unique ball court. Moreover, the ruins of two 16th-century Spanish churches are nearby. The site is set on the banks of the New River Lagoon. Since it was still occupied by the Maya when the Spanish arrived, Lamanai is one of the few sites in Belize to retain its traditional name. See "The Submerged Crocodile: Lamanai" in chapter 9.

o **Xunantunich** (Cayo District and Western Belize): Xunantunich is an impressive, well-excavated, and easily accessible Mayan site, close to San Ignacio. Xunantunich was a thriving Mayan city during the Classic Period, from about A.D. 600 to 900. You'll find carved stelae and one very tall main pyramid here. To reach the ruins, you must cross the Mopan River aboard a tiny hand-cranked car-ferry in the village of San José Succotz. See "San Ignacio" in chapter 10.

o **El Pilar** (Cayo District and Western Belize): El Pilar just may be the most underappreciated major Mayan city in Mesoamerica. The site is huge, with more than 25 known plazas, covering some 40 hectares (100 acres) that straddle the Belize and Guatemala border. Excavation and exploration here are in their early stages, and I actually think that, in time, El Pilar will join the ranks of Caracol and Tikal as one of the major Classic Mayan sites of this region. See "San Ignacio" in chapter 10.

○ **Caracol** (Cayo District and Western Belize): Caracol (www.caracol.org) is the largest known Mayan archaeological site in Belize, and one of the great Mayan city-states of the Classic era. Located deep within the Chiquibil Forest Reserve, the ruins are not nearly as well excavated as those at Tikal, Xunantunich, or any number of other sites. However, this is part of Caracol's charm. The main pyramid here, **Caana** or "Sky Palace," stands some 42m (138 ft.) high; it is the tallest Mayan building in Belize and still the tallest man-made structure in the country. See chapter 10.

○ **Tikal:** Just over the Belizean border in neighboring Guatemala, **Tikal** is the grandest of the surviving Classic Mayan cities. Tikal is far more extensively excavated than any ruins in Belize. The pyramids here are some of the most perfect examples of ceremonial architecture in the Mayan world. The peaks of several temples poke through the dense rainforest canopy. Toucans and parrots fly about, and the loudest noise you'll hear is the guttural call of howler monkeys. In its heyday, the city probably covered as much as 65 sq. km (25 sq. miles) and supported a population of more than 100,000. See "Tikal" in chapter 11.

THE best VIEWS

○ The **Blue Hole** is probably best experienced and viewed from above. A perfectly round sinkhole measuring some 305m (1,000 ft.) across in the middle of the Lighthouse Reef Atoll lagoon, the Blue Hole appears as a deep, dark blue circle in a sea of shimmering turquoise. The best way to get this bird's-eye view is with **Astrum Helicopters** (p. 45). See chapters 3 and 7 for more information.

○ If you're lucky enough to grab a seat along the railing at the **Wet Lizard** (p. 117), you'll have a ringside seat to the hustle and bustle of Belize City's busy harbor. Traditional sailboats bob at anchor, speedboats come and go to and from the cayes, and cruise ship tenders provide a steady shuttle service for passengers between the offshore ships at anchor and the city's main pier.

○ Try watching the **sun rise over the New River Lagoon** from a hammock strung on the front porch of your veranda at the **Lamanai Outpost Lodge** (p. 233). It is a view you'll always treasure. The view is lovely throughout the day, but it's worth waking up early for. See chapter 9.

○ Although the **main temple at Cerros** is just a diminutive 21m (69 ft.) tall, it offers excellent views across Corozal Bay. Moreover, this is an easy climb for most, and far easier than the climbs to the tops of most other major Mayan ceremonial pyramids. See chapter 9.

○ The main pyramid at Xunantunich, **El Castillo,** rises to 39m (128 ft.). It's a steep climb, but the view from the top is worth it. On a clear day, you'll be able to make out the twin border towns of Benque Viejo, Belize, and Melchor de Menchos, Guatemala. See chapter 10.

○ Poking their heads over the dense rainforest canopy, the **pyramids of Tikal** offer some of the best views to be found in all of Central America. Temple IV is the tallest and the preferred platform for enjoying this view (especially by *Star Wars* fans), but Temple II, just off the Great Plaza, is really just as good. Get here early and wait for the fog to clear, or stay late to enjoy the views without the hustle and bustle of busloads of tourists. See chapter 11.

THE best DESTINATIONS FOR FAMILIES

o **Belize Zoo** (near Belize City): The Belize Zoo (p. 107) houses more than 125 animals, all native Belizean species. It is considered a national treasure and a model for the possibilities of a conservation-based zoo. The zoo itself is wonderfully laid out, on meandering trails with large and well-maintained enclosures for the animals. For a real treat, you can stay in some cozy cabins here and take a private night tour of the zoo.

o **Old Belize** (Belize City): Old Belize (p. 105) is part museum, part playground, part beach, and part adventure attraction. There's something here for everyone, and plenty for the kids, including a large water slide. It's easy to spend several hours, if not a whole day, here.

o **Ambergris Caye** (Northern Cayes and Atolls): Ambergris Caye is the most developed of Belize's beach and diving destinations. As such, it has the greatest selection of hotels and activities, many of them either geared toward or just plain great for kids. From snorkeling and paragliding to touring the island on golf carts and visiting the Not-So-Secret Beach, there's plenty to keep families and kids of all ages occupied here. **Xanadu Island Resort** (p. 142) and **Mahogany Bay Village** (p. 141) are good choices for families.

o **Almond Beach Resort & Spa and Jaguar Reef Lodge & Spa** (p. 189): These mid-size beachfront resorts, both Viva Belize properties, have a range of amenities and activities that will make parents happy and keep kids occupied. In addition to a couple of pools and a long beach, they have sea kayaks and mountain bikes, and an extensive menu of daily tours and activities.

o **The Inn at Robert's Grove** (p. 202): This is another small beach resort that is well-suited for families. As at Almond Beach & Jaguar Reef, there's a wide enough range of activities available here to keep families active and interested for a full vacation. What makes this place trump Jaguar Reef are two private cayes, excellent restaurants, and outstanding service.

o **Cayo District** (Western Belize): The Cayo District is the heart of Belize's Mayan world, as well as its prime ecotourism destination. Between a full plate of active adventure activities and a steady diet of Mayan ruins and ancient burial caves, families will find this a great place to spend time in Belize. Not only is **Chaa Creek** (p. 275) extremely comfortable for families, but they also have their own butterfly breeding project and natural history museum on-site. And if parents need a little pampering, they also have an excellent spa.

o **Caves Branch** (Cayo District and Western Belize): You'll be heroes in your kids' eyes after you take them inner tubing through the dark and spooky network of limestone caves traversed by the slow-moving Caves Branch River. Families with a real hankering for adventure should head to **Ian Anderson's Caves Branch** (p. 258), which offers a wide range of guided cave adventures and accommodations that are plush, but almost always include bunk beds for the kids.

THE best LUXURY HOTELS & RESORTS

- o **Turneffe Island Lodge** (The Outer Atolls; p. 168): Gilligan and his lost friends never had it so good. At this near-deserted island lodge guests stay in luxurious digs (there's even a glam swimming pool), eat food that's grown on site or caught nearby, and engage in some of the best fishing, snorkeling, and scuba diving in Belize, with an expert, attentive staff leading excursions.
- o **Mahogany Bay Village** (Ambergris Caye; p. 141): Belize's first truly large-scale resort, this "townlet" is brand new and holds nothing back when it comes to providing a high-end experience, with an on-site spa, private beach club, and beautifully-appointed colonial rooms with modern amenities.
- o **Matachica** (Ambergris Caye; p. 144): This intimate beachfront hotel has a refined and relaxed air of style. The individual cabins are very inviting and artistically designed. The excellent restaurant, chic bar, large pool, and intuitive staff make this my top choice on northern Ambergris Caye.
- o **Cayo Espanto** (just off the coast of Ambergris Caye; p. 145): What could be more decadent and luxurious than staying in a private villa with a private swimming pool, a private dock, and a personal butler, all on an almost private island? (There are seven villas here, and if you really want to go all out, you can rent out the whole island if you like.) This place pulls out all the stops, providing all the conveniences, perks, and pampering possible on a desert-island getaway.
- o **Turtle Inn** (Placencia; p. 202): Building on the experience gained from his Blancaneaux Lodge (Cayo; p. 284) and building upon the ruins of a hotel destroyed by Hurricane Iris, director Francis Ford Coppola has created one of the top high-end hotels in Belize. The individual villas here are some of the most beautiful and spacious in the country. The hotel is set right on an excellent stretch of beach, and the service and dining are top-notch.
- o **Copal Tree Lodge** (Punta Gorda; p. 215): This is by far the most luxurious option around Punta Gorda, and one of the top rainforest lodges in the country. This place features a series of large and plush individual cabins set on a thickly forested hillside.
- o **Belize Boutique Resort and Spa** (off the Old Northern Hwy.; p. 224): Set in a patch of lush forest and flowering gardens, the entire operation is an eclectic orgy designed to please the eyes and all other senses. The individual villas here are spectacular. A wide range of spa treatments is available, and excellently and professionally done. Don't miss out on their signature Mood Mud Massage, perhaps one of the few massage experiences for

which you'll want to bring a camera. This is also the only place in Belize where you'll find a Tesla charger.

o **Chaa Creek** (off the road to Benque Viejo, Cayo District; p. 275): A pioneer nature lodge in Belize, this collection of individual and duplex cottages was also a pioneer in the whole concept of rustic luxury. Cool terra cotta tile floors, varnished wood, thatched roofs, and beautiful Guatemalan textiles and handicrafts are elegantly yet simply combined. The property is set on a steep hillside over the lovely Macal River. Service is very friendly and personable, and the lodge provides easy access to a wealth of natural adventures and ancient Mayan wonders.

o **Ka'ana** (on the outskirts of San Ignacio, Cayo District; p. 269): This boutique resort offers an enticing blend of creature comforts and easy access to the region's many adventures, Mayan ruins, and natural treasures. The individual bungalows and rooms are packed with amenities, and the restaurant here is the best in the region.

o **Hidden Valley Inn** (Mountain Pine Ridge Reserve, Cayo District; p. 285): Hidden Valley Inn sits on a tremendous amount of acreage in the Mountain Pine Ridge area, with waterfalls, stunning vistas, and seemingly endless hiking trails to explore. The property is wonderfully serene, with only 12 cottages, an on-site pool, comfortable lodge, and surrounding gardens.

o **La Lancha** (Lago Petén Itzá, Petén; p. 307): Set on a steep, high hillside overlooking the lake, this is the most luxurious option close to the amazing ruins of Tikal. Another of Francis Ford Coppola's regional resorts, this place has rooms once again decorated with style, featuring furniture and artwork from around the world. The food is also excellent.

THE best MODERATELY PRICED HOTELS

o **San Pedro Holiday Hotel** (Ambergris Caye; p. 140): This brilliantly white three-building complex with painted purple and pink trim sits in the center of San Pedro town. This was the first hotel on Ambergris Caye when Celi McCorkle opened it more than 40 years ago, and it's still one of the best. Grab a room with an oceanview balcony, and you'll be in tropical vacation heaven.

o **Seaside Cabanas** (Caye Caulker; p. 161): Comfy rooms, a fabulous location, a complete range of amenities, and an oceanview pool, all at a great price—what could be better?

o **Ranguana Lodge** (Placencia; p. 203): These simple, comfortable, and cool individual cabins are located just off the "sidewalk" in the center of Placencia Village. Some of them are beachfront cabins, and the others are just a few steps farther away from the sea.

o **Coral House Inn** (Punta Gorda; p. 216): By far the best option in the town of Punta Gorda itself, this little bed-and-breakfast is facing the sea across a well-tended lawn and garden. The hotel offers neat rooms, a refreshing pool, and a friendly, welcoming vibe.

o **Almond Tree Hotel Resort** (Corozal Town; p. 242): The best option in Corozal, this small, oceanfront inn has a friendly vibe with guests quickly feeling part of the family.

o **Cahal Pech Village Resort** (San Ignacio, Cayo District; p. 270): With a commanding hillside perch, this collection of individual cabins and hotel rooms is an excellent option in the San Ignacio area. The resort is located just beyond the entrance to the Cahal Pech Mayan ruins, and a whole host of tours and activities can be arranged here.

o **Black Rock Jungle River Lodge** (Cayo District; p. 276): Located down a long dirt road on the edge of a cliff overlooking the Macal River, it offers all the benefits and amenities of a top-notch ecolodge at very reasonable rates.

o **Gaia River Lodge** (Mountain Pine Ridge, Cayo District; p. 287). You'll be lulled to sleep each night by the crashing waves of the waterfall right outside your window, at what may well be one of the most glam moderately priced options in Belize. You'll get to explore the waterfall, and the rest of the lush grounds here, on nightly (and morning) nature hikes, led by the resort's crack staff of naturalists, or when you take the on-site tram down to the water to swim. An idyllic resort.

THE best BUDGET HOTELS

o **Belcove Hotel** (Belize City; p. 115): This budget hotel is set on the banks of Haulover Creek, just a block from the Swing Bridge and the heart of downtown Belize City. The old wooden building is in funky shape, but the riverview balconies are one of my favorite spots in all of Belize to sit and read a book, or watch the sporadic action on the river and streets below.

o **Ruby's** (Ambergris Caye; p. 141): Located right on the waterfront in the center of San Pedro, most of the rooms here overlook the ocean, and the best ones come with a balcony. This is one of the older and more historic hotels on the island, and you just can't do much better on Ambergris Caye for this price.

o **Maxhapan Cabanas** (Caye Caulker; p. 162): There are only three rooms here, but if you score one, you'll be treated to a clean, cozy wooden cabin in a tranquil little oasis just on the outskirts of Caye Caulker's hustle and bustle.

o **Tree Tops Guest House** (Caye Caulker; p. 162): While the best rooms here actually fall into the moderately priced category (and are some of the best rooms on Caye Caulker), the whole place offers such good value for your money that it's getting a listing in this category. The budget rooms here continue to set the standard on Caye Caulker, and the service is friendly, knowledgeable, and attentive.

o **Tipple Tree Beya** (Hopkins Village; p. 191): There are just seven simple rooms at this friendly hostel-like option at the southern end of Hopkins Village. However, if the rooms are full, you can also camp. The hotel sits on a lovely section of beach and is within easy walking distance of the small Garífuna village of Hopkins.

o **Jungle Jeanie's by the Sea** (Hopkins Village; p. 191): Located at the southern end of this small traditional Garífuna fishing village, the individual wooden cabins are just steps from the ocean on a beautiful patch of beach.

o **Lydia's Guesthouse** (Placencia; p. 203): An oceanview room with a balcony in this price range? That's just one of the perks of staying in this convivial lodging, which offers kitchen use to guests, and is located right on the boardwalk that leads to the town's restaurants and bars (but is removed enough from the action to be nice and quiet).

o **Mirador Hotel** (Corozal Town; p. 243): While the large concrete building is a bit imposing and lacking in warmth, you can't beat the view or location of this downtown hotel. And the price is pretty right as well.

o **Midas Tropical Resort** (San Ignacio, Cayo District; p. 271): Sure, you can stay in San Ignacio for a little less, but this collection of cottages and hotel rooms is just a half-mile or so from downtown, right on the banks of the Macal River. The big pool and attached grotto make the whole thing feel like a slice of Miami.

o **The Trek Stop** (Benque Viejo, Cayo District; p. 277): A great choice for active travelers, college kids, and anyone looking to commune with nature and have a little adventure. This little hotel is located just across the road from a beautiful section of the Mopan River and near the ferry crossing for Xunantunich.

o **Rock Farm Inn** (Belmopan, Cayo District; p. 256): Stays in this bird sanctuary allow guests to get up-close-and-personal with our fluttering friends at dusk, and first thing in the morning when they're out in numbers, and the outside visitors haven't yet arrived. It also allows you to socialize with the extraordinary British couple who run both the sanctuary and the inn. Erudite and charming, they are a delight, and create an atmosphere at the inn that's unusually social and lively.

THE best RESTAURANTS

o **Wet Lizard** (Belize City; p. 117): This often-rowdy little restaurant and bar serves up excellent fresh seafood and burgers in an open-air setting overlooking the Swing Bridge and Belize Harbor. This is a great place to savor some late-afternoon conch fritters and a refreshing drink.

o **Elvi's Kitchen** (San Pedro, Ambergris Caye; p. 148): Elvia Staines has come a long way since she began selling hamburgers out of a takeout window more than 44 years ago. Today her friendly and very popular restaurant oozes island charm. The restaurant is a thatched, screened-in building with picnic tables, with a large flamboyant tree growing up through the roof and a floor of crushed shells and sand. No visit to Ambergris Caye is complete without a meal here.

o **Palmilla** (Ambergris Caye; p. 149): This is easily the most elegant and finest dining to be had on Ambergris Caye, if not in all of Belize. The atmosphere is island formal, meaning relaxed yet refined at the same time, and the chefs here prepare the freshest of local ingredients with a creative blend of techniques, spices, and cuisines from around the world. When the weather's nice, you can dine under the stars by candlelight.

o **Jyoto Japanese Restaurant** (Ambergris Caye; p. 146): Mahogany Bay Village has assembled a fine team of all kinds of purveyors, but they really knocked it out of the park by bringing Chef Toshiya on board to build out a sushi restaurant. Frankly the food here is so superior that it's worth making a trip out just for a meal.

o **Errolyn's House of Fry Jacks** (Caye Caulker; p. 164): Almost every restaurant sells fry jacks in some form or another, which is what makes Errolyn's stand out: She has fry jacks worth skipping all the others for. Find her on Middle Street on Caye Caulker.

o **Amor y Cafe** (Caye Caulker; p. 164): This little cafe serves one of the best breakfasts in Belize. It has a solid Belizean menu, strong coffee, and excellent people watching: a perfect way to start the day.

o **Maya Beach Hotel Bistro** (Placencia; p. 204): This unassuming hotel restaurant serves up my favorite food on the Placencia peninsula. The menu is peppered with creative concoctions and hearty favorites, and the open-air main dining room is set just a few steps from the sea.

o **Chef Rob's** (Hopkins Village; p. 192): For decades, Chef Rob garnered fame in top kitchens around Belize before finally setting up shop in the sleepy Garífuna village of Hopkins. The creative and eclectic menu changes nightly, with Chef Rob working his magic in a tiny show kitchen just off the even tinier bar.

o **Marian's Bayview** (Punta Gorda; p. 218): The ambience and decor here are basic—at best—but the mix of Indian and Belizean cuisine is some of the most spectacular in southern Belize. The small menu changes regularly but always includes some of Marian's expertly prepared spicy East Indian fare.

o **Patty's Bistro** (Corozal Town; p. 244): Set in a simple room in the heart of downtown Corozal, this homey place has earned a well-deserved reputation as the best restaurant in northern Belize. Traditional Belizean and Mexican standards are done to perfection.

o **Pop's Restaurant** (San Ignacio; p. 273): This beloved breakfast joint has just expanded into dinner service, and people are overjoyed. Cayo's best fry jacks can be found here; any breakfast choice will be the right one.

o **La Ceiba** (at Ka'ana, just outside San Ignacio; p. 272): Exceptional food is served in a seriously beautiful setting. The cooking showcases traditional regional cuisine, updated with classical French and contemporary fusion touchs.

o **La Luna** (Flores, Guatemala; p. 318): If you find yourself in Flores, Guatemala, be sure to seek out this hip little restaurant. The eclectic decor varies from room to room, but like the food, it is consistently creative and tasteful.

THE best AFTER-DARK FUN

Belize isn't really a nightlife destination in the traditional sense, but that's not to say there isn't plenty of living to do after the sun goes down. It's true that most towns are relatively quiet by most international standards, making you hard-pressed to find a truly notable bar or club. Even so, there are plenty of after-dark destinations and activities that are unique to Belize and should not be missed.

o **Stargazing:** This is one of my favorite nighttime activities, but it is especially rewarding when there is no (or little) ambient light. Given its sparse development and low population density, Belize offers a wealth of opportunities for some truly spectacular stargazing. Your best spots are the isolated beach getaways of Belize's three mid-ocean atolls, but you can also enjoy the astronomical splendor from any number of deserted beaches or rural mountain getaways. Watching the Milky Way form over a bonfire at **Cayo Frances** (p. 143) is a visual I'll never forget.

o **Night Diving:** If you've come to Belize to scuba dive, you should definitely try a night dive. Many creatures are nocturnal, and the reefs here come alive at night. Moreover, the brilliant colors of the coral and sea life really shine under the strong glare of an underwater light, and there's something truly eerie about the experience. All of the major dive destinations and resorts offer night diving. See chapter 5 and the destination chapters for more details.

o **Safari After Dark:** Belize's land animals are more active after dusk, like the elusive jaguar or the spooky owls that fly silently through the night sky. My favorites of these experiences are the night safari with **Chan Chich Lodge** (p. 235), searching for the shining eyes of crocodiles with **ACES** aka American Crocodile Education and Sanctuary (p. 135), and a night tour of the **Belize Zoo** (p. 107).

o **Riverside Tavern** (Belize City; p. 119): Featuring excellent steaks, fresh fish, and the country's best burgers and bar food, this place is a local favorite. There are TV screens for sporting events, and there's always an interesting mix of locals, expatriates, and tourists alike.

o **Havana Cigars** (Ambergris Caye; p. 138): Havana Cigars is one of a kind. If you can handle the scent of smoke, join locals and repeat visitors in sampling an excellent whiskey and rum collection in a sociable lounge setting. See "Ambergris Caye" in chapter 7.

o **Barefoot Beach Bar** (Placencia; p. 206): Located on the beachfront, just off the central sidewalk, this casual outdoor spot is the best place in Placencia to enjoy live music or a drink with friends in a delightfully tropical setting.

o **Moonrise at Tikal:** Watching the full moon rise from the top of Temple IV in Tikal is one of the highlights of my many travels to this region. You'll have to stay at one of the hotels on-site to do this, and you may even have to persuade or bribe a park guard. You'll also have to time your visit with the moon phase. But if all these things come together, you're in for a memorable and awe-inspiring evening. See "Tikal" in chapter 11.

THE best WEBSITES ABOUT BELIZE

o **Latin American Network Information Center** (http://lanic.utexas.edu): Hosted by the University of Texas Latin American Studies Department, this site houses a vast collection of links to all sorts of information about Belize. This is hands down the best one-stop shop for Web browsing on the country, with helpful links to a wide range of tourism, government, local media, and general information sites.

o **Caribya** (www.caribya.com): This website has a near comprehensive database of all the restaurants, hotels, tours, and everything else one might be searching for in Belize. That said, plenty of the information is out of date, so double check if it seems like it might need an update.

o **The Belize Forums** (www.belizeforum.com/belize/): These are active and informative forums on living in and traveling around Belize. Several regular posters are quite knowledgeable and are generous with that knowledge.

o **My Beautiful Belize** (www.mybeautifulbelize.com): This is a travel publication run by the folks of the San Pedro Sun (www.sanpedrosun.com), an Ambergris Caye–focused newspaper. The stories here are in-depth features detailing aspects of Belize that most tourists don't get to see, but would certainly like to know. Their wildlife stories are especially wonderful.

o **Belize News** (www.belizenews.com): This site provides access to all of Belize's major online news sources, including the online editions of all the major Belizean print newspapers.

o **Belize Bus Blog** (http://belizebus.wordpress.com): This site offers the best and most up-to-date info on bus travel inside of Belize, as well as other tips, recommendations, and helpful links.

o **The San Pedro Scoop** (www.sanpedroscoop.com): Searching for travel tips or specific Belize curiosities will inevitably lead you to Rebecca Coutant's ex-pat/Belize travel blog. It's an excellent resource for seeing the country's hotels, restaurants, and activities from a keen, local eye.

o **United States Embassy in Belize** (http://bz.usembassy.gov): This is the official site of the U.S. Embassy in Belmopan. In addition to handy contact information, you'll find a range of useful information, news reports, and links here.

o **Belize Tourism Board** (www.travelbelize.org): This is the official site of the Belize Tourist Board. It has its fair share of information and links, although you'll probably end up being directed to one of the other sites mentioned earlier.

o **Facebook:** It's quite common for Belizean businesses to maintain an active Facebook presence in lieu of maintaining a website. If you're having trouble finding information or getting in touch with a restaurant or hotel, try here first. A tremendous amount of Belize's information sharing takes place through this medium.

BELIZE IN DEPTH

Belize is the second-youngest nation in the Western Hemisphere, having been granted independence from Britain in 1981. It's also a decidedly sparsely populated country, with just more than 350,000 citizens and no large cities. Belize is the only country in Central America where English is the official and predominant language.

Originally a major part of the ancient Mayan empire, Belize was next settled by pirates and then colonized by the British, who used slave labor. The descendants of each of these groups are woven into the historical lore and cultural fabric of modern Belize. Add to the mix the independent Garífuna people, who settled along the remote southern shore in the early part of the 19th century, and the more recent waves of Mexican, Chinese, and East Indian immigrants, and you have an idea of the cultural mishmash that constitutes this unique Central American country. Surprisingly, Belizeans of all cultural stripes tend to get along a lot better and with far fewer outward and untoward shows of racism than citizens of most other nations. This is a small country. The sense of community is strong and, even in the big city, people know their neighbors and almost everyone is somehow related.

Tourism is a major social, economic, and cultural force in Belize, and the country offers a wide range of attractions for visitors, from sun-'n'-fun beach vacations to active adventures and ecotourism explorations. This chapter will help you get acquainted with the history, people, culture, and natural environment of this small yet very diverse and exciting Central American nation.

BELIZE TODAY

Belize is a developing nation, limited by a small economy, a tiny industrial base, a huge trade deficit, widespread unemployment, and a historic dependence on foreign aid. These problems have only been compounded since independence. Sugar, bananas, and citrus are the principal cash crops, though seafood exports also help. A modest oil find in 2005 allowed the country to produce and export as much as 3,500 barrels of crude oil per day. Tourism is also an important source of income and jobs, responsible for providing 34% of the nation's jobs and 38% of its GDP, as of 2016. Increasingly, Belizeans whose fathers and grandfathers were farmers or fishermen find themselves hotel owners, tour guides, waiters, and cleaning personnel.

speaking OF TONGUES

English is the official language of Belize, but a traveler will most likely run across a wide range of languages. Three centuries of colonization have given the Queen's English some foothold here; however, a large percentage of the local population, particularly black Kriols, speak a Kriol English that is downright unintelligible to most English-speaking visitors. In recent years there have been attempts to standardize and record the Kriol dialect, and you may see it written out on billboards and in newspapers. *How Fi Rite Bileez Kriol (How to Write Belize Creole)* is a helpful pamphlet that can sometimes be found at local gift shops, and is an excellent and entertaining reference if you want to take a stab at Kriol.

Moreover, this is still Central America, and Spanish is widely spoken in Belize, especially in the northern and western regions near the borders with Mexico and Guatemala. If that's not enough, Belize has three relatively homogenous ethnic groups, the Garífunas and the Kekchi and Mopan Mayas, each of whom has a distinct language. Finally, rounding out this polyglot pastiche, you may also hear some Chinese, Arabic, Hindi, or even the archaic German used by the country's small Mennonite community.

Check out chapter 12 for some useful terms and phrases in Kriol and Spanish.

Belize has a population of some 367,000, roughly half of whom live in one of the six major towns or cities, with the rest living in rural areas or small villages. About 45% of the population is considered mestizo, descendants of mixed Spanish, Mexican, and/or Mayan blood. Making up 30% of the population are the Kriols, predominantly black descendants of slaves and the early British colonists. Belize's three Mayan tribes—Yucatec, Mopan, and Kekchi—make up around 10% of the population. The Garífuna constitute approximately 6.5% of the population, while a mix of whites of British descent, Mennonites, Chinese, and East Indians fill out the rest.

In general, the pace of life and business is slow in Belize. You'll seldom find people rushing down the sidewalks or dirt streets. There are only four major highways in the country, and traffic is never heavy. In fact, all of these highways actually have speed bumps along their length, as they pass through the many roadside towns and villages.

Belize is a British commonwealth country, and held its first parliamentary elections in 1984. Since then, power has ping-ponged back and forth between the United Democratic Party (UDP) and the People's United Party (PUP). The former is a more conservative, free market–oriented party, while the latter champions a more liberal, social-democratic agenda. The country is currently headed up by the UDP, with Dean Barrow as prime minister, who has held the position since 2008. The Government of Belize (often referred to or written as GoB) has been plagued by scandal since its inception, but the recent tourism boom has focused more international attention on the small country, making systemic corruption easier to call out. In general the further north you go in Belize, the more likely you are to find citizens willfully engaged in politics, but overall Belizean culture avoids the topic.

LOOKING BACK AT BELIZE

Early History

Before the arrival of the first Europeans, this was the land of the ancient Mayas. Although most people think of Mexico's Mayan cities in the Yucatán and Guatemala's Tikal when they think of *El Mundo Maya,* or the Maya World, ongoing archaeological discoveries show that what is today known as Belize was once a major part of the Mayan Empire. River and coastal trade routes connected dozens of cities and small towns throughout this region to each other and to the major ceremonial and trading cities of Mexico and Guatemala. Caracol, a Maya ruin in the Cayo District of western Belize, is a huge ceremonial city that defeated Tikal in battle in A.D. 562. Other sites, such as Lamanai, Altun Ha, and Xunantunich, were thriving ceremonial and trade centers, with impressive ruins and artifacts. Moreover, ongoing excavations at sites such as Pilar and La Milpa may eventually reveal other cities and ceremonial sites of equal or greater importance.

One of the earliest known Mayan cities in Mesoamerica, Cuello is located just outside of Orange Walk Town and has been dated to 2000 B.C. or earlier. Mayan history is often divided into several distinct periods: Archaic (10,000–2000 B.C.), Pre-Classic (2000 B.C.–A.D. 250), Classic (A.D. 250–900), and Post-Classic (900–1540). Within this timeline, the Classic Period itself is often divided into Early, Middle, Late, and Terminal stages. At the height of development, as many as two million Maya may have inhabited the region that is today known as Belize. No one knows for sure what led to the decline of the Classic Maya, but somewhere around A.D. 900 their society entered a severe and rapid decline. Famine, warfare, deforestation, and religious prophecy have all been cited as possible causes. Nevertheless, Belize is somewhat unique in that it had several major ceremonial or trading cities still occupied by Maya when the first Spanish conquistadors arrived.

Spanish Attempts at Conquest

Christopher Columbus sailed past the Belize coast in 1502, and even named the Bay of Honduras, but he never anchored or set foot ashore here, and the Spanish never had much success in colonizing Belize. In fact, they met with fierce resistance from the remaining Maya. Part of their problem may have come from Gonzalo Guerrero, a Spanish sailor who was shipwrecked off the coast of Belize and the Yucatán in the early years of the 16th century. Originally pressed into slavery, Guerrero eventually married the daughter of a Mayan ruler, and became an important warrior and military advisor in the Maya battles with the Spanish.

To be sure, the Spanish led various attacks and attempts at conquest and control of the territory that is present-day Belize. Many of these were brutal and deadly. They were also able to set up some missionary outposts, most notably those near Lamanai, where travelers today can still see the ruins of these early Spanish churches. Nevertheless, by the mid-1600s, the Spanish had been militarily forced to abandon all permanent settlements and attempts at colonialism in Belize, concentrating their efforts on more productive regions around Central and South America and the Caribbean Sea.

The British Are Coming

Belize likes to play up the fact that it was founded by pirates and buccaneers, and indeed, these unsavory characters were among the first to make this region their base of operations. Many of these pirates and buccaneers used the Belize coastline and its protected anchorages as hideouts and bases following their attacks on Spanish fleets transporting gold and silver treasures from their more productive colonies.

By the mid–17th century, British loggers were settling along the coast and making their way up the rivers and streams in search of mahogany for shipbuilding and other types of wood for making dyes. Proud and independent, these early settlers called themselves "Baymen" (after the Bay of Honduras). Politically, the Baymen trod a delicate balance between being faithful British subjects and being fiercely independent settlers.

Throughout this period and into the 18th century, the Spanish launched regular attacks on pirate bases and Baymen settlements in Belize. Spanish attacks devastated early settlements in Belize in 1679, 1717, 1730, and 1754, although after the dust cleared and the Spanish fleet moved on, the Baymen would always return. As the attacks increased in intensity, the Baymen sought more and more support from the British. In 1763, Spain and Britain signed the Treaty of Paris, which granted Britain official rights to log in Belize, but maintained Spanish sovereignty. Still, in 1779, Spain attacked the principal Belizean settlement on St. George's Caye, capturing 140 British and Baymen settlers and 250 slaves and shipping them off into custody on Cuba.

Belize by Any Other Name

There's some debate as to the origin of the name "Belize." Some claim it is the timeworn corruption of the name Wallace, one of the early buccaneer captains to set anchor here. Others claim it comes from the Mayan word *beliz*, which translates as "muddy water." Or it may be an evolution of the Spanish *belleza*, meaning "beauty."

Diplomatic and military give and take between Spain and Britain ensued until 1798, when the Baymen won a decisive military victory over a larger Spanish fleet, again just off the shores of St. George's Caye. The Battle of St. George's Caye effectively ended all Spanish involvement and claim to Belize, and it solidified Belize's standing within the British Empire.

In 1862, with more or less the same borders it has today, Belize was formally declared the colony of British Honduras (after functioning as a colony for the previous century). This small colonial outpost became a major source of hardwood and dyewood for the still-expanding British Empire. The forests were exploited, and agriculture was never really encouraged. The British wanted their colony to remain dependent on the mother country, so virtually all the necessities of life were imported. Few roads were built, and the country

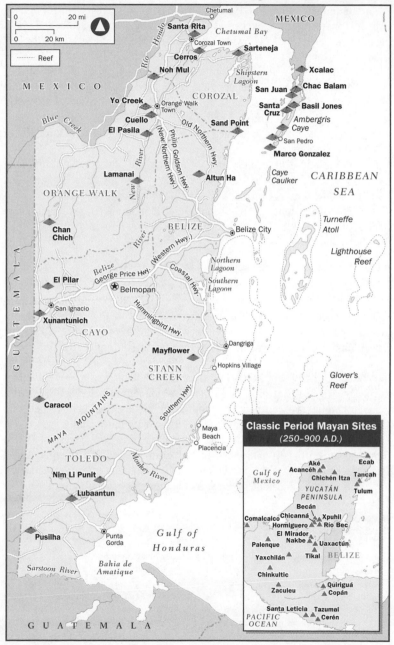

Maya Sites in Belize

0   20 mi
0   20 km

Reef

Chetumal

MEXICO

Santa Rita

Chetumal Bay

Rio Hondo

Corozal Town

Sarteneja

Cerros

Noh Mul

Shipstern
Lagoon

Xcalac

MEXICO

COROZAL

San Juan

Chac Balam

Yo Creek

Orange Walk
Town

Santa
Cruz

Basil Jones

Blue Creek

Cuello

Old Northern Hwy.

Sand Point

Ambergris
Caye

El Pasila

Philip Goldson Hwy.)

New Northern Hwy.)

San Pedro

Marco Gonzalez

New River

Lamanai

Altun Ha

Caye
Caulker

CARIBBEAN
SEA

ORANGE WALK

River

BELIZE

Belize City

Turneffe
Atoll

Chan
Chich

Belize River

George Price Hwy. (Western Hwy.)

Lighthouse
Reef

GUATEMALA

El Pilar

Belmopan

Northern
Lagoon

Coastal Hwy.

Southern
Lagoon

San Ignacio

Xunantunich

CAYO

Hummingbird Hwy.

Dangriga

Mayflower

STANN
CREEK

Hopkins Village

Glover's
Reef

MAYA MOUNTAINS

Caracol

Southern Hwy.

TOLEDO

Monkey River

Maya
Beach
Placencia

Nim Li Punit

Lubaantun

Pusilha

Punta
Gorda

Gulf of
Honduras

Sarstoon River

Bahia de
Amatique

GUATEMALA

Classic Period Mayan Sites
(250–900 A.D.)

Gulf of
Mexico

Aké
Acancéh

Ecab

Chichén Itza

Tancah

YUCATÁN
PENINSULA

Tulum

Becán

Comalcalco

Chicanná

Xpuhil

Hormiguero

Río Bec

El Mirador

Palenque

Nakbe

Uaxactún

Yaxchilán

Tikal

BELIZE

Chinkultic

Zaculeu

Quiriguá

Copán

Santa Leticia

Tazumal

Cerén

PACIFIC
OCEAN

remained unexplored and undeveloped, with a tiny population mostly clustered along the coast.

Throughout the 18th and 19th centuries, African slaves were brought to British Honduras. The slave period was marked by several revolts and uprisings. Black Caribs, today known as Garífuna, also migrated here from the Bay Islands of Honduras, although they originally hailed from the Caribbean island of St. Vincent. Beginning in the early 1800s, the Garífuna established their own villages and culture along the southern coast, predominantly in the towns of Dangriga and Punta Gorda. The Abolition Act of 1833 abolished slavery throughout the British Empire, and former Belizean slaves and Garífuna villagers slowly began to integrate into the economic and cultural life of this budding colony.

During the mid–19th century, many Mexican and Guatemalan refugees of the bloody Caste Wars fled across the borders into British Honduras and founded such towns as Corozal Town and Benque Viejo. A century later, further waves of Guatemalan, Salvadoran, and Honduran refugees, who were fleeing civil wars and right-wing death squads, immigrated to Belize during the 1970s and 1980s.

From Independence to the Present

In the early 1960s, groundwork was laid by the People's United Party for granting British Honduras independence. In 1973, the country's name was officially changed to Belize. Although the 1964 constitution granted self-government to the British colony, it was not until September 21, 1981, that Belize finally gained its true independence, making it Central America's newest nation. The delay was primarily due to Guatemala's claim on the territory. Guatemala actually sent troops into the border Petén Province several times during the 1970s. Fearful of an invasion by Guatemalan forces, the British delayed granting full independence until an agreement could be reached with Guatemala. Although to this day no final agreement has actually been inked, tensions cooled enough to allow for the granting of full sovereignty in 1981. British troops officially pulled out of Belize in 1994. The British legacy in Belize is a relatively stable government with a parliamentary system and regular elections that are contested by two major parties and several smaller

Place Your Bet

Whether or not you're the gambling type, a lot of people wager a few bucks on a **chicken drop.** This very loose variation on roulette involves wagering on a number written on a wooden board. Once all the bets are in, a chicken is set free over the board, and the number where the chicken's poop lands wins the pot. The "lucky" winner, however, usually must clean up the board before collecting. There's a chicken drop every Thursday night at 6pm at the **Wahoo's Lounge** (p. 151), set to the backdrop of live music. Some people love it, some people hate it, but no matter how you feel, it is an experience that is decidedly unique to Belize.

parties. The country is still a member of the Commonwealth, and Guatemala continues to make land claims.

It was big news when oil was discovered near the Mennonite community of Spanish Lookout in 2005. It has quickly become a major export and economic boon, with international crude prices helping substantially on that front. The country currently exports approximately 5,000 barrels of oil per day.

THE LAY OF THE LAND

Belize is a narrow strip of land on the Caribbean coast of Central America, located due south of Mexico's Yucatán Peninsula. It covers an area of just under 23,210 sq. km (9,000 sq. miles), about the same size as the state of Massachusetts, and is bordered on the west and south by Guatemala and on the east by the Caribbean Sea. Offshore from mainland Belize are hundreds of tiny islands, known as cayes (pronounced "keys"), which rise from the world's second-longest barrier reef, which extends for more than 298km (185 miles) along the Belizean coast. From the broad, flat coastal plains, Belize rises to form the **Maya Mountains,** mountain peaks of more than 914m (3,000 ft.) and the source of the many rivers that wind through the country. For centuries these rivers were the principal means of transportation within Belize. Moreover, most of these mountains are limestone karst formations, which has left them coursed with caves, caverns, and underground rivers.

Even though much of Belize's primary forest and tropical hardwoods were harvested throughout the past 3 centuries, population density has always been extremely low, and the forest reclaims ground quickly. Though Belize lacks much true primary tropical rainforest, it does possess large expanses of tropical moist and lowland secondary rainforest, as well as mangrove, swamp, and even highland pine forests. In fact, nearly 65% of Belize is uninhabited, while more than 20% of the country and its offshore reefs are considered protected land, private reserve, or marine reserve. The combination of a low level of human population and conscious conservation efforts has been a boon for a wide range of flora and fauna.

Flora & Fauna

At least 618 species of migratory and resident birds have been identified in Belize, including the massive jabiru stork, the scarlet macaw, and the keel-billed toucan, Belize's national bird. Belize is also home to the densest concentration of jaguars on the planet. Revered by the ancient Maya and feared by most jungle dwellers, the jaguar is the largest new-world cat, and can reach more than 1.8m (6 ft.) in length and weigh more than 113kg (250 lb.). The **Cockscomb Basin Wildlife Sanctuary** (p. 184) was created as the world's first and only jaguar preserve.

In addition to the jaguar, Belizean forests are home to four other wild cats—the puma, ocelot, margay, and jaguarundi—as well as such quintessential jungle dwellers as howler monkeys, green iguanas, and boa constrictors. The tapir is the country's national animal. Also called a mountain cow, the tapir is docile, curious, and entirely vegetarian. Still, these wild creatures stand nearly 1.5m (5 ft.) tall and can weigh more than 227kg (500 lb.).

Bird-watchers will want to visit several of Belize's lowland and offshore sanctuaries, including **Crooked Tree Wildlife Sanctuary** (p. 225), the **Shipstern Nature Reserve** (p. 240), **Río Bravo Conservation Area** (p. 234), and the **Half Moon Caye National Monument** (p. 167).

Off Belize's coast, the barrier reef is a world all its own, and thanks to the recent moratorium on oil explatoration here, it should remain a true wonder for generations to come. Though the cayes are little more than low, flat coral and limestone outcroppings, the myriad of underwater flora and fauna here is truly astounding. Colorful angelfish, parrotfish, and triggerfish feed on the multicolored coral. Giant sponges provide homes and feeding grounds for hundreds of smaller fish and delicate coral shrimp. Under the rocks and caverns dwell lobsters, moray eels, and octopuses. Larger predators such as sharks and barracudas cruise the reefs for their plentiful prey, while manta and spotted eagle rays glide gracefully over the sand bottoms and conch thrive in the sea grass. The **Gladden Spit** area, off the coast from Placencia, is quickly being recognized as one of the world's top spots to snorkel and dive with giant whale sharks, while Belize's three mid-ocean atolls are wonderlands for a wide range of nature-loving adventurers and travelers.

Although it might seem strange to think of it, the cayes also support a unique and endangered forest environment, the **littoral forest,** as well as rich **mangroves.** These saltwater-tolerant environments are major breeding and life-support grounds for a broad range of fauna.

See "Tips on Health, Safety & Etiquette in the Wilderness" in chapter 5 for additional tips on enjoying Belize's natural wonders.

ART & ARCHITECTURE

With its tiny population and relative isolation from the outside world, Belize lacks the vibrant cultural scene found in larger, more cosmopolitan countries. Still, if you poke around, you'll find some respectable local music, literature, art, and architecture to enjoy. For current information about the arts and what might be happening while you're in Belize, contact the **National Institute of Culture and History** (www.nichbelize.org; ℭ **227-0518**), which has offices in Belmopan and Belize City.

Architecture

Only a few colonial buildings of any interest survive in Belize City. Most of the rest have succumbed to the ravages of time or were destroyed in the major hurricanes of 1931 and 1961. The most prominent survivor is the brick **St. John's Cathedral** in Belize City. **Clapboard houses** built on stilts are the most typical architectural feature, and quite a few of these buildings, often painted in the pastel colors that are so popular throughout the Caribbean, can be seen in Belize City and in small towns around the country, but most commonly along the coast and out on the cayes.

If you're looking for classic monumental architecture, however, you're in luck. Stone fares better than wood in these parts, and there is plenty of it. The two tallest structures in Belize remain the Mayan pyramids at **Caracol** and **Xunantunich.** Moreover, the country is dotted with lesser sites, and one almost entirely unexcavated city, **Pilar,** which might prove to be the largest Classic-era Mayan city in the region. For those looking to see perhaps the finest example of Classic Mayan ceremonial architecture, a trip to neighboring Guatemala and the ruins at **Tikal** are a must.

Art

Belizean artists range from folk artists and artisans working in a variety of forms, materials, and traditions to modern painters, sculptors, and ceramicists producing beautiful representational and abstract works.

Out in the western Cayo district, the traditional Mayan arts are kept alive by several talented artisans working in carved slate bas-reliefs. Of these, the **García sisters,** who run a gallery and small museum in the Mountain Pine Ridge area, are the prime proponents.

Perhaps the most vibrant place to look for modern art is Dangriga, where Garífuna painters such as **Benjamín Nicholas** and **Pen Cayetano** have produced wonderful bodies of work depicting local life in a simple style. **Walter Castillo** is another excellent modern painter whose colorful works can be found throughout the country.

Several galleries in Belize City and San Pedro carry a wide range of locally produced art; see chapters 6 and 7, respectively, for more information.

BELIZE IN BOOKS, FILM & MUSIC

Literature

Belize doesn't have a strong literary tradition. However, most gift shops and bookstores around the country have a small collection of locally produced short stories, poetry, fiction, and nonfiction. In recent years, there has been a trend to resuscitate and transcribe the traditional Mayan and Garífuna tales and folklore, along with the publication of modern pieces of fiction and nonfiction either set in Belize or written by Belizeans.

RECOMMENDED BOOKS

For a good, comprehensive look at the country's history, check out *Understanding Belize: A Historical Guide* (Harbour Publishing, 2006), by Alan Twigg. For a more firsthand, somewhat opinionated and local take on the subject, you could turn to Assad Shoman's *Thirteen Chapters of a History of Belize* (Angelus Press, 2000).

If you're more interested in a mix of modern history and the environment, don't miss *The Last Flight of the Scarlet Macaw* (Random House, 2008), by Bruce Barcott, which tells the story of Sharon Matola's fight to stop the Chalillo dam on the Macal River. Matola is the founder and director of the Belize

Zoo, and the dam destroyed important habitat of the fragile and endangered Belizean macaw population. The book is far more interesting and better written than the above description might lead you to believe.

To prepare your eyes for possible sensory overload when you arrive in Belize, you may want to get your hands on a copy of Thor Janson's coffeetable book of photography, *Belize: Land of the Free by the Carib Sea* (Bowen and Bowen Ltd., 2000). This book is chock-full of beautiful photos of Belizean countryside, wildlife, local festivities, and people.

If the wildlife and nature pictures in Janson's book move you and leave you anxious to see the real deal, there are a slew of books dedicated to observing the wonders of Belizean flora and fauna. Les Beletsky's *Belize and Northern Guatemala: The Ecotravellers' Wildlife Guide* (Natural World Academic Press, 2004), features descriptions and color plates of most of the commonly spotted mammals, birds, amphibians, reptiles, fish, and corals, and is probably the best all-around field guide for first-timers and armchair naturalists. Those with more specific interests in, say, birds, butterflies, or ocean species can find any number of more specific field guides.

Jaguar: One Man's Struggle to Establish the World's First Jaguar Preserve (Island Press, 2000), by Alan Rabinowitz, is an account of the author's time in Belize studying and working to protect jaguars. As you might have already guessed from the title, Rabinowitz was a major force in the establishment of the world's first jaguar preserve in the Cockscomb Basin Wildlife Sanctuary.

Maya-philes will want to have some reference material handy when visiting the many Belizean ruins. *The Maya* (Thames and Hudson, 2005), by Michael D. Coe, is a good primer on the history of this advanced and enigmatic culture, as is *Chronicle of the Maya Kings and Queens* (Thames and Hudson, 2005), by Simon Martin and Nicolai Grube. However, I find *A Forest of Kings: The Untold Story of the Ancient Maya* (Harper Perennial, 1992), by David Freidel and Linda Schele, to be a better read, and one that gives a good feel for what life might have been like in the Mayan world. To delve into the intricacy and reasoning behind the Mayan aesthetic legacy, check out Mary Ellen Miller's book, *Maya Art and Architecture* (Thames and Hudson, 1999). Anabel Ford has published a helpful pamphlet/book titled *The Ancient Maya of Belize: Their Society and Sites* that is available at many bookstores and gift shops in Belize.

There is also a host of excellent books on the Maya and Tikal. *Tikal: An Illustrated History of the Ancient Maya Capital*, by John Montgomery (Hippocrene Books, 2001), is a good place to start. *The Lords of Tikal: Rulers of an Ancient Maya City* (Thames & Hudson, 2000), by Peter D. Harrison et al., is a similar option.

The history of Ix Chel Farm is chronicled in *Sastun: My Apprenticeship with a Maya Healer* (HarperOne, 1995), by Rosita Arvigo, who spent years studying with Mayan bush doctor Don Elijio Panti. If this book on Belizean natural medicine doesn't satisfy your shamanistic tendencies, don't fret: there are several additional books on the subject. Check out *One Hundred Healing*

Herbs of Belize (Lotus Press, 1993), by Arvigo and Michael Balick; or *Rainforest Home Remedies: The Maya Way to Heal Your Body and Replenish Your Soul* (HarperOne, 2001), by Rosita Arvigo and Nadine Epstein.

Belize, A Novel (BookSurge Publishing, 2008), by Carlos Ledson Miller, is a lively novel covering 4 decades of life in a family, beginning with the disastrous consequences and events of Hurricane Hattie. Meanwhile, *Belize Survivor: The Darker Side of Paradise* (NK Marketing, 2007), by Nancy Koerner, is a stark and well-written account of a woman's personal struggle with spousal abuse, set within the framework of an expatriation to Belize.

If you're bringing along the little ones, or even if you're leaving them behind but want to share a little bit of Mayan culture with them, look for Pat Mora's beautifully illustrated book *The Night the Moon Fell: A Maya Myth* (Groundwood Books, 2000). Or, for a handy little picture book filled with photographs of Mayan daily life, check out *Hands of the Maya: Villagers at Work and Play* (Henry Holt & Company, 2002), by Rachel Crandell. Older children and adults alike should read *Beka Lamb* (Heinemann, 1986), by Zee Edgell; it's a beautiful coming-of-age story by one of Belize's most prolific modern fiction writers.

Serious language lovers should seek out *A Grammar of Belizean Creole: Compilations from Two Existing United States Dialects* (Peter Lang Inc., International Academic Publishers, 1999) by Laurie A. Greene. It takes a linguistic approach to analyzing the cultural and social impacts of the Belizean Creole language, including a lot of examples of why certain words and phrases are the way they are, which can be useful in trying to learn the language.

Music

The most distinctive and popular form of Belizean music you will come across is **Punta** and **Punta Rock.** Punta is similar to many Afro-Caribbean and Afropop music forms, blending traditional rhythms and drumming patterns with modern electronic instruments (Punta is usually more rootsy and acoustic than Punta Rock, which features electric guitars and keyboards). Pen Cayetano is often credited as being the founder of Punta Rock; you will find his music for sale throughout Belize, as well as those by his successors Andy Palacio, the Garífuna Kids, Travesia Band, Peter Flores (aka Titiman), and Chico Ramos. Punta music is usually sung in the Garífuna dialect, although the latest incarnations feature lyrics in English and even Spanish. Dancing to Punta and Punta Rock is sensuous and close, often settling into a firm butt-to-groin grind.

Paranda is another modern yet more traditional offshoot of Garífuna music and culture. Featuring acoustic guitars and rhythm ensembles, paranda is a lively, syncopated musical form. Paul "Nabby" Nabor is a popular paranda artist. A similar and rootsy form of contemporary folk music that comes from the Kriol tradition is known as **brukdown.**

In northern and western Belize, near the Mexican and Guatemalan borders, the local **mestizo** musical forms reflect their Spanish roots with marimba bands and Spanish-language folk songs influenced by the mariachi and ranchero traditions.

There is very little in the way of a club or live music scene in Belize. However, at the hotels in the southern Garífuna region, you are likely to be treated to a performance of traditional Garífuna drumming and dance, and at a few clubs around Belize City, San Pedro, and other popular tourist destinations, you should be able to find various rock, reggae, and Punta Rock bands playing.

Younger generations have been exploring the metal side of the music world, forming bands and playing in mini-festivals and at other live music events. Although not a Belize-specific genre, it is fun to watch live.

Film

Although it wasn't a box-office hit, you might want to rent a copy of *The Mosquito Coast* (1986), which was filmed in Belize. Starring Harrison Ford and River Phoenix and directed by Peter Weir, the film is about an inventor who relocates his family to the Central American jungle. Other films shot in Belize include *Dogs of War* (1980), which features Christopher Walken, and *Heart of Darkness* (1994), with John Malkovich.

Perhaps the most relevant and readily available film for most tourists is *Three Kings of Belize* (Stonetree Records, 2007). Directed by Katia Paradis, this documentary provides an intimate look into the lives of Belizean musicians Paul Nabor, Florencio Mess, and Wilfred Peters. All three of these men are distinct. Nabor is a Garífuna singer, songwriter, and guitarist; Mess plays a traditional Mayan harp; and the recently deceased Kriol accordionist Mr. Peters was known across Belize as the "King of Brukdown." You will find *Three Kings of Belize* on DVD for sale at bookstores and gift shops all over Belize.

Palacio R.I.P.

Perhaps the best known and most popular proponent of Punta music, Andy Palacio, died on January 19, 2008, at the age of 48. In addition to his musical fame, Palacio, who was born in the southern village of Barranco, was a tireless prominent proponent of all facets of Garífuna culture. His final album, *Wátina*, was released in 2007 to critical acclaim and was awarded the prestigious WOMEX award for World Music.

Another good selection is *Sastun* (Create Space, 2009), Guido Verweyen's documentary look into the relationship between Rosita Arvigo and famed Mayan healer Don Elijio Panti. This provides an excellent compliment to Arvigo's book (see above).

BELIZEAN FOOD & DRINK

While it is hard to pin down any truly distinctive Belizean cuisine, what you will find in Belize is a mix of Caribbean, Mexican, African, Spanish, and Mayan culinary influences. You'll also find burgers, pizzas, Chinese food, and even Indian restaurants.

Belize's strongest suit is its **seafood.** Fresh fish, lobster, shrimp, and conch are widely available, especially in beach and island areas. Belize has historically been a major exporter of lobster, but overharvesting has caused the population to decline. It is still readily available and relatively inexpensive, but there is a lobster season, from June 15 to February 14.

Rice and beans is a major staple, often served as an accompaniment to almost any main dish. A slight difference is to be inferred between "rice and beans," which are usually cooked (sometimes in coconut milk) and served together, and "beans and rice," which are usually cooked and served separately. Belizeans tend to use a small red bean, but black beans are sometimes used.

Aside from rice and beans, if there were such a thing as a national dish it would be **stew chicken** and its close cousins stew beef and stew fish. These Kriol-based recipes are dark stews that get their color from a broad mix of spices, as well as red *recado,* which is made from annatto seed or achiote. A similar and related stew commonly found around Belize is **chimole,** which is sometimes called black gumbo.

Perhaps the most distinctive element of Belizean cuisine and dining is **Marie Sharp's Hot Sauce.** Almost no dining table is complete without a bottle of Marie Sharp's. The original Marie Sharp's is a very spicy sauce made from a base of habanero peppers, carrots, and onions. Currently, Marie Sharp's has a wide range of different hot sauces, jams, and chutneys. If you have a hankering for the hot stuff, you will find that your options aren't confined to Marie Sharp's. More and more hotels and restaurants are making their own version of the hot stuff, each adding their own twist to the classic, and while not quite hot sauce, many restaurants will have a jar of habanero peppers and onions marinating in simple white vinegar. One other local hot sauce you might see is **Hot Mama's,** which is also quite good.

A new local product to look out for is homemade organic chocolate, which you'll see in supermarkets and gift shops around the country under the label **Goss Chocolate** (www.goss-chocolate.com).

Meals & Dining Customs

Belizeans tend to eat three meals a day, in similar fashion and hours to North Americans. Breakfast tends to be served between 6:30 and 9am; lunch, between noon and 2pm; and dinner, between 6 and 10pm. Most meals and dining experiences are quite informal. In fact, there are only a few restaurants in the entire country that could be considered semiformal, and none requires a jacket or tie, although you could certainly wear them.

I have separated restaurant listings throughout this book into three price categories based on the average cost per person of a meal, including tax and service charge. The categories are **Expensive,** more than BZ$50; **Moderate,** BZ$20 to BZ$50; and **Inexpensive,** less than BZ$20. Note, however, that individual items in the listings—entrees, for instance—do not include the sales or service taxes. Keep in mind that there is an additional 12.5% GST tax, and a 10% service charge is often added. Belizeans rarely tip, but that doesn't mean you shouldn't. If the service is particularly good and attentive, you should probably leave a little extra.

FOOD

BREAKFAST The typical breakfast in Belize is quite simple, usually anchored by some scrambled eggs and refried red or black beans. However, instead of toast, you will often have a choice of tortillas, **johnnycakes,** or **fry jacks** to accompany them. A johnnycake is a semidry, baked, round flour biscuit, served with butter or stuffed with ham and/or cheese. Fry jacks are a similar batter and shape, but deep-fried, and served as is or dusted with confectioner's sugar. Tortillas will usually be corn.

APPETIZERS **Conch fritters** are by far the country's most popular and tastiest appetizer. These deep-fried balls of flour batter and chopped conch meat are on most bar and restaurant menus in the country, particularly on the cayes and along the coast. Try some.

SANDWICHES & SNACKS Belize's light menus show a heavy Mexican and American influence. Many simple eateries and roadside carts will feature simple tacos, tamales (also called *dukunu*), or *garnaches.* The latter, a fried corn tortilla topped with beans, cheese, or shredded meat or chicken, would probably be considered a tostada by many. Popular stuffed pastries include meat pies and *panades,* small, deep-fried empanadas.

You can also get traditional sandwiches, often served on sliced white bread, as well as American-style burgers. I personally recommend looking for fish, shrimp, or conch burgers, which are available at most beach and island destinations.

MEAT, POULTRY & WILD GAME Belizeans also eat a fair amount of meat and poultry, as well as some more interesting game. Because Belize only recently began to raise its own beef, the country relied for a long time on wild game. Some of the more interesting game items you might see on a Belizean menu include **gibnut** (paca) and **iguana.** The gibnut is a large rodent, *Agouti paca,* which some say tastes like rabbit, although I find it a bit gamier. Iguana is frequently called "bamboo chicken," and it does actually taste a bit like chicken. Occasionally, you may also come across wild boar, armadillo, or some other forest-dwelling creature.

Another popular wild animal found in restaurants is the **sea turtle,** endangered all over the world, including in Belize. It's not yet illegal to sell sea turtle within Belize, but international agreements prohibit its export. Please don't order turtle steak, turtle soup, or turtle eggs. In fact, I'm a little hesitant to recommend the eating of wild game at all. This includes the **hicatee turtle,** or Central American river turtle, which is a traditional favorite but critically endangered and only getting worse. So far, there's no reliable data on the impact that the hunting of wild game has had or could have, but there is reason for concern. Belize is struggling to preserve its natural environment, and as long as people order wild game, it will continue to show up on menus. Exceptions would be any farm-raised wild animals, such as iguanas. When harvested from commercial "iguana farms," this wild game actually has the potential to mix sustainable yield with modern conservation.

SEAFOOD   Seafood is the basic staple of most of the country's coastal and island destinations. It is fresh and plentiful. Shrimp, conch, lobster (in season), and a variety of fish are almost always on the menu. You're best off sticking to simple preparations, either grilled or fried. My favorite fishes are grouper, snapper, and dorado (or mahi-mahi). You will also come across barracuda, shark, and marlin. **Lionfish** is popping up on menus nationwide, largely because it is an invasive species that everyone is eager to remove from the sea, but also because it tastes good.

> ### The Queen's Rat
>
> The gibnut is often called "The Queen's Rat" or "The Royal Rat" because Queen Elizabeth was served gibnut during a visit here. Headlines in London read "Queen Eats Rat."

If you are in a Garífuna region, you should not miss the chance to try *hudut,* a fish stew or whole fish preparation served in a coconut-milk broth, often accompanied by mashed, fried green plantains. *Sere* is a very similar Kriol dish that seems more like a traditional fish or seafood stew, but again, based on a coconut-milk broth.

Ceviche, a cold marinade of fish, conch, and/or shrimp "cooked" in lime juice and seasoned, is a great treat for lunch or as an appetizer.

VEGETABLES   On the whole, you'll find vegetables surprisingly lacking in Belizean meals. Fresh garden salads are rare and hard to come by. A lack of fresh ingredients makes other vegetable dishes and sides almost as uncommon. Most restaurant meals come accompanied by a simple slaw of grated cabbage, or a potato or beet salad. Bear in mind that lettuce and other vegetables are sometimes washed with unfiltered water, so check before digging in.

FRUITS   Belize has a wealth of delicious tropical fruits. The most common are mangoes (the season begins in May), papayas, pineapples, melons, and bananas. Other fruits you might find include the **fruit of the cashew tree,** which has orange or yellow glossy skin, and **carambola** (star fruit), a tart fruit whose cross sections form perfect stars.

DESSERTS   Belize doesn't have a very extravagant or refined dessert culture. After all, the country was colonized by the British, not the French. However, you can find homemade coconut pie, chocolate pie, or bread pudding on most menus. Flan, an egg-and-condensed-milk custard imported from Mexico, is also popular.

DRINKS
BEVERAGES   Most major brands of soft drinks are available—including some Fanta flavors that aren't sold in the U.S.—as are fresh lime juice (limeade) and orange juice. You're in the tropics, so expect to find fresh shakes made with papaya, pineapple, or mango.

One of the most unique drinks you're likely to sample anywhere is a **seaweed shake,** a cooling concoction made of dried seaweed, evaporated and condensed milk, cinnamon, and nutmeg, and blended with ice. Seaweed shakes are sometimes kicked up with a shot of rum or brandy.

WATER Much of the drinking water in Belize is **rainwater.** People use the roofs of their houses to collect water in a cistern, which supplies them for the year. Tap water isn't generally considered safe to drink, even in most cities and popular tourist towns. The water in Belize City and San Ignacio is relatively safe to drink, but travelers often get a touch of diarrhea whenever they hit a foreign country, so always play it safe. Ask for bottled drinking water at your hotel, and whenever you can, pick up a bottle of spring or purified water (available in most markets) to have handy. This is especially recommended on Ambergris Caye, which has water systems that go underground through quite a bit of trash, which can seep in and make a fun vacation unpleasant quickly.

BEER, WINE & LIQUOR The Belize Brewing Company's **Belikin** beer is the national beer of Belize. It comes in several varieties, including Belikin Lager, Belikin Premium, and Belikin Stout. The recipes and original brew masters all came from Germany. Both the lager and the premium are full-bodied, hearty beers. The Belikin brewery also bottles a **locally produced Guinness Stout,** as thick and rich as its brand name demands.

As you'll find throughout the Caribbean, rum is the liquor of choice in Belize. There are several brands and distilleries producing rum in Belize. Probably the finest Belizean rum is the 5-year-aged **Prestige.** One of the most popular brands you'll come across is **1 Barrel,** which has a hint of vanilla, and is slightly sweet for my taste. **Caribbean Rum** is also quite popular, particularly with budget booze buyers.

Belize doesn't produce any traditional wines of note. The climate and soil are not well suited for growing the right kinds of grapes. On Ambergris Caye, the **Rendezvous Restaurant & Winery** does in fact import grape juice for the purpose of producing and bottling their own wines, although they are really more of a novelty than a delicacy. **Wine de Vine** on Ambergris Caye has a great selection of wines from more traditional regions, plus some otherwise hard-to-find premium cheeses to go with them.

Several different **fruit wines** are produced in Belize using native fruits, including pineapple and even banana. These wines are very sweet and are more a novelty than anything else. In remote parts of the country, you'll find homemade fruit wines that are a bit like hard cider.

PLANNING YOUR TRIP TO BELIZE

Belize offers a wealth of vacation options, including sun-and-fun beach time, dedicated scuba diving or fishing trips, and themed vacations exploring the ancient Mayan culture and archaeology. Moreover, given the compact size of the country, it's very possible to cover a lot of ground in a short time, and to mix and match these options. Whatever your interests, this chapter (as well as chapter 5) will provide you with all the tools and information necessary to plan and book your trip.

WHEN TO GO

Belize's high season for tourism runs from late November to mid-April, which coincides almost perfectly with the chill of winter in the United States, Canada, and Great Britain. The high season is also the dry season. If you want some unadulterated time on a tropical beach or private island and a little less rain during your rainforest experience, this is the time to visit. During this period (and especially around the Christmas and Easter holidays), the tourism industry operates at full tilt—prices are higher, attractions are more crowded, and reservations need to be made in advance.

The weather in Belize is subtropical and generally similar to that of southern Florida. The average daytime temperature on the coast and cayes is around 80°F (27°C), although it can get considerably warmer during the day during the summer months. During the winter months, when northern cold fronts extend their grip south, it can get downright nippy. In fact, from late December to February, "northers" can hit the coastal and caye areas hard, and hang around for between 3 and 5 days, putting a severe crimp in any beach vacation. The best months for guaranteed sun and fun are March through May.

The rainy season runs from June to mid-November, while the hurricane season runs from July to October, with the most active months being August, September, and October. For the most part, the rainy season is characterized by a dependable and short-lived afternoon shower. However, the amount of rainfall varies considerably with the regions. In the south, there may be more than 150 inches of rain per year, while in the north, it rarely rains more than 50 inches per year. Usually there is also a brief dry period in mid-August, known as the *mauger.* If you're skittish about rain and hurricanes, don't come to Belize between late August and mid-October, the height of both the rainy and hurricane seasons. However, if you do come, you should be able to land some good bargains.

The Cayo District and other inland destinations tend to be slightly cooler than the coastal and caye destinations, although since there is generally little elevation gain, the differences tend to be slight.

Average Monthly Temperatures & Rainfall in Belize

	JAN	FEB	MAR	APR	MAY	JUNE	JULY	AUG	SEP	OCT	NOV	DEC
Temp (°F)	73	76	78	80	82	82	82	82	81	79	75	74
Temp (°C)	23	24	26	27	28	28	28	28	27	26	24	23
Days of Rain	12	6	4	5	7	13	15	14	15	16	12	14

Public Holidays

Official holidays in Belize include **January 1** (New Year's Day), **March 9** (Baron Bliss Day), Good Friday, Holy Saturday, Easter Sunday, Easter Monday, **May 1** (Labour Day), **May 24** (Commonwealth Day), **September 10** (St. George's Caye Day), **September 21** (Independence Day), **October 12** (Pan American Day), **November 19** (Garífuna Settlement Day), **December 25** (Christmas Day), **December 26** (Boxing Day), and **December 31** (New Year's Eve).

Government offices and banks are closed on official holidays, transportation services are reduced, and stores and markets may also close.

Belize Calendar of Events

Some of the events listed here might be considered more of a community celebration or tradition than an event—there's not, for instance, a Deer Dance Festival PR Committee that readily dispenses information. If I haven't listed a contact number, your best bet is to visit www.travelbelize.org for additional information.

JANUARY

Krem New Year's Cycling Classic. This New Year's Day road race starts in Corozal Town and ends in Belize City. The competitors are mostly Belizean, although Guatemalan and Mexican teams occasionally enter. The winners usually take around 3½ to 4 hours to cross the finish line; crowds usually form at the start and finish points. January 1.

FEBRUARY

International Billfish Tournament. Hosted by the Radisson Fort George Hotel and Marina (www.radisson.com; © **800/333-3333** in the U.S., or 223-3333), this multiday event features cash prizes. Early February.

Valentine's Day Cycle Race. This is Belize's premier road race. Starting in San Ignacio, cyclists pedal to Benque Viejo, turn around, and race all the way back to Belize City. For more information, check out **www.belize cycling.com**. February 14.

Carnival. San Pedro celebrations take place during the week before Lent, which will be February 26-March 1 in 2019, while in the rest of the country it happens throughout September. Larger towns have parades and dance competitions. In San Pedro, watch out for getting "painted" (see more on p. 139).

MARCH

La Ruta Maya Belize River Challenge. This 4-day canoe race begins in San Ignacio in the Cayo District and ends at the Swing Bridge in Belize City. For more details, visit www.larutamayabelize.bz. Early March.

Baron Bliss Day. The day is marked with nationwide celebrations of Belize's benefactor. The greatest festivities are held in Belize City, which hosts a regatta, as well as horse-and footraces. Second week in March.

MAY

Labour Day. After a national address by the prime minister or minister of labor (carried on all local radio and television stations), the rest of Labour Day is filled with street celebrations, regattas, and horse races. May 1.

Cashew Festival, Crooked Tree Village. Celebrating the cashew harvest, this weekend celebration features local booths selling everything possible under the sun made with this coveted nut, including cashew wine and cashew jelly. Live music and general revelry accompany the celebrations. First weekend in May.

National Agriculture & Trade Show, Belmopan. This national fair is geared toward farmers, cattle ranchers, large-scale agribusiness, and buyers, but it's still an interesting event to tour or visit if you're in the country at the time. Mid-May.

Toledo Cacao Fest, Punta Gorda. Chocolate lovers should head to southern Belize in late May for this festival. In addition to food and desserts, there are concerts, games, parades, and tour activities planned. For exact dates, see www.belize.com/toledo-cacao-fest.

JUNE

Día de San Pedro, San Pedro, Ambergris Caye. This is a 3-day celebration of the island's patron saint, Saint Peter, or San Pedro. Boats are blessed, and there are parades and processions. June 27 to 29.

Lobster Festival, San Pedro. During this 10-day celebration, the reopening of the lobster season brings cooking competitions, street fairs, and concerts on Ambergris Caye. Businesses and locals get involved in all things lobster-themed, culminating in a fun block party. Check www.sanpedrolobsterfest.com for the latest details. June 15-24.

JULY

Lobster Festival, Caye Caulker. Not to be outdone by San Pedro, Caye Caulker also puts on a long weekend celebration of the start of lobster season. Food, music, and dancing are all served up in hearty portions around town. Early July.

AUGUST

Costa Maya Festival, San Pedro, Ambergris Caye. This is perhaps the largest festival in the country. Drawing participants from the neighboring countries of El Salvador, Mexico, Guatemala, and Honduras, this celebration features a steady stream of live concert performances, street parades, beauty pageants, and water shows and activities. Early August.

Deer Dance Festival, San Antonio, Toledo District. This 9-day Mayan festival is celebrated in the small Mayan village of San Antonio. Highlights include costumed and dance performances. Late August to early September.

SEPTEMBER

Independence Day. Patriotic parades and official celebrations are mixed with street parties, beauty pageants, and open-air concerts. September 21.

OCTOBER

Pan American Day. Formerly known as Columbus Day, this day now celebrates mestizo and Mayan culture with parades, street fairs, and concerts. October 12.

NOVEMBER

Garífuna Settlement Day. The greatest Garífuna celebration occurs in Dangriga, where Garífunas from across Belize and throughout the region gather to commemorate their arrival from St. Vincent in 1832. Street parades, religious ceremonies, and dance and drumming performances are all part of the celebrations throughout the southern coastal zone. November 19.

Boxing Day. While Christmas Day is predominantly for family in Belize, Boxing Day is a chance to continue the celebration with friends, neighbors, and strangers. Dances, concerts, horse races, and general festivities are put on around the country. December 26.

ENTRY REQUIREMENTS

Passports

A current passport, valid for at least 3 months following entry date, is required for entry into Belize. Driver's licenses and birth certificates are not valid travel documents. In some cases you may be asked to show an onward or return plane ticket.

VISAS

No visas are required for citizens of the United States, the European community (including Ireland), Great Britain, South Africa, Australia, or New Zealand. Nationals of certain other countries do need a visa or consular permission to enter Belize. For a current list, see the Belize Tourism Board website (www.travelbelize.org), or call the nearest Belizean consulate or embassy.

Tourists are permitted a maximum stay of 30 days. The **Belize Department of Immigration and Nationality** in Belmopan (www.ins.gov.bz; ✆ 822-3860) will sometimes grant an extension of up to 3 months. These extensions are handled on a case-by-case basis and cost BZ$25 for a maximum extension of 3 months.

If you have additional travel or visa questions about Belize, you can contact any of the following Belizean embassies or consulates: in the **United States** or **Canada** (www.embassyofbelize.org; ✆ 202/332-9636); in **Great Britain,** (www.belizehighcommission.com; ✆ 020/7723-3603); and in **Australia** (✆ 02/9905-8144). There is no Belizean embassy or consulate in New Zealand.

Customs

WHAT YOU CAN BRING INTO BELIZE

Visitors to Belize may bring with them any and all reasonable goods and belongings for personal use during their stay. Cameras, computers, and electronic equipment, as well as fishing and diving gear for personal use, are permitted duty-free. The one exception is drones, which are not allowed into the country. Customs officials in Belize seldom check arriving tourists' luggage.

WHAT YOU CAN TAKE HOME FROM BELIZE

It is expressly illegal to take out any pre-Columbian artifact or jaguar product from Belize, whether you bought it, you discovered it, or it was given to you.

For information on what you're allowed to bring home, contact one of the following agencies:

U.S. Citizens: U.S. Customs & Border Protection (CBP) (www.cbp.gov; ✆ 877/227-5511).

Canadian Citizens: Canada Border Services Agency, (www.cbsa-asfc.gc.ca; ✆ 800/461-9999 in Canada, or 204/983-3500).

U.K. Citizens: HM Customs & Excise (www.hmce.gov.uk; ✆ **0845/010-9000,** or 020/8929-0152 from outside the U.K.).

Australian Citizens: Australian Customs Service (www.customs.gov.au; ✆ **1300/363-263,** or 612/6275-6666 from outside Australia).

New Zealand Citizens: New Zealand Customs (www.customs.govt.nz; ✆ **64/9-927-8036** from abroad, or 0800/428-786 from New Zealand).

Medical Requirements

No shots or inoculations are required to enter Belize. For more on medical concerns and recommendations, see "Health & Safety," p. 47.

GETTING THERE & GETTING AROUND

Getting There

BY PLANE

Belize City's **Philip S. W. Goldson International Airport** (www.pgiabelize. com; ✆ **225-2045;** airport code BZE) is serviced by several airlines out of

FINDING A GOOD airfare

Book well in advance. It sounds odd, but you can often save a good amount by booking international airfare 57 days in advance of departure. That figure comes from a study of 26 million airfare transactions that an industry group called the Airlines Reporting Corporation undertook in 2017. Book earlier than that, and you won't have access to the lowest-priced seats, as the airlines only release them when they have an idea of how the plane is selling. Book too close to departure, and the airline knows they've "got you" and will charge more. As with so many things in life, timing is truly essential.

Book on a Sunday. That same study found that those flyers who booked airfares on Sunday saved up to 17% (statistically) over those who booked on other days of the week. The most expensive day to book is Friday. And to clarify, when I say book, I'm not talking about the day you fly, I'm talking about the day on which you put the money down to secure the ticket.

Do a smart Web search. On Frommers. com we did an extensive study of airline search engines, conducting hundreds of fare comparisons. We found that not all are alike, and that the less well-known engines usually did better than the brand names. The "winners"? Momondo.com and Skyscanner.net found the lowest prices far more often than better known websites. Each searches all of the discount sites, as well as the airline sites directly, returning a broad and impartial search, and most importantly, one that consistently turned up the lowest fares on the market.

Be careful of cookies. Though they'll deny it, the airlines track customers and raise prices when interest is shown in a particular itinerary. So consider using several browsers, and perhaps even more than one computer, when you're searching for airfares. You increase your likelihood of seeing the lowest fares on the market that way.

major U.S. hubs. **American Airlines, Delta, Southwest,** and **United** all have regular direct service to Belize. **WestJet** and **Air Canada** have direct flights from Toronto with a flight time of 5½ hours. Flying time from Miami is just more than 2 hours.

There are no direct flights to Belize from Europe, Australia, New Zealand, mainland Asia, or Africa. To get to Belize from any of these points of origin, you will have to connect through one of the U.S. hubs.

GETTING INTO TOWN FROM THE AIRPORT

The **Philip S. W. Goldson International Airport** is located 16km (10 miles) northwest of the city on the Northern Highway. There is no public bus service or shuttle van service. However, taxis are there to meet every flight. A taxi into town will cost BZ$50, a government-mandated price.

By Cruise Ship

As many as one million tourists stop in Belize as part of a cruise itinerary per year. All ships call at Belize City and offer a wide range of day-tour options around the country. Cruise lines that offer stops in Belize as part of their Caribbean and Panama Canal routes include **Celebrity Cruises** (www.celebrity cruises.com; ℭ 888/751-7804), **Crystal Cruises** (www.crystalcruises.com; ℭ 888/722-0021), **Holland America** (www.hollandamerica.com; ℭ 877/932-4259), **Princess** (www.princess.com; ℭ 800/774-6237), **Regent Seven Seas Cruises** (www.rssc.com; ℭ 844/473-4368), **Royal Caribbean** (www.rccl.com; ℭ 866/562-7625), and **Silversea Cruises** (www.silversea.com; ℭ 888/978-4070).

It might pay off to book through a travel agency that specializes in cruises; these companies are rewarded by the cruise lines when they sell a lot of inventory with perks they pass on to their customers (like free upgrades, a waiving of gratuities, and more). Try **CruisesOnly** (www.cruisesonly.com), **Vacations To Go** (www.vacationstogo.com) or **GalaxSea Cruises and Tours** (www.cruisestar.com).

Note: **Norwegian Cruise Lines** (www.ncl.com; ℭ 866/234-7350) also calls in Belize just south of Placencia, but their terminal, Harvest Caye, is not the ecotourism destination that it's marketed as. Not only was a manatee mating habitat dredged to build this terminal, scarlet macaws and keel-billed toucans are caged as an attraction for arriving guests, and neither bird species is equipped for life by the sea. Plus, with barely 300 macaws living in the wild in Belize, reducing their population by any amount has major consequences. Wildlife lovers might want to consider cruising with another company for this reason.

Getting Around
BY PLANE
Traveling around Belize by commuter airline is common, easy, and relatively economical. Two local commuter airlines serve all the major tourist destina-

HOW TO SAVE ON cruises

Use a travel agency. This is one case in which booking with a cruise agent can actually save you money. That's because agents who sell a lot of cruises are often rewarded by the cruise lines with money-saving perks, like free upgrades, a waiving of gratuities, free meals in the specialty restaurants, and more. If you book directly with the cruise lines, you won't be eligible for these extras.

Early bird & late booking discounts. Cruise fares can vary drastically, month to month on the same sailings. The best way to snag the lowest rates is either to book well in advance, thus snagging an early bird price, or by buying your cruise within a month before sailing, which is often when fares are being slashed to move cabins. The problem with the second strategy is that airfares to the first and final ports will rise in the last 30 days before a departure, and that cost could wipe out any savings you might find on the cruise.

Don't buy the cruise lines' shore excursions. Shore excursions are one of the biggest rip-offs in the travel industry. They cost far more than you would pay on your own for a similar excursion with a local vendor, and certainly far more than you'd pay to simply get off the boat and explore on your own. Because you won't want to spend too much time in Belize City (there's more interesting sightseeing and activities the farther you go from the port), you *will* however need a tour, for the simple reason that you won't have time to rent a car, return it at the end of the day, and sightsee.

We recommend working with either **CruisingExcursions.com** or **ShoreTrips.com**. Both companies work with local, vetted operators in Belize and offer the very same excursions that the cruise lines do, with some significant differences. Book with ShoreTrips or CruisingExcursions and you'll pay about a third less than you will with the cruise lines. And you'll be touring around with a maximum of 12 people in a van rather than 40 in a bus. Because of that you'll likely see more during your time ashore. Both companies offer a guarantee that if for some reason you miss getting back to the ship on time they will make sure you get to the next port, and on their dime.

tions around Belize. The carriers are **Maya Island Air** (www.mayaislandair.com; © **223-1140**) and **Tropic Air** (www.tropicair.com; © **800/422-3435** in the U.S. or Canada, or 226-2012 in Belize). They operate out of both the **Philip S. W. Goldson International Airport** and the Belize City **Municipal Airport.** In both cases, flights are considerably less expensive into and out of the Municipal Airport. See the destination chapters for specific details on schedules and costs.

BY CAR

There are only four major roads in Belize: the Philip Goldson Highway (formerly Northern), the George Price Highway (formerly Western), Southern Highway, and Hummingbird Highway. All are just two-lane affairs, and all actually have speed bumps as they pass through various towns and villages along their way. Belize is only 113km or so (70 miles) wide, and around 402km (250 miles) long. Renting a car is an excellent way to see the country.

If you are going to the Mountain Pine Ridge area of the Cayo District, or to the Gallon Jug or Lamanai areas, you will certainly need a four-wheel-drive vehicle. However, if you're just visiting the major towns and cities of San Ignacio, Placencia, Corozal, or Punta Gorda, you'll probably be fine in a standard sedan. That said, it's always nice to have the extra clearance and off-road ability of a four-wheel-drive vehicle, particularly during the rainy season (June through mid-Nov).

Among the major international agencies operating in Belize are **Avis** (www.avis.com; ℂ **225-4400**), **Budget** (www.budget-belize.com; ℂ **223-2435**), **Hertz** (www.hertz.com; ℂ **223-5395**), and **Thrifty** (www.thrifty.com; ℂ **225-2436**). **Crystal Auto Rental** ★ (www.crystal-belize.com; ℂ **936/307-1325** in the U.S., or 223-1600) is a local company, with an excellent fleet and good prices. Prices run between BZ$110 and BZ$250 per day for a late-model compact to a compact SUV, including insurance. Most of the rental companies above have a 25-year-old minimum age requirement for renting, although Crystal Auto Rental will rent to 21- to 24-year-olds, but with twice the security deposit.

> ### Hit The Spot
>
> As you drive around Belize, keep an eye out for "cool spots." These roadside stands serve up cold drinks, a bit of shade, and sometimes food. Most are little more than simple shacks or a shady thatch-roof over a few rustic wooden tables and chairs or plastic lawn furniture. Many have colorful names such as Bamboo Cool Spot, Yam Wit Cool Spot, or Last Chance Cool Spot.

Often included in the price, car-rental insurance runs about BZ$25 to BZ$40 per day with an average deductible of around BZ$1,500, although sometimes for a few extra dollars per day you can get no-fault, no-deductible coverage.

Before driving off with a rental car, be sure that you inspect the exterior and point out to the rental-company representative every tiny scratch, dent, tear, or any other damage.

Note: It's sometimes cheaper to reserve a car in your home country than to book when you arrive in Belize. If you know you'll be renting a car, it's always wise to reserve it well in advance for the high season, as the rental fleet can't match demand. We HIGHLY recommend working with **AutoSlash.com**, which will apply discount codes to the rental, and re-book you should the price drop.

MAPS   There are so few roads in Belize that you will probably be fine using the maps in this book, or GPS on your phone. However, data services and GPS can be slow or downright unavailable, especially in the western part of the country, so it might be worth picking up the Belize map produced by the **International Travel Maps and Books** (www.itmb.com). Locals are generally pretty helpful so if you get lost you can also ask someone for directions.

GASOLINE   Gas stations can be found in all the major towns and tourist destinations. Gasoline is sold as "unleaded" and "super." Both are unleaded; super is just higher octane. Diesel is available at most gas stations as well. At press time, a gallon of super costs around BZ$11, about double the U.S. average.

DRIVING RULES   A current foreign driver's license is valid for the time you are in Belize. Despite having been a British colony and current member of the Commonwealth, cars drive on the right-hand side of the road, just as in the United States. Seatbelt use is mandatory in Belize, and failure to comply carries a fine. One odd driving law in Belize is that drivers wishing to make a left-hand turn while traveling along any of the country's "highways" must first pull over to the right-hand shoulder until all oncoming and following traffic has cleared. As with obeying the speed limits (55mph on the highway, 25mph on country roads), this is not always what actually happens.

RENTER'S INSURANCE   Even if you hold **your own car-insurance policy** at home, coverage doesn't always extend abroad. Be sure to find out whether you'll be covered in Belize, whether your policy extends to all persons who will be driving the rental car, how much liability is covered in case an outside party is injured in an accident, and whether the *type* of vehicle you are renting is included under your contract.

Most **major credit cards** provide some degree of coverage as well—provided that they were used to pay for the rental. Again, terms vary widely, so be sure to call your credit card company directly before you rent. Usually, if you are **uninsured** or are **driving abroad,** your credit card provides primary coverage as long as you decline the rental agency's insurance. This means that the credit card will cover damage or theft of a rental car for the full cost of the vehicle. If you already have insurance, your credit card will provide secondary coverage, which basically covers your deductible. *Credit cards will not cover liability* or the cost of injury to an outside party and/or damage to an outside party's vehicle.

BREAKDOWNS   Be warned that emergency services, both vehicular and medical, are extremely limited in Belize, and their availability is directly related to the remoteness of your location at the time of breakdown. You'll find service stations spread over the entire length of the major highways, and a fair number of these have tow trucks and mechanics. Car rental companies typically have a phone number for you to call their preferred roadside assistance, but these are still subject to the same delays. The major towns

Road Distances from Belize City	
Belmopan	84km (52 miles)
Benque Viejo	130km (81 miles)
Corozal Town	138km (86 miles)
Dangriga	116km (72 miles)
Orange Walk Town	89km (55 miles)
Placencia	241km (150 miles)
Punta Gorda	330km (205 miles)
San Ignacio	116km (72 miles)

car-rental TIPS

While it's preferable to use the coverage provided by your home auto-insurance policy or credit card, **check carefully to see if the coverage really holds in Belize.** Many policies exclude four-wheel-drive vehicles and off-road driving—but good portions of Belize can in fact be considered off-road. While it's possible at some car-rental agencies to waive the insurance charges, you will have to pay all damages before leaving the country if you're in an accident. If you do take the insurance, you can expect a deductible of between US$750 and US$1,500. At some agencies, you can buy additional insurance to lower the deductible.

Also, when you pick up your car, **be sure to check it for any dings or dents.** It's not uncommon for local agencies to try and charge customers for damage they didn't inflict. If you find any scratches or dents on the car, alert the employee who is checking you out and also take a photo of the damage with your cellphone, adding a time stamp to the photo so that there's no argument about when the damage was done.

of Belize City, Belmopan, Orange Walk, Corozal, Dangriga, Punta Gorda, and San Ignacio all have hospitals, and most other moderately sized cities and tourist destinations have some sort of clinic or health-services provider.

Note: It should go without saying, but you cannot rent a car on or drive to any of the cayes or outer atolls.

BY BUS

Belize has an extensive network of commuter buses serving all the major villages and towns and tourist destinations in the country. However, this system is used primarily by Belizeans. The buses tend to be a bit antiquated, and they'll be familiar to many: They are almost all secondhand Blue Bird school buses used in the United States. Buyouts and bankruptcies within the industry have left the status of buses squarely in the hands of private companies: There is no national bus service. See the destination chapters for specific details on schedules and costs, and be sure to check in advance, or as soon as you arrive, as schedules (and costs) do change regularly. One of the most reliable online resources about transportation is http://belizebus.wordpress.com, which has timetables, rates, fuel prices, and even the latest news about roads and airlines. That said, asking a local for help is often the best way to learn what the buses are up to.

BY BOAT

While it's possible to fly to a few of the outer cayes, most travel between mainland Belize and the cayes and atolls is done by high-speed launch. There are regular water taxis between Belize City and Ambergris Caye, Caye Caulker, Caye Chapel, and St. George's Caye. Hotels and resorts on the other islands either have their own boats or can arrange transport for you. See the destination chapters for specific details on how to get to the cayes and atolls by boat.

BY HELICOPTER

Astrum Helicopters ★ (www.astrumhelicopters.com; ☎ **888/278-7864** in the U.S. and Canada, or 222-5100 in Belize) has a small fleet of sleek and modern helicopters. They will take you to just about any destination in Belize, including remote lodges, islands, and atolls. They will also take you out on sightseeing tours. Rates run between BZ$2,400 and BZ$7,200, depending upon the distance and number of passengers.

MONEY & COSTS

It's always advisable to bring money in a variety of forms on a vacation: a mix of cash, credit cards, and debit cards.

Currency

The Belize dollar, abbreviated BZ$, is the official currency of Belize. It is pegged to the U.S. dollar at a ratio of 2 Belize dollars to 1 U.S. dollar. Both currencies are acceptable at almost any business or establishment around the country. As long as you have U.S. dollars, it is entirely unnecessary to change for Belize dollars in advance of your trip. However, travelers from Canada, Europe, Australia, New Zealand, or anywhere else will want to change a sufficient amount of their home currency to U.S. dollars before traveling. To check the very latest exchange rates before you leave home, check online at **www.oanda.com/convert/classic**.

Once you are in Belize, the change you receive will most likely be in Belize dollars, although it is not uncommon for it to be a mix of both currencies. However, do try to have some small-denomination bills for paying taxis, modest meal tabs, and tips.

The branch of the **Atlantic Bank** (☎ **225-3331**) at the international airport is open Monday through Friday from 9am to 3:30pm, and Saturday 9am to 2:30pm. If you are flying out on a Sunday, or outside of these hours, be sure to spend or exchange any Belize dollars beforehand.

Tip: Be careful to note whether the price you are being quoted is in Belize or U.S. dollars. Many hotels, restaurants, and tour operators actually quote in U.S. dollars. If in doubt, ask. At a two-to-one ratio, the difference can be substantial.

BZ$	US$	Can$	UK£	Euro(€)	Aus$	NZ$
1.00	0.50	0.61	0.35	0.40	0.62	0.68

WHAT THINGS COST IN BELIZE	BZ$	US$
Taxi from the airport to Belize City	50.00	25.00
Local taxi ride	6.00–20.00	3.00–10.00
Water taxi ride to Ambergris Caye	46.00	23.00
One-way flight to San Pedro from Municipal Airport	116.00	58.00
One-way flight to San Pedro from International Airport	179.50	89.75
Double room, expensive	250.00–400.00+	125.00–200.00+
Double room, moderate	120.00–250.00	60.00–125.00
Double room, inexpensive	50.00–120.00	25.00–60.00
Dinner for one without wine, expensive	80.00	40.00
Dinner for one without wine, moderate	40.00	20.00
Dinner for one, inexpensive	16.00	8.00
Bottle of Belikin beer	3.00–5.00	1.50–2.50
Bottle of Coca-Cola	2.00	1.00
Cup of coffee	1.50	0.75
Gallon of premium gas	11.00	5.50
Admission to most national parks	10.00	5.00
Admission to Belize Zoo	30.00	15.00
Two-tank dive with equipment	150.00–240.00	75.00–120.00
Airport exit tax	111.00	55.50
Ground exit tax	40.00	20.00

ATMs

ATMs aren't consistent throughout the country: your card may work well at the Atlantic Bank in Caye Caulker, but be unusable at the San Ignacio branch. There isn't really any rhyme or reason to it, which is why you always want to have a backup plan for payment.

Currently, in Belize, you will find internationally accessible ATMs in major cities or towns and tourist destinations, including Belize City, San Pedro, Caye Caulker, Placencia, Punta Gorda, San Ignacio, Belmopan, Dangriga, and Corozal Town. It's best to assume you will have to use cash, but then charge when possible, which will be the case at most tourist-oriented businesses.

Tip: It's probably a good idea to change your PIN to a four-digit PIN. While many ATMs in Belize will accept five- and six-digit PINs, some will accept only four-digit PINs.

Credit Cards

Most major credit cards are accepted in Belize, although MasterCard and Visa are much more widely accepted than American Express, especially by smaller hotels, restaurants, and tour operators. While there are some exceptions, Diners Club and Discover are rarely accepted around Belize.

You can withdraw cash advances from your credit cards at banks or ATMs, but high fees make credit card cash advances a pricey way to get cash. Keep in mind that you'll pay interest from the moment of your withdrawal, even if you pay your monthly bills on time. Also, note that many banks now assess a 1% to 3% "foreign transaction fee" on **all** charges you incur abroad (whether you're using the local currency or your native currency).

Beware of hidden credit card fees while traveling. Check with your credit or debit card issuer to see what fees, if any, will be charged for overseas transactions. Recent reform legislation in the U.S., for example, has curbed some exploitative lending practices. But many banks have responded by increasing fees in other areas, including fees for customers who use credit and debit cards while out of the country—even if those charges were made in U.S. dollars. Fees can amount to 3% or more of the purchase price. Check with your bank before departing to avoid any surprise charges on your statement.

Some credit card companies recommend that you notify them of any impending trip abroad so that they don't become suspicious when the card is used numerous times in a foreign destination and block your charges. Even if you don't call your credit card company in advance, you can always call the card's toll-free emergency number if a charge is refused—a good reason to carry the phone number with you. But perhaps the most important lesson here is to carry more than one card with you on your trip; a card might not work for any number of reasons, so having a backup is the smart way to go.

HEALTH & SAFETY

Staying Healthy

The only major modern hospitals in Belize are located in Belize City, although there are smaller hospitals or clinics in every major town or city. In general, you should bring any prescription drugs you will need with you, although there are reasonably well-stocked pharmacies in most major towns and tourist destinations.

GENERAL AVAILABILITY OF HEALTHCARE

There are two major hospitals in Belize City: **Belize Medical Associates,** 5791 St. Thomas Kings Park (www.belizemedical.com; © **223-0302**), a modern, 24-hour private hospital, with emergency care and numerous private-practice physicians; and the city's main public hospital, the **Karl Heusner Memorial Hospital** on Princess Margaret Drive (www.khmh.bz; © **223-1548**), which is also open 24 hours and has a wide range of facilities and services.

Most of the other towns and major tourist destinations have either a small hospital or a local health clinic, in addition to private-practice doctors. Any foreign consulate can provide a list of area doctors. If you get sick, consider asking your hotel concierge or front desk staff to recommend a local doctor—even his or her own. We list **additional emergency numbers** in the "Fast Facts" section below and I've listed hospitals and emergency numbers under "Fast Facts" in the regional destination chapters.

BEFORE YOU GO

Pack **prescription medications** in your carry-on luggage, and carry prescription medications in their original containers, with pharmacy labels—otherwise they won't make it through airport security. Also bring along copies of your prescriptions in case you lose your pills or run out. Carry the generic name of prescription medicines, in case a local pharmacist is unfamiliar with the brand name. Don't forget an extra pair of contact lenses or prescription glasses.

If you worry about getting sick away from home, consider purchasing **medical travel insurance** and carry your ID card in your purse or wallet. In most cases, your existing health plan will provide the coverage you need.

COMMON AILMENTS

TROPICAL ILLNESSES   None of the major tropical illnesses is epidemic in Belize, and your chance of contracting any serious tropical disease in the country is slim. However, several mosquito-borne illnesses are present, particularly malaria and dengue.

Although **malaria** is found in Belize, it's far from epidemic—in fact it's extremely rare. It is most common along the coastal lowlands, as well as in some of the more remote southern inland communities. Malaria prophylaxes are available, but several have side effects, and others are of questionable effectiveness. Consult your doctor as to what is currently considered the best preventive treatment for malaria. Be sure to ask whether a recommended drug will cause you to be hypersensitive to the sun—it would be a shame to come down here for the beaches and then have to hide under an umbrella the whole time. Because malaria-carrying mosquitoes usually come out at night, you should do as much as possible to avoid being bitten after dark. If you are in a malarial area, wear long pants and long sleeves, use insect repellent, and either sleep under a mosquito net or burn mosquito coils (similar to incense but with a pesticide).

Of greater concern may be **dengue fever,** which has had periodic outbreaks in Latin America since the mid-1990s. Dengue fever is somewhat similar to malaria and is spread by an aggressive daytime mosquito. This mosquito seems to be most common in lowland urban areas, and Belize City and Dangriga have been the hardest-hit cities in Belize. Dengue is also known as "bone-break fever" because it is usually accompanied by severe body aches. The first infection with dengue fever will make you very sick but should cause no serious damage. However, a second infection with a different strain of the dengue virus can lead to internal hemorrhaging and may be life-threatening. As with malaria, your best protection is to not get bitten. Use plenty of repellent, and wear light long-sleeved shirts and long pants, especially on bird-watching tours or nature hikes. Like most of Latin America, Belize has also reported cases of the **Zika virus** spread by mosquitos, so the Centers for Disease Control (CDC) advises pregnant women against visiting Belize (or any other Zika-stricken country). New instances of the disease seem to be decreasing overall, so treat this like any other illness: protect yourself as much as possible, but know that you are unlikely to contract it.

Many people are convinced that taking B-complex vitamins daily will help prevent mosquitoes from biting you. The American Medical Association has not endorsed this idea yet, but there is some ongoing debate on the topic.

DIETARY RED FLAGS Even though the water around Belize is relatively safe, you still may encounter some intestinal difficulties even when sticking to bottled water, because food can carry bugs such as salmonella and E. coli. And despite the heavy tourist presence on Ambergris Caye, there is a lot of trash buried underground surrounding the water pipes, and waterborne bugs can leach in. This water can then be used to wash produce or form ice cubes, and you won't know without asking. Still, much of this sensitivity is due to tender northern stomachs coming into contact with Cenrtral American intestinal flora. In extreme cases of diarrhea or intestinal discomfort, it's worth taking a stool sample to a lab for analysis. The results will usually pinpoint the amoebic or parasitic culprit, which can then be readily treated with available over-the-counter medicines.

If you have any strict dietary restrictions, be it for health, religious, or ethical reasons, be sure to check with your hotel in advance to ensure that you don't starve while on vacation.

BUGS, BITES & OTHER WILDLIFE CONCERNS Although Belize has Africanized bees (the notorious "killer bees" of fact and fable) and several species of venomous snakes, your chances of being bitten are minimal, especially if you refrain from sticking your hands into hives or under rocks in the forest. If you know that you're allergic to bee stings, consult your doctor before traveling.

Snake sightings, much less snakebites, are very rare. Moreover, the majority of snakes in Belize are nonvenomous, and even those aren't aggressive, excepting the Fer-De-Lance. If you do encounter a snake, stay calm, don't make any sudden movements, and absolutely do not handle it. If you're bitten, seek medical attention immediately—don't try to bleed the area of the wound or suck the poison out. Staying calm will keep the venom from circulating quickly, giving you more time to get help.

Scorpions, black widow spiders, tarantulas, bullet ants, and other biting insects can all be found in Belize. In general, they are not nearly the danger or nuisance most visitors fear. (If you're a serious arachnophobe, stick to the beach resorts.) You should be fine if you watch where you stick your hands;

in addition, you might want to shake out your clothes and shoes before putting them on to avoid any painful surprises. It's also best practice to keep your bags and luggage sealed at night so you don't take on any accidental passengers, such as cockroaches.

The most prevalent and annoying biting insect you are likely to encounter (besides mosquitos), especially on the cayes and along the coast, are sand flies or "no-see-ums." These tiny biting bugs leave a raised and itchy welt, but otherwise are of no significant danger. Sand flies and no-see-ums tend to be most active around sunrise and sunset, or on overcast days. The black fly, or "botlass," is their inland equivalent, and for many, much more irritating. Your best protection is to wear light long-sleeved shirts and long pants when these bugs are biting. If you have any exposed skin, these little devils will find it.

Belize does have ticks in and around the jungle areas, but the good news is that unlike their northern counterparts, these ones don't carry Lyme disease. In most bug-bite cases locals will advise treating the itch with fresh lime juice, and there is definitely something to that.

TROPICAL SUN   Limit your exposure to the sun, especially during the first few days of your trip and, thereafter, from 11am to 2pm. Use a sunscreen with a high protection factor and apply it liberally. Remember that children need more protection than adults do, and that water magnifies the sun's rays, so be excessive with that SPF when doing water activities.

Drink plenty of water and other fluids to avoid dehydration. Also, this may seem counterintuitive, but add extra salt to your meals or bring rehydration tablets, which are essentially flavored salt. The humidity and consistently high temperatures will make you sweat, draining you of water and sodium, both of which are needed to keep you hydrated. Belizeans will be quick to remind you that if you feel thirsty, then you're already behind on staying hydrated.

WHAT TO DO IF YOU GET SICK AWAY FROM HOME

Your hotel will be your best resource if you fall ill while traveling in Belize. Most hotels will be able to refer you to a local doctor, clinic, or hospital.

For travel abroad, you may have to pay all medical costs upfront and be reimbursed later. Medicare and Medicaid do not provide coverage for medical costs outside the U.S. Before leaving home, find out what medical services your health insurance covers.

To protect yourself, consider buying medical travel insurance. When searching for a specific policy, we highly recommend the websites **Square Mouth.com** and **InsureMyTrip.com**. Both act as online marketplaces for reliable insurance companies. Thanks to their sophisticated designs, all the user needs to do is insert their dates of travel, age, and destination before being provided with an extensive list of policy options. We do recommend medical evacuation insurance for Belize, particularly for those with pre-existing conditions.

We list **additional emergency numbers** in the "Fast Facts" section below as well as in the "Fast Facts" sections of the chapters on major towns and tourist destinations.

Safety

Belize City itself has a deserved reputation for being a sketchy city for travelers, especially after dark, and especially in neighborhoods off the beaten path. See "Safety" in "Fast Facts: Belize City" in chapter 6 for more details. That said, if you use basic common sense and take standard precautions, you should have no problems staying safe in Belize.

Despite a seemingly relaxed and open drug culture at some of the popular beach and caye destinations, visitors should be very careful. Drugs are strictly illegal, even in small quantities, and the laws are applied firmly to foreigners. It's not uncommon for travelers to be sold drugs by someone who then immediately turns them in to the police for a reward.

WHAT ABOUT MARIJUANA?

You may have heard that marijuana became legal in October 2017, but that's not exactly true. The government did indeed decriminalize possession of up to 10 grams of marijuana, and the consumption of it on private property, but locals are wary of this change, and for good reason. It's still illegal to buy, sell, and grow marijuana, so there's no legal way to come by it. As a tourist, it's also very unlikely that you will find an owner of private property willing to let you smoke there. So while you probably won't be penalized for having 10 grams or less on you, I still heavily recommend proceeding with caution in this arena.

PROSTITUTION IN BELIZE

You may discover that prostitution is legal in Belize, but like marijuana, there is no legal way to obtain sexual services. Sex trafficking, including of children, is a problem in Belize, so sex workers are almost guaranteed to be exploited victims, and it goes without saying that the practice should not be supported.

HIV is also on the rise in Belize, with a known prevalence of 2.5% of the population, so practice safe sex in every aspect of the word: don't further victimize other people, and don't victimize yourself.

SPECIALIZED TRAVEL RESOURCES

LGBTQ Travelers

Belize is a small, socially conservative, provincial country where public displays of same-sex affection are rare and considered somewhat shocking. Homosexuality was illegal up until 2016, when the country's Supreme Court declared the anti-sodomy law unconstitutional, thanks to the brave work of one Caleb Orozco. Although Belize's first pride parade proceeded the following year, the country is still culturally and religiously opposed to homosexuality, even among younger generations. There is virtually no open gay or lesbian bar or club scene in Belize City or any of the major tourist destinations. Gay and lesbian travelers should choose their hotels with care and be discreet in most public areas and situations.

The **International Gay and Lesbian Travel Association (IGLTA;** www.iglta.org; © **954/630-1637**), the trade association for the gay and lesbian travel industry, offers an online directory of gay- and lesbian-friendly travel businesses and tour operators.

Travelers with Disabilities

Most disabilities shouldn't stop anyone from traveling. There are more options and resources out there than ever before. However, in general, there are relatively few handicapped-accessible buildings or transport vehicles in Belize. A very few hotels offer wheelchair-accessible accommodations, and there are no public buses, commuter airlines, or water taxis thus equipped. The only wheelchair-friendly outdoor experience in the country is exploring the **Belize Zoo** (p. 107). In short, it's relatively difficult for a person with disabilities to get around in Belize.

Family Travelers

Hotels in Belize often give discounts for children 11 and under, and children under 3 or 4 years old are usually allowed to stay for free. Discounts for children and the cutoff ages vary according to the hotel, but in general, don't assume that your kids can stay in your room for free.

Many hotels, particularly on the cayes, offer rooms equipped with kitchenettes or full kitchen facilities. These can be a real money saver for those traveling with children, and I've listed many of these accommodations in the destination chapters that follow.

Hotels offering regular, dependable babysitting services are few and far between. If you will need babysitting, make sure your hotel offers it before you make your reservation.

Senior Travelers

Although it's not common policy in Belize to offer senior discounts, don't be shy about asking for one anyway. You never know. Always carry some kind of identification, such as a driver's license, that shows your date of birth, especially if you've kept your youthful glow.

Many reliable agencies and organizations target the 50-plus market. **Road Scholar** (www.roadscholar.org; © **800/454-5768**) arranges worldwide study programs for those ages 55 and older. **ElderTreks** (www.eldertreks.com;

Specialized Travel Resources

PLANNING YOUR TRIP TO BELIZE

© **800/741-7956,** or 416/558-5000 outside North America) offers small-group tours to off-the-beaten-path or adventure-travel locations, restricted to travelers 50 and older. Both of the above-mentioned companies have periodic trips to Belize.

Due to its temperate climate, stable government, low cost of living, and friendly retiree incentive program, Belize is popular with retirees from North America and Europe. The country's retirement and incentive program is run by the **Belize Tourism Board** (www.belizetourismboard.org; © **800/624-0286** in the U.S. and Canada, or 227-2420 in Belize).

Student Travel

Check out the **International Student Travel Confederation** (**ISTC;** www. istc.org) website for comprehensive travel services information and details on how to get an **International Student Identity Card** (**ISIC),** which qualifies students for some savings on plane tickets, entrance fees, and more. It also provides students with basic health and life insurance and a 24-hour help line. The card is valid for a maximum of 12 months. You can apply for the card online or in person at **STA Travel** (www.statravel.com; © **800/781-4040** in North America; © 132-782 in Australia; © 0871/230-0040 in the U.K.), the biggest student travel agency in the world; check out the website to locate STA Travel offices worldwide.

Although you won't find any discounts at the national parks, most museums and other attractions around Belize do offer discounts for students. It always pays to ask.

Female Travelers

I would love to tell you that Belize is a totally safe place for women to travel, particularly alone, but it's not. Misogyny runs deep in Belizean culture, revealing itself in the frequent cat-calling, to the most extreme of situations, such as sexual assault. It's easy to let your guard drop because of the relaxed vibe of the country, but the same kind of vigilance you would keep anywhere else should be maintained here. The police are not known for taking reports of sexual assault seriously, so prevention is your safest bet. Don't walk around alone at night, stick to populated areas, and avoid situations that leave you alone with an unknown man.

If you are assaulted, I recommend confiding in a sympathetic woman, who is more likely to understand and believe you. You can ask her to accompany you to a public hospital, where rape kits are free, and do not require the police to order it. Another option is **Mary Open Doors** at 1 Church Street in San Igancio, Cayo District (© **804-4562**). While technically a shelter for people escaping domestic violence, their forte is in addressing immediate survival needs and they can help you. Even if you're not in Cayo, and even if you're male, they can guide you in the right direction over the phone. Note that the police will need to be involved if you want to file charges.

sustainable PROPERTIES IN BELIZE

Following is a selection of hotels that I feel are making real efforts to implement sustainable practices. Throughout the book, I've tried to highlight hotels, as well as restaurants and other attractions, that pay more than mere lip service to sustainability.

Belize City:
Radisson Fort George Hotel & Marina (p. 114)
The Great House (p. 114)

The Northern Cayes & Atolls:
Xanadu Island Resort (p. 142)
The Phoenix (p. 139)

South:
Manatee Lodge (p. 177)
Thatch Caye (p. 184)
Hamanasi (p. 189)
Copal Tree Lodge (p. 215)
The Lodge at Big Falls (p. 215)
Coral House Inn (p. 216)
Hickatee Cottages (p. 216)
Nature's Way Guest House (p. 217)
The Maya Village Homestay Network (p. 214)

Northern Belize:
Lamanai Outpost Lodge (p. 233)
La Milpa Field Station (p. 235)
Chan Chich Lodge (p. 235)

Cayo District & Western Belize:
Monkey Bay Wildlife Sanctuary (p. 254)
Ian Anderson's Caves Branch (p. 258)
Pook's Hill (p. 258)
Ka'ana Resort (p. 269)
Chaa Creek (p. 275)
Black Rock Jungle River Lodge (p. 276)
The Trek Stop (p. 277)
Mountain Equestrian Trails (p. 286)
Blancaneaux Lodge (p. 284)
Hidden Valley Inn (p. 285)
Table Rock Camp & Cabañas (p. 285)
Crystal Paradise Resort (p. 286)

Tikal & Guatemala's Petén:
La Lancha Resort (p. 307)
Hotel Gringo Perdido (p.307)
La Casa de Don David (p. 308)

SUSTAINABLE TOURISM

Belize is a popular ecotourism destination. Some of the small hotels, isolated nature lodges, and tour operators around the country are pioneers and dedicated professionals in the sustainable tourism field. Other hotels, lodges, and tour operators are honestly and earnestly jumping on the bandwagon and improving their practices, while still others are simply "green-washing," using the terms "eco," "green," and "sustainable" in their promo materials, but doing little real good in their daily operations.

Belize's ranking in the Environmental Performance Index (EPI; http://epi. yale.edu) has fallen over the past decade, but hopefully the 2017 oil moratorium for the Belize Barrier Reef will reverse this. There are substantial amounts of good work being done, and ongoing advances being made in the field, but Belize faces severe environmental threats. Given the fact that the cayes are virtually flat islands, at sea level, protected by a fragile barrier reef, the dangers of ocean pollution and rising sea levels due to climate change pose a real and present danger to Belize.

To date there is no overall organizational structure or classification system to rate, train, and assist local hotels, restaurants, and tourism operators in sustainable tourism practices. The **Sustainable Tourism Program** was launched in 2013, and revised in 2016, with the hopes of supporting genuine ecotourism around the country, but it hasn't yet translated to an easy or accurate way to navigate responsible tourism in the country. Still, they're working on it, and all signs point to optimistic results.

Recycling is just beginning to gather momentum in Belize. You can now occasionally find separate bins for plastics, glass, and paper on town and city streets, at national parks, and at the country's more sustainable hotels and restaurants. This is a nascent phenomenon, but I expect it to continue to grow and spread. Your hotel will be your best bet for finding a place to deposit recyclable waste, especially if you choose a hotel that has instituted sustainable practices.

In addition, organic and sustainably grown fruits and vegetables (as well as coffee) are becoming more available. Very few restaurants feature organic produce, although it's becoming a trend in higher-end hotels, so hopefully that will spread to other businesses.

Several of the tour operators listed in the "Organized Adventure Trips" in chapter 5 (p. 76) have trips specifically geared toward ecotourists. You might also focus on specific hotels and lodges that have an ecotourism bent or have implemented sustainable practices, such as those I recommend in the box above.

Finally, another great way to make your tourism experience more sustainable is to volunteer. For specific information on volunteer options in Belize, see "Ecologically Oriented Volunteer & Study Programs" in chapter 5.

See "The Lay of the Land" in chapter 2 for additional information on the various ecosystems and geographical highlights you'll find around the country. For information on Belize's national parks and info about what to expect and how to take care of yourself in the Belizean forests, caves, rivers, and seas, turn to chapter 5.

Animal-Rights Issues

For information on animal-friendly issues throughout the world, visit **Tread Lightly** (www.treadlightly.org). Mostly, be wary of any experience that would enable you to touch or interact with a wild animal, especially in an unofficial capacity. Scarlet macaws (or any parrot), jaguars (or any big cat), monkeys, and other wild animals placed in cages will never be considered ethical, and these experiences should be avoided. The exception is the **Belize Zoo,** which only takes on native rescue animals.

STAYING CONNECTED
Telephones

Belize has a standardized seven-digit phone numbering system. There are no city or area codes to dial from within Belize.

To call Belize:

1. Dial the international access code: 011 from the U.S.; 00 from the U.K., Ireland, or New Zealand; or 0011 from Australia.
2. Dial the country code: 501.
3. Dial the seven-digit number.

To make international calls: To make international calls from Belize, first dial 00 and then the country code (U.S. or Canada 1, U.K. 44, Ireland 353, Australia 61, New Zealand 64). Next dial the area code and number. For example, if you wanted to call the British Embassy in Washington, D.C., you would dial 🕾 00-1-202-588-7800.

For directory assistance: Dial 🕾 **113** if you're looking for a number inside Belize; for numbers to all other countries, dial 🕾 **115** and (for a charge) an operator will connect you to an international directory-assistance operator.

For operator assistance: If you need operator assistance in making a call, dial 🕾 **115,** whether you're trying to make a local or an international call.

Toll-free numbers: Numbers beginning with 0800 and 800 within Belize are toll-free, but calling a 1-800 number in the States from Belize is not toll-free. In fact, it costs the same as an overseas call.

Mobile Phones

Belize uses both **GSM** (Global System for Mobile Communications) and **CDMA** (Code Division Multiple Access) networks. If your cellphone is on a GSM or CDMA system, and you have a world-capable multiband phone such as newer iPhones and many Android phones, you can make and receive calls across civilized areas around much of the globe. Activate an international plan on your account: data and calling prices will vary depending on your provider.

Belize Telecommunications Limited (BTL) and their cellular division **Digi-Cell** (www.digicell.bz; ✆ 227-7085) have a virtual monopoly on GSM cellular service in Belize. Luckily, DigiCell offers affordable packages for SIM card activation. If you have an unlocked GSM phone, they sell local prepaid phone cards in various denominations, although the initial SIM card and activation cost BZ$45, including BZ$20 of calls. You can buy subsequent minutes by topping up in grocery stores or on the DigiCell website. Calls anywhere within Belize are BZ50¢, and you are not charged for incoming calls. The SIM chips and calling cards are sold at their desk at the airport or at one of their many outlets around Belize. Their website also has information on setting up your home phone for roaming in Belize.

Internet

In Belize, you'll find free Wi-Fi readily available in almost every restaurant and hotel. It's rare to be charged for Internet use. In fact, these days it's rare to find a business of any kind in Belize that doesn't offer high-speed Wi-Fi access. Throughout the book, I list which hotels provide free, or for a fee, Wi-Fi access. Note that high-speed in Belize is not like high-speed in North America, so be prepared for slower, often spotty Wi-Fi service.

Belize uses standard U.S.-style two- and three-prong electric outlets with 110-volt AC current.

TIPS ON ACCOMMODATIONS

Belize has no truly large-scale resorts or hotels. For all the loyalty point collectors, there are some chain hotels: the Radisson in Belize City, Mahogany Bay Village (a Hilton Curio Collection Hotel, but not actually owned by Hilton) in Southern Ambergris Caye, and in December 2018 the Wyndham Grand Resort on Northern Ambergris Caye is supposed to be completed. Upscale travelers looking for over-the-top luxury have very few options here, unless they're willing to go boutique. True budget hounds will also find slim pickings, especially in the beach and caye destinations, though hostels abound

PLANNING A BELIZE wedding

Getting married in Belize is simple and straightforward. In most cases, all you need are current passports and a copy of the bride and groom's birth certificate (same-sex marriage is unfortunately still illegal). You'll also need a Belizean marriage license, which can be acquired after spending at least 3 days in the country, for BZ$200. A Special Belize Wedding License can be obtained for couples in the country for fewer than 3 days at an additional cost. For marriage license info, contact the **Registrar General's Office** (© **501/227-7377**). The marriage license must be signed by both participants in the presence of a justice of the peace and two witnesses. The justice of the peace also must notarize the license.

Things are only slightly more complicated if one or more of the partners was previously married or widowed. In such a case, the previously married partner must provide an official copy of the divorce decree. In the case of widows and widowers, an official copy of the deceased's death certificate is required.

Most travelers who get married in Belize do so in a civil ceremony officiated by the aforementioned local justice of the peace, although priests and ministers from most major Christian religious denominations can be found to perform the ceremony. If you're Jewish, Muslim, Buddhist, or a follower of some other religion, bringing your own officiant is a good idea.

For something different, you might try an extreme or adventurous wedding in Belize. Options include tying the knot at a Mayan ceremonial site or surrounded by coral reefs and sea creatures, while the bride, groom, witnesses, and officiant breathe through scuba gear. There are many beautiful natural wedding sites around the country, and your choices range from pristine beaches to lush tropical forests to candle-lit caves.

Most of the higher-end and romantic hotels in Belize have ample experience in hosting weddings. Many have an in-house wedding planner. Top choices include **Victoria House** (p. 142), **Matachica** (p. 144), **Cayo Espanto** (p. 145), **Turtle Inn** (p. 202), and **Robert's Grove Beach Resort** (p. 202). If you want a remote, yet plush, rainforest lodge to serve as host and backdrop, try **Chaa Creek** (p. 275), **Blancaneaux Lodge** (p. 284), **Copal Tree Lodge** (p. 215), or **Belize Boutique Resort and Spa** (p. 224). **Hidden Valley Inn** (p. 285) has a great waterfall backdrop for weddings, too.

If you're looking for service beyond what your hotel can offer, or if you want to do it yourself, check out www. belizeweddings.com, www.dulcebelize weddings.com, or www.signaturebelize weddings.com.

---

for travelers who can handle dorms. What the country does have is a host of intimate and interesting **small to midsize hotels** and **small resorts.** Most of these are quite comfortable and reasonably priced by international standards, although nowhere near as inexpensive as neighboring Mexico.

Belize is a noted ecotourism and bird-watching destination, and there are small nature-oriented **ecolodges** across the inland portion of the country. These lodges offer opportunities to see wildlife (including monkeys, hundreds of species of birds, and sometimes jaguars) and learn about tropical forests.

TURNING TO THE internet or apps FOR A HOTEL DISCOUNT

It's not impossible to get a good deal by calling a hotel, but you're more likely to snag a discount online and with an app. Here are some strategies:

1. **Browse extreme discounts on sites where you reserve or bid for lodgings without knowing which hotel you'll get.** You'll find these on Priceline.com and Hotwire.com, and they can be money-savers, particularly if you're booking within a week of travel (that's when the hotels get nervous and resort to deep discounts). These feature major chains, so it's unlikely you'll book a dump.

2. **Review discounts on the hotel's website.** As we said above, the hotels are giving the lowest rates to those who book through their sites rather than through a third party. But you'll only find these truly deep discounts in the loyalty section of these sites—so join the club.

3. **Use the right hotel search engine.** They're not all equal, as we at Frommers.com learned in the spring of 2017 after putting the top 20 sites to the test in 20 destinations around the globe. We discovered that **Booking.com** listed the lowest rates for well-located hotels, and in the under $200 range, 16 out of 20 times—the best record, by far, of all the sites we tested. And Booking.com includes all taxes and fees in its initial results (not all do, which can make for a frustrating shopping experience). For top-end properties, again in the city center, both Priceline.com and HotelsCombined.com came up with the best rates, tying at 14 wins each.

They range from Spartan facilities catering primarily to scientific researchers to luxury accommodations that are among the finest in the country.

At the more popular beach and resort destinations, specifically Ambergris Caye, Caye Caulker, and Placencia, you might want to look into renting a **condo** or efficiency unit, especially for longer stays.

Throughout this book, I've separated hotel listings into several broad categories: **Expensive,** BZ$252 and up; **Moderate,** BZ$122 to BZ$250; and **Inexpensive,** under BZ$120 for a double. *Rates given in this book do not include the 9% hotel tax unless otherwise stated.* This tax will add to the cost of your room, so do factor it in.

One item you're likely to want to bring with you is a beach towel. Your hotel might not provide one at all, and even if it does, it might be awfully thin.

For tips on surfing for hotel deals online, visit Frommers.com.

[FastFACTS] BELIZE

Area Codes There are no area codes in Belize. All local phone numbers are seven-digit numbers.

Business Hours Banks are generally open Monday through Friday from 8am to 4:30pm, with a few now open on Saturdays. However, in many small towns, villages, and tourist destinations, bank hours may be limited. Belizean businesses tend to be open Monday through Friday from 8am to noon and from 1 to 5pm. Some businesses do not close for lunch, and some open on Saturday. Most bars are open until 1 or 2am, although some go later.

Drinking Laws The legal drinking age in Belize is 18, although it is often not enforced. Beer, wine, and liquor are all sold in most supermarkets and small convenience stores Monday through Saturday. No liquor is sold on Good Friday or Easter Sunday. On Election Day, no liquor can be sold until 6pm.

Drugstores There are a handful of pharmacies around Belize City and in most of the major towns and tourist destinations. Perhaps the best-stocked pharmacy in the country can be found at **Belize Medical Associates,** 5791 St. Thomas Kings Park, Belize City (www.belizemedical. com; ℂ **223-0303**).

Electricity Electricity is 110-volt AC, and most outlets are either two- or three-prong U.S.-style outlets.

Embassies & Consulates The **United States Embassy** is located in Belmopan on Floral Park Road (http://bz.usembassy.gov; ℂ **822-4011**). The **British High Commission** is located in Belmopan at Embassy Square (www.ukin belize.fco.gov.uk; ℂ **822-2147**). You can contact the **Canadian Honorary Consul**

in Belize City at 80 Princess Margaret Dr. (ℂ **223-1060**).

Emergencies In case of an emergency, dial ℂ **90** from anywhere in Belize. This will connect you to the police. In most cases, ℂ **911** will also work. I've listed the various numbers for fire departments, ambulances, and hospitals in the "Fast Facts" sections throughout the book.

Gasoline (Petrol) Gasoline is sold as "unleaded" and "super." Both are unleaded; super is just higher octane. Diesel is available at most gas stations as well. At press time, a gallon of super costs around BZ$11.

Hospitals Belize Medical Associates, 5791 St. Thomas Kings Park, Belize City (www.belizemedical. com; ℂ **223-0303**), is a modern, 24-hour private hospital, with emergency care and numerous private-practice physicians. The country's main public hospital, the **Karl Heusner Memorial Hospital,** Princess Margaret Drive, Belize City (ℂ **223-1548**), is also open 24 hours and has a wide range of facilities and services.

Language English is the official language of Belize, and it is almost universally spoken. However, Belize is a very polyglot country, and you are likely to hear and come across Spanish, Creole, and Garífuna. For some help in communicating in Spanish and Creole, see chapter 12.

Laundromats Most folks rely on their hotel's laundry and dry-cleaning services, although these can be expensive. Where they exist, I've listed laundromats and laundry options in the "Fast Facts" sections of the destination chapters.

Legal Aid If you need legal help, your best bet is to first contact your local embassy or consulate. Alternatively, ask at your hotel.

Lost & Found Be sure to tell all your credit card companies the minute you discover that your wallet has been lost or stolen, and file a report at the nearest police precinct. Your credit card company or insurer may require a police report number or record of the loss. Most credit card companies have an emergency toll-free number to call if your card is lost or stolen; they may be able to wire you a cash advance immediately or deliver an emergency credit card in a day or two. It's a good idea to write this number down and carry it someplace separate from your wallet or credit cards. **Visa**'s emergency number is ℂ **800/847-2911** toll-free in the U.S., or call 410/581-9994 collect from Belize. **American Express** cardholders and traveler's check holders should call ℂ **800/221-7282** toll-free in the U.S., or 336/393-1111 collect from Belize. **MasterCard** holders should call ℂ **800/627-8372** toll-free in the U.S., or 636/722-7111 collect from Belize.

If you need emergency cash over the weekend when all banks and American Express offices are closed, you can have money wired to you via **Western Union** (www.westernunion. com; ☏ **800/325-6000** in the U.S. and Canada, or **227-1818** in Belize), although the service charges are substantial.

Mail Most hotels will post a letter for you, and there are post offices in the major towns. It costs BZ$.60 to send a letter to the United States, and BZ$.75 to send a letter to Europe. Postcards to the same destinations cost BZ$.30 and BZ$.40, respectively.

If your postal needs are urgent, or you want to send anything of value, several international courier and express-mail services have offices in Belize City, including **DHL**, Puma St. and Coney Dr. (www.dhl.com; ☏ **223-1070**), and **FedEx,** Fort St. (www.fedex.com; ☏ **223-11577**). Either can arrange pickup and delivery services to any hotel in town, and sometimes in the different outlying districts.

Newspapers & Magazines Belize has no daily newspaper. There are several primary weeklies: *Amandala* (www.amandala. com.bz), the *Reporter* (www. reporter.bz), and the *Guardian* (www.guardian.bz). Most come out on Friday, and all are relatively similar in terms of content, although with some differing and usually obvious political leanings.

Amandala and the *Reporter* actually publish twice weekly and are my favorites.

Police The police in Belize can be helpful, but corruption does exist so make sure to advocate for yourself; there is a dedicated tourism police force in Belize City. Dial ☏ **90** or **911** in an emergency. You can also dial ☏ **227-2222.**

Smoking In 2015 Belize enacted a smoking ban that makes smoking illegal in places such as government buildings, banks, hotel lobbies, schools, public transportation, and in non-designated smoking areas in restaurants.

Taxes There is a BZ$37.50 departure fee that must be paid in cash (in either U.S. or Belize dollars) at the international airport upon departure, although the fees are almost always already included in your airline ticket; the land exit fee is US$20. There is a 9% hotel tax added to all hotel bills, and there is a 12.5% GST tax on all goods and services. A 10% service charge is sometimes added to restaurant bills. Take this into account when deciding how much to tip (if the service is really good, an extra 5%–10% is fine).

Telephones Belize has a standardized seven-digit phone numbering system. There are no city or area codes to dial from within Belize; use the country code, 501 (not to be confused with the area code for

the state of Arkansas), only when dialing a Belizean number from outside Belize.

For directory assistance: Dial ☏ **113** if you're looking for a number inside Belize; for numbers to all other countries, dial ☏ **115** and (for a charge) an operator will connect you to an international directory assistance operator.

For operator assistance: If you need operator assistance in making a call, dial ☏ **115,** whether you're trying to make a local or an international call.

Toll-free numbers: Numbers beginning with 0800 and 800 within Belize are toll-free, but calling a 1-800 number in the States from Belize is not toll-free. In fact, it costs the same as an overseas call.

See "Staying Connected," on p. 56, for tips on calling to and from Belize.

Time Belize is on Central Standard Time, 6 hours behind Greenwich Mean Time. Belize does not observe daylight saving time.

Tipping Most Belizeans don't tip. Many restaurants add a 10% service charge. However, if the service is particularly good, or if the service charge is not included, tipping is appropriate. If you look like you're from the U.S., you will probably be asked for a tip at some point, as hospitality workers are aware that tipping is the status quo in the States.

Toilets There are very few public toilets or restrooms in Belize. About the only ones I know of are located at the little cruise-ship tourist village on Fort Street in the Fort George section of Belize City, and at the water taxi terminal by the swing bridge. However, most hotels and restaurants will let tourists use their facilities.

Water Many travelers react adversely to water in foreign countries, and it is probably best to drink bottled water throughout your visit to Belize. It's also normal and expected to ask if your ice has been filtered, and your greens washed with clean water.

SUGGESTED BELIZE ITINERARIES

D on't be fooled by its size—there's a lot to see and do in Belize. And the fact that the country is so compact makes it quick to get around and do a lot in a short time. The following itineraries are meant to serve as rough outlines to help you structure your time and get a taste of some of the country's must-see destinations. Other options include specialized itineraries focused on a particular interest or activity. Bird-watchers could design an itinerary that visits a series of prime bird-watching sites. Cave enthusiasts and spelunkers could design a trip to take in several of Belize's caves, including both wet and dry cave explorations. In Belize, there's something for everyone.

4

THE REGIONS IN BRIEF

BELIZE CITY Belize City is a modest-size coastal port city located at the mouth of the **Belize River.** It's Belize's transportation hub, with the only international airport, an active municipal airport, a cruise-ship dock, and all the major bus-line and water-taxi terminals. Still, Belize City is of limited interest to most visitors, who quickly seek the more beachy and pastoral charms of the country's various tourist destinations and resorts. Belize City has a reputation as a rough and violent urban center, and visitors should exercise caution and stick to the most popular tourist areas of this small city.

THE NORTHERN CAYES & ATOLLS This is Belize's primary tourist zone and attraction. Hundreds of palm-swept offshore islands lie between the coast of the mainland and the protection of the 298km (185-mile) **Belize Barrier Reef.** The reef, easily visible from many of the cayes, offers some of the world's most exciting snorkeling, scuba diving, and fishing. The most developed cayes here, **Ambergris Caye** and **Caye Caulker,** have numerous hotels and small resorts, while some of the less developed cayes maintain the feel of fairy-tale desert isles. In addition to the many cayes, there are two open-ocean atolls here, **Turneffe Island Atoll** and **Lighthouse Reef Atoll.** Each of these unique rings of coral, limestone, and mangrove cayes surrounds a central, protected saltwater lagoon.

For those whose main sport is catching rays, not fish, it should be mentioned that the cayes, and Belize in general, lack wide, sandy beaches. Although the water is as warm and clear blue as it's touted to be, most of your sunbathing will be on docks, deck chairs, or imported patches of sand fronting a sea wall or sea-grass patch of shallow ocean. Large-scale resorts like those in the rest of the Caribbean are only just finding their way to Belize, with the completion of Mahogany Bay Village (p. 141) on Ambergris Caye in 2018.

SOUTHERN BELIZE   Southern Belize encompasses two major districts, Stann Creek and Toledo. The former includes the **Cockscomb Basin Wildlife Sanctuary** and the coastal towns of **Dangriga, Hopkins Village, Placencia,** and the best access to private islands within the Belize Barrier Reef. Dangriga is the country's major center of **Garífuna culture** (p. 172), while Hopkins Village is a quaint, oceanfront Garífuna village, and Placencia boasts what is arguably the country's best beach. Farther south, the Toledo District is Belize's final frontier. The inland hills and jungles are home to numerous Kekchi and Mopan Mayan villages. Hidden in these hills are some lesser known and less visited Mayan ruins, including **Lubaantun** and **Nim Li Punit.** The Toledo District is also emerging as an **ecotourism destination,** with the country's richest, wettest, and most undisturbed rainforests. Off the shores of southern Belize lie more cayes and yet another mid-ocean atoll, **Glover's Reef Atoll.** The cayes down here get far less traffic and attention than those to the north, and they are perfect for anyone looking for all of the same attractions, but fewer crowds.

NORTHERN BELIZE   Anchored on the south by Belize City, this is the country's business and agricultural heartland. Toward the north lie **Orange Walk Town** and **Corozal Town.** Both of these small cities have a strong Spanish feel and influence, having been settled largely by refugees from Mexico's Caste War. The Maya also lived here, and their memories live on at the ruins of **Altun Ha, Lamanai, Cerros,** and **Santa Rita,** all in this zone. This is a land that was once submerged and is still primarily swamp and mangrove. Where the land is cleared and settled, sugar cane is the main cash crop, although bananas, citrus fruits, and pineapples are also grown. Toward the western section of this region lies the **Río Bravo Conservation Area,** a massive tract of virgin forest, sustainable-yield managed forest, and recovering reforestation areas. Northern Belize has some of the country's premier isolated nature lodges, as well as some of the prime destinations for bird-watchers, including the **Shipstern Nature Reserve** and **Crooked Tree Wildlife Sanctuary.**

CAYO DISTRICT & WESTERN BELIZE   This mountainous district near the Guatemalan border has become Belize's second-most-popular destination.

Belize

Here you'll find some of Belize's most beautiful countryside and most fascinating natural and man-made sights. The limestone mountains of this region are dotted with numerous caves, sinkholes, jagged peaks, underground rivers, and waterfalls. There are clear-flowing aboveground rivers that are excellent for swimming and canoeing, as well as mile after mile of unexplored forest full of wild animals and hundreds of bird species. Adventurers, nature lovers, and bird-watchers will definitely want to spend some time in the Cayo District. This is also where you'll find Belize's largest and most impressive Mayan ruins. In the remote **Mountain Pine Ridge** section of the Cayo District lies **Caracol,** one of the largest known Classic Maya cities ever uncovered. Closer to the main town of San Ignacio, you'll find **Xunantunich, El Pilar,** and the smaller **Cahal Pech.**

TIKAL & GUATEMALA'S PETÉN   Just over Belize's western border lies Guatemala's **Petén province,** a massive and remote area of primary forest and perhaps Mesoamerica's most spectacular Maya ruin, **Tikal.** The level of preservation, restoration, and rich rainforest setting make Tikal one of the true wonders of the world, and an enchanting stop for anyone even remotely interested in the ancient Maya or archaeology. The surrounding jungles and small Guatemalan villages are easily accessible from Belize and allow travelers the chance to add yet another unique adventure to any itinerary.

BELIZE IN 1 WEEK

The timing is tight, but this itinerary packs a trio of Belize's best destinations into 1 week. It allows for a chance to visit major Maya ruins, snorkel on the barrier reef, ride an inner tube on an underground river, and relax a bit on the waterfront.

Day 1: Arrive & Head to San Ignacio

Arrive in **Belize City** and pick up a rental car for the drive to the **Cayo District ★★.** Stop at the **Belize Zoo ★★** (p. 107) or for a **cave tubing adventure** (p. 250) near Nohoch Che'en en route. If it's a hot day, cave tubing is a great way to cool down, while the zoo is perfect for rainy days (and times when water levels don't allow tubing). Settle into one of the hotels in San Ignacio or one of the lodges located out on the way to Benque Viejo. For dinner, be sure to treat yourself to the creative cuisine offered in the beautiful outdoor eating area of **La Ceiba ★★★** (p. 272).

Day 2: Cross the Border to See Tikal

Wake up early to cross the border into Guatemala for a day trip to **Tikal ★★★** (p. 290), where you can explore a vast ancient Mayan city. This will be an all-day adventure, which will be just enough time to see the main highlights. Take it easy when you get back, as tomorrow will be another early day.

Belize in 1 Week & 2 Weeks

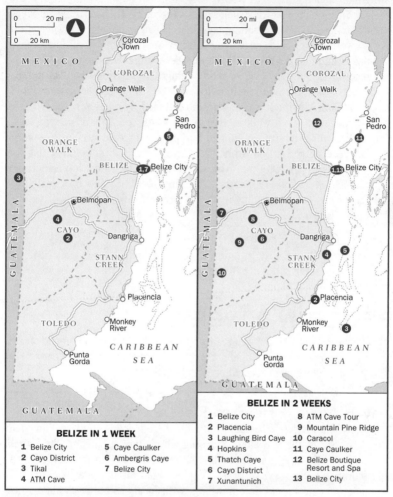

BELIZE IN 1 WEEK

1 Belize City
2 Cayo District
3 Tikal
4 ATM Cave
5 Caye Caulker
6 Ambergris Caye
7 Belize City

BELIZE IN 2 WEEKS

1 Belize City
2 Placencia
3 Laughing Bird Caye
4 Hopkins
5 Thatch Caye
6 Cayo District
7 Xunantunich
8 ATM Cave Tour
9 Mountain Pine Ridge
10 Caracol
11 Caye Caulker
12 Belize Boutique Resort and Spa
13 Belize City

Day 3: Actun Tunichil Muknal Cave Tour

If you want to get up close and personal with Mayan history, there is no more exhilarating way to do so than the extremely popular **ATM cave tour ★★★** (p. 251). It involves hiking, wading, and squeezing through tight spaces, but the reward is burial sites over 1,000 years old, preserved skeletons included. Because cameras are not allowed inside the cave, taking this trip yourself is the only way you'll get to see the wonders inside.

Days 4, 5 & 6: Fly to the Cayes

Before heading back to Belize City, stop by **Pop's Restaurant** ★★★ (p. 273) for a breakfast of their famous fry jacks. Then head for the cayes, dropping off the car before boarding an airplane—the view is from above. Choose between **Caye Caulker** ★★★, with its intimate, laid-back charm, and **Ambergris Caye** ★★, with its wider choice of hotels, resorts, and restaurants. A whole range of activities and adventures awaits you at both. From either location be sure to try the snorkel trip to **Hol Chan Marine Reserve** ★★ and **Shark-Ray Alley** ★★ (p. 132). On another day, you'll want to visit **Koko King** ★★ (p. 159) if you're on Caye Caulker or go for a longer, bumpy golf cart ride to **Not-So-Secret Beach** ★★ (p. 136) on Ambergris Caye. And the best nightlife in these parts is to go out with the **American Crocodile Education Sanctuary (ACES)** ★★★ (p. 135) crew, searching for crocodiles by the light of their eyes. That alone may make it worth picking Ambergris Caye over Caye Caulker.

Day 7: Going Home

Return to **Belize City** in time for your international connection. If you have time, stop off at the **Belize Tourism Village** (p. 112) for some last minute souvenir hunting.

BELIZE IN 2 WEEKS

If you have 2 weeks, you'll be able to hit all the highlights mentioned above, as well as some others, including a trip out to a private island. And you can do all this at a slightly more relaxed pace to boot.

Day 1: Arrive & Head to Placencia

Arrive into **Belize City** and grab a quick connecting flight to **Placencia** ★★. Spend the afternoon strolling along the beach and the town's famous sidewalk. For dinner, try the tapas and fusion fare served up at **Rumfish y Vino** ★★ (p. 205). Then head back to the sidewalk after dinner, and enjoy some time mingling with locals and tourists alike at the **Barefoot Beach Bar** ★ (p. 206).

Day 2: Way Down upon the Monkey River

Take a snorkel trip to **Laughing Bird Caye** ★★ (p. 197) and enjoy a picnic lunch on this tiny little gem of an island. If you happen to be here during **whale-shark season** (p. 197), swap out the Laughing Bird Caye trip for a chance to snorkel or scuba dive with the world's largest fish.

Day 3: Hop over to Hopkins

Make your way up to **Hopkins Village** ★★★, a lovely seaside Garífuna settlement. Spend the day relaxing on the beach or exploring the town, because at night is when this little village comes alive. Head to the **Lebeha Drumming Center** ★ (p. 188) to try your hand at Garífuna drumming and dancing—it's impossible not to get caught up in the rhythm. If you're going to be here close to a new moon, schedule a **bioluminescence river tour** ★★★ (p. 188) to witness a dark lagoon coming to life.

Days 4 & 5: Live that Private Island Life

Venture just a little bit further north to Dangriga to catch the boat out to **Thatch Caye Resort** ★★★ (p. 184). Join a small handful of other visitors in sipping rum cocktails out of coconuts while surrounded by the calm turquoise water of the Caribbean Sea. Spend your time here either relaxing in a hammock, swimming off of the docks, or having a spa treatment—how you relax is totally up to you. For those interested in a more active experience, you can go fishing, catching conch, kayaking, and more.

Days 6, 7 & 8: Cayo Calling

From Dangriga head to the **Cayo District** ★★ either by driving the beautiful Hummingbird Highway or flying via Belize City. Spend what remains of the day with an exploration of the Mayan ruins of **Xunantunich** ★★★ (p. 264). On day 7 delve deeper into Mayan history with an all-day spelunking of Actun Tunichil Muknal, aka the **ATM Cave Tour** ★★★ (p. 251). For the last day in this area, choose between **Belize Botanic Gardens** ★★ (p. 267) and nearby **Chaa Creek Natural History Centre and Blue Morpho Butterfly Farm** ★ (p. 267), or heading out to **Mountain Equestrian Trails** (p. 286) for a jungle horseback ride. The former is ideal for those who are tired from the previous day's excursions, while the horseback ride is for those who want to keep their energy up. At night experience local music and art with the co-operative **Belize Soul Project** ★★ (p. 274), and for breakfast stop by **Pop's Restaurant** ★★★ (p. 273) for (arguably) the best fry jacks in Belize.

Day 9: Tikal

Head across the border to view the most extraordinary ruins in Central America. For a full description, and all the how to's, see p. 290.

Day 10: Climb Caana

Venture into the **Mountain Pine Ridge** ★★ area, staying either at **Hidden Valley Inn** ★★★ (p. 285) or **Blancaneaux Lodge** ★ (p. 284). Visit the ruins at **Caracol** ★★ (p. 282) and climb to the top of the tallest man-made structure in Belize. Stop at **Río On Pools** ★★ (p. 281) on your way back from the ruins.

Days 11, 12 & 13: Go Slow in the Cayes

It's time to head to either funky **Caye Caulker** ★★★ or larger **Ambergris Caye** ★★. Follow the suggestions in the weeklong itinerary for what to see and do.

Day 14: Head Home

Time to head to **Belize City** and home. You may want to pick up some last-minute souvenirs at **Belize Tourism Village** (p. 112) before hitting the airport.

BELIZE FOR FAMILIES

Belize doesn't have many well-staffed children's programs, nor will you find many activities or attractions specifically geared for the very young. Still, this English-speaking country is a great destination for families, especially if your children have an adventurous streak or love animals.

Day 1: Head for Hopkins

Arrive into **Belize City** and head straight to **Hopkins Village ★★★** (p. 186). Settle into a comfortable suite at **Jaguar Reef Lodge & Spa ★★** (p. 189). Kids can play in the children's pool while parents take advantage of the swim up Tiki bar.

Day 2: Go Garífuna

Sign up for a class in traditional Garífuna drumming and dancing at the **Lebeha Drumming Center ★** (p. 188). Afterwards make use of the resort's ample facilities and activity options, which include free sea kayaks, Hobie Cats, and snorkel gear. At night the entire family will enjoy seeing the glowing blue waters of the **bioluminescence river tour ★★★** (p. 188).

Days 3 & 4: A Nearly Deserted Island

Head out to **South Water Caye ★★★**. The island here is tiny, and the kids will no doubt fantasize about being stranded on a deserted island. The waters here are extremely calm and protected by the barrier reef, which lies just offshore. This is a great place to introduce the family to snorkeling, and to head out in individual or tandem kayaks.

Days 5 & 6: Into the Dark

On your way back north, stop off at **Ian Anderson's Caves Branch ★★** (p. 258). Accommodations here are plush but kid friendly (bunk beds in most suites), and the resort's guided experiences lean toward the adventurous. Most revolve around the surrounding forest and the area's namesake river, which runs through a series of underground caves. The cave tubing adventure is exciting for kids and adults alike, and sitting in an inner tube as it floats down a lazy river through caves means it's easy to keep track of the whole family.

Days 7, 8 & 9: Sun & Fun in San Pedro

Head for **Ambergris Caye ★★**, first stopping at the **Belize Zoo** (p. 107) for a quick face-to-face with jaguars and tapir. With its wide choice of

Belize for Families & Mayan Ruins Highlights Tour

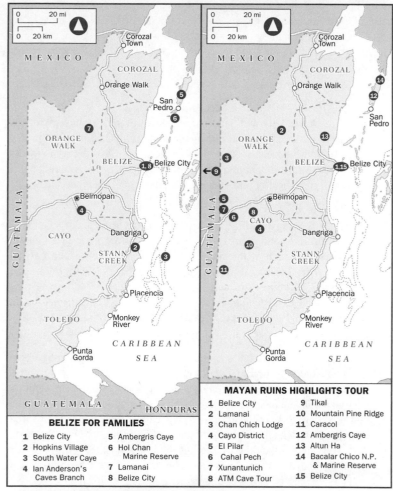

BELIZE FOR FAMILIES

1 Belize City	5 Ambergris Caye
2 Hopkins Village	6 Hol Chan
3 South Water Caye	Marine Reserve
4 Ian Anderson's	7 Lamanai
Caves Branch	8 Belize City

MAYAN RUINS HIGHLIGHTS TOUR

1 Belize City	9 Tikal
2 Lamanai	10 Mountain Pine Ridge
3 Chan Chich Lodge	11 Caracol
4 Cayo District	12 Ambergris Caye
5 El Pilar	13 Altun Ha
6 Cahal Pech	14 Bacalar Chico N.P.
7 Xunantunich	& Marine Reserve
8 ATM Cave Tour	15 Belize City

hotels, resorts, and restaurants, there's a whole range of activities and adventures available for the family on Ambergris Caye. Be sure to schedule in a snorkel trip to **Hol Chan Marine Reserve** ★★ and **Shark-Ray Alley** ★★ (p. 132). More adventurous members of the family can try parasailing or windsurfing. Reserve 1 day for a visit to the Mayan ruins at **Lamanai** ★★ (p. 231). You'll also want to explore the mangroves on an **American Crocodile Education Sanctuary** (ACES) nighttime crocodile tour ★★★ (p. 135). Fly directly from San Pedro to the international airport in **Belize City** in time for your return flight home.

MAYAN RUINS HIGHLIGHTS

Belize boasts dozens of known Mayan ruins of varying sizes and in varying states of excavation and exploration. The following itinerary hits most of the major ruins, and even allows you some time to visit the cayes. You could easily add on a side trip to the northern or southern zones, where there are several lesser-known ruins.

Day 1: The Sleeping Crocodile

Arrive in **Belize City** and head straight to **Lamanai,** staying right next door to the ancient Mayan city at the **Lamanai Outpost Lodge** ★★ (p. 233). You'll probably arrive in the afternoon. Save the ruins for the next day, but take a boat tour on the New River Lagoon around sunset, and you'll see a host of bird species, and, most likely, a crocodile or two.

Days 2 & 3: Life in Ruins

Spend the morning exploring the **Lamanai ruins** ★★ (p. 231). Get there early before the tour groups arrive, and enjoy the peace and quiet of the site. Have lunch at the hotel and then head over to **Chan Chich Lodge** ★★ (p. 235). Settle into your room here, which is set on the central plaza of a Mayan ruin. Spend the following day exploring the ruins at and around Chan Chich. If you have time, head over to nearby **La Milpa** ★ (p. 234), a large site with an active and ongoing excavation.

Days 4, 5 & 6: Cayo Calling

Head to the **Cayo District** ★★ and stay at one of the lodges in San Ignacio or on the way to Benque Viejo. Be sure to take a trip to **Actun Tunichil Muknal** ★★★ (p. 251), an almost full day hiking and spelunking tour, which includes a look at ancient Mayan pottery shards and calcified skeletons. Still, in the afternoon, you can squeeze in a visit to **Cahal Pech** (p. 263), which is right in the town of San Ignacio. Over the next 2 days, you can visit the ruins of **Xunantunich** ★★★ (p. 264), **El Pilar** ★★ (p. 277), and the Mayan ceremonial burial cave at **Chechem Ha** ★ (p. 264). Caving is hard work, so be sure to treat yourself to a spa treatment at **Chaa Creek** ★★ (p. 275).

Days 7 & 8: Tikal Time

Take a 2-day/1-night trip to **Tikal** ★★★ (p. 290). Stay at one of the lodges right at the ruins. Get an early start in order to beat the crowds and because the ruins here are so extensive. Make sure you set aside plenty of time to explore the amazing ruins here, but also schedule some time to enjoy the quaint little island city of Flores. Return to Belize in the afternoon of Day 8, and head to the **Mountain Pine Ridge** ★★ area (p. 278), staying at either **Blancaneaux Lodge** ★★★ (p. 284) or **Hidden Valley Inn** ★ (p. 285). Horseback riders should stay at **Mountain Equestrian Trails** (p. 286) and do the following day's activity by horseback.

Day 9: Caracol

Get an early start for your visit of the ruins at **Caracol** ★★ (p. 282). And remember, at one point, Caracol defeated Tikal in battle. Stop at the **Río Frío Cave** and **Río On Pools** ★★ (p. 281) on your way back from the ruins.

Days 10 & 11: Enjoying the Cayes

Unwind for a couple of days on **Ambergris Caye** ★★. If you didn't get to visit **Altun Ha** ★ (p. 222) during your inland stint, you can easily visit as a day tour by boat and minivan from here. You can also arrange boat trips to the tiny ruins of Chac Balam in the **Bacalar Chico National Park & Marine Reserve** or to **Cerros** (p. 240) outside Corozal.

Day 12: Heading Home

Return to **Belize City** in time for your international connection.

WILDLIFE HIGHLIGHTS

Belize is one of the best place on the planet for wildlife lovers, not only because of the many species that can be spotted here, but because Belizeans take great care to conserve the creatures they share their country with. This itinerary includes a wide range of both marine and terrestrial animals, and because looking for wildlife in their natural habitat requires patience, most of these recommendations are over several day periods.

Days 1 & 2: A Jaunt into the Jungle

From Belize City head into the Río Bravo forest in western Belize to the luxurious **Chan Chich Lodge** ★★ (p. 235), a hotel with an excellent track record for jaguar sightings. Although it's quite rare, sometimes the nocturnal cats reveal themselves during one of the hotel's night safaris. This deep into the jungle plenty of other creatures will come out at night to say hello, too. During the day, birding walks and hiking reveal plenty of other wildlife.

Days 3, 4 & 5: Cayo Calling

Continue down to the **Cayo District** ★★ (p. 246), using **Hidden Valley Inn** ★★★ (p. 285) in the Mountain Pine Ridge area as a launchpad for wildlife adventures. The hotel itself offers birding and animal tours on its vast grounds; this is where you'll find the rare orange-breasted falcon, which is being reintroduced on the hotel's property. In the nearby town of San Ignacio take selfies with reptiles at the **Green Iguana**

Top Wildlife Areas

MEXICO

COROZAL

Orange Walk

San Pedro

ORANGE WALK

BELIZE — Belize City

Belmopan

CAYO

Dangriga

STANN CREEK

Placencia

TOLEDO

Monkey River

Punta Gorda

CARIBBEAN SEA

GUATEMALA

1 Belize City
2 Chan Chich Lodge
3 Cayo District
4 Green Iguana Conservation Project
5 Blue Morpho Butterfly Farm
6 Xunantunich
7 Mountain Pine Ridge
8 Belize Zoo
9 Ambergris Caye
10 Hol Chan Marine Reserve
11 Belize City

0   20 mi
0   20 km

Conservation Project ★★ (p. 267), which houses iguanas that cannot be returned to the wild, typically due to disability. Stepping into the world of iridescent butterflies at the **Blue Morpho Butterfly Farm** ★★ (p. 267) at Chaa Creek on the road between San Ignacio and Benque is as magical as it gets. Slightly further up the road is the Mayan ruin of **Xunantunich** ★★★ (p. 264), a favorite spot for howler and spider monkeys to congregate.

Day 6: Rest with Rescues

The **Belize Zoo** ★★ (p. 107) is one of those rare zoos that houses only local species which have arrived as rescues. This is your best opportunity to see the widest range of animal types, jaguars and tapir included. Stay at the onsite jungle lodge in order to take the night tour, which brings a whole new perspective to zoo exploration.

Days 7, 8 & 9: Catch the Cayes

Head to **Ambergris Caye** ★★ to experience Belize's populous marine wildlife along the Belize Barrier Reef. Start with a snorkeling trip to **Hol Chan Marine Reserve** ★★ and **Shark-Ray Alley** ★★ (p. 132) to swim with nurse sharks and stingrays. A sunset cruise is your best shot at seeing playful bottlenose dolphins, which love to cruise among the wake of touring boats. A nighttime trip with **American Crocodile Education Sanctuary** (ACES) ★★★ (p. 135) not only gets you up close and personal with the American crocodile, it supports essential conservation efforts for the misunderstood creature.

Day 10: Heading Home

Return to **Belize City** in time for your international connection.

THE ACTIVE VACATION PLANNER

5

Belize is a fantastic destination for the active and adventurous traveler. The range of available sport and tour options is wide; the quality of the adventures and local tour operators is high; and the fact that the country is so compact allows travelers to mix and match. Whether their interests are scuba diving, snorkeling, fishing, sailing, spelunking, mountain biking, horseback riding, or bird-watching, Belize has terrain and opportunities that are perfect for all active travelers. I hope that the following chapter, combined with the regional and destination chapters that follow it, will help you design and enjoy your dream vacation.

ORGANIZED ADVENTURE TRIPS

Because many travelers have limited time and resources, organized ecotourism or adventure-travel packages are a popular and efficient way of combining several activities. Bird-watching, cave exploring, and hiking can be teamed with, say, visits to classical Mayan ruins and a few days on an outlying caye for snorkeling and diving, sea kayaking, and more bird-watching.

Traveling with a group on an organized trip means that your accommodations and transportation are arranged, and most (if not all) of your meals are included in the cost of a package. If your tour operator has a reasonable amount of experience and a decent track record, you should proceed to each of your destinations quickly without the snags those traveling on their own can occasionally face. You'll also have the opportunity to meet like-minded souls who are interested in nature and active sports. Of course, you'll pay more for the convenience of having all your arrangements handled in advance. So skip this chapter if you're a planner (and a saver); you'll find all the info you need to put together your own adventurous trip in the destinations chapters of this guide.

In the best cases, group size is kept small (10–20 people), and the tours are conducted by knowledgeable guides who are either naturalists or biologists. Be sure to ask about difficulty levels when you're choosing a tour. While most companies offer "soft adventure" packages that those in moderately good (but not phenomenal) shape can handle, others focus on more hard-core activities geared toward only seasoned athletes or adventure travelers.

North America–Based Tour Operators

These agencies and operators specialize in well-organized and coordinated tours that cover your entire stay. *Note:* Most of these operators are not cheap, with 10-day tours generally costing in the neighborhood of US$2,000 to US$3,500 per person, not including airfare to Belize.

Bike Hike Adventures ★ (www.bikehike.com; ℂ **888/805-0061** in the U.S. and Canada) is a Canada-based company specializing in multiday, multiadventure tours for small groups. Their Belize offering is a 9-day tour that includes horseback riding, rappelling, cave tubing, and either snorkeling or diving. The cost is around US$2,800 per person, not including airfare to Belize.

G Adventures ★★ (www.gadventures.com; ℂ **888/800-4100** in the U.S. and Canada) offers a huge range of trips around the world, but only a handful of them are partnered with National Geographic Journeys. Their 10-day Belize trip is not only one of those few, it's also a great deal at US$1,900, not including airfare to Belize. Culture, food, and outdoor adventure are balanced equally on this locally-designed and -led experience.

International Expeditions ★ (www.ietravel.com; ℂ **877/392-0878** in the U.S. and Canada) specializes in independent programs and natural history group tours. They run a regular 10-day tour to Belize and Tikal that takes in several of the major Mayan sites and tropical ecosystems, while staying in top-end lodges. The cost is US$3,500 per person, not including airfare to Belize.

Island Expeditions ★★ (www.islandexpeditions.com; ℂ **800/667-1630**) runs various adventurous multiday land and sea tours around Belize. Kayaking the atolls is one of their strong suits, but they also combine this with inland adventures. These trips usually involve some island camping. Prices run around US$2,400 for a 7-day trip, not including airfare to Belize.

Journeys International ★ (www.journeysinternational.com; ℂ **800/255-8735** in the U.S. and Canada, or 734/665-4407 in the U.S.) offers small-group natural history and adventure packages around Belize, including trips especially geared toward families. Their 8-day family trip costs US$3,075 per adult, and US$2,450 for children 12 and under. Airfare to Belize is extra.

Magnum Belize ★ (www.magnumbelize.com; ℂ **800/446-2735** in the U.S. and Canada) is one of the largest wholesalers specializing in Belize. With years of experience and excellent staff on the ground, these folks offer a wide range of tour and adventure options, and good deals.

Sea & Explore Belize ★ (www.seaexplore.com; ☏ **800/345-8786** in the U.S. and Canada) has more than 20 years' experience booking travel to Belize, and offers both custom tours and well-priced packages for both adventure travelers and more traditional vacationers.

Slickrock Adventures ★★ (www.slickrock.com; ☏ **800/390-5715** toll-free in the U.S. and Canada, or 435/259-4225 in the U.S.) offers a variety of multiday land and sea tours around Belize. They specialize in sea-kayak and dive extravaganzas based out of their camp and lodge on the private Long Caye in Glover's Reef atoll. A full 8 days, 9 nights with these folks, not including international airfare, costs around US$2,350.

U.K.-Based Tour Operators

Imaginative Traveller ★ (www.imaginative-traveller.com; ☏ **44/1728-862-230** in the U.K.) is a good-value operator specializing in budget student, group, and family travel. Their offerings in Belize focus on the entire Mundo Maya, and usually also take in parts of southern Mexico and Guatemala. These trips range in duration from 17 to 58 days.

Journey Latin America ★ (www.journeylatinamerica.co.uk; ☏ **020/8747-8315** in the U.K.) is a large British operator specializing in Latin American travel. They offer a range of escorted tours around Latin America, including a few that touch down in Belize. They also design custom itineraries and often have excellent deals on airfare.

Belize-Based Tour Operators

Because many U.S.-based companies subcontract portions of their tours to established Belizean companies, it makes sense to set up their tours directly with these companies, thereby cutting out the middleman. While that means these packages are often less expensive than those offered by U.S. companies, it doesn't mean they are cheap. You're still paying for the convenience of having all your arrangements handled for you.

There are scores of tour agencies in Belize City and at all of the major tourist destinations around the country that offer adventure options. These agencies, and the tour desks at most hotels, can arrange everything from cave tubing and Mayan-ruins tours to scuba diving and snorkeling. While it's generally quite easy to arrange most of these popular tours and adventures on the spur of the moment during your vacation, some are offered only when there are enough interested people or on set dates. If you have a very specialized tour or activity in mind, it pays to contact the hotel you will be staying at or a few of the companies listed here before you leave home, to find out what they might be doing when you arrive.

Belize Trips ★★★ (www.belize-trips.com; ☏ **561/210-7015** in the U.S., or 610-1923 in Belize) is the place to come to set up a custom tour. Owner and longtime resident Katie Valk is extremely knowledgeable, friendly, and responsive. She knows the country inside and out, and is adept at designing one-off itineraries, perfectly matched to her clients' needs and desires.

Organized Adventure Trips

THE ACTIVE VACATION PLANNER

Destinations Belize ★★ (www.destinationsbelize.com; ✆ **561/315-6161** in the U.S., or 610-4718 in Belize) is an excellent Belize-based company specializing in creating custom itineraries and tours.

Discovery Expeditions ★ (www.discoverybelize.com; ✆ **671-0748,** or 671-2882) is a long-standing and well-respected Belizean company with a broad offering of soft adventure and natural history tours. They have offices in Belize City and San Pedro.

S & L Travel & Tours ★ (www.sltravelbelize.com; ✆ **227-7593**) is one of the original tour operators in Belize, with some 40 years of experience in both adventure and regular tours. It's still one of the best, with excellent on-staff guides, a good working relationship with all the hotels, and a focus on ecotourism.

ACTIVITIES A TO Z

Each listing in this section describes the best places to practice a particular sport or activity and lists tour operators and outfitters. If you want to focus on only one active sport during your time in Belize, these companies are your best bets for quality equipment and knowledgeable service.

Adventure activities by their very nature carry certain risks. In the past couple of years there have been several deaths and dozens of relatively minor injuries in activities ranging from freshwater fishing to jetskiing to boating. I try to list only the most reputable and safest of companies. However, if you ever have any doubt as to the safety of the guide, equipment, or activity, it's better to be safe than sorry: there's no OSHA in Belize. Moreover, know your limits and abilities and don't try to exceed them.

Biking

Belize is not a major biking destination. In fact, there are only four or so major paved roads in the entire country—the Philip Goldson (Northern), George Price (Western), Southern, and Hummingbird highways. Except for the wild Maya Mountains and Mountain Pine Ridge areas, the country is almost entirely flat. It would be possible to tour Belize's major mainland destinations on a touring bike, but the heat and humidity are often oppressive, and those few highways get plenty of traffic and generally don't have very wide shoulders. Serious (but not professional) road cyclists may enjoy watching or even participating in the Cross Country Cycling Classic, a 142-mile race ridden east to west and back every year on the day before Easter.

The options are slightly more appealing for mountain bikers and off-track riders. Fat-tire explorations are relatively new and underexploited in Belize. Just about every major hotel in the Cayo District and the southern zone has mountain bikes for guest use or rental, or can hook you up with a local rental company. These bikes are fine for day trips and nontechnical riding. However, if you plan to do any serious biking, you might consider bringing your own rig, as quality mountain bike rentals are still a rarity in Belize. The **Mountain**

Pine Ridge Forest Reserve and the area around it win my vote as the best place for mountain biking in Belize. The scenery's great, with primary and secondary forests, waterfalls, and plenty of trails. Truly hearty bikers can make it all the way to Caracol. See "Mountain Pine Ridge & Caracol" in chapter 10 for details.

Bird-Watching

With some 618 recorded species of resident and migrant birds identified throughout the country, and a wide variety of ecosystems and habitats, Belize abounds with great bird-watching sites. Even amateur bird-watchers should have little trouble checking off upwards of 100 species in a week's worth of watching.

Lodges with the best bird-watching include **Chan Chich Lodge** (p. 235) near Gallon Jug; **Lamanai Outpost Lodge** (p. 233) on the New River Lagoon; **Chaa Creek** (p. 275); **duPlooy's** (p. 274) or any of the nature lodges outside of San Ignacio; **Hidden Valley Inn** (p. 285) or any of the lodges in the Mountain Pine Ridge area; **Rock Farm at Belize Bird Rescue** (p. 256) outside of Belmopan; and **Copal Tree Lodge** (p. 215), **Hickatee Cottages** (p. 216), and **The Lodge at Big Falls** (p. 215), all in the Toledo District.

Some of the best parks and reserves for serious birders are **Cockscomb Basin Forest Reserve ★**, for scarlet macaws and a host of primary forest dwellers; **Shipstern Nature Reserve ★★**, for scores of different sea- and shorebirds; **Crooked Tree Wildlife Sanctuary ★★★**, for large varieties of wading birds, including the jabiru stork; **Man-O-War Caye ★★**, a major nesting site for the magnificent frigate; **Caracol** Mayan ruins and the **Chiquibil National Park ★★**, for many different resident and migratory forest species; **Half Moon Caye,** for the vast nesting flocks of red-footed boobies; and the **Río Bravo Conservation Area ★★**, for ocellated turkeys and trogons. You'll also find excellent bird-watching in neighboring Guatemala's **Petén ★★** province and around the **Tikal ★★** area.

Bird-watchers staying on Ambergris Caye should certainly head to the **Bacalar Chico National Park & Marine Preserve.**

A Bird-Watcher's Bible

Any serious bird-watcher will want to pick up a copy of *Birds of Belize* (University of Texas Press), by H. Lee Jones. Published in January 2004, this dedicated guide to the birds of Belize is updated regularly. The book is wonderfully illustrated by Dana Gardener, and includes 574 species of birds.

TOUR OPERATORS

In addition to the operators listed below, the **Belize Audubon Society** (www. belizeaudubon.org; ✆ **223-5004**) is an active and informative organization worth contacting.

Birding in Belize (Paradise Expeditions) ★★ (www.birdinginbelize. com; ✆ **610-5593**) is the go-to choice for anyone wanting to focus their adventure on Belize's beautiful birds. Based in country, this organization's guides have experience in leading tours as well as advanced avian knowledge. The 8-day tour goes through some of the best birding spots in the country, and costs US$2,195 for double occupancy, not including airfare.

Victor Emanuel Nature Tours ★★ (www.ventbird.com; ✆ **800/328-8368,** or 512/328-5221 in the U.S. and Canada) is a very well-respected small-group tour operator specializing in bird-watching trips, and a pioneer of the genre in Belize. These tours focus primarily on the area around Chan Chich Lodge and Crooked Tree Wildlife Sanctuary, two of the country's prime bird-watching destinations, though some of their other tour options touch down around Lamanai and the Mountain Pine Ridge region.

Caving

Belize is an excellent destination for spelunking. Whether you're passionate about cave exploration or you've never been underground in the dark, you should not leave Belize without venturing into one or more of its vast cave systems. The ancient Mayans believed caves to be a mystical portal between the world of the living and the underworld of spirits and the dead. They called this mystical realm Xibalba. In almost every explored cave in Belize, some evidence of use by the Mayans has been uncovered. Fire pits, campsites, burial mounds, and ritual altars have all been found. Numerous pieces of pottery, as well as skeletons, bones, and religious artifacts, have also been encountered.

The aptly named **Caves Branch region** ★★, just outside of Belmopan, is a prime (and certainly the most popular) place to go caving. The cave tube trips here, including the spectacular **Crystal Cave** ★★, are excellent introductions to the underworld. There are also several great caves for exploring in the Cayo District, including the **Barton Creek Cave** ★ and **Chechem Ha** ★. Perhaps the most adventurous and rewarding cave to explore is **Actun Tunichil Muknal** ★★★. For more information, see chapter 10.

A SPECIALIZED CAVE TOUR OPERATOR

The premier cave adventure operator in Belize is **Ian Anderson's Caves Branch** ★★, Hummingbird Highway, Mile Marker 41½ (www.cavesbranch.com; ✆ **610-3451**). The company has a lovely forested setting at a far upstream entrance to the Caves Branch River, and a wide variety of cave tours and explorations are offered; most full-day trips run from US$85 to US$125.

Cruising

Belize is blessed with some wonderful cruising grounds. Steady yet gentle trade winds, combined with protected internal passages and innumerable isolated islands and anchorages, make this a perfect place to explore by boat. Cruising options in Belize range from bareboat charters of modern catamarans and monohulls to funky converted Belizean fishing sloops pressed into the snorkel-and-sunset cruise market. Belize is also a major port of call for many Caribbean cruise lines. For information on the major cruise lines that ply the waters of Belize, see "By Cruise Ship" under "Getting There & Getting Around" in chapter 3.

Virtually any section of Belize's coast and its outlying cayes and barrier reef are perfect for sailing. At nearly every beach or dive destination, it is possible to get out on the water for a cruise. Given the choice, I'd say the more remote and isolated cayes of southern Belize are the best places to venture out to sea. The two operations listed below are by far your best bets for bareboat cruising.

YACHT OUTFITTERS

With their operations based in Ambergris Caye, **TMM** ★ (www.sailtmm.com; © **800/633-0155** in the U.S. and Canada, or 226-3026 in Belize) offers mostly catamarans, with the option for either bareboat or crewed chartering.

The Moorings ★ (www.moorings.com; © **888/952-8420** in the U.S. and Canada) has its main base in Placencia. They offer bareboat and crewed charters on both monohull and catamaran yachts.

Depending on the season and boat size, rates for a bareboat run between US$2,000 and US$7,000 per week, and crewed charters cost from US$3,000 to US$9,000 per week. Before you settle on a price, go to www.getmyboat.com, a marketplace website where boat owners often give discounted rates to draw customers.

Fishing

Any angler worth his or her saltwater fly rod already knows that Belize is a world-class fishing destination. Fly-fishing on the flats for permit, tarpon, and bonefish is the main draw, and the fish are excellent all up and down the coast and on the saltwater flats the length of the barrier reef. Bonefish- and permit-fishing are good year-round, while tarpon are best sought from April to November, with July and August being the best months. The southern zone around Punta Gorda and Placencia is prime fishing grounds for permit, while the coastal mangroves and rivers are excellent spots to land lively snook.

Just beyond the barrier reef, anglers can land snapper, barracuda, jack, and grouper, while those who head farther out can stalk sailfish and marlin.

Action Belize (www.actionbelize.com; © **701/544-0214**) is a Belize City–based operation offering a vast array of package and custom tour options. They are especially good with fishing itineraries, and even have their own boats and captains. A 7-day/6-night trip with 4 full days of fishing costs US$1,869 per person, double occupancy. A full day of fishing starts at US$150 per person for cruise-ship passengers and independent travelers.

By Belizean law all sport-fishing enthusiasts over the age of 16 must have a fishing license. The cost of the license is BZ$20 per day and BZ$50 per week. Since its passage the law has been controversial, with locals and visitors alike confused as to where to obtain the license, who it pertains to, and whether certain fish are game fish. Officially, the licenses must be obtained from the **Ministry of Agriculture's Fisheries Department** (www.agriculture.gov.bz; $\textcircled{C}$ **822-2241**). However, most licensed fishing guides and tour operators around the country can help you get a license.

FISHING LODGES

Cayo Frances Farm & Fly ★★ (www.belizeflyfishcamp.com; $\textcircled{C}$ **610-3841**) is a remote, rustic camp on the leeward side of northern Ambergris Caye. Surrounded by still, clear water, it's perfect for practicing and perfecting the art of fly fishing.

El Pescador ★ (Ambergris Caye; www.elpescador.com; $\textcircled{C}$ **804/661-2259**) is a luxury lodge on the northern end of Ambergris Caye, specializing in fishing packages. They have excellent guides and boats.

Turneffe Flats ★★ (www.tflats.com; $\textcircled{C}$ **888/512-8812** in the U.S., or 232-9022) is a beautiful fishing lodge with a privileged position right on the ring of the Turneffe Island Atoll and its extensive mid-ocean lagoon and openwater flats. See p. 167 for a complete review.

Copal Tree Lodge ★★★ (www.copaltreelodge.com; $\textcircled{C}$ **844/238-0216**) is by far the most luxurious lodge that accommodates fishermen. Permit is the prime game sought here, and the hotel's guides are some of the best in the area. See p. 215 for a complete review.

Golf

Belize is not one of the world's great golfing destinations; in fact, it's not a golf destination at all. The country's only regulation course was shuttered in 2010 and has since been turned into high-end housing that may one day have a private golf course, but not now.

Belize's only operational golf course is located on the outskirts of Belmopan. The **Roaring River Golf Course** (www.belizegolfcourses.com; $\textcircled{C}$ **664-5441**) is a par-64, 18-hole executive course. Greens fees run BZ$50 for 18 holes, and there's no charge for a set of clubs. A 9-hole round will run you BZ$35. The course is open every day of the year from dawn to dusk.

Horseback Riding

Although Belize is very sparsely populated, and much of it is ideal for exploring on the back of a horse, horseback riding is still a relatively undeveloped sport. The best place to grab a mount and explore is the Mountain Pine Ridge Forest Reserve, and the best outfitter to tour with here is **Mountain Equestrian Trails** (www.metbelize.com; $\textcircled{C}$ **669-1124**). A half-day trip including lunch costs BZ$132 per person; a full-day trip costs up to BZ$200. Even if you're not staying here, most of the lodges in this area also offer horseback riding. For more information on riding in this region, see chapter 10.

Kayaking & Canoeing

Belize lacks the major white water necessary for serious rapid enthusiasts. Most of the rivers here are rated Class I, II, or III. Still, many of these rivers are quite well suited for gentle canoe explorations and less technical kayaking adventures. The Macal and Mopan rivers in the Cayo District are perfect for these types of adventures, and most of the hotels and tour operators in the area offer a range of these types of tours. See chapter 10 for more information.

However, sea kayaking in Belize is excellent. The relatively calm waters and protection provided by the barrier reef and mid-ocean atoll lagoons, combined with a string of small, relatively closely spread cayes, makes this a perfect place to tour and explore by sea kayak. **Glover's Reef Atoll** is probably the most popular and best place for a sea kayak adventure; see "Dangriga" in chapter 8 for more information.

OUTFITTERS

Island Expeditions ★★ (www.islandexpeditions.com; © **800/667-1630**) runs various multiday kayaking tours to the outer atolls, Glover's Reef Atoll, and the coral islands along the southern stretch of Belize's barrier reef. These folks offer up quite a bit of flexibility, allowing you to design a trip that is part guided, part independent exploration, and part inland adventure. An 8-day/7-night excursion runs US$1,950 to US$2,400.

Slickrock Adventures ★★ (www.slickrock.com; © **800/390-5715**) specializes in multiday kayak tours around Glover's Reef Atoll, and they even have their own rustically comfortable base camp and lodge on a private caye here. An 8-day/7-night trip costs US$2,350 per person.

Kiteboarding

Its steady trade winds and calm waters make Belize a good place to learn how to kiteboard. More advanced boardsailors would probably want more extreme conditions, but this is a great place to learn and perfect your skills. That said, this is still a relatively minor activity in Belize. If you're interested, contact **Kitexplorer** (www.kitexplorer.com; © **652-7308**) on Caye Caulker. They offer top-notch equipment rentals and lessons in this sport.

Scuba Diving & Snorkeling

Belize is one of the world's top spots for scuba diving and snorkeling. It has the second-longest barrier reef in the world, as well as three spectacular mid-ocean atolls (there is only one other atoll in the entire Caribbean). In general, the reef is in very healthy shape and the water quality and visibility are consistently excellent.

Amateur or casual divers and snorkelers should really be happy almost anywhere in Belize, and every major beach and island destination has easy access to some fabulous dive and snorkel sites. Truly dedicated divers will probably want to head to one of the outer atolls. **Glover's Reef** ★★, **Turneffe Island** ★★, and **Lighthouse Reef atolls** ★★ all offer outstanding diving opportunities. The Blue Hole and several other sites on Lighthouse Reef Atoll make it the top choice for scuba divers, among a crowded field. **Shark-Ray Alley** ★★ and **Hol Chan Marine Reserve** ★★ are two deservedly popular snorkel spots just off of Ambergris Caye, although overpopularity and overcrowding are threatening the experience there. And finally, only just becoming known to cognoscenti, the **Gladden Spit** ★★ area, off the coast from

THE ACTIVE VACATION PLANNER | Activities A to Z

Placencia, is one of the top spots on the planet to snorkel or dive with giant whale sharks.

There are several dedicated dive resorts around Belize. Another option for hard-core divers is to stay on a live-aboard dive boat. These midsize vessels usually carry from 10 to 20 divers in private staterooms. The boats feature fully equipped dive operations and a host of amenities. One of the advantages here is that you get to hit several of the top reef and atoll sites in a weeklong vacation.

Information on snorkeling, scuba diving, and local operators is in each of the destination chapters that follow. Almost every beach resort in Belize, as well as most hotels in Belize City, either has its own dive shop and operation or can hook you up with a local crew. Below are listed a couple of live-aboard operations, and a couple of the best dedicated dive resorts in Belize.

Note: While many of the beach and island hotels and all of the dive shops in Belize have snorkeling and diving gear for rent, you might consider bringing your own. If nothing else, bring your own mask. A good, properly fitting mask is the single-most-important factor in predicting the success of a dive outing. Faces come in all sizes and shapes, and I really recommend finding a mask that gives you a perfect fit. Fins are a lesser concern, as most operators should have fins to fit your feet. As for your own snorkel, well, in this day and age, I think you should want your own. If you plan on going out snorkeling or diving more than a few times, the investment will more than pay for itself.

LIVE-ABOARD DIVE BOATS

Aggressor Fleet ★★ (www.aggressor.com; © **800/348-2628,** or 706/993-2531 in the U.S. and Canada) has the 34m (112-ft.) *Aggressor III and Aggressor IV,* comfortable dive boats with deluxe staterooms. Rates are around US$2,995 to US$3,095 per week.

Tip: Both boats are very comfortable and well-equipped, with full dive and photo-lab operations, rental equipment, attentive service, and plenty of deck and lounge areas. Each boat has one or two master staterooms with a queen-size bed for couples. The *Aggressor III* features TVs in every stateroom, and even has a hot tub on the upper deck. Couples will enjoy the *Aggressor III*'s wider lower bunk of their staggered quasi–bunk bed arrangement.

When a Package Isn't a Deal

While it's often tempting to purchase all-inclusive dive packages before coming to Belize, this limits your flexibility. For example, if the weather and water are really rough, you're already committed, even though you might prefer taking an inland tour to a Mayan ruin instead of a rough dive.

DIVING RESORTS & OUTFITTERS

In addition to the folks listed below, check the listings at specific beach and island destinations in the regional chapters, particularly those in Placencia, Ambergris Caye, Caye Caulker, and the outer cayes and atolls.

Hamanasi ★★★ (www.hamanasi.com; © **844/235-4930** in the U.S., or 520-7073 in Belize) is an excellent dive resort located on a beautiful patch of beach south of Hopkins Village. The location grants good access to a wide range of dive sites, including the outer atolls. See p. 189 for a complete review.

Isla Marisol Resort ★★ (www.islamarisolresort.com; © **888/623-5403** in the U.S. and Canada, or 610-4204 in Belize) has the distinct advantage of being located on Glover's Reef Atoll, an isolated spot loaded with world-class dive sites. See p. 183 for a complete review.

Capturing It on Film

No longer is underwater photography and video the exclusive realm of professionals with very expensive equipment. Generic and custom waterproof housings can be purchased for most modern digital still and video cameras, including for GoPro cameras. Alternatively, many dive shops will rent professional or semiprofessional underwater still and video cameras for about US$20 to US$40 per day.

St. George's Caye Resort ★★ (www.belizeislandparadise.com; © **800/813-8498** in the U.S. and Canada) is a boutique resort located close to Belize City and well located for trips to most major dive destinations in the country. See p. 165 for a complete review.

The Inn at Robert's Grove ★★ (www.robertsgrove.com; © **800/565-9757** in the U.S., or 523-3565 in Belize) is a luxury resort in Placencia, with a top-notch dive operation. See p. 202 for a complete review.

Spas & Retreats

So far the trend toward destination spas and yoga or tai chi retreats hasn't caught on in Belize. In fact, there are no true dedicated destination spas or retreats in the country yet. However, the two places listed below do a pretty good job at what they do.

Primarily a nature lodge and ecotourism resort, **Chaa Creek** ★★, off the road to Benque Viejo in the Cayo District (www.chaacreek.com; © **824-2037**), has a very nice full-service day spa offering a wide range of body and skin treatments to guests and non-guests alike. Multiday packages are available and can be designed to give the feel of a full-destination spa experience. See p. 275 for a complete review of the resort.

Belize Boutique Resort and Spa ★★ (www.belizeresortandspa.com; © **800/861-7001** in the U.S. and Canada, or 225-5555 in Belize) is a true spa, offering a wide range of treatments and packages. Their various massages, their mud and exfoliating treatments, and the general feeling of sensual overload and pampering are all top-notch. Aside from this, they don't really offer any of the classes or active exercise programs that you would expect at a destination spa. This is a popular option for cruise visitors and others looking for a spa experience (you don't have to be a hotel guest). For more information, see p. 224 in chapter 9.

THE ACTIVE VACATION PLANNER | Activities A to Z

5

BELIZE'S TOP PARKS & BIORESERVES

Belize has a broad mix of national parks, forest reserves, marine reserves, natural monuments, wildlife sanctuaries, archaeological reserves, and private reserves. All told, more than one-fifth of the country's landmass and much of its offshore waters are, to some extent, protected areas. In fact, the entire Belize Barrier Reef was declared a World Heritage Site by UNESCO in 1996.

Most of the national parks charge a BZ$10 per-person per-day fee for any foreigner, although some have begun charging slightly more and a few slightly less. Belizeans and foreign residents often pay less. At parks where camping is allowed, an additional charge of around BZ$4 per person per day is usually charged. Fees at private reserves vary, but are similar to those listed above.

The following section is not a complete listing of all of Belize's national parks, protected areas, and private reserves, but rather a selective list of those parks that are of greatest interest and accessibility. They're the most popular, but they're also among the best. You'll find detailed information about food and lodging options near each of the individual parks in the regional chapters that follow.

Northern Cayes & Atolls

BACALAR CHICO NATIONAL PARK & MARINE RESERVE This is one of the newer additions to Belize's national park system. In addition to being home to scores of bird, animal, and plant species (many of which are endemic), the park also features several ancient Mayan ceremonial and trading sites. Nearly 200 species of birds have been spotted here, and the park allegedly contains all five wildcat species found in Belize, including the jaguar. The park is accessible only by boat, but once you get here, there are several trails. **Location:** On the far northern end of Ambergris Caye. For more details, see "Ambergris Caye" in chapter 7.

HALF MOON CAYE NATIONAL MONUMENT A combined land and marine reserve, Half Moon Caye itself is the principal nesting ground for the red-footed booby, as well as for both hawksbill and loggerhead turtles. There is a visitor center here, and overnight camping is permitted with prior arrangement. **Location:** On the southern tip of the Lighthouse Reef Atoll. For more information, see "The Outer Atolls" in chapter 7.

HOL CHAN MARINE RESERVE *Hol chan* is a Mayan term meaning "little channel," which is exactly what you'll find here—a narrow channel cutting through the shallow coral reef. The reserve covers 7.8 sq. km (3 sq. miles) and is divided into three zones: the reef, the sea-grass beds, and the mangroves. The walls of the channel are popular with divers, and the shallower areas are frequented by snorkelers. Some of the exciting residents of the area are large green moray eels, stingrays, and nurse sharks (harmless).

Location: 6.4km (4 miles) southeast of San Pedro on Ambergris Caye. For more details, see "Ambergris Caye" in chapter 7.

Southern Belize

COCKSCOMB BASIN WILDLIFE SANCTUARY The world's first jaguar reserve, this sanctuary covers nearly 389 sq. km (150 sq. miles) of rugged, forested mountains and has the greatest density of jaguars on the planet. Other resident mammals include tapirs, otters, coati-mundi, tayra, kinkajous, deer, peccaries, anteaters, armadillos, and four other species of wildcats, as well as nearly 300 species of birds. The sanctuary is part of the even larger Cockscomb Basin Forest Reserve. Trails inside the park range from gentle and short to quite arduous and long. During the dry season, you can even climb Victoria Peak here, which, at 1,122m (3,681 ft.), is the country's highest mountain. **Location:** 10km (6¼ miles) west of the Southern Highway, at a turnoff 32km (20 miles) south of Dangriga. For more information, see "Dangriga" in chapter 8.

FIVE BLUES LAKE NATIONAL PARK The main attraction here is a stunning cenote, whose various hues of blue give the park its name. All around the park lie forested lands and beautiful karst hill formations. **Location:** Mile Marker 32 on the Hummingbird Highway. For more information, see "Dangriga" in chapter 8.

GLOVER'S REEF ATOLL MARINE RESERVE This stunning and isolated mid-ocean coral formation features an oval-shaped central lagoon nearly 35km (22 miles) long. The steep-walled reefs here offer some of the best wall diving anywhere in the Caribbean. The entire atoll was declared a World Heritage Site by the United Nations. **Location:** 121km (75 miles) southeast of Belize City; 45km (28 miles) east of Dangriga. For more information, see "Dangriga" in chapter 8.

Northern Belize

CROOKED TREE WILDLIFE SANCTUARY This swampy lowland is home to more than 250 resident species of birds and serves as a resting spot for scores of migratory species. During a visit here, you are sure to spot any number of interesting water birds. However, the sanctuary was established primarily to protect Belize's main nesting site of the endangered jabiru stork, the largest bird in the Western Hemisphere. Crocodiles, iguanas, coati-mundi, and howler monkeys are all frequently sighted. There are six major lagoons here connected by a series of creeks, rivers, and wetlands. The best way to explore the preserve is by dugout canoe. **Location:** 53km (33 miles) northwest of Belize City. For more information, see "En Route North: Crooked Tree Wildlife Sanctuary" in chapter 9.

RÍO BRAVO CONSERVATION AREA This 105,218-hectare (260,000-acre) tract is a mix of virgin forest, sustainable-yield managed forest, and recovering reforestation areas. The land is home to nearly 400 bird species

Belize's National Parks & Nature Reserves

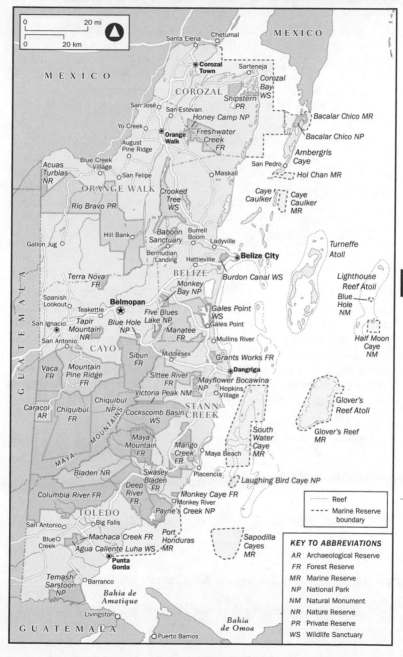

0   20 mi
0   20 km

MEXICO

Santa Elena   Chetumal   **MEXICO**

● **Corozal Town**   Sarteneja

MEXICO

Corozal Bay WS

COROZAL

Shipstern PR

San José○   San Estevan

Honey Camp NP

Yo Creek○   Freshwater Creek FR

● **Orange Walk**

August Pine Ridge○

Bacalar Chico MR

Bacalar Chico NP

Ambergris Caye

San Pedro○

Hol Chan MR

Acuas Turbias NR

Blue Creek Village○   ○San Felipe

ORANGE WALK

Maskall○

Caye Caulker   Caye Caulker MR

Rio Bravo PR

Crooked Tree WS

Gallon Jug○

Hill Bank○

Baboon Sanctuary   Burrell Boom

Ladyville

Bermudian Landing   Hattieville

BELIZE

● **Belize City**

Turneffe Atoll

Terra Nova FR

Monkey Bay NP

Burdon Canal WS

Lighthouse Reef Atoll

Blue Hole NM

Spanish Lookout○

● **Belmopan**

Teakettle○   Tapir Mountain NR

San Ignacio●

San Antonio○

Five Blues Lake NP

Blue Hole NP

Gales Point WS

○Gales Point

GUATEMALA

Vaca FR   Mountain Pine Ridge FR

Sibun FR

Middlesex○

Manatee FR

Mullins River○

Half Moon Caye NM

CAYO

Grants Works FR

Caracol AR   Chiquibul FR

Chiquibul NP

Sittee River FR

Victoria Peak NM

Mayflower Bocawina NP

○Hopkins Village

●Dangriga

Cockscomb Basin WS

STANN CREEK

Glover's Reef Atoll

MAYA MOUNTAINS

Maya Mountain FR

Mango Creek FR

Maya Beach○

South Water Caye MR

Glover's Reef MR

Bladen NR

Swasey Bladen FR

Deep River FR

○Placencia

Laughing Bird Caye NP

Columbia River FR

Monkey Caye FR

○Monkey River

Payne's Creek NP

TOLEDO

San Antonio○   ○Big Falls

Blue○ Creek

Machaca Creek FR

Port Honduras MR

Sapodilla Cayes MR

Agua Caliente Luha WS

● **Punta Gorda**

Temash-Sarstoon NP

○Barranco

Bahia de Amatique

Livingston○

Bahia de Omoa

GUATEMALA

○Puerto Barrios

········· Reef

‐ ‐ ‐ Marine Reserve boundary

KEY TO ABBREVIATIONS

AR   Archaeological Reserve
FR   Forest Reserve
MR   Marine Reserve
NP   National Park
NM   Natural Monument
NR   Nature Reserve
PR   Private Reserve
WS   Wildlife Sanctuary

and more than 200 species of tropical trees. It also supports a healthy population of most of the new-world cat species, and is one of the best areas in the Americas for spotting a jaguar, even better than Cockscomb Basin. La Milpa, one of Belize's largest known Mayan sites, is located within this reserve, and Río Bravo is bordered by some 101,171 hectares (250,000 acres) of private reserve at Chan Chich, as well as the Kalakmul Reserve in Mexico and the Maya Biosphere Reserve in Guatemala, making it part of a massive regional biological and archaeological protected area. **Location:** 89km (55 miles) southwest of Orange Walk Town. For more information, see "Going West" in chapter 9.

SHIPSTERN NATURE RESERVE The 8,903 hectares (22,000 acres) of this reserve protect a variety of distinct ecosystems and a wealth of flora and fauna. Shipstern Nature Reserve is home to more than 250 bird species, and its mangroves, lagoons, and flat wetlands offer some of the best bird-watching sites in Belize. The lagoons and wetlands here are home to manatees and Morelet's crocodiles. The reserve also has lowland tropical dry forest unique to Belize. **Location:** 60km (37 miles) north of Orange Walk Town. For more information, see "Corozal Town" in chapter 9.

Cayo District & Western Belize

ST. HERMAN'S BLUE HOLE NATIONAL PARK This park gets its name from a crystal-clear pool, or cenote, formed in a collapsed cavern. A short, well-marked trail leads to the main attraction here. Dense jungle surrounds a small natural pool of deep turquoise. This park also features **St. Herman's Cave,** one of the largest and—at one time—most easily accessible caves in Belize. The trail that connects the cenote and the cave passes through lush and beautiful primary and secondary tropical forests that are rich in flora and fauna. **Location:** 19km (12 miles) south of Belmopan on the Hummingbird Highway. For more information, see "Belmopan" in chapter 10.

CARACOL ARCHAEOLOGICAL RESERVE Caracol is the largest known Mayan archaeological site in Belize, and one of the great Mayan city-states of the Classic era. So far three main plazas with numerous structures and two ball courts have been excavated. Caracol is located deep within the **Chiquibil Forest Reserve,** which is a largely undeveloped tract of primary and secondary tropical rain and pine forests. The bird-watching here is excellent. **Location:** 80km (50 miles) from the Western Highway at a turnoff just south of San Ignacio. For more information, see "Mountain Pine Ridge & Caracol" in chapter 10.

GUANACASTE NATIONAL PARK This 20-hectare (50-acre) park is named for a huge old guanacaste, or tubroos, tree that is found within the park. There are nearly 3.2km (2 miles) of well-marked and well-maintained trails in the park. The park is bordered on the west by Roaring Creek and on the north by the Belize River. Among the animals you might see are more than

120 species of birds, large iguanas, armadillos, kinkajous, deer, agoutis (large rodents that are a favorite game meat in Belize), and jaguarundis (small jungle cats). **Location:** 3.2km (2 miles) north of Belmopan, where the Hummingbird Highway turns off the Western Highway. For more information, see "Belmopan" in chapter 10.

MONKEY BAY   The combined Monkey Bay Wildlife Sanctuary and Monkey Bay Nature Reserve represent more than 1,344 hectares (3,320 acres) of private, protected reserve of forest and wetlands. More than 250 species of birds have been recorded here so far, and the number is growing. There are hiking trails, as well as canoe tours on the Sibun River. **Location:** 50km (31 miles) west of Belize City, just off the Western Highway. For more information, see "Belmopan" in chapter 10.

Tikal, Guatemala

TIKAL NATIONAL PARK   While it's obviously not in Belize, the close proximity and convenient access have earned this spectacular Guatemalan national park and ancient Mayan ceremonial city a place on this list and in this book. Surrounded by dense, virgin tropical rainforest, the Tikal ruins are perhaps the most spectacularly preserved and restored Mayan ruins yet uncovered. **Location:** 100km (62 miles) northwest of the Belize border; 64km (40 miles) north of Flores. For more information, see "Tikal" in chapter 11.

TIPS ON HEALTH, SAFETY & ETIQUETTE IN THE WILDERNESS

Much of what is discussed below is common sense. For more detailed information, see "Health & Safety" in chapter 3.

Taking Care

While most tours are safe, there are risks involved in any adventurous activity. Know and respect your own physical limits before undertaking any strenuous activity. Be prepared for extremes in temperature and rainfall and for wide fluctuations in weather. A sunny morning hike can quickly become a cold and wet ordeal, so it's usually a good idea to carry along some form of rain gear when hiking in the rainforest, or to have a dry change of clothing waiting at the end of the trail. Make sure to bring along plenty of sunscreen when you're not going to be covered by the forest canopy.

If you do any backcountry packing or camping, remember that it really *is* a jungle out there. Don't go poking under rocks or fallen branches. Snakebites are very rare, but don't do anything to increase the odds. If you do encounter a snake, stay calm, don't make any sudden movements, and *do not* try to handle it. Also, avoid swimming in major rivers unless a guide or local operator can vouch for their safety. Though white-water sections and stretches in mountainous areas are generally pretty safe, most mangrove canals and river mouths in Belize support healthy crocodile populations.

Bugs and bug bites will probably be your greatest health concern in Belize, and even they aren't as big a problem as you might expect. Mostly bugs are an inconvenience, although mosquitoes can carry malaria or dengue (see "Health & Safety" in chapter 3, for more information). A strong repellent and proper clothing will minimize both the danger and the inconvenience; you may also want to bring along some cortisone or Benadryl cream to soothe itching. At the beaches, you'll probably be bitten by sand fleas, or "no-see-ums." These nearly invisible insects leave an irritating welt. Try not to scratch, as this can lead to open sores and infections. No-see-ums are most active at sunrise and sunset, so you might want to cover up or avoid the beaches at these times.

And remember: Whenever you enjoy nature, you should tread lightly and try not to disturb the natural environment. There's a popular slogan well known to most campers that certainly applies here: "Leave nothing but footprints, take nothing but memories." If you must take home a souvenir, take photos. Do not cut or uproot plants or flowers. Pack out everything you pack in, and *please* do not litter.

5 | Searching for Wildlife

Animals in the forests are predominantly nocturnal. When they are active in the daytime, they are usually elusive and on the watch for predators. Birds are easier to spot in clearings or secondary forests than they are in primary forests. Unless you have lots of experience in the tropics, your best hope for enjoying a walk through the jungle lies in employing a trained and knowledgeable guide. (By the way, if it's been raining a lot and the trails are muddy, a good pair of rubber boots comes in handy. These are usually provided by the lodges or at the sites, where necessary.)

Here are a few helpful hints:

- **Listen.** Pay attention to rustling in the leaves; whether it's monkeys up above or pizotes on the ground, you're most likely to hear an animal before seeing one.
- **Keep quiet.** Noise will scare off animals and prevent you from hearing their movements and calls.
- **Don't try too hard.** Soften your focus and allow your peripheral vision to take over. This way you can catch glimpses of motion and then focus in on the prey.
- **Bring your own binoculars.** It's also a good idea to practice a little first to get the hang of them. It would be a shame to be fiddling around and staring into space while everyone else in your group oohs and aahs over a trogon or honeycreeper.
- **Dress appropriately.** You'll have a hard time focusing your binoculars if you're busy swatting mosquitoes. Light, long pants and long-sleeved shirts are your best bet. Comfortable hiking boots are a real boon, except where

heavy rubber boots are necessary. Avoid loud colors; the better you blend in with your surroundings, the better your chances are of spotting wildlife.

o **Be patient.** The jungle isn't on a schedule. However, your best shots at seeing forest fauna are in the very early-morning and late-afternoon hours.

o **Read up.** Familiarize yourself with what you're most likely to see. Most lodges and hotels have a copy of *Birds of Belize* (University of Texas Press, 2004), by H. Lee Jones, and other wildlife field guides, although it's always best to have your own. A good all-around book to have is Les Beletsky's *Belize and Northern Guatemala: The Ecotravellers' Wildlife Guide* (Natural World Academic Press, 2004).

ECOLOGICALLY ORIENTED VOLUNTEER & STUDY PROGRAMS

Below are some institutions and organizations that are working on ecology and sustainable development projects.

Belize Bird Conservancy ★★ (www.belizebirdconservancy.org) brings people deep into the Chiquibul Forest Reserve near the Guatemalan border to camp beneath nesting macaws for several weeks, protecting the babies from poachers in the illegal pet trade. It's free to volunteer, but know that the conditions are extremely primitive. With the help of volunteers, scarlet macaws are returning from the brink of being extinct in Belize. It's an incredible experience, and I highly recommend it.

Cornerstone Foundation ★★ (www.cornerstonefoundationbelize.org; ✆ 667-0210), based in San Ignacio in the Cayo District, is an excellent and effective nonreligious, nongovernmental peace organization with a variety of volunteer and cultural exchange program opportunities. Programs range from AIDS education to literacy campaigns to renewable resource development and use. Overall, costs are pretty low and reflect the costs of basic food, lodging, and travel in country, with some extra going to support the organization and its work.

Earthwatch Institute ★ (www.earthwatch.org; ✆ 800/776-0188 in the U.S. and Canada) organizes volunteers to go on research trips to help scientists collect data and conduct field experiments in a number of scientific fields and a wide range of settings. Current expeditions to Belize focus on the study and field research on sharks. Fees for food and lodging average around US$3,000 for a 8-day expedition, excluding airfare.

International Zoological Expeditions ★★ (www.izebelize.com; ✆ 508/655-1461 in the U.S. and Canada) has two research and educational facilities in Belize, on South Water Caye and in Blue Creek Village. IZE organizes and administers a variety of educational and vacation trips to these two stations, for both school groups and individuals. A 10-day program usually costs about US$1,300 to US$1,800 per student.

Maya Research Program at Blue Creek ★ (www.mayaresearchprogram. org; ✆ **817/831-9011** in the U.S.) runs volunteer and educational programs at an ongoing Mayan archaeological dig. Two-week sessions allow participants to literally dig in and take part in the excavation of a Mayan ruin. The cost is US$1,850 for the 2-week program; discounts are available for students and longer stays.

Monkey Bay Wildlife Sanctuary (www.monkeybaybelize.com; ✆ **822-8032**) is a private reserve and environmental education center that specializes in hosting study-abroad student groups. They also run their own in-house educational programs and can arrange a variety of volunteer stays and programs, including homestays with local Belizean families. See "Belmopan" in chapter 10 for complete details.

Sustainable Harvest International ★★ (www.sustainableharvest.org; ✆ **207/669-8254** in the U.S. and Canada) offers unique programs based on sustainable farming techniques and practices. Their Belize program focuses on organic cacao production in the southern Stann Creek and Toledo districts. The 8-day program usually costs about US$2,000 per person, with discounts available for students and children.

Toledo Institute for Development and Environment ★ (www.facebook. com/TIDEBZE; ✆ **722-2274**) is a small, grassroots environmental and eco-tourism organization working on sustainable development and ecological protection issues in the Toledo District. Contact them directly if you are interested in volunteering.

BELIZE CITY

L ong ago stripped of its status as the country's capital,
Belize City remains Belize's business, transportation, and
cultural hub. Sooner or later you'll spend at least some
time here, unless you do all your in-country traveling by air or
have a very precisely planned itinerary. As the country's most
urban area, it can be rough around the edges, and doesn't
offer quite the same draw as destinations along the coast or
in the jungle, but there are still treasures all their own to be
explored here.

With a population of some 50,000, plus another 20,000 in the
surrounding area, Belize City is surrounded on three sides by water,
and at high tide it is nearly swamped. It's a strange, dense warren
of narrow streets and canals (the latter being little more than open
sewers, and pretty pungent in hot weather), modern stores, dilapidated shacks, and quaint colonial mansions, coexisting in a seemingly chaotic jumble.

The city was originally settled by the ancient Mayans, who lived
up and down the coast here. By the mid-1600s, pirates were using
the current site of Belize City as a hideout and provisioning spot.
Soon after, the British arrived and set up a logging base here, fueled
by slave labor. Logs were harvested inland and floated down the
Belize River for milling and shipping. This logging base soon
became a colonial settlement and the seat of Britain's colonial
empire on the Central American isthmus. Belize City itself is said
to sit on a foundation of wood chips, discarded ships' ballast, and
empty rum bottles.

Belize City has historically been a hotbed of bad luck. The entire
population abandoned the city and moved to St. George's Caye in
1779 following a Spanish attack. The Baymen, as the British settlers called themselves, returned and resettled the city in 1784.
Massive fires razed much of the city in 1804, 1806, and 1856.
Deadly hurricanes inflicted heavy damage in 1931 and 1961.
Between these events, the residents endured smallpox, yellow
fever, and cholera epidemics. Belize City had been declared the
capital of British Honduras in 1892, but after Hurricane Hattie
struck in 1961, the country's capital was relocated inland to
Belmopan.

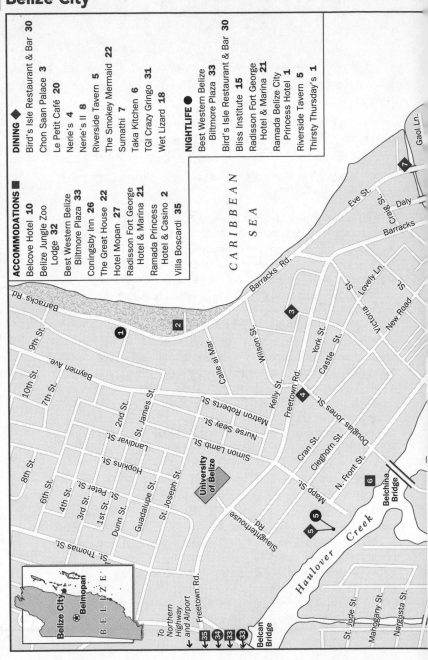

DINING ◆
Bird's Isle Restaurant & Bar **30**
Chon Saan Palace **3**
Le Petit Café **20**
Nerie's **4**
Nerie's II **8**
Riverside Tavern **5**
The Smokey Mermaid **22**
Sumathi **7**
Taka Kitchen **6**
TGI Crazy Gringo **31**
Wet Lizard **18**

NIGHTLIFE ●
Best Western Belize
Biltmore Plaza **33**
Bird's Isle Restaurant & Bar **30**
Bliss Institute **15**
Radisson Fort George
Hotel & Marina **21**
Ramada Belize City
Princess Hotel **1**
Riverside Tavern **5**
Thirsty Thursday's **1**

ACCOMMODATIONS ■
Belcove Hotel **10**
Belize Jungle Zoo
Lodge **32**
Best Western Belize
Biltmore Plaza **33**
Coningsby Inn **26**
The Great House **22**
Hotel Mopan **27**
Radisson Fort George
Hotel & Marina **21**
Ramada Princess
Hotel & Casino **2**
Villa Boscardi **35**

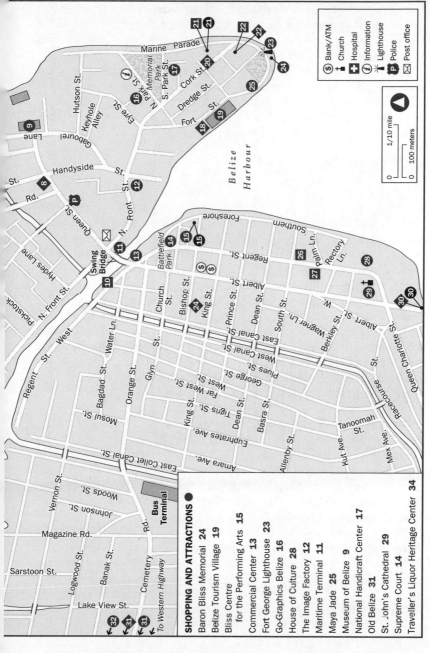

Marine Parade

Memorial Park

Cork St.

Dredge St.

Fort St.

Belize Harbour

Foreshore

Southern

N. Park St.

S. Park St.

Eyre St.

Hutson St.

Keyhole Alley

Gabourel Lane

Handyside St.

Queen St.

N. Front St.

Swing Bridge

Battlefield Park

Regent St.

Albert St.

Church St.

Bishop St.

King St.

Prince St.

Dean St.

South St.

Wagner Ln.

Berkley St.

Palm Ln.

Rectory Ln.

Albert St.

Queen Charlotte St.

Racecourse St.

East Canal St.

West Canal St.

Plues St.

George St.

West St.

Far West St.

Tigris St.

Dean St.

Basra St.

Allenby St.

Kut Ave.

Tanoomah St.

Mex Ave.

King St.

Euphrates Ave.

Amara Ave.

Mosul St.

Bagdad St.

Orange St.

Glyn St.

Water Ln.

West St.

Regent St.

Pickstock St.

Hydes Lane

N. Front St.

Gabourel Lane

Handyside St.

Rd.

St.

East Collet Canal St.

Vernon St.

Woods St.

Johnson St.

Bus Terminal

Magazine Rd.

Sarstoon St.

Logwood St.

Banak St.

Cemetery Rd.

Lake View St.

To Western Highway

(S) Bank/ATM
† Church
✚ Hospital
(i) Information
⚓ Lighthouse
P Police
⊠ Post office

0   1/10 mile
0   100 meters

SHOPPING AND ATTRACTIONS ●

Baron Bliss Memorial **24**
Belize Tourism Village **19**
Bliss Centre
  for the Performing Arts **15**
Commercial Center **13**
Fort George Lighthouse **23**
Go-Graphics Belize **16**
House of Culture **28**
The Image Factory **12**
Maritime Terminal **11**
Maya Jade **25**
Museum of Belize **9**
National Handicraft Center **17**
Old Belize **31**
St. John's Cathedral **29**
Supreme Court **14**
Traveller's Liquor Heritage Center **34**

97

Today, most people who know it well will encourage you to pass through without a second thought. A common nickname among locals is something that rhymes with "Belize Gritty," which is sadly fitting. This is an urban area in a developing nation, and the gang violence here has earned Belize one of the highest homicide rates in the world. While tourists are typically spared from this, precautions must be taken to avoid victimization of any kind.

That being said, Belize City remains the urban heart and soul of Belize, and a surprisingly fruitful place for shopping. Belize City is also the best place to see the culture of the country concentrated in one place, whether it's the local arts community, fishermen pulling in their daily haul, or even just people-watching at hole-in-the-wall restaurants.

ORIENTATION

Arriving

BY PLANE

All international flights into Belize land at the **Philip S. W. Goldson International Airport** (www.pgiabelize.com; ℂ **225-2045;** airport code BZE), which is located 16km (10 miles) northwest of the city in Ladyville, on the Philip Goldson Highway (formerly the Northern Highway). See chapter 3 for details about airlines that service Belize City.

In the baggage claim area, there's an information booth maintained by the **Belize Tourism Board.** This booth supplies maps and brochures, and will often make a call for you if you need a hotel or car-rental reservation. Inside the international departure terminal is a branch of **Atlantic Bank** (www.atla bank.com; ℂ **225-3331**), open Monday through Friday from 9:30am to 1pm and 1:30 to 3:30pm, Saturday from 9am to 1pm and 1:30 to 2:30pm.

Across the parking lot, you'll find 14 car-rental desks, as well as tour agencies.

A taxi into town, including to the water taxi or bus station, will cost BZ$50, a non-negotiable price mandated by the government. A taxi agent at a wooden podium just outside baggage claim will help arrange the ride for you. Unlike other international airports, this one does not have the problem of scammers tricking newcomers into expensive or dangerous rides. The cars may be in disrepair, but green license plates mean that these are official taxis that won't take you for a ride (so to speak).

If you fly in from somewhere else in Belize, you'll probably land at the **Sir Barry Bowen Municipal Airport** (airport code TZA and usually referred to just as the Municipal Airport), which is on the edge of town. A taxi from here costs just BZ$15 to most hotels in the city. There's no bank or any other services at the Municipal Airport, although most car-rental agencies can arrange to have a car there for you. See p. 101 for taxi info.

There is no direct bus service to either airport.

BY CAR

There are only two highways into Belize City: the Philip Goldson Highway, which leads to the Mexican border (166km/103 miles away), and the George Price (formerly Western) Highway, which leads to the Guatemalan border (132km/82 miles away). Both are well-marked and in good driving condition. If you arrive by car from the north, stay on the road into town, paying close attention to one-way streets, and you'll end up at the Swing Bridge. If you're arriving on the George Price Highway, stay on it after it becomes Cemetery Road, and you'll end up at the intersection with Albert Street, a block away from the Swing Bridge.

BY BUS

If you arrive in town by bus, you'll probably end up at the main **bus terminal** on West Collet Canal Street. This is an easy walk to downtown, but it is not recommended after dark. A taxi from the bus station to any hotel in town will cost around BZ$8 to BZ$10; see p. 101 for taxi info.

Tip: For excellent info on bus travel around Belize, check out http://belize bus.wordpress.com.

Visitor Information

The **Belize Tourism Board** (www.belizetourismboard.org or www.travel belize.org; ℭ **800/624-0686** toll-free in the U.S. and Canada, or 227-2420 in Belize) has its main office at 64 Regent St., in the heart of the business district of Belize City. If you missed their desk at the airport, they have another information desk here with regional brochures, basic maps, and a score of hotel and tour fliers; the office is open Monday through Friday from 8am to 4pm. Local travel agencies are another good source of information. Two in Belize City to try are **Discovery Expeditions,** 5916 Manatee Dr., Buttonwood Bay (www.discoverybelize.com; ℭ **671-0748**), and **S&L Travel and Tours,** 91 N. Front St. (www.sltravelbelize.com; ℭ **227-7593**).

City Layout

Belize City is surrounded on three sides by water, with Haulover Creek dividing the city in two. The Swing Bridge, near the mouth of Haulover Creek, is the main route between the two halves of the city, as well as the city's principal landmark. At the south end of the bridge is Market Square and the start of Regent Street and Albert Street. This is where you'll find most of Belize City's shops and offices. Unfortunately, this can also be the city's most dangerous area, so exercise caution, especially after dark. To the west and east of these two major roads is a grid of smaller roads lined with dilapidated wooden houses. On the north side of the bridge and to the right is the Fort George area, the more affluent section of the city. From the southern side of the city, Cemetery Road heads out of town to the west and becomes the George Price Highway, while from the northern side of the city, Freetown Road becomes Haulover Road and then the Philip Goldson Highway.

The Neighborhoods in Brief

NORTH SIDE

Fort George Anchored by the Fort George Lighthouse and Radisson Fort George Hotel & Marina at the eastern tip of the city, the Fort George neighborhood encompasses the area south of Queen Street, beginning at the northern side of the Swing Bridge, until it ends at Gabourel Lane. This neighborhood is easily the most upscale and picturesque in Belize City, with stately houses and mansions reflecting the colonial era, some kept in good repair, others not as much. Most of the best hotels in the city are located here. It also includes the small triangular Memorial Park and the Belize Tourism Village, as well as the lovely seaside Marine Promenade. The area was originally an island, but was deliberately connected to the mainland with landfill. This area should probably be your first choice for a stay in Belize City.

Barrack Road Located a mile or so north of downtown, Barrack Road runs along the Caribbean Sea for a good stretch before curving inland and becoming Princess Margaret Drive. This is where you'll find the Princess Hotel & Casino, as well as a couple of good restaurants. Much of the land on either side of Barracks Road is set aside as public parkland, while just inland is an area that is made up mostly of modern middle-class homes. While not within easy walking distance of downtown, it's just a very short taxi ride away. The seaside setting and parks make this a relaxing option for those wanting to avoid the bustle of downtown.

SOUTH SIDE

Commercial District Belize City's downtown business district runs from the south end of the Swing Bridge between Regent and Queen Charlotte streets, though most of the action is contained to Albert and Regent streets, which curves around with the water. In addition to a busy mix of banks and businesses, this area is home to a host of inexpensive hotels, as well as the Supreme Court and the Bliss Institute. Visit this area with caution, as this is where much of the city's crime takes place. Just south of this area, you will find the House of Culture and St. John's Cathedral. This is a decent option for budget travelers, but if you can afford it, we highly recommend lodging across the river in the Fort George neighborhood.

GETTING AROUND

By Foot

Belize City's downtown hub is compact and easy to navigate on foot. However, the city has a rather nasty reputation for being unsafe for visitors, and you'd be wise to stick to the busiest sections of downtown and obvious tourist districts. You can easily walk the entire Fort George neighborhood, as well as the compact business area just south of the Swing Bridge. If you need to venture any farther, or if you feel unsafe, take a taxi. Be careful when you walk,

---

Hauled Over Haulover

Haulover Creek is actually just what locals call the final few miles of the Belize River, before it joins the Caribbean Sea. It got its name as an outgrowth of common usage, as this is the area where goods and cattle used to be "hauled over" by early settlers, before a bridge was built.

as sidewalks are often in bad shape and sometimes quite narrow. It's wise to stow flashy jewelry, and avoid making visible cash transactions. And don't walk anywhere at night.

By Taxi

Taxis are plentiful and relatively inexpensive. A ride anywhere in the city should cost between BZ$7 and BZ$10, plus BZ$1 for each additional passenger. There's no standardized look or color to taxis in Belize: Many are old, some are sedans and some are vans, and most are in some stage of disrepair. Licensed taxis will have green license plates, and some have roof ornaments or "TAXI" written on the doors. Almost all have friendly drivers. Very few taxis use meters, so be sure to negotiate your fare in advance—you shouldn't be spending more than BZ$10 while staying within the city limits. If you need to call a cab, ask at your hotel or try **Cinderella Plaza Taxi Stand** (✆ **203-3340**), **Taxi Garage Services** (✆ **227-3031**), or **Majestic Taxi** (✆ **203-4465**).

By Car

You shouldn't need to navigate Belize City in a car. If you do find yourself driving around Belize City, go slowly, as pedestrians can appear out of nowhere and it's easy to get turned around. Pay attention to the general flow of traffic and the wealth of one-way streets. Despite being members of a former British colony, Belizeans drive on the right-hand side of the road, and road distances are listed in miles. Parking will be a challenge, particularly on the south side of the city. Cars parked on the street are targeted for theft throughout the city.

Most rental-car agencies are based at the Philip S. W. Goldson International Airport, although a couple have offices downtown or at the Municipal Airport, and almost all will arrange to deliver and pick up your vehicle at any Belize City hotel. The most reputable rental-car agencies in Belize include **Avis** (www.avis.com; ✆ **225-4400**), **Budget** (www.budget-belize.com; ✆ **223-2435**), **Crystal Auto Rental** ★ (www.crystal-belize.com; ✆ **936/307-1325** from the U.S., or 223-1600 in Belize), **Hertz** (www.hertz.com; ✆ **225-3300**), and **Thrifty** (www.thrifty.com; ✆ **225-2277**). Prices run between BZ$120 and BZ$250 per day for a late-model compact car to a compact SUV, including insurance. For more information on renting a car in Belize, see chapter 3.

Note: There is no way to bring a car with you from the mainland to the cayes. The best place to stash your vehicle is at the fenced-in international airport lot.

By Bus

Buses are few and far between in Belize City, but the services that do run operate on a schedule that can be found on http://belizebus.wordpress.com. Note that this site is not updated with frequency, and timetables are not always adhered to. Often your best bet is to ask locals for bus information.

[FastFACTS] **BELIZE CITY**

Babysitters Your hotel front desk is your best bet for finding a babysitter.

Bookstores Bibliophiles will be disappointed in Belize. You'd be best off purchasing any specific reading material, for either pleasure or research, before arriving in the country. Many gift shops carry a small selection of locally produced fiction and poetry, as well as guidebooks and maps. Your closest bet for books will be in San Pedro or San Ignacio, and all will be secondhand.

Cellphones DigiCell (www.digicell.bz; ☏ **0800/ DIGICELL** [344-4235]) has a booth at the airport. If you have an unlocked phone, they'll sell you a local pre-paid SIM chip with a local number. The chip and initial activation cost BZ$35, including BZ$10 of calls and data. You can top up in most grocery stores, some restaurants, and DigiCell outlets in whatever amount you like by speaking with an employee. It's also possible to add minutes online at the DigiCell website. The SIM chips and calling cards are sold at their desk at the airport or at one of their many outlets around Belize. Their website also has information on setting up your home phone for roaming in Belize.

Currency Exchange Most banks will exchange money for a small service charge. It is unnecessary to exchange U.S. dollars for Belize dollars while in Belize, as U.S. dollars are universally accepted at the official two-to-one exchange rate. The exception to this is upon leaving the country, when you will want to convert your remaining Belize dollars. There is a branch of **Atlantic Bank** (www.atla bank.com; ☏ **225-3331**), open Monday through Friday from 9:30am to 1pm and 1:30 to 3:30pm, Saturday from 9am to 1pm and 1:30 to 2:30pm, at the international airport. If you are flying out on a Sunday or outside of these hours, be sure to exchange any Belize dollars beforehand.

Dentists Call your embassy, which will have a list of recommended dentists, or ask at your hotel.

Doctors Contact your embassy for information on doctors in Belize City, or see "Hospitals," below.

Drugstores There are a handful of pharmacies around Belize City. In downtown, try **Brodie Pharmacy** on Regent Street by Battle Field Park (☏ **227-7070**); it's open Monday through Friday from 9am to 5pm. Perhaps the best-stocked pharmacy can be found at **Belize Medical Associates,** 5791 St. Thomas St. (www.belize medical.com; ☏ **223-0302**); it's open Monday through Friday from 7:30am to 7:30pm, Saturday from 7:30am to 5pm, Sunday from 10am to 1pm, and it makes emergency deliveries at any hour.

Embassies & Consulates See "Fast Facts" in chapter 3.

Emergencies In case of an emergency, dial ☏ **90** from anywhere in Belize City. This will connect you to the police, fire department, and ambulance central switchboard. You can also dial ☏ **911.**

Express Mail Services Several international courier and express-mail services have offices in Belize City, including **DHL,** 31 New Rd. (www.dhl.com; ☏ **223-1070**); and **FedEx as operated by Gutierrez Logistics,** 6 Fort St. (www.fedex.com/bz/contact; ☏ **223-1577**). Both can arrange pickup and delivery services to any hotel in town.

Eyeglasses The **Hoy Eye Center** is a small nationwide chain of opticians and eyeglass stores. Their Belize City branch (www.hoyeye center.bz; ☏ **223-0994**) is located at the corner of St. Thomas and St. Joseph streets.

Hospitals Belize Medical Associates, 5791 St. Thomas Kings Park (www.belizemedical.com; ☏ **223-0303**), is a modern, 24-hour private hospital, with emergency care and numerous private-practice physicians. The city's main public hospital, the **Karl Heusner Memorial Hospital,**

Princess Margaret Drive (www.khmh.bz; ☏ 223-1548), is also open 24 hours and has a wide range of facilities and services.

Internet Access Pretty much every hotel listed in this chapter and the rest have either Wi-Fi or a small business center with Internet connections. Internet cafes are also scattered around the principal business and tourist districts of Belize City. Though mostly used by locals who don't have home computers, they still get the job done.

Laundry & Dry Cleaning Most folks rely on their hotel's laundry and dry cleaning services. If your hotel is lacking in this arena, you can try **Belize Dry Cleaners & Laundromat,** 3 Dolphin St. (www.belizedry cleaners.com; ☏ 227-3396).

Maps The **Belize Tourism Board** (☏ 227-2420) can provide you with good maps to both the city and the country either at their kiosk at the international airport, or at their main office at 64 Regent St. Also, most gift shops sell maps of the country.

Newspapers & Magazines Belize has no daily newspaper. There are four primary weeklies: *Amandala* (www.amandala. com.bz), the *Reporter* (www. reporter.bz), *Belize Times* (www.belizetimes.bz), and the *Guardian* (www. guardian.bz). Most are relatively similar in terms of content, although with some differing, and usually obvious, political leanings.

Police The main Belize City station is at 9 Queen St.; the tourist police is a division of the small force. Dial ☏ **90** or **911** in the case of emergency. You can also call ☏ **227-2222.**

Post Office The main post office (☏ **227-4917**) is located at 3 N. Front St. It costs BZ$1 to send a letter to the United States, and BZ$1.20 to send a letter to Europe. Postcards to the same destinations cost BZ$.50 and BZ$.60, respectively.

Safety Belize City has a reputation for being a rough and dangerous city. Tourist police do patrol the busiest tourist areas during the day and early evenings. Still, while most populous downtown areas and tourist attractions are relatively safe during the daytime, travelers are strongly advised not to walk around at night, except in the best-lit and most popular sections of downtown. Basic common sense and street smarts are to be employed. Don't wear flashy jewelry or wave wads of cash around. Be aware of your surroundings, and avoid any people and places that make you feel uncomfortable.

Rental cars generally stick out and are easily spotted by thieves, who know that such cars are likely to be full of expensive camera equipment, money, and other valuables. Don't ever leave anything of value in an unattended parked car.

Taxes There is a BZ$37.50 departure fee that must be paid in cash (in either U.S. or Belize dollars) at the international airport upon departure, although usually the fee is already included in your airline ticket; the land exit fee is US$20. There is a 9% hotel tax added on to all hotel bills, and there is a 12.5% GST tax on all goods and services. A 10% service charge is sometimes added on to restaurant bills. Take this into account when deciding how much to tip (if the service is really good, an extra 5%–10% is fine).

Time Zone Belize City is on Central Standard Time, 6 hours behind Greenwich Mean Time. Belize does not observe daylight saving time.

Toilets There are very few public restrooms in Belize City. The best one I know of is in the water taxi terminal at 111 N. Front St. Most hotels and restaurants will let travelers use their facilities, although they are happiest about providing the service to clients.

Useful Telephone Numbers For directory assistance, call ☏ **113;** for an international operator, call ☏ **115;** for the exact time, date, and temperature, call ☏ **121.**

Water The water in Belize City is safe to drink for Belizeans. Many travelers react adversely to water in foreign countries, so stick with filtered or bottled water during your visit to Belize.

Weather The weather in Belize City is subtropical,

and generally similar to that of southern Florida. The average daytime temperature is around 80°F (27°C), although it can get considerably warmer during the summer months, as well as more humid. During the winter months, when northern cold fronts extend their grip south, it can get downright nippy. For more details, see "When to Go" in chapter 3.

WHAT TO SEE & DO

When cruise ships are in town, you'll find a line of trolley cars and horse-drawn carriages just outside the Belize Tourism Village offering rides around the city. Most of these include a stop, with entrance fee included, to the Museum of Belize (see below). If you really feel the need for a guided tour of the city and there's no cruise ship in town, you can contact **Belize Horse & Carriage Tours** (☏ 602-3048), **Discovery Expeditions** (www.discovery belize.com; ☏ 671-0748), or **S & L Travel and Tours** (www.sltravelbelize. com; ☏ 227-7593). A half-day city tour should cost around BZ$60 to BZ$100 per person, but can easily be combined with a visit to one of the several popular near-to-the-city attractions.

That being said, there really isn't much reason to *take* a guided tour of Belize City. The downtown center is extremely compact and lends itself to self-directed exploration. There are only a handful of interesting attractions, and all are within easy walking distance of the central Swing Bridge. Below you'll find reviews of the most intriguing attractions, as well as a walking tour of the city.

The Top Attractions

Belize City is very light on true attractions. The museums mentioned below are provincial by most standards, although they are worth a visit if you are spending a day getting to know the city, residents, and local history.

Bliss Centre for the Performing Arts ★ A busy little complex that is the cultural heart of Belize City, the Bliss Centre houses a performing arts space, rehearsal halls, a cafeteria, the National Institute of the Arts, and a couple of gallery spaces. If there are live theater, dance, and music performances while you're in town, they'll most likely be here. It also occasionally hosts worthwhile exhibits of art or photography. The main building's circular design takes advantage of the complex's setting, with large picture windows overlooking the Belize Harbour. The gallery spaces are fairly small, so you will need only about a half-hour, possibly less, to tour the institute.

Southern Foreshore, btw. Church and Bishop sts. www.nichbelize.org. ☏ **227-2110.** Free admission. Shows BZ$10–BZ$40. Mon–Sat 8:30am–5pm.

The Image Factory ★ This is Belize City's top art gallery. With a large stable of local and regional artists to choose from, this nonprofit gallery and arts organization has regularly rotating exhibitions, as well as a semi-permanent collection of art, photography, sculpture, and craft works.

91 N. Front St. www.imagefactorybelize.com. ☏ **223-4093.** Free admission. Mon–Fri 9am–5pm.

Museum of Belize ★★ Housed in what was once "Her Majesty's Prison," this museum features a collection of historical documents, photographs, currency, stamps, and other artifacts, as well as exhibits of Mayan pottery and archaeological finds. Although somewhat small, the collection of Mayan ceramic, jade, and both ornamental and functional pieces is worth the price of admission. There are also traveling exhibits and a room featuring attractively mounted insects from Belize. Just so you won't forget the building's history, a prison cell has been restored to its original condition. The museum takes up the two floors of this historic brick building. Plan on spending between 1 and 2 hours here.

8 Gabourel Lane, in front of the Central Bank building. www.nichbelize.org. ⓒ **223-4524.** Admission BZ$10 adults, BZ$4 students, free for children. Mon–Thurs 8:30am–5pm; Fri & Sat 8:30am-4:30pm; closed Sundays.

Old Belize ★ This attraction aims at providing a comprehensive experience of the natural, cultural, and political history of Belize, with exhibits re-creating everything from a rainforest and a Mayan ceremonial cave to a logging camp and a Garífuna home. Admission includes a 45-minute guided tour, but you'll probably want to stay longer to explore some exhibits on your own, visit the gift shop, or eat at the restaurant here (p. 119). There's even a pretty decent little beach, with a large water slide and children's playground area, and separate zipline cable adventure. While it's certainly touristy, if you have only a limited amount of time in Belize City, or the country in general, this place does give a good overview.

George Price Hwy., Mile 5. www.oldbelize.com. ⓒ **222-4129.** Admission to full-access package BZ$30 adults, BZ$15 children 6–12; museum-only admission BZ$10 adults, BZ$3 children. Tues–Thurs 7:30am–4:30pm; Fri–Sun 9:30am–4:30pm.

St. John's Cathedral ★ This old brick church is the oldest Anglican cathedral in Central America, and the oldest standing structure in Belize. Built in 1812 by slaves using bricks brought over as ballast, it is also the only Anglican church outside of England where kings have been crowned—during the 1800s, four Mosquito Indian kings held their coronation ceremonies here. The bell in the high bell tower here was brought over in 1826. In the small yard surrounding the church you'll find a few graves of prominent Anglican clergy.

At the corner of Albert and Regent sts. ⓒ **227-2098.** Free admission. Daily 8:30am–5pm.

Traveller's Liquor Heritage Center ★ Belize's world famous spirit producer offers the opportunity to learn a bit about the history, lore, and production process of the country's ubiquitous One Barrel Rum at this small museum-like exhibit. You can also get a glimpse into the contemporary production operation at the factory located behind the Heritage Center. At the end of the tour, you can taste various products and shop for bottles, T-shirts, and other souvenirs.

Mile 2½ Philip Goldson Hwy. www.onebarrelrum.com. ⓒ **223-2855.** Free admission. Mon–Sat 8am–5pm.

Why do they call this Belize City icon the "Swing Bridge"? Some expect to find a suspension bridge, thinking it might rock back and forth. In actuality, this bridge used to "swing" open twice daily to let tall masted sailboats pass through. Boat traffic has gone down, and because it's a hassle to open, it no longer does so unless there's a particular need. When it does open, the entire process takes approximately 20 minutes, and in addition to being a minor spectacle because it requires at least four people to operate it, it is a major traffic hassle. It is more commonly used as a reference point when describing where to find nearby businesses.

A Walking Tour

The following walking tour covers both the north and south sides of Belize City, which together comprise the entire historic downtown center. For most of its length, you'll be either right on the water or just a block or two away. As described, the walking tour should take you anywhere from 2 to 4 hours, depending on how much time you take visiting the various attractions. The only major attraction not right on the route below is the Museum of Belize, although it's only a 4-block detour east from the Swing Bridge. The route laid out on this walking tour is pretty safe during daylight hours, but should not be attempted after dark.

Begin your stroll at the **Fort George Lighthouse** and **Baron Bliss Memorial,** out on the northeastern tip of the city. A small slate stone marks the grave of Henry Edward Ernest Victor Bliss (see "Baron Bliss," below). After soaking up the view of the Caribbean and some fresh sea air, head toward downtown on Fort Street. On your left, you'll find the **Belize Tourism Village** (© 223-7786), which was built to accommodate the rising tide of cruise-ship passengers. Stop in and shop if you like, though most of the items are cheaply made and overpriced. There is also a public restroom here.

As you continue, Fort Street becomes North Front Street. Just north of the Belize Tourism Village you'll find **Fine Arts** (p. 111) and **The Image Factory** (p. 112), by far the two best galleries and fine arts gift shops in the country. Just before reaching the Swing Bridge, you'll pass the **Maritime Terminal** on your left.

Now, cross the **Swing Bridge** and head south. On your left is the **Commercial Center.** Wander through the stalls of fresh vegetables, butcher shops, and fish stands. You'll also find some gift shops and souvenir stands.

The **Supreme Court building,** off the small **Battlefield Park** (or Market Sq.) just a block south of the Swing Bridge, is a real prize of English colonial architecture with the city's only clock tower. Walk around the four sides and see if any are accurately telling the time.

Down at the southern end of Regent Street, you'll find the **Government House** and **St. John's Cathedral** (see above), also known by its more officious-sounding moniker, the Anglican Cathedral of St. John the Baptist. Both of these buildings were constructed with slave labor in the early 19th century, and they remain the most prominent reminders of the 3 centuries of British colonial presence here. The Government House has been converted into a **House of Culture** (✆ 227-3050), with the mission of encouraging and sponsoring local participation in the arts, music, and dance. You will occasionally find lecture series or an odd concert going on here.

For your return to downtown, head toward the water and come back on the Southern Foreshore Road, stopping in at the **Bliss Institute** (p. 104) to see if there's an interesting exhibit on display or a performance scheduled for later in the evening.

Attractions Outside Belize City

The attractions listed below are within an hour of Belize City; both can be reached by public transportation. In addition, the Mayan ruins of **Altun Ha ★** (p. 222) and **Lamanai ★★** (p. 231) and the **Crooked Tree Wildlife Sanctuary ★** (p. 225) are all easily accessible from Belize City. All are popularly sold as day tours, often in various mix-and-match combinations. If you're interested in visiting one or more of these attractions as part of an organized tour, ask at your hotel, or call **Discovery Expeditions** (www.discoverybelize. com; ✆ 223-0748) or **S & L Travel and Tours** (www.sltravelbelize.com; ✆ 227-7593). Prices range from about BZ$100 to BZ$280 per person, depending on the tour, means of transportation, and attraction(s) visited. Tours, especially those to Altun Ha and Crooked Tree, are often combined with lunch and an optional spa treatment at Belize Boutique Resort and Spa (formerly known and still referred to as Maruba Resort Jungle Spa), which is quite possibly the most quirky hotel in the country, and worth visiting on that merit alone (p. 224). For more information on Altun Ha, Lamanai, Crooked Tree Wildlife Sanctuary, and Belize Boutique Resort & Spa, see chapter 9.

Belize Zoo ★★   Founded in 1983 as part of a last-ditch and improvised effort to keep and care for a host of wild animals that were being used in a

baron **BLISS**

Henry Edward Ernest Victor Bliss, the fourth Baron Bliss of the Kingdom of Portugal, anchored his yacht, *Sea King*, off of Belize City on January 14, 1926. Within 2 months, the baron would be dead, never having set foot on Belizean soil. Nonetheless, the eccentric Baron Bliss is this tiny country's most beloved benefactor. His time spent anchored in Belize Harbour was enough to convince him to rewrite his will and leave a large chunk of his estate—nearly $2 million at the time—to the country of Belize (then

known as British Honduras). The trust he set up stipulated that the principal could never be touched, and only the interest was to be used. The ongoing bequest has funded numerous public works projects around the country, and today it's hard to miss the baron's legacy. There's the Baron Bliss Memorial, Baron Bliss Nursing School, Bliss Institute, and the Bliss (Fort George) Lighthouse. Every year on March 9, a large regatta is held in Belize Harbour in honor of the baron.

documentary film shoot, the **Belize Zoo** is a national treasure. Gentle paths wind through some 12 hectares (30 acres) of land, where the zoo houses more than 200 animals, all native Belizean species. According to them, "the zoo keeps animals which were either orphaned, born at the zoo, rehabilitated animals, or sent to the Belize Zoo as gifts from other zoological institutions." They are seriously invested in education, helping future generations appreciate and protect these wild animals.

Exploring the zoo, you'll see several species of Belizean cats, April the tapir, crocodiles, and other critters in idealized natural surroundings. The animals here are some of the liveliest and happiest looking I've ever seen in a zoo. It's obvious that they're well cared for. This is your best shot for ethically experiencing jungle wildlife if you're not planning to visit the actual jungle. All the exhibits have informative hand-painted signs accompanying them.

I highly recommend booking a VIP tour by appointment only with founding director Sharon Matola, the dedicated American woman who initially began the zoo. She is a wealth of information and very special to the Belize community. In 2008 she became the subject of Bruce Barcott's book, *The Last Flight of the Scarlet Macaw: One Woman's Fight to Save The World's Most Beautiful Bird.* It's a short, enthralling read outlining wildlife conservation efforts in Belize, and conveniently sold in the zoo's gift shop.

Tip: It's best to visit early in the morning or close to closing time, when the animals are at their most active and the Belizean sun is at its least oppressive. In addition, the zoo can get crowded at times; on days when cruise ships are visiting Belize City, busloads of tourists begin to arrive around 10am, but often are packed up and gone by 3pm.

Note: This is the first, and currently only, nature destination in Belize that is accessible to wheelchairs.

The entrance is a couple of hundred yards in from the George Price Highway. Any bus traveling between Belize City and Belmopan or San Ignacio will drop you off at the zoo entrance.

George Price Hwy., Mile Marker 29. www.belizezoo.org; ✆ **220-8000**). Admission BZ$30 adults, BZ$10 children. Daily 8:30am–5pm.

Community Baboon Sanctuary ★ There aren't really baboons in Belize; this is just the Kriol name for the black howler monkeys who reside in this innovative sanctuary. The sanctuary is a community program run by local landowners in eight villages to preserve the local population of these vociferous primates. The howlers are an endangered endemic subspecies found only in Belize. There's a visitor's center and natural history museum in the village of Bermudian Landing; admission includes a guided hike, which will start here. If you want a longer guided hike, you should hire one of these guides for a modest fee, as they can provide more context to what you're seeing and make sure you don't get lost or touch a plant that might harm you. The preserve stretches for some 32km (20 miles) along the Belize River, and there are several trails that wind through farmland and secondary forest. You will undoubtedly hear the whooping and barking of the howler monkeys as they make their way through the treetops feeding on fruits, flowers, and leaves. In addition to the nearly 1,500 howler monkeys that make their home in the sanctuary, there are numerous other bird and mammal species to be spotted here, including peccaries, anteaters, pacas, and coati-mundi. Bring binoculars if you have them. Wayward guides may let you touch the monkeys for extra money, but this is extremely unethical, and should not be supported.

At the visitor's center, you can also hire a canoe for a leisurely paddle and float on the Belize River. The cost is around BZ$50 for an hour or so paddle in a canoe that will hold two passengers in addition to the guide. Other guided tours offered include specialized bird-watching excursions and night canoe outings to spot crocodiles. Finally, the several small villages that compose the conservation project are wonderful examples of rural Kriol villages. Be sure to visit one or two, stroll around, talk to the residents, and see what kind of craftwork and food you can find. In each village, there are families that rent out simple rooms. Ask at the museum and information center, or reserve in advance via their website.

Bermudian Landing village, site of the sanctuary's visitor center, is about 32km (20 miles) west of Belize City. If you are driving, head north on the Philip Goldson Highway and watch for the Burrel Boom Road turnoff. Buses to Bermudian Landing leave Belize City several times a day. Call the sanctuary's visitor's center for current schedule and departure point.

Bermudian Landing Village. www.facebook.com/BermudianLandingVillage. ✆ **660-3545.** Admission BZ$14, which includes a short guided hike.

OUTDOOR ACTIVITIES

Due to the crime, chaos, and often oppressive heat and humidity, you'll probably want to get out of the city, or onto the water, before undertaking anything too strenuous. But if you want to brave the elements, there are a few outdoor activities for you to try in and around Belize City. See chapter 5 for more info on adventure sports in Belize.

CAVING The **Caves Branch ★★★** region is about a 50- to 90-minute drive from Belize City, depending on where you enter the cave systems. Several tour operators offer a variety of hiking and tubing trips through an extensive network of caves here. The **Caves Branch River** is a slow, meandering river that should probably be called a creek. Nevertheless, it passes through a series of long caves, making it perfect for a slow float on an inner tube through this dark and mysterious world. However, I recommend hiking because it allows more time for close examination of the geological formations and Mayan relics than tubing. **Actun Tunichil Muknal ★★★**, located near Teakettle Village north of Belmopan (p. 251), and the **Crystal Cave ★★**, located adjacent to what was once the Jaguar Paw Jungle Resort (now Nohoch Che'en, p. 254), are two of the more spectacular caves you will ever visit. Most tour operators and tour desks in Belize City can arrange these trips, or you can call **Ian Anderson's Caves Branch Adventure Company ★★**

(www.cavesbranch.com; © **610-3451**) directly. These folks run, by far, the most extensive cave adventure tour operation in the country. See "Belmopan" in chapter 10 for more information on the Caves Branch region.

FISHING   While most serious fishermen head to one of the cayes or southern Belize destinations, it's possible to line up fishing charters out of Belize City. The marinas at the **Radisson Fort George Hotel & Marina** (© **223-3333**), **Old Belize** (© **222-4129**), and **Princess Hotel & Casino** (© **223-2670**) all have regular sport charter fleets and can arrange a variety of options. You could also check in with the folks at the **Belize River Lodge** (www.belizeriver lodge.com; © **888/275-4843** in the U.S. and Canada, or 225-2002 in Belize). Expect to pay around US$1,000 to US$1,800 per day for a boat that can accommodate up to four fishermen. To get the best rates, try a service like **GetMyBoat.com** which serves as a marketplace for both private owners and charter tour operators to rent their boats.

GOLF   Your options are limited if you want to hit the links in Belize. There's only one public golf course in the country, the **Roaring River Golf Course** (www.belizegolfcourses.com; © **664-5441**), a par-64 executive course, located just outside of Belmopan. Greens fees here are just BZ$50 for 18 holes.

JOGGING   Belize City is not very amenable to jogging. If you must run, you could try a loop around the Fort George neighborhood, hugging the coast from the Fort George Lighthouse to Memorial Park, then heading to Fort Street, which will bring you back to the lighthouse. It's best to jog very early, before there's much street traffic and before it gets too hot. Another nice stretch for jogging is on the sidewalk and parks that line Barrack Road where it fronts the sea.

SAILING   The waters off Belize Harbour are theoretically perfect for day sailing excursions, although it is not a very common launch point. If you're interested in trying to line up a day sail, ask at your hotel desk or check in with the marinas at the **Radisson Fort George Hotel & Marina** (© **223-3333**), **Old Belize** (© **222-4129**), and **Princess Hotel & Casino** (© **223-2670**). See chapters 7 and 8 for details on longer charter options.

SCUBA DIVING & SNORKELING   The recently protected Belize Barrier Reef lies just off the coast from Belize City. It's a short boat ride to some excellent scuba diving and snorkeling. While most serious divers choose to stay out on one of the cayes for really close proximity to the reefs, it is still possible to visit any number of excellent sites on day trips from Belize City, including the Blue Hole and Turneffe and Lighthouse atolls. Check in with **Hugh Parkey's Belize Dive Connection** (www.hpbelizeadventures.com; © **223-4024**).

SPAS & GYMS   **Best Western Belize Biltmore Plaza** (p. 116) and **Radisson Fort George Hotel & Marina** (p. 114) have small gym facilities and offer basic spa services. However, only the Radisson allows nonguests use of their facilities, with a daily fee of BZ$20.

SWIMMING   Most of the higher-end hotels in Belize City have pools. If yours doesn't, you can head out to the **Cucumber Beach ★** at Old Belize (p. 105). The beach here has both an open-water section and an enclosed, and hence calmer, lagoon. There are also a water slide and a children's playground, as well as chaise longues and palm-thatch shade shelters. Admission is BZ$20 for both the beach and water-slide privileges. Children's admission is half-price.

SHOPPING

You won't be bowled over by shopping options here in Belize City, and very few people come to Belize specifically to shop. You will find a modest handicraft industry, with different specialties produced by the country's various ethnic communities. The Kriol populations of the coastal area and outer cayes specialize in coral and shell jewelry, as well as woodcarvings with maritime (dolphins, turtles, and ships) themes. The Belizean Mayan population produces replicas of ancient petroglyphs and different modern designs on various-sized pieces of slate. Finally, the Garífuna peoples of the southern coastal villages are known for their small dolls.

My favorite gift item in Belize continues to be **Marie Sharp's Hot Sauce ★★★**, which comes in several heat gradations, as well as some tropical fruit flavors. But Hillary Clinton and I agree: the original blend of habanero peppers, carrots, and vinegar is the best of the lot. The company also produces mango chutney and an assortment of jams. You can pick up Marie Sharp's products at any supermarket and most gift shops; I recommend you stick to the supermarkets, though, to avoid price gouging. In addition to Marie Sharp's, Lizette's and Hot Mama brands of locally produced hot sauces are also a good bet.

Please do not buy any kind of sea-turtle products (including jewelry); wild birds; lizard, snake, or cat skins; corals; or orchids (except those grown commercially). No matter how unique, beautiful, insignificant, or inexpensive it may seem, your purchase will directly contribute to the further hunting and destruction of endangered species.

The Shopping Scene

Most shops in the downtown district are open Monday through Saturday from about 8am to 6pm. Some shops close for lunch, while others remain open (it's just the luck of the draw for shoppers). Since the cruise ships are such a big market for local merchants, many adjust their hours to specifically coincide with cruise-ship traffic and their particular shore times.

Shopping A to Z
ART
Fine Arts ★★   This is the best gallery and gift shop I've found in Belize City. They have a large selection of original art works in a variety of styles, formats, and sizes. Browse primitivist works by Walter Castillo and Pen

Cayetano, alongside more modern abstract pieces, traditional still lifes, and colorful representations of Belize's marine, natural, and human life. 1 Fort St., next to the Belize Tourism Village. (© **674-5868.**

The Image Factory Shop ★ Attached to the excellent gallery and exhibition space of the same name, this shop offers up prints, paintings, photographs, and craft pieces by prominent Belizean and regional artists, as well as books, music CDs, and more traditional souvenir items. 91 N. Front St. (© **223-4093.**

HANDICRAFTS & SOUVENIRS

By far the largest selection of gift shops and souvenir stands can be found at the **Belize Tourism Village** (8 Fort St.; (© **223-2767**).

In addition to housing the best collections of fine art for sale in the city, **Fine Arts** and **The Image Factory Shop** (see "Art," above) also feature some of the best handicrafts and handmade jewelry. The quality and selection are a definite step above what you'll find at most other gift shops and tourist traps in town, and around the country.

Go-Graphics Belize ★ This long-standing design and production company has a shop and factory in the city, where you'll find an extensive collection of T-shirts, visored hats, and local textiles. They also sell a range of handmade jewelry, Guatemalan textiles, Mexican hammocks, and Belizean crafts. 64B N. Front St., Buttonwood Bay. www.gographicbelize.com (© **223-4660.**

National Handicraft Center ★ This place houses a wide selection of local and regional crafts and souvenirs all under one roof, but it's no longer the main game in town. In fact, it's lost a lot of its luster and traffic to the Belize Tourism Village. Still, you'll find a good selection of Mayan stone carvings, coconut shell jewelry, and wooden knickknacks, as well as some oil paintings, prints, and a small selection of books. Moreover, the prices here are slightly better than those at the Belize Tourism Village, and if you see something you really like, you might even be able to bargain for it. 2 S. Park St. (© **223-3636.**

JEWELRY

Coral is a very delicate, rapidly disappearing living organism that grows very slowly; please avoid buying coral jewelry, as it just feeds demand and inevitably leads to the destruction of the spectacular Belizean reefs, the only barrier reef to be legally protected from oil drilling by its government in the world. The same goes for jewelry made from the endangered Hawksbill sea turtle.

Maya Jade ★ This place bills itself as a museum and gallery, and while there is a whole room of museum-style displays explaining the history of Mesoamerican Mayan jade use and artistry, this is nonetheless predominantly a retail operation. That said, the small selection here includes some very pretty necklaces and earrings that you won't find elsewhere. 8 Fort St. (© **203-1222.**

LIQUOR

Your best bet for liquor shopping is at local supermarkets, or the duty-free shop at the airport. There are several brands of Belizean rum available; the most popular is **One Barrel,** which has a hint of coconut and vanilla. Other brands produce some more heavily flavored coconut rums. The **Prestige** brand aged rum is pretty good, if you're looking for a straight, dry rum. Belize doesn't produce any wines or other spirits of note, although you may want to pick up a bottle of locally produced wine, or cashew wine, for the sake of novelty.

MARKETS

The only real market of note is the **Commercial Center,** located just over the Swing Bridge, on the southern side of the city. This two-story modern concrete structure houses a mix of stalls and enclosed storefronts. The first floor is predominantly devoted to fresh produce, fish stalls, and butcher shops, but you'll also find stands selling flowers, fresh herbs, and some souvenir shops. There are more souvenir shops and some restaurants on the second floor. The Commercial Center is open daily from 7:30am to 7pm.

MUSIC

Punta Rock is the most Belizean of music styles. A close cousin to soca and calypso, Punta is upbeat dance music. Popular proponents include Andy Palacio, Chico Ramos, Pen Cayetano, the Garífuna Kids, Travesia Band, and Peter Flores (aka Titiman). For a taste of traditional Kriol folk music, try to track down a copy of *Mr. Peters' Boom & Chime.* You also might be able to find some traditional Garífuna music, which tends to be ceremonial dance music, very similar to traditional West African music.

The best place to find Belizean music is a gift shop. Still, these are very hit or miss. Check at the **Belize Tourism Village** (p. 112). You might also try online music stores; one good source is **www.facebook.com/stonetree records**. I'd avoid the various vendors selling bootleg cassettes and CDs on the side of the road, since the quality can be sketchy, and the artists don't receive a dime.

WHERE TO STAY

Belize City is small, and your options for where to stay are limited, though you will find some of the largest hotels in the country here. The most picturesque and safest neighborhood by far is the area around the Fort George lighthouse. Here you'll find most of the city's best shopping, dining, and accommodations. Still, since the city is so compact, and it's not really recommended to walk around anywhere at night, you're best off choosing a hotel that best meets your needs, style, and budget. There are really only three large, modern hotels in town, and they're all listed below. If your tastes tend toward smaller, more intimate lodgings, there are several good options in different price ranges to choose from. Travelers staying in lower-priced hotels should take extra precautions when it comes to safety.

When getting a price quote from or negotiating with a hotel in Belize, be clear about whether you are being quoted a price in Belize or U.S. dollars. There is a 9% tax on all hotel stays in Belize, which isn't included in the rates listed below.

Fort George

EXPENSIVE

The Great House ★   This stately, colonial-style, small hotel is aptly named. Set a block from the water, near the Fort George lighthouse, this three-story converted mansion was originally built in 1927. It has been well maintained and restored. All rooms are on either the second or third floor, and there are no elevators, if that is an issue for you. The rooms on the top floor are my favorites, with high ceilings, wood floors, and a large, shared wraparound veranda. In fact, there are wraparound verandas on both the second and third floors. While the rooms vary in size, most are very spacious; room no. 1 is one of the largest. Room no. 8 is the smallest room, but it just may have the best view. Throughout the building you'll find a mix of wicker, neocolonial, and locally-made modern wood furniture.

13 Cork St. (opposite the Radisson Fort George), Belize City. www.greathousebelize. com. ℂ **223-3400.** 16 units. BZ$400 double. Free parking. **Amenities:** Restaurant; bar; lounge; concierge; room service; tour desk; in-house shops; Wi-Fi (free).

Radisson Fort George Hotel & Marina ★★   Located in the quiet Fort George neighborhood fronting the ocean, out by the lighthouse, just 1 block from the cruise-ship tourist village, this is Belize City's finest business-class and luxury hotel. The most view-rich rooms are located in the six-story Club Tower. All are spacious and relatively modern, and feature marble floors and plush furnishings. Rooms on the ground floor come with a small, private garden terrace. The poolside bar here is one of the more popular spots in town, and often features live music. The hotel also has a full-service marina and dive shop. Service here is excellent, and they've got a comprehensive on-site recycling program.

2 Marine Parade, Belize City. www.radisson.com. ℂ **800/333-3333** in the U.S., or 223-3333 in Belize. 102 units. BZ$440 double. Rates slightly lower in the off season. Free parking. **Amenities:** 3 restaurants; 2 bars; lounge; babysitting; concierge; well-equipped exercise room; 2 midsize outdoor pools; room service; Wi-Fi (free).

Barrack Road

EXPENSIVE

Ramada Princess Hotel & Casino ★   The largest hotel in Belize City, the Princess has a massive lobby area that lets out into the hotel's casino, two movie theaters, a shopping arcade, an eight-lane bowling alley, a salon, and various restaurants and bars. Outside is an Olympic-size swimming pool. The hotel is set right on the water's edge on the northern edge of downtown and is built as one long, six-story structure so that every room has an ocean view. All rooms are large, but junior suites offer more space and have private oceanfront balconies. The casino is definitely one of the prime nightlife spots in the country, attracting far more locals than tourists. The Princess also has a full-service marina and dive shop. The Radisson (above) is definitely more elegant and better maintained, with far more personalized service and ambience, but the Princess does have a bit more in the way of facilities and nightlife.

1758 Newtown Barracks Rd., Belize City. www.wyndhamhotels.com. © **223-2670.** 181 units. BZ$255 double. Rates include breakfast buffet. Free parking. **Amenities:** 2 restaurants; 2 bars; casino; concierge; fitness center; large outdoor pool; room service; smoke-free rooms.

Commercial District

INEXPENSIVE

Belcove Hotel ★ This funky canal-front hotel is my preferred budget choice in town. You just can't beat the charm of grabbing a seat on one of the upstairs balconies overlooking Haulover Creek and the Swing Bridge, especially at these prices. Sure, the rooms are simple and very basic, but they are neatly kept with shiny, varnished wood floors,. The old wooden building is usually covered in a coat of fresh yellow paint with blood-red trim, yet still feels weathered and historic. The budget rooms have shared bathrooms, whereas the deluxe rooms are en suite with air conditioning.

9 Regent St., Belize City. www.belcove.com. © **227-3054.** 12 units. BZ$60–BZ$95 double. Free street parking. **Amenities:** Airport shuttle; Wi-Fi (free).

Coningsby Inn ★ Housed in a converted old home toward the western end of Regent Street, the rooms here are compact and rather nondescript. Still, they are clean and comfortable. I prefer those on the second floor, although don't choose one of these for the view, which is over an abandoned lot. I would definitely recommend a splurge for one of the air-conditioned rooms. There's a convivial hostel-like vibe to this operation, and the second-floor bar and lounge area is the social hub of the joint.

76 Regent St. coningsby_inn@btl.net. © **227-1566.** 10 units. BZ$110 double without A/C; BZ$120 double with A/C. Free street parking. **Amenities:** Bar; pet-friendly rooms; Wi-Fi (free)

Hotel Mopan ★ Located a block or so from the water toward the western end of Regent Street, this longstanding and humble little hotel is a good option in downtown Belize City. The rooms are clean and comfortable, and most of them have air-conditioning. It's definitely worth the slight splurge—I'd say it's necessary—for one of the air-conditioned rooms. Those on the third floor are the best, with the end units, nos. 301 and 304, the best of these. There's no true restaurant here, but breakfast is served in the large first-floor dining room and common area, which also serves as the social hub of the hotel throughout the day and as a bar at night.

55 Regent St., Belize City. © **227-7351.** 12 units. BZ$90–BZ$150 double. Free street parking. **Amenities:** Bar; tour desk; laundry service; Wi-Fi (free).

Just outside the city

In addition to the places listed below, **D'Nest Inn** ★ (www.dnestinn.com; ℗ 223-5416) is a cute, well-run little bed-and-breakfast located about 4.8km (3 miles) outside of downtown, just off the Goldson Highway.

EXPENSIVE

Best Western Belize Biltmore Plaza ★ Located on the northern outskirts of the city, this chain hotel is simple and straightforward. It's a fine choice if you want to be a little closer to the airport and avoid the crowds and commotion of downtown. The rooms are contemporary and comfortable, with tile floors and heavy wood furnishings, and there is a pool. All face the hotel's central courtyard and pool area. As at the Radisson and Ramada hotels, the bar here is a popular meeting place for locals, after work and on weekends.

Goldson Hwy., Mile Marker 3½. www.belizebiltmore.com. ℗ **223-2302.** 75 units. BZ$320 double. Free parking. **Amenities:** Restaurant; 2 bars; small exercise room; small outdoor pool; room service; Wi-Fi (free).

MODERATE

Villa Boscardi ★★ This small and elegant bed-and-breakfast is the plushest lodging you'll find near the airport. Housed in a converted private home, the rooms here are spacious and decorated with a sense of style. Most have interesting artwork and headboard treatments over the beds. The best room here is actually a detached cottage. The hotel is located on the northern outskirts of Belize City, in a quiet neighborhood, just a block or so from the water, though not too close to many places to eat. The staff here is top-notch.

6043 Manatee Dr., Buttonwood Bay, Belize City. www.villaboscardi.com. ℗ **223-1691.** 7 units. BZ$218–BZ$254 double. Rates include full breakfast. Free parking. **Amenities:** Wi-Fi (free).

Belize Zoo Jungle Lodge ★★ Part of, and adjacent to the **Belize Zoo** (p. 107), this unique lodge is set on 34 hectares (84 acres) of untouched savannah. It boasts a nature trail, an observation platform, a classroom, and a range of guest rooms including four cabanas and a 30-person dorm, where international wildlife hero Steve Irwin once stayed. All are woodsy, pleasant, and far from luxurious, which seems appropriate—you're not here for the pampering, but for the nature experience. Camping-inclined travelers can pitch a tent here for BZ$16, too. Folks who stay here can take a nocturnal tour of the zoo for BZ$200 for 1-4 people.

Next to the Belize Zoo. George Price Highway, Mile Marker 29. www.belizezoo.org. ℗ **663-5378.** 3 units and dorm space for up to 30. BZ$148–BZ$332 double. Rates include full breakfast and dinner. **Amenities:** Shared kitchen; Wi-Fi (free).

Near the Airport

The airport is located just 16km (10 miles) north of downtown Belize City, a 15- to 20-minute drive, depending on traffic. The area around the airport is decidedly undeveloped and of little interest to visitors. Few international flights arrive late enough or leave early enough to necessitate a stay near the airport. While you'll see the large **Global Village Hotel** (www.globalvillage hotel.com; © 225-2555) right next to the airport, I find this a desultory and unappealing option. I really recommend you take the short taxi ride into Belize City, or stay at one of the places listed below.

The **Belize River Lodge** (www.belizeriverlodge.com; © **888/275-4843** in the U.S. and Canada, or 225-2002 in Belize) is an upscale fishing lodge located on the banks of the Belize River, just a few miles from the airport, while the **Black Orchid Resort** ★ (www.blackorchidresort.com; © **225-9158**) is a small resort hotel named for the national flower, also on the banks of the Belize River near the town of Burrell Boom.

WHERE TO DINE

Despite its small size, Belize City actually has an excellent and varied selection of dining options. While Belizean cuisine and fresh seafood are most common, you can also get top-notch Chinese, Indian, and other international fare throughout the city.

Note: When the cruise ships are in town, the restaurants in the Fort George area can get extremely crowded, especially for lunch.

Fort George

In addition to the places listed below, you can get good burgers and bar food at the **Baymen's Tavern** at the Radisson Fort George Hotel.

MODERATE

The Smokey Mermaid ★ INTERNATIONAL Who doesn't like to eat in the open air? The Smokey Mermaid has a couple of raised decks and gazebos and a few fountains, spread out among heavy wooden tables and chairs under broad canvas umbrellas in the shade of large seagrape and mango trees and a wealth of other lushly planted ferns and flowers. The food isn't quite as good as the setting but we've found if you stick to classics like the Jamaican jerk pork, shrimp thermidor, or the yucca-crusted catch of the day, you'll do fine. Breakfasts are filling and varied, and there's a lunch menu, daily specials, and a range of soups, salads, and sandwiches.

13 Cork St., in The Great House. www.smokymermaid.com. © **672-4759.** Reservations recommended. Main courses BZ$20–BZ$82. Daily 6:30am–10pm.

Wet Lizard ★ BELIZEAN/INTERNATIONAL And here's another lively *al fresco* dining opportunity, this time in a prime setting on a second-floor covered deck overlooking the Swing Bridge and Belize City's little harbor. When the cruise ships are in town, this raucous restaurant is the most popular spot in town. Comfort food is the order of the day, with most going for sandwiches, burgers, and American-style bar food. But the restaurant does do some tropical specials, too, like coconut shrimp, conch fritters, and fried calamari. If you like sweets, save room for the banana chimichanga. The best seats here are the small tables and high stools ringing the railing and overlooking the water. Everything is painted in bright primary colors, and the walls are covered with graffiti and signatures from guests.

1 Fort St. ℂ **620-5933.** Reservations not accepted. Main courses BZ$20–BZ$30. Mon–Thurs 8:30am–4pm.

Taka Kitchen ★★ SUSHI/JAPANESE   Belize has fourteen Japanese residents, two of whom are chefs, and one of those chefs runs this restaurant. Seafood can be found anywhere in the country, but sushi made in the traditional Japanese style is rare. Chef Takayuki Yanai serves up standard fare such as nigiri and sashimi, and hot Japanese cuisine as well, such as ramen noodles and a chicken teriyaki rice burger. Located on the second floor of the Northern Shops, it's probably not a restaurant you'll just happen across, so make sure to seek it out when you're craving Japanese food.

Mile 1 on the Goldson Highway, 2nd floor of Northern Shops. ℂ **604-9154.** Main courses BZ$15–BZ$35. Tues–Sun 11am–6pm; closed Mon and first Sun of month.

INEXPENSIVE

Le Petit Café ★ COFFEEHOUSE   This place does a brisk business for breakfast, especially among local workers. A variety of both sweet and savory baked goods are available, as well as a wide range of coffee drinks. For lunch, you'll find a selection of sandwiches, filled pastries, and a daily special or two. Seating is available in an air-conditioned dining area, as well as an open-air courtyard, under shade trees and flower-covered trellises. These folks also have a small kiosk in the departure lounge of the international airport.

2 Marine Parade, at the Radisson Fort George Hotel. ℂ **223-3333.** Reservations not accepted. Main courses BZ$4–BZ$20. Daily 6am–8pm.

Barrack Road
MODERATE

Sumathi ★ INDIAN   If you're familiar with Indian cuisine, you won't be disappointed here. And if you like it hot and spicy, you're in the right place. With a location near the heart of downtown, this remains the best Indian restaurant in Belize City. The menu features a wide selection of northern Indian and tandoori specialties. There are also excellent options for vegetarians, who probably won't find as broad a selection to fit their dietary needs in any other restaurant in the city.

No. 31 Eve St. ℂ **223-1172.** Main courses BZ$20–BZ$30. Tues–Sun 11am–10pm.

Commercial District
INEXPENSIVE

Nerie's ★ BELIZEAN   Very popular with locals, Nerie's serves traditional favorites such as cow-foot soup and a fry jack breakfast for under BZ$10. Also tops on the menu: refreshing fruit juices and savory stew chicken with rice and beans. The Daly St. location has a bar called Bodega Lounge known for its karaoke and frozen drinks. Nerie's has three locations, one of which is up north in Corozal.

Corner of Queen and Daly sts. (second location at Douglas Jones St.) www.neries.bz. © **223-4028** (Daly St. location), or 224-5199 (Douglas Jones St. location). Main courses BZ$10–BZ$15. Mon–Sat 8am–8:30pm; closed Sun.

Around Town
MODERATE

Bird's Isle Restaurant & Bar ★ BELIZEAN   This relaxed restaurant has arguably the best location in the city, seaside on a small island just over a tiny bridge at the far southern end of Regent Street. The main dining hall is a circular wooden deck under a soaring thatch roof, though I prefer the open-air seats under large shade umbrellas on the wooden deck closer to the water. You can get a range of Belizean staples, fresh seafood, and grilled meats. Portions are hefty. Be careful when leaving at night, as the neighborhood can be dicey.

90 Albert St. © **207-6500.** Main courses BZ$10–BZ$16; lobster BZ$24. Mon–Fri 10:30am–2:30pm; Wed 5:30–9pm; Thurs 5:30pm–midnight; Fri 5:30–10pm; Sat 10:30am–10pm; closed Sun.

Chon Saan Palace ★ CHINESE   If you're in the mood for Chinese food in Belize City, you can't do better than this local favorite. The room and the menu are immense. You'll find plenty of chow mein and Cantonese dishes, but there's also a substantial Szechuan section and a showstopping sizzling steak that comes hissing and screaming to your table. If you're primed for seafood, you'll love the large fish tanks stocked with live lobster (in season), shrimp, and the daily catch. This is a great place to come with a group, as there are plenty of large, round tables with built-in Lazy Susans, perfect for sharing food and a good time.

1 Kelly St. © **223-3008.** Main courses BZ$15–BZ$40. Daily 11am–11:30pm.

Riverside Tavern ★★★ INTERNATIONAL   One of the most happening spots in Belize City, this large place has both indoor and outdoor seating on a spot overlooking Haulover Creek. The restaurant specializes in hefty steaks and delicious ribs. But you can also get seared tuna, grilled snapper, coconut shrimp, or jerk shrimp. Owned by the Bowen family of Belikin brewing, this is a top place for beer. There are TVs showing sporting events, and at times this place can get quite boisterous.

2 Mapp St. © **223-5640.** Lunch BZ$12–BZ$50; dinner main courses BZ$30–BZ$75. Mon–Sat 11am–10pm; closed Sun.

TGI Crazy Gringo ★ BELIZEAN/INTERNATIONAL   What this restaurant lacks in creativity and fancy fare, it makes up for in portion size. The servings are huge. There's an emphasis on fried foods here—chicken and shrimp are favorites. But you can also get pizzas, burritos, burgers, hot dogs, and buffalo wings. The best seats are on the long, open-air deck fronting the lagoon here. This is a great spot for lunch. You'll see a lot of families here as it's part of the Old Belize complex, with an attached museum, beach, and children's play area.

Western Hwy., Mile 5. www.oldbelize.com. © **222-4129.** Main courses BZ$30–BZ$60. Daily 9am–10pm.

BELIZE CITY AFTER DARK

Again, Belize City is a small, provincial city, so don't expect to find a raging nightlife scene. The most popular nightspots—for both locals and visitors alike—are the bars at the few high-end hotels in town.

The Performing Arts

It's really the luck of the draw as to whether you can catch a concert, theater piece, or dance performance—they are the exception, not the norm. To find out if anything is happening, ask at your hotel, read the local papers, or check in with the **Bliss Institute** (p. 104).

The Bar Scene

The bar and club scene in Belize City is rather lackluster. The most happening bar in town is the **Riverside Tavern ★★** (see above). This is especially true on weekends, and whenever there's an important soccer, basketball, or cricket match on. The **Bird's Isle Restaurant & Bar ★** (see above) is another lively option, with karaoke on Thursday nights and live music on Fridays. For a casual bar scene, you can also try **Thirsty Thursday's** (© **223-1677**), located out on Newtown Barracks Road.

Travelers and locals alike also tend to frequent the bars at the major hotels and tourist traps. The liveliest of these are the bars at the **Radisson Fort George Hotel & Marina** (p. 114), the **Best Western Belize Biltmore Plaza** (p. 116), and the **Ramada Belize City Princess Hotel** (p. 114), all of which often have a live band on weekend nights. Of these, I prefer the **Club Calypso ★** (© **223-0638**), an open-air affair built over the water at the Princess Hotel & Casino, although it's sort of a crapshoot as to which bar will be hopping on any given night.

Casinos

For gaming, the **Ramada Belize City Princess Hotel** (p. 114) is the only game in town, and the casino here is large, modern, and well equipped. While it's not on the scale of Vegas or Atlantic City, the casino is certainly respectable, with enough gaming tables, slots, and other attractions to make most casual gamblers quite happy to drop a few dollars.

SIDE TRIPS FROM BELIZE CITY

Given the fact that Belize is so small, it is possible to visit any of the country's major tourist destinations and attractions as a side trip from Belize City. Most are easily reached in less than 2 hours by car, bus, or boat taxi. Other attractions are accessible by short commuter flights. All in all, you can visit almost any destination or attraction described in this book as a day trip, except for the far southern zone.

For a listing of active adventures that make good day trips, see "Outdoor Activities," earlier in this chapter; for a description of the most popular attractions within close proximity to Belize City, see p. 107. Other possible destinations for side trips out of Belize City include **Caye Caulker** and **Ambergris Caye,** dive excursions to the nearby reefs, and even trips to the more isolated dive destinations such as the **Blue Hole** and the **Lighthouse** and **Turneffe atolls** ★★. You can also visit the Mayan ruins of **Altun Ha, Lamanai, Xunantunich, Cahal Pech,** and even **Caracol** and **Tikal.**

Most hotels can arrange any of the day trips suggested above. In addition, you can check in with **Discovery Expeditions** (www.discoverybelize.com; ✆ **671-0748**) or **S & L Travel and Tours** (www.sltravelbelize.com; ✆ **227-7593**). *Note:* Most of the tours and activities mentioned here and in "Outdoor Activities," earlier in this chapter, are also sold to visiting cruise-ship passengers. When the cruise ships are in town, a cave-tubing adventure, a snorkel trip to Hol Chan Marine Reserve and Shark-Ray Alley, or a visit to either Altun Ha or Lamanai ruins can be a mob scene. It's often possible to avoid these crowds by starting your tour or activity very early, or in the late afternoon. If you are organizing your tour or activity with a local operator, mention that you want to avoid the cruise-ship groups, if at all possible.

THE NORTHERN CAYES & ATOLLS

7

The cayes (pronounced "keys") are a series of small islands strung along the length of the Belize Barrier Reef, set amid waters that are at once crystal clear and brilliantly turquoise. Seen firsthand, there's something truly mesmerizing and almost unbelievable about the clarity and color of this water. But as they say around here: "You betta Belize it."

With the reef providing protection from the open ocean, and the government providing protection to the reef, the cayes are literally islands of tranquility in a calm blue sea. Aside from sunbathing and slow strolling, scuba diving, snorkeling, and fishing are the main attractions in the cayes. They are all world-class. From the bustling mini-resorts (and one regular resort) of **Ambergris Caye ★★** to the funky Rastafarian charm of tiny **Caye Caulker ★★★** to the deserted-isle feel of the **Turneffe Islands ★★** and **Lighthouse Reef atolls ★★**, it's the idyllic combination of sun and sea, as well as adventure and relaxation, that attracts and captivates most visitors to Belize. Most of the cayes are small enough to walk from one end to the other in less than 20 minutes. On others, it won't take you nearly as long.

Jacques Cousteau put Belize on the diving map back in 1971, with his explorations of the **Blue Hole ★★**. The country has almost 322km (200 miles) of continuous barrier reefs and visibility of up to 61m (200 ft.) on some days. It's hard to open a diving magazine without finding an article on diving in Belize. For those sticking a little closer to the surface, the snorkeling is just as rewarding, with **Hol Chan Marine Reserve ★★** and **Shark-Ray Alley ★★** considered two of the best snorkeling experiences on the planet.

On the plentiful flats found inside the reefs and up in nearby estuaries, anglers find action with tarpon, snook, permit, and feisty bonefish. There's more tarpon as well as giant snapper and grouper found along the reefs, while out on the open ocean the tackle and game get bigger, with marlin, sailfish, tuna, and wahoo as the principal prey.

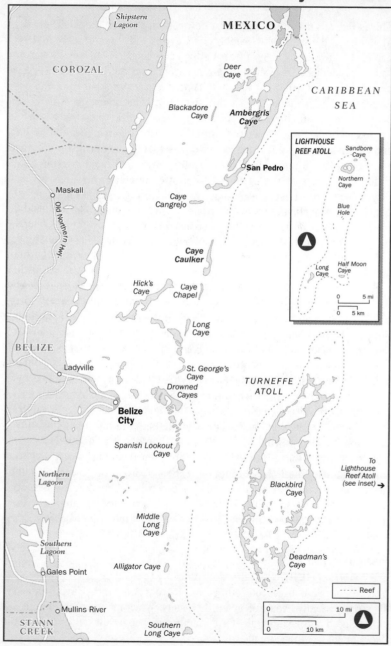

AMBERGRIS CAYE ★★

This is Belize's most popular tourist destination. Dubbed "La Isla Bonita" by Madonna in the late 1980s, Ambergris Caye is truly a sight to behold. The compact "downtown" area of **San Pedro** is a playground of hotels, souvenir shops, restaurants, dive shops, tour agencies, and the docks that serve as launch points for exploring the reef. The vibe is at once laid back and energized, its long-time identity as a chill fishing village contending with a ratcheting up of construction projects and golf cart traffic jams. As a separate byproduct of the boom, wooden Caribbean houses are giving way to concrete and cinder-block buildings, and even Belize's first large-scale resort. Development has reached both ends of Ambergris Caye, and rapid construction is filling in the blanks from north to south, offering greater housing variety to visitors and expats alike. Unfortunately, waste management has not caught up with the tourism boom, so you may notice trash scattered throughout the caye, piled into heaps or caught in the branches of mangroves. Even so, the surrounding sea remains in near-pristine condition, making Ambergris Caye an excellent destination for water-based activities such as diving, fly-fishing, and kayaking.

Long before the British settled Belize, and long before the sun-seeking vacationers and zealous reef divers discovered Ambergris Caye, the Maya were here. In fact, the Maya created Ambergris Caye when they cut a channel through the long, thin peninsula that extended down from what is now Mexico. The channel was cut to facilitate coastal trading and avoid the dangerous barrier reef that begins not too far north of San Pedro. Ambergris Caye is 40km (25 miles) long and only .8km (½ mile) wide at its widest point.

San Pedro reflects the dichotomies of Belize's identity. Yes, the tourism boom has led to construction projects that displace mangroves, negatively effecting the nearby coral and other wildlife, but in turn this has driven conservation awareness, with the caye's population of some 20,000 leading the charge when the Belize Barrier Reef was threatened with the possibility of oil drilling in late 2016. More and more San Pedro businesses are getting involved in cleaning up trash, investing in eco-friendly buildings, and relocating crocodiles instead of just killing them. It's a remarkable time to witness the evolution of this community, all while enjoying the bright sunshine, sparkling sea, and maybe a Belikin beer or two.

Essentials
GETTING THERE & DEPARTING
You've got two options for getting to and from Ambergris Caye: sea or air. The trip is usually beautiful by either means. When the weather's rough, it's bumpy both ways, although it's certainly quicker by air, and you're more likely to get wet in the boat.

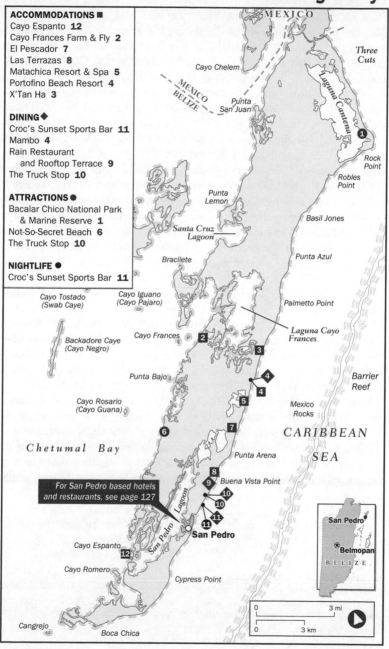

Ambergris Caye

ACCOMMODATIONS ■
Cayo Espanto **12**
Cayo Frances Farm & Fly **2**
El Pescador **7**
Las Terrazas **8**
Matachica Resort & Spa **5**
Portofino Beach Resort **4**
X'Tan Ha **3**

DINING ◆
Croc's Sunset Sports Bar **11**
Mambo **4**
Rain Restaurant
   and Rooftop Terrace **9**
The Truck Stop **10**

ATTRACTIONS ●
Bacalar Chico National Park
   & Marine Reserve **1**
Not-So-Secret Beach **6**
The Truck Stop **10**

NIGHTLIFE ●
Croc's Sunset Sports Bar **11**

MEXICO

Cayo Chelem

Three Cuts

MEXICO
BELIZE

Punta
San Juan

Cayo Espanto **12**

Cayo Frances Farm & Fly **2**

Laguna Cantena

Rock Point

Robles Point

Punta Lemon

Basil Jones

Santa Cruz Lagoon

Punta Azul

Bracilete

Cayo Tostado
(Swab Caye)

Cayo Iguano
(Cayo Pajaro)

Palmetto Point

Cayo Frances

Laguna Cayo Frances

Backadore Caye
(Cayo Negro)

Punta Bajo

Barrier
Reef

Cayo Rosario
(Cayo Guana)

Mexico
Rocks

CARIBBEAN

Chetumal Bay

Punta Arena

SEA

For San Pedro based hotels
and restaurants, see page 127

Buena Vista Point

San Pedro

Cayo Espanto

Cayo Romero

Cypress Point

San Pedro

Belmopan

BELIZE

Cangrejo

Boca Chica

0   3 mi
0   3 km

7

THE NORTHERN CAYES & ATOLLS | Ambergris Caye

BY PLANE   There are frequent daily flights between Belize City and San Pedro Airport (airport code SPR) on Ambergris Caye. Flights leave from both Philip S. W. Goldson International Airport and Municipal Airport several times an hour between 6:40am and 9:10pm. If you're coming in on an international flight and heading straight for San Pedro, you should book a flight from the international airport. If you're already in Belize City or in transit around the country, it's cheaper to fly from the Municipal Airport, which is also closer to downtown, and quicker and cheaper to reach by taxi. During the high season, and whenever possible, it's best to have a reservation. However, you can usually just show up at the airport and get a seat on a flight within an hour. Baggage is addressed quite casually, so if the plane is too full, your luggage may be hitching a ride on the next flight.

Maya Island Air (www.mayaislandair.com; ✆ **223-1140,** or 223-1146) has 11 flights daily between Goldson International Airport and San Pedro Airport, with two extra evening flights running between March and October. The flights depart every hour beginning at 7:40am, with the last flight at 5:40pm. Flight time is around 15 minutes; the fare is BZ$140 each way. These flights actually originate at the Belize City Municipal Airport 10 minutes earlier. From the Municipal Airport, the fare is just BZ$72 each way. When you're ready to leave, flights from San Pedro to Belize City run from 7:30am to 5:30pm on Tropic Air and 7am to 5pm on Maya Air. Both airlines offer discounts for children.

Tropic Air (www.tropicair.com; ✆ **800/422-3435** in the U.S. or Canada, 226-2012 in Belize) has five daily flights between Corozal Town and San Pedro, leaving Corozal Town at 7:30 and 10:30am, and 1:30, 3:30, and 5:30pm. Flights from San Pedro to Corozal Town leave at 7 and 10am, and 1, 3, and 5pm. The fare is BZ$150 each way.

There is an airstrip at Caye Caulker, however as of early 2018 all flights have been suspended due to a faulty runway. The project has been unable to secure funding to fix it so there is no timeline for when flights will resume.

Maya Island Air has daily flights between Corozal and San Pedro, leaving San Pedro at 7 and 9am (11am seasonally), and 3 and 4:30pm, and returning at 7:30 and 9:40am, and 3:25 and 5pm, with an 11:30am seasonally. Flight duration is 20 minutes. The fare is BZ$85 each way.

Connections to and from all the other major destinations in Belize can be made via the Municipal and international airports in Belize City. There are also charter helicopter options, some of which can be arranged directly with the hotels that have helipads.

Add It Up

Because a taxi into Belize City from the international airport costs BZ$50, and the boat to Ambergris Caye costs about BZ$34–BZ$56 one-way, it is only a bit more expensive to fly if you are heading directly to the cayes after arriving on an international flight. Plus, the aerial view during the trip can't be beat.

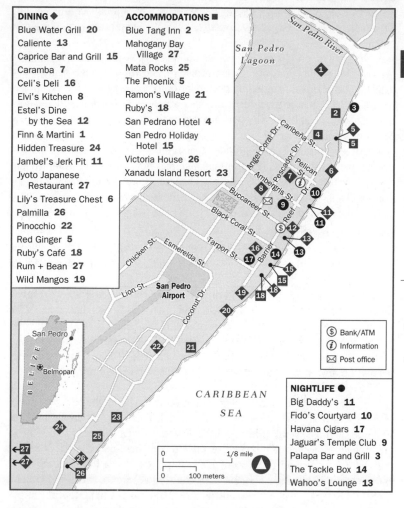

DINING ◆
Blue Water Grill **20**
Caliente **13**
Caprice Bar and Grill **15**
Caramba **7**
Celi's Deli **16**
Elvi's Kitchen **8**
Estel's Dine
  by the Sea **12**
Finn & Martini **1**
Hidden Treasure **24**
Jambel's Jerk Pit **11**
Jyoto Japanese
  Restaurant **27**
Lily's Treasure Chest **6**
Palmilla **26**
Pinocchio **22**
Red Ginger **5**
Ruby's Café **18**
Rum + Bean **27**
Wild Mangos **19**

ACCOMMODATIONS ■
Blue Tang Inn **2**
Mahogany Bay
  Village **27**
Mata Rocks **25**
The Phoenix **5**
Ramon's Village **21**
Ruby's **18**
San Pedrano Hotel **4**
San Pedro Holiday
  Hotel **15**
Victoria House **26**
Xanadu Island Resort **23**

San Pedro
Lagoon

San Pedro River

San Pedro
Airport

San Pedro

BELIZE

Belmopan

CARIBBEAN
SEA

$ Bank/ATM
ⓘ Information
✉ Post office

NIGHTLIFE ●
Big Daddy's **11**
Fido's Courtyard **10**
Havana Cigars **17**
Jaguar's Temple Club **9**
Palapa Bar and Grill **3**
The Tackle Box **14**
Wahoo's Lounge **13**

0   1/8 mile
0   100 meters

BY BOAT   Ocean Ferry Belize (www.oceanferrybelize.com; ☏ **223-0033**) and **San Pedro Belize Express Water Taxi** (www.belizewatertaxi.com; ☏ **223-2225**) are the two water taxi companies that will get you to Ambergris Caye from Belize City. Both depart near the Swing Bridge: Ocean Ferry from the Marine Terminal, and the San Pedro Belize Express from Brown Sugar Terminal, both on North Front Street. Both provide covered speedboats powered by huge, loud engines, with space for 50 to 100 passengers. No matter the weather, water almost always enters the cabin somehow, but on sunny days it's worth it to open the window because the cramped interior gets steamy with body heat in a matter of minutes. The ride takes about an hour and a half, always including a stop at Caye Caulker. The fare is BZ$34 to BZ$56 one-way, or BZ$64 to BZ$76 round-trip, Ocean Ferry being the cheaper of the two options. Ocean Ferry offers 5 trips a day, compared with the San Pedro Belize Express' 9, but does offer Wi-Fi on board which is a nice perk.

Tickets can be purchased in advance online or by visiting their terminals in person, though this is generally unnecessary. Stowing luggage is free, and bags will be taken and tagged by porters prior to boarding, so hold on tight to the claim ticket you're given. Pets are also welcome, but they need to be contained in kennels or bags. All boats arrive at their respective destinations in the center of town.

Tip: It's worth it to arrive no later than a half-hour early to queue up and get first pick of the seats. The front is a bumpier ride, and wetter if the weather's bad, but the back is louder and smells more like the gasoline that fuels the engines. Those prone to motion sickness will either want to sit next to a window for the fresh air, or on one of the center seats that faces forward.

GETTING AROUND

The downtown section of San Pedro is easily navigated by foot. Some of the hotels located on the northern or southern ends of the island can be quite isolated, however.

Most hotels arrange pickup and drop-off for guests, whether they are arriving or departing by air or sea. Taxis are waiting for all flights that arrive at the airport and are available for most trips around the island. If your hotel can't call you one, try **Amber Isle Taxi** (℮ **226-4060**), **Felix Taxi** (℮ **226-2041**), or **Island Taxi** (℮ **226-3125**). Fares run between BZ$10 and BZ$20 for rides nearby the downtown area, but BZ$25 to BZ$50 when going north over the BZ$10 toll bridge.

Golf carts, which are the most common vehicle type on the caye, are available for rent from several outlets on the island. This is by far the best choice if you're staying several miles from the downtown area and want to be able to get around. However, it's expensive to ship carts here and the prices reflect that. Rates run around BZ$130 to BZ$180 per day for a four-seat cart, and BZ$160 to BZ$280 for a six-seat cart. Hourly rates are between BZ$50 and BZ$100. Several dependable outfits are **Moncho's Cart Rental** (http://monchosbze.com; ℮ **226-4490**) near the airstrip, **Cholo's Golf Cart Rental** (℮ **226-2406**), and **Carts Belize** (www.cartsbelize.com; ℮ **226-4090**). Some hotels also offer their guests on-site cart rental services, something to consider when picking a place to stay. The roads on the north side are in pretty bad condition, so be prepared for a bumpy ride.

Bicycles are another good option. Most hotels have their own bikes, available for free or for a small rental fee. If your hotel doesn't have a bike, call or head to **Joe's Bike Rental** on the south end of Pescador Drive (℮ **226-4371**) between Caribena and Pelican streets. Rates run BZ$40 per day.

Depending on where your hotel is located, a water taxi may just be your best means for commuting between your accommodations and shops of San

Pedro or the restaurants of other resorts. **Coastal Xpress** (www.coastalxpress. com; © **226-2007**) runs regularly scheduled launches that cover the length of the island, cruising just offshore between Amigos Del Mar in town and Blue Reef Island Resort up north. The launches are in radio contact with all the hotels and restaurants, and they stop to pick up and discharge passengers as needed. These boats run at regular intervals, roughly every half-hour, from 5:30am to 10pm. Rates are between BZ$10 and BZ$28 one-way per person (double that for round-trip), depending on the length of the ride. Chartered water taxis with Coastal Xpress are also available, and usually charge around BZ$100 to BZ$350, depending on the length of the ride and size of your group.

ORIENTATION

San Pedro (the only town on the island of Ambergris Caye) is just three streets wide. The streets, from seaside to lagoonside, are Barrier Reef Drive (Front St.), Pescador Drive (Middle St.), and Angel Coral Street (Back St.). The airport is at the south end of the busy little downtown. The island stretches both north and south of San Pedro. Less than a mile north of San Pedro there is a small channel, or cut, dividing the island in two. The northern section of the island is much less developed and is where you will find more of the higher-end isolated resorts, though it's becoming increasingly more popular for day visitors with the discovery of **Not-So-Secret Beach** (p. 136).

A bridge connects the northern and southern sections of Ambergris Caye. Pedestrians and bicycles can cross the bridge for free, but golf carts and other vehicles must pay a toll of BZ$5 each way.

FAST FACTS   For the local **police,** dial © **911,** or 226-2022; for the **fire department,** dial © **226-2372.** In the case of a medical emergency, call the **San Pedro PolyClinic** (© **226-2536**), which is the closest thing the island has to a hospital.

International Costa Maya Festival

Begun as the San Pedro Sea & Air Festival, the annual **International Costa Maya Festival** ★★ is the largest public celebration on Ambergris Caye, even larger and more popular than Carnival. Celebrated from Thursday to Sunday in early August, the festival offers a steady stream of live concert performances, street parades, beauty pageants, and water shows and activities. When the festivities reinvented themselves several years ago, they had been transformed into a regional affair, honoring and inviting the peoples from around the Mayan world. Performers, participants, and festivalgoers come from around Belize, as well as from Mexico, Honduras, El Salvador, and Guatemala, the five countries that compose the Mundo Maya. San Pedro's football field is converted into the fairgrounds, and a large stage is set up at one end. Food stalls and arts and crafts booths are set up as well. A 3-day pass costs BZ$175; per night it's between BZ$50 and BZ$100. Pricey, but worth it—it's quite the party. Find specific dates and events at www. internationalcostamayafestival.com.

Atlantic Bank (☏ 226-2195) and **Belize Bank** (☏ 226-2450) are both located on Barrier Reef Drive in downtown San Pedro and open on weekdays, though Atlantic Bank has a second branch on the corner of Pescador Drive and Black Coral Street that is open on Saturday mornings from 9am to noon. The **post office** (☏ 226-2260) is located on Barrier Reef Drive; it's open Monday through Friday from 8am to noon and from 1 to 4:30pm. Wi-Fi is easily found in hotels, restaurants, and bars around the island.

Most hotels also provide laundry service, but pricing varies widely, so ask first. **Nellie's Laundromat** (☏ 226-2454) is located on Pescador Drive toward the south end of town next to Atlantic Bank. They charge around BZ$2.25 per pound, and they even offer pickup and delivery service.

What to See & Do

Before you book your vacation, you should be aware that there really isn't much beach to speak of on Ambergris Caye. Around most of the island, there's just a narrow band of sand where the land meets the sea. In some spots, even at low tide, it's barely wide enough for you to lay out a beach towel. Some of the beachfront hotels create their own beaches by building retaining walls and filling them in with sand. You'll find the best of these at the resorts on the northern part of the island, at Victoria House, and at Mahogany Bay Village's private club, which is actually a 15-minute boat ride north of the hotel proper. **Not-So-Secret Beach** (p. 136) is the best public option on Ambergris Caye, even though it's pretty rocky for a sandy beach.

Likewise, swimming is not what you might expect. For 100 yards (300 ft.) or more out from shore, the bottom is covered with sea grass. In a smart move that prioritizes the environment over tourism, the local and national government has decided to protect the sea grass, which supports a wealth of aquatic life. Beneath the grass is a layer of spongy roots and organic matter topped with a thin layer of white sand. Walking on this spongy sand is somewhat unnerving; there's always the possibility of a sea urchin or stingray lurking, and it's easy to trip and stumble. Swimming is best off the piers, and many of the hotels here have built long piers out into the sea, with steps down into the water, and usually a roped-off little swimming area. Beyond this, good swimming can be had from boats anchored out in the turquoise waters between the shore and the reef, or by taking a kayak offshore a little way.

There is a lot of boat traffic (some of it quite fast and furious) running up and down the coast of Ambergris Caye, so do not try to swim or snorkel from shore out to the reef. Unfortunately, over the years, more than one swimmer or snorkeler has been run over by a speeding motorboat.

FUN IN THE WATER
Scuba Diving & Snorkeling
So why do people bother to come here if there is no beach and you can't go swimming right off the shore? They come for the spectacular coral reef, turquoise waters, and seemingly endless visibility. Less than a quarter-mile offshore is the longest coral reef in the Western Hemisphere. The Belize Barrier

Taking the Lion's Share

While underwater you may catch sight of the beautiful lionfish, a venomous creature with ornate spines and fins that spread out in a mane-like fashion. While on land you may also hear or see people encouraging guests to kill as many of these fish as possible, as they are invasive in Caribbean waters, threatening native fish and coral populations without having many natural predators of their own. The lionfish is not just unwelcome; it is also delicious, so spearing a few will be great for the reef and for your belly.

Reef is second only to Australia's Great Barrier Reef, yet is receiving far better treatment thanks to a recent moratorium designed to protect the fragile ecosystem from oil interests. Snorkeling, scuba diving, and fishing are the main draws here, and all are consistently spectacular.

Within a 10- to 20-minute boat ride from the piers lie scores of **world-class dive sites** ★★★, including **Mexico Rocks, Mata Rocks, Tackle Box, Tres Cocos, Esmeralda, Cypress Tunnel,** and **Rocky Point.** A day's diving will almost always feature a mix of steep wall drops and coral caverns and tunnels. You'll see brilliant coral and sponge formations, as well as a wealth of colorful marine life. On good dives, you might see schools of spotted eagle rays, watch an octopus slither among the coral and rocks, or have the chance to swim face to face with a sea turtle. Nurse sharks, moray eels, and large barracuda are also commonly sighted.

There are scores of dive operators in San Pedro, and almost every hotel can arrange a dive trip, because either they have their own dive shop or they subcontract out. Rates are pretty standardized, but you should be able to get deals on multiday, multidive packages. While it's often tempting to purchase all-inclusive dive packages before coming to Belize, this limits your flexibility; for example, if the weather and water are really rough, you're already committed, although you might prefer taking an inland tour to a Mayan ruin over a rough dive.

For reliable scuba-diving service and reasonable rates, contact **Amigos del Mar** (www.amigosdivebelize.com; ✆ **226-2706**), **Aqua Scuba Belize** (www.aquascubabelize.com; ✆ **226-2775**), or **Ecologic Divers** ★ (www.ecologicdivers.com; ✆ **226-4117**). Most of these companies, as well as the individual resorts, charge BZ$160 to BZ$220 for a two-tank dive, with equipment rental included.

For more adventurous and truly top-rate diving, you'll probably want to head out to the **Turneffe Island Atoll** ★★★, **Lighthouse Reef** ★★★, and **Blue Hole** ★★. For more information on these sites, see p. 166. Most of the dive operations on the island offer this trip or will subcontract it out. It's about a 2- to 3-hour ride each way (in a fast boat) over sometimes rough seas. You'll definitely want to choose a seaworthy, speedy, and comfortable boat. Most day trips out to Turneffe Island or Lighthouse Reef and Blue Hole run around

BZ$380 to BZ$600 per person, including transportation, two or three dives, and tanks and weights, as well as lunch and snacks.

If you've always dreamed of learning to scuba dive and plan on spending any time on Ambergris Caye, you should consider taking a course here. Resort courses will give you a great one-day introduction into the world of scuba diving, including a very controlled shallow-water boat dive. These courses cost BZ$320 to BZ$400. In 3 to 4 days, however, you can get your full open-water certification. These more extensive courses run between BZ$700 and BZ$1,000, including all equipment rentals, class materials, and the processing of your certification, as well as four open-water and reef dives. All the above-mentioned dive centers, as well as many of the individual resorts here, offer these courses.

There are a host of boats offering snorkeling trips, and most of the hotels on the island, as well as the above dive operators, also offer snorkel trips and equipment rental. Trips to other sites range in price from BZ$30 to BZ$60 for short jaunts to half-day outings, and BZ$100 to BZ$140 for full-day trips. One of the operators who specializes in snorkeling trips here is the very personable Alphonse Graniel and his launch *Li'l Alphonse* ★ (℗ 226-3136). Another good snorkel operator is **Grumpy & Happy** (www.grumpyandhappy.com; ℗ 226-3420), a husband-and-wife team that offers private personalized outings. Snorkel gear is available from most of the above operators and at several other sites around town. A full set of mask, fins, and snorkel will usually cost BZ$16 to BZ$30 per person per day.

Tip: Hol Chan and Shark-Ray Alley are extremely popular. If you really want to enjoy them, try to find a boat leaving San Pedro at or before 8am, and head first to Shark-Ray Alley. Most boats dive Hol Chan first, and this is the

THE PERFECT plunge

If you're hesitant to take a tank plunge, don't miss a chance to at least snorkel. There's good snorkeling all along the protected side of the barrier reef, but some of the best is at **Shark-Ray Alley ★★** and **Hol Chan Marine Reserve ★★**, which are about 6.4km (4 miles) southeast of San Pedro. Shark-Ray Alley provides a nice adrenaline rush, even though the nurse sharks are essentially big catfish. Here you'll be able to snorkel above and between schools of the sharks and several species of stingrays, which are baited with chum by almost all tour operators. *Hol chan* is a Mayan term meaning "little channel," which is exactly what you'll find here—a

narrow channel cutting through the shallow coral reef. The walls of the channel are popular with divers, and the shallower areas are frequented by snorkelers. Some of the exciting residents of the area are large, green moray eels; stingrays; and nurse sharks (harmless). The reserve covers 13 sq. km (5 sq. miles) and is divided into three zones: the reef, the sea-grass beds, and the mangroves. Most combination trips to Shark-Ray Alley and Hol Chan Marine Reserve last about 2½ to 3 hours, and cost around BZ$90 to BZ$120. There is a BZ$20 park fee for visiting Hol Chan, which may or may not be included in the price of boat excursions to the reserve.

best way to get a dive with the greatest concentration of nurse sharks and stingrays. By all means, avoid snorkeling or diving these sites at times when the cruise ships are running excursions there, which is usually mid-day (doublecheck with the tour operator when booking). Alternatively, you may want to consider visiting a different snorkeling site, such as Mexico Rocks Coral Gardens, Tres Cocos, or Mata Rocks, where the snorkeling is just as good, if not better, and you're more likely to have the place to yourself.

COMBINING SNORKELING WITH MANATEE VIEWING Another popular option is a day trip to see manatees and do some snorkeling at a remote caye. These trips include a leisurely tour of famed manatee feeding and mating sites at Swallow Caye on the way to the isolated Goff's Caye, which is little more than a football field–size patch of sand, with a few palm trees. These trips include all transportation, lunch on the caye, and several snorkeling stops, and cost around BZ$150 to BZ$200. Most hotels and tour agencies in town offer this trip; or check with **SEAduced ★** (www.seaducedbybelize. com; ✆ **226-2254**) or **Sea-Rious Adventures** (www.seariousadventures.com; ✆ **226-4202**).

GLASS-BOTTOM BOATS If you really don't want to take a plunge of any sort, you can still get a good view of the reef and its undersea wonders aboard a glass-bottom boat. There are a few glass-bottom boats working Ambergris Caye, but the *Reef Runner* (reefrunnerbz@yahoo.com; ✆ **226-2172,** or 602-0858), is the most popular, having been around the longest, providing consistently fun experiences. Most hotels and tour agencies on the island can book them for you, or you can contact the glass-bottom boat operator directly. Rates run between BZ$110 and BZ$130, depending on the length of the tour, and whether a meal or drink is involved. Most of the glass-bottom boat tours allow time for a snorkeling break as well.

Sailing

The crystal-clear waters, calm seas, and isolated anchorages and snorkeling spots all around Ambergris Caye make this an excellent place to go out for a sail. Your options range from crewed yachts and bareboat charters for multi-day adventures to day cruises and sunset sails. A day cruise, including lunch, drinks, and snorkeling gear, should run between BZ$180 and BZ$300 per person. Most hotels and tour operators around town can hook you up with a day sail or sunset cruise.

Although not a true sailboat, the *Winnie Estelle* (winnie_estelle@yahoo. com; ✆ **226-2427**), a 20m (66-ft.) motor-sailer operated by Captain Roberto Smith, does a day cruise to Caye Caulker with several snorkeling stops for BZ$110. There's a lunch stop on Caye Caulker, where you can dine at the restaurant of your choice, on your own account, while snacks and drinks are included on the cruise. This boat can also be chartered for longer trips to the outer atolls, or to southern cayes.

If you're looking for a longer and more adventurous time on the high seas, **TMM** (www.sailtmm.com; ✆ **800/633-0155** in the U.S., or 226-3026 in Belize) is a large-scale charter company with operations on Ambergris Caye. Options include monohulls, catamarans, and trimarans of varying sizes. Given the shallow draft, increased interior space, and reduced drag, a multihull is your best bet. All the boats are well-equipped and seaworthy. Rates for a weeklong charter run between BZ$4,400 and BZ$12,000, depending on the size of the boat and whether you charter it bareboat or with a crew.

Also be sure to look at **www.GetMyBoat.com**, a rental marketplace that allows owners of all sorts to rent their crafts (often for very good prices).

Fishing

Sport fishing for tarpon, permit, and bonefish is among the best in the world around these cayes and reefs, and over the years a few record catches have been made. If you prefer deep-sea fishing, there's plenty of tuna, mahi-mahi, and marlin to be had beyond the reefs. Both **Fishing San Pedro** (www.fishing sanpedro.com; ✆ **607-9967**) and **Go Fish Belize** ★ (www.gofishbelize.com; ✆ **226-3121**) can fix you up with a guide and equipment. A half-day of reef trolling, casting, or fly-fishing for bonefish or tarpon runs around BZ$300 to BZ$600, a full day BZ$600 to BZ$1,000. Deep-sea trolling for larger game costs between BZ$800 and BZ$1,600 for a half-day, and between BZ$1,600 and BZ$3,000 for a full day. These prices are per boat for two to four fishermen and usually include drinks, tackle, and lunch.

Hard-core fishermen might want to check out one of the dedicated fishing lodges, such as **El Pescador** ★ (www.elpescador.com; ✆ **800/242-2017** in the U.S. and Canada, or 226-2398) on Ambergris Caye, or **Turneffe Flats** ★★ (www.tflats.com; ✆ **888/512-8812** in the U.S., or 220-4046) out on the Turneffe Island Atoll.

Serious fans of fly-fishing should explore **Cayo Frances** (www.belize flyfishcamp.com; ✆ **610-3841**), a tranquil, off-the-grid fly-fishing camp on the far north end of Ambergris Caye, accessible only by boat. One of the guides they match guests with is **Lori-Ann Murphy** (www.loriannmurphy. com), though she can be hired directly no matter where on Ambergris Caye you're staying. She is also specialized in leading women in fly-fishing through the company she co-founded, Reel Women Fly Fishing Adventures.

Windsurfing, Parasailing & Watercraft

Ambergris Caye is a good place for beginning and intermediate windsurfers. The nearly constant 15- to 20-knot trade winds are perfect for learning on and for easy cruising. The protected waters provide some chop, but are generally pretty gentle on beginning boardsailors. If you're looking to do some windsurfing, or to try the latest adrenaline boost of kiteboarding, your best bet is to check in with the folks at **KiteXplorer** (✆ **632-6355**). Kiteboard rentals run BZ$200 for a half-day and BZ$300 for a full day. Weekly rates are also available. These folks offer a variety of courses for kiteboarding, as well as windsurfing and stand-up paddle boarding.

Most resort hotels here have their own collection of all or some of the above-mentioned watercraft. Rates run around BZ$60 to BZ$100 per hour for a Hobie Cat, small sailboat, or windsurfer, and BZ$150 to BZ$200 per hour for a jet ski. Parasailing can be booked through **Castaway Caye WaterSports** (www.castawaycaye.com; ✆ **671-3000,** or 671-3001), which goes from Wet Willy's dock and costs BZ$198 per person.

FUN ON DRY LAND

Spas, Yoga, Fitness & Body Work

There is one full-scale resort on the island with a spa, and that is Mahogany Bay Village, a "townlette" with everything. Its brand new spa, **Science and Soul Wellness** (www.scienceandsoulwellness.com; ✆ **615-0089**), is a holistic yoga studio and spa, which offers a wide array of soothing, pampering bodywork and treatments, including Ayurvedic. Traditional massage begins at BZ$180, while facials cost BZ$150. They offer the full range of possible spa treatments, so whether you're staying at Mahogany Bay or not, head here if you're really looking to relax.

If you want to work out, there's a modest health club and gym in the town proper at the **Train Station Fitness Club** at 41 Laguna Dr. (✆ **226-4222**), which has a great selection of machines and weights, as well as locally famous protein shakes. The club also has an upstairs area for classes or private workouts.

Finally, if you're in the mood for a good yoga session, you'll want to head just north of the bridge to **Ak'Bol Yoga Retreat** ★ (www.akbol.com; ✆ **226-2073**), which offers a regular schedule of classes for BZ$30 and intensive retreats. Rooms and individual cabins are also available here for rent, along with a largely vegetarian restaurant and small spa. Staff rebuilt the beautiful wooden oversea yoga platform after Hurricane Earl took the last one in 2016; it's an energizing spot to do yoga.

ANIMAL EXPERIENCES

American Crocodile Education Sanctuary (ACES) tour

The secret to Belize's wildlife conservation success lies in the people who fight for the species that matter to them most. The future of crocodiles in this small country is being secured by **ACES** ★★★ (www.americancrocodile sanctuary.org; ✆ **623-7920**) a San Pedro-based non-profit that performs research, provides education, and relocates crocodiles as a means for conservation. An important source of funding comes from a BZ$100 per person crocodile tour ACES leads on Ambergris Caye; up to 10 guests join croc wranglers on a nighttime expedition to catch, record, and relocate the big reptiles. This is one of the best opportunities in Belize to witness (and support) conservation up close, and you'll come away with a lot of knowledge about the misunderstood animals. Tours are scheduled by request, so contact them directly to get your time set up, and for instructions on where to find the boat.

Volunteer with the Saga Humane Society

Like many other Caribbean and Central American countries, street dogs in San Pedro are a noticeable thread in the fabric of the community. Cats are everywhere to be found as well, usually skulking around looking for a meal. **Saga** (www.sagahumanesociety.org; © **226-3266**) takes in these homeless animals, treats them in their non-profit veterinary clinic, and adopts out those that can be rehomed—BZ$50 for dogs and BZ$35 for cats. Taking adopted pets back to the U.S. (except Hawaii) is fairly common as Saga takes care of the paperwork, which consists of a simple rabies certificate. Airlines have rules and fees associated with transporting pets, so be sure to contact them in advance of departure. If you're not looking for a new friend, they always appreciate tourists donating supplies brought from abroad, but visitors are also welcome to stop by and volunteer their time by walking the dogs. This is a unique, and free, opportunity to give back to the community, as well as meet locals and learn more about life on the island.

OTHER ATTRACTIONS
A National Park

Occupying the northern end of Ambergris Caye and its surrounding waters, **Bacalar Chico National Park & Marine Reserve** (© **605-1633**) is home to scores of bird, animal, and plant species (many of which are endemic), as well as several ancient Mayan ceremonial and trading sites. The ranger station is, in fact, located at the diminutive Chac Balam ruins. Bacalar Chico is the name of the channel cut 1,500 years ago by the Maya to facilitate coastal trading. Just across the channel is Mexico. Nearly 200 species of birds have been spotted here, and the park allegedly contains all five wildcat species found in Belize, including the jaguar—although your odds of seeing a cat are remote at best. However, you've got decent odds of seeing a crocodile or wild deer, and of course numerous bird species. The park is only accessible by boat. All the local tour outfits offer half- and full-day trips to Bacalar Chico. Depending on your needs, these trips usually provide a mix of bird- and nature-watching, snorkeling, and Mayan ruin explorations. Specialist guides can be hired around San Pedro, if you want to focus primarily on any one of these pursuits.

Swim at Not-So-Secret Beach

Sandy beaches are at a premium, which is why the closest thing to one on Ambergris Caye was called **Secret Beach** ★★ up until the past year or so.

This spit of lagoon-side land was once a locals' swimming hole at the end of a bumpy, unmarked ride through the swamps. The drive hasn't changed much, but the beach has transformed into a popular tourist destination with changing rooms, restaurants, and bars. Two short docks extend over the water from the rocky shore, and the lack of sea grass and warm, calm, and shallow water make it a really nice place to swim. Drive carefully to and from the beach, as potholes and surprisingly deep puddles can leave you stranded. This area will be developed soon enough, so enjoy it while it's still hard to reach, even if it's no longer a secret.

Visit the Truck Stop

Drive 1 mile north of San Pedro and you'll see something that looks like a slice of Portland, Oregon (think: brightly painted, repurposed container ships). It's **The Truck Stop** (www.facebook.com/truckstopbz; ✆ **226-3663**), an extremely popular food park and beer garden. Five stationary food trucks serve up a range of cuisines, including pizza and ice cream. In the back, a deck overlooks the lagoon—arguably the best sunset spot on the island. In addition to serving food they offer a Wednesday night movie, Thursday trivia, host farmer's markets and live music, and about a million other activities that delight tourists and locals alike.

Excursions Farther Afield

A host of tour operators on Ambergris Caye offer excursions to all the major attractions and destinations around the country, including Altun Ha, Lamanai, Xunantunich, Mountain Pine Ridge, and even Tikal. You can also go cave tubing in the Caves Branch region. Most of these tours involve a flight in a small charter plane.

One of the most popular day trips is to the Mayan ruins at **Altun Ha.** This is also one of the most economical, as it doesn't require a flight. The day begins on a powerful little boat that will whisk you over to the mainland. You'll then take a taxi to the ruins and have lunch before returning to San Pedro. Most operators offering the Altun Ha trip include a lunch stop at Belize Boutique Resort and Spa (formerly Maruba Resort, p. 224), with the option of adding on a decadent jungle spa treatment. Prices for these trips run around BZ$150 to BZ$350. A similar trip by boat and land is offered to the ruins at Lamanai. **Tanisha Eco Tours** (www.tanishatours.

What's up, San Pedro?

Because of its high population density and general popularity, Ambergris Caye exists as something of a separate entity, which is why it requires its own media to fully grasp. My go-to sites of information are the San Pedro Scoop (www.sanpedroscoop.com), a blog that gives the expat perspective of exploring Belize, and the San Pedro Sun (www.sanpedrosun.com), a more traditional news source that is always on top of the latest changes to the caye.

com; ✆ **226-2314**) is a great choice for these and other mainland trips out of San Pedro, as they offer a wide range of options at reasonable prices, and can be booked without going through a middleman.

For trips involving a flight, prices range from BZ$250 to BZ$500 per person, depending on the distance traveled and number of activities and attractions crammed into 1 day. Most hotels on the island can book these tours, or you can contact **SEAduced** ★ (www.seaducedbybelize.com; ℂ **226-2254**) or **Sea-Rious Adventures** (www.seariousadventures.com; ℂ **226-4202**).

For detailed descriptions of these various destinations and attractions, see the respective regional chapters in this book.

Shopping

Most of the shopping on Ambergris Caye is typical tourist fare. You'll see tons of T-shirts and tank tops with dive logos and silk-screen prints of the Blue Hole. Beyond this, the best buy on the island is handmade jewelry sold by local Belizean artisans from makeshift display stands along Barrier Reef Drive. I'd be wary of black coral jewelry, though. Black coral is extremely beautiful, but as with every endangered resource, increased demand leads to increased harvesting of a slow-growing coral. The same goes for anything made of turtle shell, and certainly the very illegal jaguar body parts, possession of which has legal consequences. If for some reason you encounter someone selling a jaguar item, please alert the authorities immediately.

Inside Fido's Courtyard at **Belizean Arts** ★ (www.belizeanarts.com; ℂ **226-3019**), you'll find the island's best collection of original paintings and crafts. Of special note are the prints and paintings of co-owner Walter Castillo, a Nicaraguan-born artist whose simple, but bold, style captures the Caribbean color and rhythm of Belize.

Another shop at Fido's Courtyard worth checking out is **Ambar** ★★ (ℂ **226-3101**). The owner and artisan here sells handmade jewelry, with a specialty in amber. The stuff here is a significant cut above the wares you'll find in most other souvenir shops and street stands.

Cigar smokers should head straight to **Havana Cigars** (ℂ **226-4576**); on Barrier Reef Drive. This is the only authorized Cuban cigar dealer in the entire country, a distinction made by the Cuban government. The owner, Carlos, hails from Cuba, bringing his expertise to the walk-in humidor of the store. This is a required destination for cigar-loving tourists, as well as locals who enjoy the upscale but familial atmosphere.

Finally, if you just need some reading material for the beach blanket or hammock, head to **Aquarius Salon and Used Book Store** (no number), with a generous selection of used books (for Belize), right on Middle Street across from Milo's.

Where to Stay
IN SAN PEDRO

There's a score of hotel options right in the heart of San Pedro town. Most are geared toward budget travelers, and a few of these are quite comfortable and charming. Most of the more upscale resorts are located a little bit farther north or south of town. See below for these options.

paint WARS

A modest version of the traditional Caribbean Carnival or Mardi Gras is celebrated in San Pedro—with an odd twist—over the weekend preceding Ash Wednesday and the period of Lent, which is always sometime between February 4 and March 10. Sure, there are colorful and lively *comparsa* parades, with marching drum bands and costumed dancers. But over the years a tradition of painting has developed. This tradition predates paintball by decades. In times past, this was a fun and frivolous game between roaming bands of local residents using flour-based homemade "paints." Tourists were usually asked before being painted and their demurrals respected. Over the years, however, the painting fever has skyrocketed and gotten more aggressive: Fresh eggs and the occasional oil-based paint were introduced as weapons, and tourists are now often painted despite pleas to the contrary. It's definitely fun and a good way to meet some locals. If you get to a shower relatively quickly, it'll wash off without much hassle. Still, if you go out during Carnival, expect to get painted, and dress accordingly.

Tip: Almost every hotel on Ambergris Caye, and certainly all of the resorts, offers scuba packages. If you plan to do a lot of diving, these packages can sometimes provide substantial savings over paying as you go, at least if you use the hotel's operators. However, you can also buy dive packages from many of the individual dive operators, either in advance or upon arrival on the caye. Note that hotels typically add at least a small surcharge when booking through them, so cutting out the middleman can be cost effective.

Expensive

Blue Tang Inn ★★   Cheery decor, cheery staff—the Blue Tang burrows its way into the hearts of most of the guests who stay here. Housed in a three-story oceanfront building, within walking distance of town, lodgings are all suites, and big ones at that, each with a kitchenette, dining area, and living area with a foldout futon (they're an excellent option for families and groups). Boldly colored walls, and jaunty striped coverlets make the rooms very appealing. My favorite feature here is the rooftop deck, which offers panoramic views; there are few better places on Ambergris to take in the sunset. While there is no restaurant on site, the Inn does serve a daily changing complimentary breakfast. You won't go hungry later in the day: Scores of eateries are a just a few steps away from the hotel.

Sand Piper St. www.bluetanginn.com. ℂ **866/881-1020** in the U.S. and Canada, or 226-2326 in Belize. 16 units. BZ$330–BZ$530 double. Rate includes continental breakfast and San Pedro Airport transfers. Rates lower in the off season; higher during peak periods. **Amenities:** Small outdoor pool; mini-fridge; laundry service; Wi-Fi (free).

The Phoenix ★★   This is the most upscale accommodation with the closest walking distance to the downtown area, and it looks like it: the stark contemporary architecture here is striking. Within the buildings walls are mostly two-bedroom/two-bath condo units, although there are a few smaller and a few larger options. Most have huge balconies that open onto the property's large pool and common area, and the Caribbean Sea beyond. All come with full kitchens featuring handsome granite countertops and stainless-steel appliances, a washer and dryer, and large televisions in both the living room and the master bedroom. The on-site restaurant, **Red Ginger** (p. 147) is excellent. Upstairs is a hopping bar area with almost-nightly activities and a complimentary cocktail hour. Eco-conscious guests can participate in the hotel's volunteer beach trash cleanings.

Barrier Reef Dr. www.thephoenixbelize.com. © **877/822-5512** in the U.S. and Canada, or 226-2083 in Belize. 30 units. BZ$800–BZ$1,000 double. Rates lower in the off season; higher during peak periods. **Amenities:** Restaurant; bar; concierge; small spa and fitness center; 2 outdoor pools; room service; golf cart rental; Wi-Fi (free).

Ramon's Village ★   The handiwork of local son Ramón Núñez, this place is appropriately named, as there is a small-village feel to the collection of Tahitian-inspired thatch-roofed bungalows and suites. It's a little gimmicky, and feels like a theme park at times, but it's a well-run operation that sees a lot of repeat guests. At the center of the complex is a small but inviting free-form pool, surrounded by palm trees and flowering plants. Rooms vary in size and are classified as beachfront, seaside, and garden view, with the beachfront units having the best unobstructed views of the water. All are clean, modern, and comfortable, with colorful-print bedspreads and dark-varnished wood trim. Most have a private or shared balcony with a sitting chair or hammock. Be sure to ask for a bungalow away from the busy road if you value quiet. Ramon's has one of the longer and prettier beaches to be found in San Pedro, off of which is a brand new post-Hurricane Earl dock with a proprietary dive shop.

Coconut Dr. (southern edge of town). www.ramons.com. © **800/624-4215** in the U.S., or 226-2071 in Belize. 61 units. BZ$310–BZ$530 double; BZ$590–BZ$1,000 suite. Rates slightly higher during peak weeks; lower in the off season. **Amenities:** Restaurant; bar; bike and golf cart rental; full-service dive shop; small outdoor pool; room service; watersports equipment rental; small beach; Wi-fi (free).

Moderate

San Pedro Holiday Hotel ★   You can't miss this brilliantly white three-building complex, with painted purple and pink trim, in the center of town. Ms. Celi McCorkle opened this hotel almost 50 years ago, the first on the island, and the operation has the same festive and lively air that it's had for years. This despite the fact that the hotel lacks some of the amenities of other options in this price range—there's no swimming pool and not all rooms have televisions. We think the lively island vibe and friendly service make up for those shortcomings, as do the immaculate rooms, each of which comes with air-conditioning and a private balcony (most also have excellent ocean views and small refrigerators). On-site are a full-service dive shop, a popular bar and restaurant, and a small gift shop.

Barrier Reef Dr. www.sanpedroholiday.com. © **713/893-3825** in the U.S., or 604-2354 in Belize. 17 units. BZ$268–BZ$326 double; BZ$424 apt. **Amenities:** 2 restaurants; bar;

bike rental; full-service dive shop; watersports equipment rental; lounge chairs; Wi-Fi (free).

Inexpensive

There are quite a few budget options on Ambergris Caye, and almost all of them are concentrated in the compact downtown area of San Pedro. True budget hounds should just walk around and see who's got the best room for the best price. There are also Airbnb listings popping up like crazy, most for very affordable rates.

San Pedrano Hotel ★ San Pedrano is often the least expensive, decent option on the island. It's near the beach and run by one of the friendliest, most helpful staffs in Ambergris Caye. While most rooms don't have a great view, the vista from the wide veranda, overlooking the rooftops of adjacent buildings, is very nice. Regular rooms have varnished wooden floors, a single bed and a double bed in every room, and clean bathrooms with tubs. Some have air-conditioning. For those on tighter budgets, there are rooms with shared bath, and for the tightest of budgets there are hostel beds. The downside? Since it's on the main drag, San Pedrano can get loud.

10 Barrier Reef Dr. (✆ **226-2054.** 7 units. BZ$70–BZ$90 double. **Amenities:** Restaurant; bar; Wi-fi (free).

Ruby's ★ No Wi-Fi, no air conditioning, no TV's . . . but no distractions from the charms of Belize. That about sums up Ruby's where the rooms are basic, but very clean, and the welcome is warm. The long-established hotel is within walking distance of the airstrip (look for the three-story whitewashed building with blood-red gingerbread trim) and is also an easy stroll from all of the restaurants in town. Be sure to get one of the rooms overlooking the water, as the street-facing ones can be loud. Downstairs you'll find **Ruby's Deli,** which is a good place for breakfast or a casual midday meal. These folks also have a separate hotel on the lagoon side of the island, with clean, spacious, simple rooms; shared bathrooms; and even lower prices.

Barrier Reef Dr. www.rubyshotelsanpedro.com. (✆ **226-2063.** 23 units. BZ$80–BZ$120 double. **Amenities:** Restaurant; they say they have Wi-Fi, but we have found it doesn't work.

SOUTH OF SAN PEDRO
Expensive

Mahogany Bay Village ★★★ Belize's long-awaited, first large-scale resort is finally open on Ambergris Caye as of January 2018. A grand archway greets guests before they head down a long driveway to the 206-unit resort and its 20,000 sq. ft. Great House, a building designed in the British Colonial style and the largest wooden structure in Belize. Here guests can check in, dine, drink, and attend conferences. As the name suggests, Mahogany Bay really feels like a village. The property hosts a coffee shop, dive shop, beauty salon, spa, Saturday farmer's market, and **Jyoto** (p. 146), the best sushi restaurant in Belize, and several other good restaurants. Just off the main building is a stunning, large pool with its own bar. There's also a private beach club 15 minutes north by boat.

The rooms, which are either in detached or townhouse buildings, are set up along "streets" separated by canals. Each unit has its own golf cart parking spot (cart not included) and Wi-Fi network. The architecture and decor are stylishly Colonial and pretty swanky, with high ceilings, covered porches, plush king beds, big TVs, air-conditioning, and handsome hardwood floors. In the rooms are a wildlife guide with instructions on handling crocodile encounters, as well as a bird-watching list with species found specifically on Ambergris Caye.

Sea Grape Dr., lagoon-side, 3.2km (2 miles) south of San Pedro airport. www.mahogany bayvillage.com. ℂ **800/416-7339** in the U.S. and Canada, or 226-4817 in Belize. 206 units. BZ$698–BZ$848 double. Rates include continental breakfast and airport transfer. Rates lower in the off season. **Amenities:** Restaurant; 3 bars; fitness room; large outdoor pool; beach club; yoga classes; dive shop; golf cart rental; room service; Wi-Fi (free).

Victoria House ★★   This elegant and exclusive island retreat features a varied collection of rooms, suites, and villas. Everything is done with a refined sense of style and attention to detail (think: canopy beds, quality wooden furnishings, soothingly quiet color schemes). The resort is set on an expansive piece of land a couple of miles south of San Pedro, with lush tropical gardens and a surprisingly good section of soft white sand fronting it. The plantation rooms and suites are spread through several buildings, and there's a string of individual casitas aligned around a grassy lawn facing the sea. These latter feature high-pitched thatch roofs, tile floors, and wide French doors letting out onto a private balcony. The villas and suites are larger and equipped with large televisions and plush furnishings. Some have kitchenettes, and others are duplex units that can be joined or rented separately. Service is attentive, yet unintrusive. A full range of tours and activities is offered, and the **Palmilla** restaurant here (p. 149) is one of the finest on the island.

Beachfront, 3.2km (2 miles) south of San Pedro. www.victoria-house.com. ℂ **800/247-5159** in the U.S. and Canada, or 226-2067 in Belize. 42 units. BZ$420 double; BZ$710 casita or plantation room; BZ$790–BZ$1,190 suite. Rates higher during peak weeks; lower in the off season; rates include breakfast. **Amenities:** Restaurant; bar; free bikes; free kayaks; concierge; full-service dive shop; golf cart rental; 2 midsize outdoor pools; watersports equipment rental; Wi-Fi (free).

Xanadu Island Resort ★★★   Many honeymooners choose the Xanadu, and once you visit you'll understand why: The gardeners here have arranged the lush plantings so that each unit gets a sunset view, but also has enough privacy for, well, honeymooners. As for those gardens, they're Edenic in the verdant beauty. They enclose two- and three-story thatch-roof buildings set in a semicircle around a central pool area. Within each building are large and amenity-loaded suites that have the feel of independent apartments or condo units. This isn't a bad thing, and it makes this a good choice for extended stays and for families. Each features a private balcony or front porch, and a full kitchen or a kitchen and spacious living room. There are studios, single-bedrooms, and two- and three-bedroom units available. The resort has a long pier jutting into the ocean, with a wonderful swimming platform at the end. There's no restaurant on-site, but several are within close proximity, and the town of San Pedro is just 1.6km (1 mile) away. Xanadu is a certified "Green Globe" sustainable tourism project.

Oceanfront, southern end of Ambergris Caye. www.xanaduislandresort.com. Ⓒ **866/ 351-4752** in the U.S. and Canada, 226-2814 in Belize. 19 units. BZ$440–BZ$640 double; BZ$790–BZ$900 2-bedroom; BZ$970–BZ$1,300 3-bedroom. Rates slightly higher during peak periods and include breakfast. Free parking. **Amenities:** Bar; free bike usage; small outdoor pool; Wi-Fi (free).

Moderate

Mata Rocks ★ The blinding white paint and angular architecture of this intimate hotel conjure images of the Greek isles, as does the serenity of its location, about 2.4 km south of San Pedro. As a thoughtful touch, the hotel lends bicycles for free, so that guests can get into town easily. As for the resort, it's on the beach and all rooms here have at least a partial ocean view. The best is no. 53, a second-floor unit fronting the sea, with a large private balcony. There are 6 suites and 11 standard rooms; all are clean, modern, and cheery. The suites come with a fully equipped kitchenette, king and sofa beds, and a small sitting area. At the center of the hotel is a small free-form pool that is fed via a small artificial stream, which is in turn fed by a small fountain. A complimentary continental breakfast buffet is served in the open-air beachfront palapa bar, as are snacks, drinks, and light lunches. There is a friendly and relaxed air about the whole operation.

Oceanfront, southern end of Ambergris Caye. www.matarocks.com. Ⓒ **888/628-2757** in the U.S. and Canada, or 226-2336 in Belize. 17 units. BZ$330–BZ$380 double; BZ$430–BZ$460 suite. Rates include continental breakfast and airport transfers. Rates lower in the off season; higher during peak periods. **Amenities:** Bar; free bike usage; small outdoor pool; Wi-Fi (free).

ON NORTH AMBERGRIS CAYE

This is where you'll find most of the larger, more isolated, and more upscale resorts on Ambergris Caye. Several require reliance on your hotel or on the local water taxis to get to and from San Pedro town, while others are accessible with a golf cart, albeit on a very bumpy road.

In addition to the hotels listed below, **El Pescador** ★ (www.elpescador. com; Ⓒ **804/661-2259** in the U.S. and Canada, or 226-2398 in Belize) is a lovely and luxurious resort primarily geared toward hard-core fishermen and -women.

Expensive

Cayo Frances Farm & Fly ★★ Those who really want to get away from it all should look no further than Cayo Frances Farm & Fly, a fly-fishing camp 12 miles north of San Pedro accessible only by boat. It makes for a relaxing departure from civilization, and the kayaking and stand-up paddle boarding are phenomenal given the glassy, shallow water at this part of the caye. Lodging is limited, though growing, and rustic but comfortable. Sleeping areas are in cabins separate from a shared bathroom building and a common area with a kitchen, bar, and Wi-Fi. Meals are prepared by owner Jeff Spiegel, a former professional chef, and reflect his talent and experience. Perhaps my favorite experience here is the nightly bonfire, the perfect way to socialize while gazing at the beautiful, untainted night sky.

12 miles north of San Pedro, leeward side. www.belizeflyfishcamp.com. ℂ **610-3841.** 2 units. BZ$350 double. Rates include all meals and boat transfers to and from San Pedro Airport. **Amenities:** Free watercraft usage; Wi-Fi (free in communal area); cute resident dogs.

Las Terrazas ★★ And here's another Ambergris Caye lodging that seems to be channeling the Greek isles with its collection of whitewashed buildings right on the beach. Inside, all are handsomely decorated, with high quality furnishings, fixtures, and amenities. Rooms are all condo units with full kitchens, washer/dryer, and at least two flatscreen televisions. The penthouse units come with their own plunge pool or Jacuzzi. My only quibble is that the ceilings feel a bit low in many units. But the restaurant is one of the finest on the island (elegant decor, expert cooking), and there's a lovely rooftop lounge and bar right above it. Service throughout the resort is top-notch.

Oceanfront, northern end of Ambergris Caye. www.lasterrazasresort.com. ℂ **800/447-1553** in the U.S. and Canada, or 226-4249 in Belize. 39 units. BZ$690–BZ$1,190 double. Rates include transfers to and from San Pedro Airport. Rates slightly lower in the off season. **Amenities:** Restaurant; bar; outdoor pool; room service; smoke-free rooms; free watercraft usage; small spa and exercise room; Wi-Fi (free).

Matachica Resort & Spa ★★★ Perfect is a strong word, but this wonderful resort may come close. The staff is superb. Some seem to have the supernatural ability to know what guests want moments before they themselves do. The grounds, which include a beach, two swimming pools, and a Jacuzzi are serene, pretty, and well-maintained. And the rooms have the kind of contemporary styling you don't find often in Belize, each with an abstract mural behind the coquettishly mosquito-net-draped beds (they're quite romantic looking). In addition, rooms boast sculptures, ceramics, and paintings from around the world. Every lodging here is a private bungalow or villa, and all can be considered junior suites or better. My favorites are the seafront casitas, which are the closest to the ocean and feature a large sitting area, a king bed on a raised platform, and an interior garden shower. On-site is a small spa, with a full list of treatments and cures, as well as a full-service tour desk. The hotel also has an excellent restaurant, **Mambo** (p. 150). Matachica is one of the few "adults only" resorts in Belize (one of the others is their sister property Gaia, p. 287). Guests must be 16 or older.

Oceanfront, northern end of Ambergris Caye. www.matachica.com. ℂ **226-5010.** 31 units. BZ$550–BZ$920 double. Rates include continental breakfast and transfers to and from San Pedro Airport. **Amenities:** Restaurant; 2 bars; free bike, kayak and watersports equipment use; 2 outdoor pools; small spa; Wi-Fi (free).

Portofino Beach Resort ★★ Right on the shore and with thatch-roofed cabins, wood floors, bamboo beds, and large picture windows, this intimate boutique resort has a tropical feel. Every room here is massive, designed with rounded features that create a relaxing flow. The Tree Top suites are second-floor units with large private balconies, while the VIP suites are large private bungalows closer to the sea. The best room here, the Honeymoon suite, comes with a private Jacuzzi and stunning views from its seafront balcony. Service is excellent, as is the in-house **Le Bistro** restaurant. The dive shop is staffed with extremely knowledgeable instructors who are ready to go slow with first timers, or rock and roll with well-seasoned divers. I'm partial to the above-water hammocks when it comes to relaxation.

Oceanfront, northern end of Ambergris Caye. www.portofino.bz. ⓒ **800/813-7880** in the U.S. and Canada, or 678-5096 in Belize. 17 units. BZ$620 double; BZ$700–BZ$900 suite. Rates include continental breakfast and transfers to and from San Pedro Airport. **Amenities:** Restaurant; bar; free kayak use; golf-cart and bike rental; outdoor pool; room service; Wi-Fi (free).

Moderate

X'Tan Ha ★★ Wooden two-story buildings painted bright purples, blues, and reds make up this waterfront resort 7 miles north of San Pedro town. Though more sparsely decorated than other resorts in the area, every room here is oversized, with its own private veranda and a kitchenette, making it a good choice for a longer stay. There's a large pool in the center of the buildings, but the beach is refreshing as well, especially when enjoyed with the complimentary kayaks, paddleboards, and water trampoline. This is one of the more cost-effective options in the area, and just so you know, it's pronounced "Ish-tan-ha."

Oceanfront, 7.2 miles north of San Pedro. www.xtanha.com. ⓒ **844/360-1553.** 32 units. BZ$300 casita; BZ$420–BZ$650 for villas. Rates slightly lower in the off season. **Amenities:** Restaurant; bar; spa; free watercraft use; outdoor pool; sandy beach; Wi-Fi (free).

AN ISLAND OF YOUR OWN

Cayo Espanto ★★★ Whether you're a bona fide member of the jet set or you just want to pretend, this is the place for you. Seven bungalows are spread across this 4-acre private island. Each is luxurious, elegantly appointed, set on the ocean's edge, and staffed by at least one houseman, who can be contacted at any time by radio. All villas except the overwater bungalow have a private plunge pool; the borrowing of kayaks, stand-up paddleboards, or overwater trampolines can be arranged anytime. The rooms have wide French doors and windows that open onto private decks and verandas and stunning views. Six of the seven come with a private pier. There's no restaurant or common lounge area here, as most guests want to maintain their privacy. Instead, all meals are served in your villa or out on your private deck or dock area. Guests are surveyed prior to arrival so the chef can prepare meals based on preferences, housemen can know how much you want them around, and any other decadent need can be met. Service is attentive and pampering, the food is excellent, and their cigar menu is impressive, as it was designed and fulfilled by Carlos of Havana Cigars in San Pedro. Cayo Espanto is located just off the western tip of Ambergris Caye, about 7 minutes by boat from San Pedro.

Cayo Espanto. www.aprivateisland.com. © **888/666-4282** in the U.S. and Canada. 7 units BZ$3,190–BZ$3,990 double. Rates include 3 meals, all drinks (except wine and champagne), all nonmotorized watersports equipment usage, and transportation to and from San Pedro during daylight hours. Rates slightly higher during peak weeks. **Amenities:** Full-service dive operation; small exercise room; 5 small outdoor pools; room service; spa services; Wi-Fi (free).

Where to Dine
IN SAN PEDRO

Seafood is, of course, the most popular food on the island, and there's plenty of it around all year. However, please keep in mind that there are seasons for lobster and conch (because sea turtles are endangered, never order turtle). Officially, lobster season runs from June 15 to February 14, while conch is available from October 1 to June 30. Local restaurants and fishery officials have struck a deal to allow lobster to be served in the off season. Supposedly this is lobster caught and frozen during the open season, and not while they are mating in the formerly closed season.

If you're staying for an extended period, or have a room equipped with a kitchenette, you'll find several good markets around town. The best produce and specialty items can be found at **The Greenhouse Produce Market** (© **226-2084**), located on Pescador Drive.

Expensive

Jyoto Japanese Restaurant ★★★ JAPANESE   Excellent seafood is to be expected in Belize, but excellent sushi? That's brand new. We can thank Jyoto's chef Toshiya Tsujimoto, who was born in Japan and later honed his craft in San Francisco before traveling the world as a sushi chef and settling

LOBSTERFEST

Since 2007 San Pedranos have spent a week in June in total lobster frenzy, celebrating the reopening of the crustacean's season. This recent addition to Belize's festival lineup is also one of the quirkiest, with the island taken over by its homage to lobster. Ten days of celebration follow the June 15 kickoff party, with lobster-themed activities and events taking place throughout San Pedro's best bars and restaurants, and ultimately culminating in a final block party. Expect dancing in the street, singing and live music, and of course lobster used creatively in food competitions. It's a cultural experience to be sure, as lobster is a mainstay of the Belizean diet as well as a major draw for food tourism, but Lobsterfest also provides a look into the whimsy and positivity of the people of Ambergris Caye. Find out more about Lobsterfest at www.sanpedrolobsterfest.com, and if you go, don't forget to bring your bib.

in Belize. His food is utterly authentic, like what you would find in Tokyo, while incorporating such local ingredients as spiny lobster. Everything on the menu is tops, but the chef's choice sashimi of the day is a special treat, as delicious as it is exquisitely plated. Jyoto is set in a brand new two-story building with industrial architecture and subtle Japanese decor, and even though it's spacious (it can seat 120), it's often packed, having become an instant hit with locals and expats upon opening in 2017. If you can, grab a seat at the sushi bar to see the chef and his team in action.

On Seagrape Dr. at Mahogany Bay Village. www.mahoganybayvillage.com. © **628-0100.** Reservations recommended. Main courses BZ$30–BZ$60. Wed–Mon noon–2:30pm and 5:00–9:30pm, closed Tues.

Blue Water Grill ★★ INTERNATIONAL/ASIAN This popular place has a lovely setting overlooking the ocean and piers from the waterfront in the heart of San Pedro. The menu is massive: pizzas, pastas, and hearty dishes, such as grilled beef tenderloin with a bacon and garlic balsamic glaze and chicken breast served with green beans, quinoa, and a ham hock jus. But the real reason to come here is for the seafood, especially the creamy lobster chowder (best in summer when lobster is in season) and the massive mixed grill, which comes with lobster, grouper, and shrimp in a coconut reduction.

At the Sunbreeze Hotel, on the beach. www.bluewatergrillbelize.com. © **226-3347.** Reservations recommended. Main courses BZ$41–BZ$66. Daily 7–10:30am, 11:30am–2:30pm, and 5:30–9:30pm.

Red Ginger ★★ FUSION Housed in The Phoenix hotel and condo complex, this restaurant serves excellent tropical fusion fare in an understatedly elegant room. When the weather permits, you can dine on a patio just outside. The long menu offers almost too many temptations, but we've had very good luck with the Korean-style lettuce wraps and the steamed shrimp dumplings for appetizers. For a main course, I recommend the Singapore noodles with a cilantro-soy sauce. The huevos rancheros sammie is one of my favorite breakfasts on the island, and lunch is an excellent deal here, featuring daily, rotating specials.

At the Phoenix hotel, on the waterfront. www.redgingerbelize.com. © **226-4623.** Reservations recommended. Main courses BZ$26–BZ$66. Daily 7am–9:30pm.

Moderate

Caprice Bar and Grill ★ SEAFOOD/BELIZEAN This chill restaurant serves dependably good fare that tastes even better if you can get a seat on the large deck looking out at the sea. Stick to the seafood, which is reasonably priced and expertly prepared. Freshly caught fish, shrimp, and conch come with a variety of sauces, and lobster is offered seasonally. They serve an excellent brunch on Sundays from 10am to 2pm—I like the eggs Benedict and the chicken and waffles.

On the beach at the San Pedro Holiday Hotel. © **226-2014.** Reservations recommended. Main courses BZ$16–BZ$60. Daily 11am–9pm.

Finn & Martini ★★ INTERNATIONAL   The chic dinner scene has made its way to San Pedro by way of Finn & Martini, a relatively new spot that serves tapas-style dishes alongside tasty cocktails (such as their refreshing watermelon martini). There's limited seating, but the open-air layout and red painted walls makes it feel warm and inviting, not cramped. F&M marquee lights help identify where the place is. The owner, Finn, is known for his great sense of humor and superb hosting skills. Snack on the seafood wantons, artichoke dip, and carpaccio, or try out one of their daily specials.

On Laguna Drive. ⑦ **627-4789.** Main courses BZ$40–BZ$60. Wed–Mon 6–10pm.

Wild Mangos ★ INTERNATIONAL/FUSION   Chef Amy Knox is a frequent award winner in food competitions, and for good reason. Her "New Wave Latin" style of cooking brings together the best components of Latin American food, from the Caribbean all the way down to Argentina. The best seats at this down-home open-air joint are those on the outdoor, covered wooden deck. The menu is fairly broad and very creative. Start things off with the Tres Amigos, a selection of three different ceviches from their ample menu of creative ceviches. For a main course I like the cashew-crusted grouper in a green chile butter sauce, or the Budin Azteca, a vegetarian dish with mole, cheese, and more between layers of tortilla. There are often nightly specials, and the desserts are delectable. There's also a somewhat more streamlined lunch menu featuring excellent sandwiches, wraps, tacos, and burritos, as well as salads and other treats.

42 Barrier Reef Dr. ⑦ **226-2859.** Reservations recommended. Main courses dinner BZ$32–BZ$48, lunch BZ$15–BZ$65. Mon–Sat 11:30am–9pm.

Inexpensive

In addition to the places below, **Ruby's Cafe** and **Celi's Deli,** on the ground floors of Ruby's hotel (p. 141) and across from the San Pedro Holiday Hotel (p. 140), respectively, are good places to pick up a light meal, and both specialize in fresh-baked breads and pastries and sandwiches to go.

Other dependable options include **Caramba** (⑦ **226-4321**), which serves a mix of Belizean, Mexican, and Caribbean fare; and **Caliente** (⑦ **226-2170**), which is a good choice for traditional Mexican food, including chicken mole. For a seafront seat in the sand, it's hard to beat **Lily's Treasure Chest** (⑦ **226-2650**), which is great for breakfast, lunch, or dinner.

Elvi's Kitchen ★★ BELIZEAN/SEAFOOD/INTERNATIONAL   Local legend Elvia Staines began selling burgers out of a takeout window in 1974. Today, Elvi's is arguably the most popular restaurant on Ambergris Caye, with a word-of-mouth reputation built on the happy bellies of thousands of diners. The restaurant is a thatched, screened-in building with picnic tables, a large flamboyant tree growing up through the roof, and a floor of crushed shells and sand. You can get everything from Belizean stewed chicken to Oaxacan-style street corn. For lunch, there are still burgers, including traditional beef burgers, although I prefer the lobster and fish burgers. There's live music every night and a Mayan Feast every Friday, and the specials they serve reflect the style of music that's being played.

Pescador Dr. www.elviskitchen.com. © **226-2176.** Reservations recommended. Main courses BZ$18–BZ$65; fresh fish, seafood, and lobster priced according to market. Mon–Sat 11am–10pm.

Estel's Dine By the Sea ★ SEAFOOD/INTERNATIONAL   If you want to dine right by the water, it's hard to get much closer than Estel's. This casual place has a sand floor with heavy wooden tables and plastic chairs inside the main dining room, and a sand terrace outside with pure plastic patio furniture. A broad range of memorabilia and antiques lines the walls, and there's a piano in one corner. This is a popular place to start the day, with excellent huevos rancheros and breakfast burritos, as well as bloody marys. The lunch menu features plenty of fresh seafood and fish simply prepared, as well as a range of Mexican and Belizean standards. Hosts Charles and Estella Worthington are usually on hand—they live upstairs. In general, it's a mellow scene, attracting a convivial blend of locals and tourists.

Barrier Reef Dr. © **226-2019.** Main courses BZ$10–BZ$48. Wed–Mon 6am–4pm.

Jambel's Jerk Pit ★ CARIBBEAN/BELIZEAN   This long-standing beachfront restaurant serves spicy curries and jerk concoctions alongside local specialties. The coconut curry chicken is excellent, and there are several vegetarian options. Still, the spicy Jamaican-style jerk is the signature dish here, and you can get it served over fish, shrimp, chicken, or conch. Wednesday and Saturday nights feature an all-you-can-eat buffet and live reggae music for BZ$20 per person. The restaurant is housed on the second floor of an open-air two-story building just off the town's small central park.

Barrier Reef Dr. © **226-3515.** Main courses BZ$25–BZ$35; lobster BZ$44. Daily 7am–9pm.

SOUTH OF SAN PEDRO
In addition to the places listed below, if you're hankering for good Italian food, head to **Pinocchio** (© **226-4447**). The owners are from Rome, and everything from the pastas to the wood-oven pizzas is authentic and delicious. Meanwhile, the **Hidden Treasure** (www.hiddentreasurebelize.com; © **226-4111**) is earning raves for its creative local and New Latin cuisine. Coffee has been trending on the caye, but it's **Rum + Bean** (www.rumandbean.com; © **236-5102**) at Mahogany Bay Village that's getting people to flock south of town for their caffeine fix.

Expensive
Palmilla ★★ INTERNATIONAL/FUSION   This continues to be one of the most elegant and refined dining experiences to be had on Ambergris Caye. The chef here always takes the freshest of local ingredients and prepares them with a creative blend of techniques and spices, influenced by cuisines from around the world. The menu changes regularly, but might include cashew-crusted grouper or a pecan-crusted chicken breast. You can choose a table in the formal dining room, with its orgy of white linens, walls, and orchids, or

dine alfresco by candlelight at one of the heavy wooden tables on the outdoor poolside deck. Save room for dessert, as the molten chocolate cake and rum-soaked bread pudding are both to die for.

At Victoria House, south of downtown San Pedro. www.victoria-house.com. © **226-2067.** Reservations recommended. Main courses BZ$45–BZ$75. Daily 6:30am–9pm.

ON NORTH AMBERGRIS CAYE

Despite its relative isolation, the northern section of Ambergris Caye has perhaps the island's greatest concentration of truly excellent eateries. If you're staying in San Pedro or on the southern half of the island, you'll want to take a water taxi or rent a golf cart. Most of these restaurants will be able to arrange the boat ride for you, usually at a reduced rate from the going fare.

Expensive

Mambo ★★★ FUSION/INTERNATIONAL   With its groovy artworks and postcard perfect setting, the Matachica resort (p. 144), sets the standard for hipster hideaways. Its on-site restaurant furthers the cause with an eclectic menu that touches on a wide range of world cuisines. Recent winners on the menu have included seared scallops in Jamaican jerk sauce, seared peppercorn beef filet, mango-and-ginger-glazed pork chops, and a warm chocolate soufflé that is one of the best desserts I've ever had in Belize. Also on tap: an excellent and extensive wine list. And for those who want to keep on enjoying the finer things in life after dinner, Matachica offers a selection of Cuban cigars and cognacs. Service is very attentive, and complimentary boat transfers are provided.

At Matachica, on the northern end of Ambergris Caye. www.matachica.com/eat. © **223-0002.** Reservations required. Main courses BZ$35–BZ$70. Daily noon–3pm and 6:30–9pm.

Rain Restaurant and Rooftop Terrace ★★ FUSION/INTERNATIONAL   Ambergris Caye's only rooftop restaurant is 2 miles north of town atop the Grand Caribe Belize, one of the largest hotels on the island. What this place lacks in decor (some may call it modern, I call it bare-looking), it makes up for in panoramic views of the sky and the sea. The dishes incorporate ingredients and recipes that you might find in an upscale seaside restaurant in the U.S., such as cashew crusted grouper and fish tacos. Favorites include blue cheese crusted filet mignon, the changing array of handmade pastas, and the coconut-pineapple curried shrimp. Rain Restaurant is particularly welcoming to vegetarian guests with a number of thoughtful options regularly on the menu.

At Grand Caribe Belize, 2 miles north. www.rainbelize.com. © **226-4000.** Reservations recommended. Main courses BZ$40–BZ$74. Daily 7am–9pm.

Moderate

The Truck Stop ★★★ INTERNATIONAL   The Truck Stop is just that: five stationary food trucks that offer a wide range of international flavors. These include crispy, thin crust pizza from Slice of Heaven (bacon and mashed potato pizza, anyone?) and tropical or boozey ice cream flavors, served up by **The Ice Cream Shoppe** (p. 272) team from San Ignacio in the Cayo District. The Southeast Asian food at **RASA** is hearty and rich, serving some of the best noodles in the country, and the Latin specials at **Arepa** are consistently toothsome. There is a deck looking out over the lagoon, which offers a swell sunset view, and if they're swimming by, you can spot passing crocodiles. Look out for the marquee lights reading "Truck Stop" a mile north of the bridge and explore what's cooking.

One mile north. www.facebook.com/truckstopbz. ℂ **226-3663.** Main courses BZ$15–BZ$30. Wed–Sun noon–9pm.

Croc's Sunset Sports Bar ★★ AMERICAN This massive wooden sports bar is a brand new addition to the Ambergris Caye skyline, perched over the lagoon on the leeward side of the island, making for a spectacular sunset view. It has 10 flatscreen TVs playing all kinds of American sports and 215 seats spread across two bar areas. When the speakers aren't blasting recorded songs, invigorating live music is being played. I recommend trying the pulled pork tacos or the bacon-wrapped shrimp, but you also can't go wrong with the burger. There's no helping the stench of the lagoon when pulling a golf cart into the spacious parking lot, but the masterfully architected building was constructed quite high, so the smell doesn't reach the lounge area.

Five-minute drive north of the bridge. www.crocsbar.com. ℂ **631-3467.** Main courses BZ$20–BZ$45. Daily 11am–10pm.

Ambergris Caye After Dark

Ambergris Caye is a popular beach and dive destination, and as such it supports a fairly active nightlife and late-night bar scene. I recommend one of the bars here built out over the water, such as **The Tackle Box** (ℂ **226-4313**), or **Palapa Bar and Grill** ★ (ℂ **226-2528**) both located off the center of town and both occasionally with live music. Palapa Bar is also a good choice for daytime partying, as guests can sip their drinks in the water while floating on the inner tubes provided.

Alternately, you might try one of the beachside bars such as the **Wahoo's Lounge** (ℂ **226-2002**) at the Spindrift Hotel, which features bingo on Tuesday nights, karaoke on Saturday nights, and the famous chicken drop, an island version of roulette, at 6pm every Thursday night. Another popular choice is **Fido's Courtyard** (ℂ **226-2056**), which has live music every night of the week. For a lagoon-front experience, head to **Croc's** (ℂ **631-3467**) just north of the bridge for a sometimes-rowdy but always fun night.

If you're looking for a dance club and late-night action, your best bets are the two traditional San Pedro discos, **Jaguar's Temple Club** (ℂ **226-4077**) and **Big Daddy's** (no phone), which are within a stone's throw of each other on Barrier Reef Drive, near the basketball court and the church, just south of downtown on Coconut Drive. Both can be somewhat rough, so keep a level head when visiting.

Havana Cigars (ℂ **226-4576**) has an extensive whiskey selection and relaxing lounge area, a favorite place for even non-smokers to socialize.

Gamblers will want to head up north to the casino at **Captain Morgan's Retreat** (© **409/422-6156**).

CAYE CAULKER ★★★

32km (20 miles) N of Belize City; 16km (10 miles) S of Ambergris Caye

While Caye Caulker is no longer the secret hideaway of a few happy hippie backpackers and chosen cognoscenti, it remains the epitome of a small, isolated, and laid-back Caribbean getaway. Unlike neighboring San Pedro, you won't find gridlock traffic here or be constantly run off the road by cars and golf carts. In fact, golf-cart traffic is relatively light, with flip-flops and bicycles fulfilling most of the transportation needs. Let's hope it stays that way. Still, Caye Caulker has begun to experience some of the effects of the amazing boom going on just to the north on Ambergris Caye. There's more and more development on either end of the island, and the long-neglected northern section of Caye Caulker—across the Split—is becoming a destination all its own.

Essentials

GETTING THERE & DEPARTING

As of publication, the airstrip at Caye Caulker has been closed for repairs, so planes are not the way to get to the island. Construction has been stalled, and it's not clear when that will change, so check news sources like the San Pedro Sun (www.sanpedrosun.com) for updates. Fortunately, the sea provides, and there are several ways to reach Caye Caulker by water.

BY BOAT   **Ocean Ferry Belize** (www.oceanferrybelize.com; © **223-0033**) and **San Pedro Belize Express Water Taxi** (www.belizewatertaxi.com; © **223-2225**) are the two water taxi companies that will get you to Caye Caulker from Belize City. Both depart near the Swing Bridge: Ocean Ferry from the Marine Terminal, and the San Pedro Belize Express from Brown Sugar Terminal, both on North Front Street. Both provide covered speedboats powered by huge, loud engines, with space for 50 to 100 passengers. No matter the weather, water almost always enters the cabin, but on sunny days it's worth it to open the window because the cramped interior gets steamy with body heat in a matter of minutes.

The ride takes about an hour and continues on to Ambergris Caye. Similarly, rides back to Belize City will be boarding passengers from Ambergris Caye first. The fare is BZ$30 to BZ$36 one-way, or BZ$50 to BZ$56 round-trip, Ocean Ferry being the cheaper of the two options. Ocean Ferry offers five trips a day, compared with the San Pedro Belize Express' nine, but does offer Wi-Fi on board, which is a nice perk.

Tickets can be purchased in advance online or by visiting their terminals in person, though this is generally unnecessary. Stowing luggage is free, and bags will be taken and tagged by porters prior to boarding, so hold on tight to the claim ticket you're given. Pets are also welcome, but they need to be contained in kennels or bags. All boats arrive at their respective destinations in the center of town.

What's in a Name?

The Spanish called this little island "Cayo Hicaco." *Hicaco* is Spanish for the coco plum palm. Some say the name comes from the fact that ships used to be caulked in the shallow calm waters off the back side of this island, hence Caye Caulker. However, a third theory purports that the island appears as Caye Corker on several early British maps. This line of reasoning claims that early sailors and pirates stopped to fill and then "cork" their water bottles with the abundant fresh water found here. Even so, don't call it Caye Corker.

Tip: It's worth it to arrive no later than a half-hour early to queue up and get first pick of the seats. The front is a bumpier ride, and wetter if the weather's bad, but the back is louder and smells more like the gasoline that fuels the engines. Those prone to motion sickness will either want to sit next to a window for the fresh air, or on one of the center seats that face forward.

GETTING AROUND

Caye Caulker is small. You can easily walk from one end of the island to the other in around 20 minutes. If you want to cover more ground quickly, a bicycle is your best bet. Many hotels have their own for guests to use free of charge or for a slight rental fee. If not, you can rent a bicycle in town. There are several places on Front Street with rates running around BZ$15 to BZ$30 per day.

If not everyone in your group can ride a bicycle or fit in a child's seat attached to a bicycle, you can also rent a golf cart from **Caye Caulker Golf Rentals** (© **226-0237**) or **Buddy's Golf Cart Rentals** (© **628-8508**). Rates run around BZ$80 to BZ$150 per day for a four-seat cart or BZ$360 for a week. But only do this if absolutely necessary.

ORIENTATION

Most boats dock at the pier jutting off Front Street at a spot called Front Bridge—so named because this is the front side of the island facing the reef (east). The town extends north and south from here. As you debark, if you kept walking straight ahead, you'd soon come to the western side of the island and the Back Bridge or dock, where some of the boats dock. Caye Caulker consists of three main north–south sand roads, a few cross streets, and numerous paths. The closest street to the water on the east side of the island is Front Street. The next street in is called either Middle Street or Hicaco Avenue, and the next street to the west is called alternately Back Street or Langosta Avenue. The currently defunct Caye Caulker airstrip is located on the southern outskirts of the town. At the north end of town, you'll find the Split or Cut, the town's prime swimming and sunbathing spot.

Much of Caye Caulker is uninhabited. The small town and inhabited sections are quite concentrated.

Though Caye Caulker is still a relatively safe place, it is not advisable to leave money or valuables in your hotel room, except in a safe. In addition, locals here have been known to take advantage of the trusting nature of the

Caye Caulker

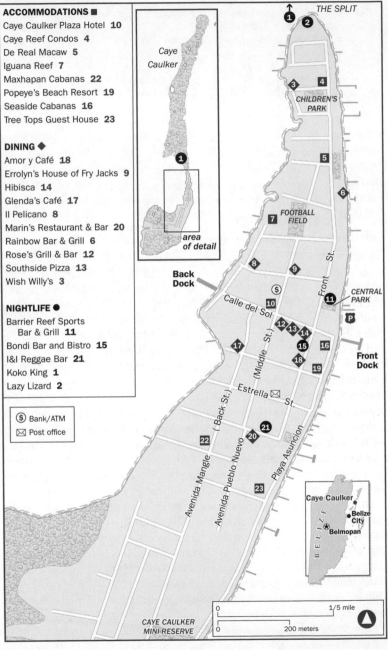

ACCOMMODATIONS ■
Caye Caulker Plaza Hotel **10**
Caye Reef Condos **4**
De Real Macaw **5**
Iguana Reef **7**
Maxhapan Cabanas **22**
Popeye's Beach Resort **19**
Seaside Cabanas **16**
Tree Tops Guest House **23**

DINING ◆
Amor y Café **18**
Errolyn's House of Fry Jacks **9**
Hibisca **14**
Glenda's Café **17**
Il Pelicano **8**
Marin's Restaurant & Bar **20**
Rainbow Bar & Grill **6**
Rose's Grill & Bar **12**
Southside Pizza **13**
Wish Willy's **3**

NIGHTLIFE ●
Barrier Reef Sports
  Bar & Grill **11**
Bondi Bar and Bistro **15**
I&I Reggae Bar **21**
Koko King **1**
Lazy Lizard **2**

Ⓢ Bank/ATM
✉ Post office

THE SPLIT

Caye
Caulker

area
of detail

CHILDREN'S
PARK

FOOTBALL
FIELD

Back
Dock

Calle del Sol

CENTRAL
PARK

Front St.

Front
Dock

Estrella St.

(Middle St.)

(Back St.)

Avenida Mangle

Avenida Pueblo Nuevo

Playa Asuncion

CAYE CAULKER
MINI-RESERVE

Caye Caulker

Belize
City

Belmopan

B E L I Z E

0   1/5 mile
0   200 meters

island's visitors, enamored as they are with the relaxed lifestyle, so put as much consideration into trusting new friends as you would anywhere else.

FAST FACTS For the local **police,** dial ℂ **911,** or 226-2022; for the **fire department,** dial ℂ **226-0353.** In the case of a medical emergency, call the **Caye Caulker Health Clinic** (ℂ **226-0166**).

Atlantic Bank (ℂ **226-0207**) is located on Back Street, near the center of the island, and has an ATM that accepts international credit and debit cards.

The **post office** (ℂ **226-0325**) is also located on Back Street; it's open Monday through Friday from 8am to noon and from 1 to 4:30pm.

> ### Slow Ride
> The unofficial, yet almost universal, motto on Caye Caulker is "Go Slow."

Most hotels provide laundry service, but pricing varies widely, so ask first. There are several coin-operated and full-service **laundromats** on Caye Caulker, all in the central downtown area. Almost all of these are a better deal than going with your hotel's service.

What to See & Do

The main activities on Caye Caulker itself are strolling up and down the sand streets, and swimming and sunbathing off the docks. The most popular spot is at the north end of the island by the **Split ★**. The Split was formed in 1961 when Hurricane Hattie literally split the island in two. Since then, the north tip of the southern half has been where the island's social activity takes place, with a bar and restaurant, dock, and calm swimming area. In 2016 Hurricane Earl knocked down a bunch of the structures here, so they decided to reimagine the whole area by clearing the mangrove and installing a seawall, creating a much larger space for people to hang out. Take care when swimming or practicing snorkeling off the docks here. The Split is an active channel with regular boat traffic. At least one swimmer has been killed by a boat, so stick to designated swimming areas, away from obvious boat channels. Also, when the tides are running strong, a strong current runs through the Split, and it's easy to get dragged along for a few hundred yards or so. If you do get caught in this current, treat it like any riptide: Don't panic, and swim diagonally across the current to get out of it.

There is a narrow strip of sand for much of the length of the island, where the land meets the sea, but even at low tide it isn't wide enough for you to unroll a beach towel. In fact, along most of its length this is a small bike and footpath that is probably the busiest thoroughfare on Caye Caulker. The one exception is the good-sized beach just north of the Split at the new day resort **Koko King** (it's on the leeward side). Just off the coast, for the first 100 yards (300 ft.) or more out from shore, the bottom is covered with sea grass, which is protected by national law. Beneath the grass is a layer of spongy roots and organic matter topped with a thin layer of white sand. Be careful when walking on this spongy sand, as you might encounter a sea urchin or stingray, and it's easy to trip and stumble.

Several of the hotels have built long piers out into the sea, with steps down into the water, and swimming is best here. Beyond this, some of the best swimming can be had from boats anchored out in the turquoise waters between the shore and the reef, or by taking a kayak offshore a little way.

As on Ambergris Caye, snorkeling, scuba diving, and fishing are the main draws here. All are excellent.

ON & UNDER THE WATER
Scuba Diving & Snorkeling ★★★

There's excellent diving and snorkeling close to Caye Caulker. Within a 5- to 20-minute boat ride from the pier lie some **world-class dive sites ★★**, including **Caye Caulker North Cut, Coral Gardens, Pyramid Flats, Sponge Avenue,** and **Amigos Wreck.** As on Ambergris Caye, a day's diving here will almost always feature a mix of steep wall drops and coral caverns and tunnels. In addition, in Caye Caulker you can dive on the wreck of a 15m (49-ft.) boat and among huge canyons of coral. You'll see brilliant coral and sponge formations, as well as a wealth of colorful marine life. The wreck and canyons are prime spots to spot giant grouper, and rays and turtles are fairly common here as well.

There are several dependable dive operators on Caye Caulker. Rates are pretty standardized, and you should be able to get deals on multiday, multidive packages. The best dive operations on the island are **Belize Diving Services ★★** (www.belizedivingservices.com; ℗ 869-0233), **Reef Friendly Tours** (www.reeffriendlytours.com; ℗ 624-2862), and **Frenchie's Diving ★** (www.frenchiesdivingbelize.com; ℗ 226-0234). Of these, Belize Diving Services is the most up-to-date, with top-notch equipment and mixed-gas and technical diving capabilities. All of these operators charge BZ$180 to BZ$210 for a local two-tank dive, with equipment rental running around BZ$50 to BZ$60 for a complete package and BZ$20 to BZ$40 for a mask, snorkel, and fins.

For more adventurous diving, you'll probably want to head out to the **Turneffe Island Atoll ★★★**, **Lighthouse Reef ★★★**, and **Blue Hole ★★**. All the dive operations on Caye Caulker offer this trip or will subcontract it out. It's about a 2- to 3-hour ride each way—depending upon the speed of your boat—over sometimes rough seas. Most day trips out to Turneffe Island or Lighthouse Reef and Blue Hole run around BZ$400 to BZ$600 per person, including transportation, two or three dives, tanks, and weights, as well as lunch and snacks. For more information on these dive sites, see p. 166.

Caye Caulker is another excellent place to learn how to scuba dive. Resort courses will give you an excellent 1-day introduction into the world of scuba diving, including a very controlled shallow-water boat dive. These courses cost BZ$200 to BZ$300. In 3 to 4 days, however, you can get your full open-water certification. Courses cost between BZ$700 and BZ$900, including all equipment rentals, class materials, and the processing of your certification, as well as four open-water and reef dives. All of the above-mentioned dive operations offer these courses.

CHOCOLATE & THE manatees

Sure, you can get candy bars, cakes, and a whole host of products derived from the fruit of the cacao tree here. But on Caye Caulker, when someone mentions "Chocolate," they are almost inevitably referring to pioneering guide and boat captain Lionel "Chocolate" Heredia. Chocolate began his career as a fisherman, but he soon dedicated himself to the fledgling business of taxiing folks by speedboat back and forth between Belize City and Caye Caulker. This business soon expanded to include guided tours, snorkeling outings, and fishing adventures. Chocolate was also probably the first guide to introduce the popular day trip to see manatees and do some snorkeling at remote cayes. He and his wife, Annie, also led the battle to protect these gentle sea mammals and their feeding grounds, finally seeing the creation of the Swallow Caye Wildlife Sanctuary (www.swallowcaye.org) in 1999. Chocolate kept his manatee tours going until passing away in 2013. The best way to honor his legacy is to refrain from patronizing businesses that allow guests to swim with manatees.

There are a host of boats on Caye Caulker offering snorkeling trips, and most of the above dive operators also offer snorkeling trips and equipment rental. Snorkeling tours range in price from BZ$70 to BZ$80 for short jaunts to half-day outings, and BZ$130 to BZ$180 for full-day trips—a bit more if you want to jump on a trip all the way out to the Blue Hole. A full set of mask, fins, and snorkel will usually cost from BZ$20 to BZ$40 per person per day.

All of the Caye Caulker dive and snorkel operators offer trips to **Shark-Ray Alley ★★** and **Hol Chan Marine Reserve ★★**, though **Reef Friendly Tours ★★★** (www.reeffriendlytours.com; © 624-2862) does them in the most ethical fashion. They're currently the only outfitter on the island that can reasonably be called eco-friendly. Captain Amado was the first to stop chumming the water for sharks and rays, enforcing a strict "no touching" policy to reduce stress on the animals. Trips to these two spots cost between BZ$130 and BZ$280 per person, depending on whether it is a snorkel or scuba dive trip, how long the tour lasts, and whether there is a stop on Ambergris Caye. Many of these include a stop for lunch and a quick walk around town in San Pedro. See "What to See & Do" on p. 130 for more information and a detailed description of Shark-Ray Alley and Hol Chan Marine Reserve.

Sailing ★★

The crystal-clear waters, calm seas, and excellent snorkeling spots around Caye Caulker make this an excellent place to go out for a sail. Unlike on Ambergris Caye, there are no organized bareboat charters available here, but you can go out on any number of different vessels for a half- or full-day sail, a sunset cruise, a moonlight cruise, a combined sailing and snorkeling adventure, or even a multi-day adventure that takes you down the coast.

A day cruise including lunch, drinks, and snorkeling gear should run between BZ$140 and BZ$280 per person; a half-day tour including drinks, a snack, and snorkeling gear should cost between BZ$80 and BZ$130. Most hotels and tour operators around town can hook you up with an appropriate captain and craft. Don't miss sailing with **Raggamuffin Tours** ★ (www.raggamuffintours.com; ℭ **226-0348**). These folks run one of my favorite adventures in Belize, a 3-day/2-night sailing trip down to Dangriga with a camping stay on Rendezvous Caye and a dorm sleepover on Ragga Caye, snorkeling gear, food, and endless drinks included.

Fishing

Despite originally being a fishing village, Caye Caulker is not particularly developed or popular for sport fishing. Even so, fishing for tarpon, permit, and bonefish is still excellent around the caye, and on the reefs and flats. There are several dedicated fishing guides on the island, and almost every hotel, tour operator, or dive shop can hook you up with a captain and crew for some angling. Bear in mind you will need to secure a fishing license; your hotel or guide can help you do this. If you're a serious fisherman, **Angler's Abroad Fly Shop** ★★ (www.anglersabroad.com; ℭ **226-0602**) should be your first stop.

A half-day of reef trolling, casting, or fly-fishing for bonefish or tarpon costs between BZ$200 and BZ$400, a full day between BZ$400 and BZ$800. Deep-sea trolling for larger game runs around BZ$800 to BZ$1,200 for a half-day, BZ$1,600 to BZ$2,400 for a full day. These prices are per boat for two to four fishermen and usually include drinks, tackle, and lunch.

Kitesurfing & Sailboarding

With strong, steady, but not overpowering winds, Caye Caulker is a top place to learn or practice kitesurfing. The folks at **Kitexplorer** (www.kitexplorer.com; ℭ **632-6355**) rent out both kitesurfing and sailboarding equipment. They also offer an intensive multi-day course in kitesurfing for BZ$980 that is guaranteed to get you up and skimming across the sea. A three-hour intro will run you BZ$360.

Kayaks & Other Watercraft

The calm, protected waters just offshore are wonderful for any number of watersports vehicles. Several hotels and tour operators around Caye Caulker have various types of watercraft for guest use, or general rental. Rates run around BZ$20 to BZ$30 per hour for a kayak and BZ$240 per hour for a jet ski.

FUN ON DRY LAND

Sunbathing, reading, and relaxing are the primary land-based activities on Caye Caulker. However, you should be sure to head south of town to the **Caye Caulker Mini-Reserve,** located on the southern outskirts of the town. The term "mini" is certainly fitting. Nevertheless, this local endeavor features a few gentle and well-cleared paths through a small stand of littoral forest. More serious bird-watchers might want to grab a boat and a guide and head to the northern half of the island, where 40 hectares (100 acres) on the very northern tip have been declared the **Caye Caulker Forest Reserve.** In all, more than 130 species of resident and migrant birds have been spotted on and around

Caye Caulker. Another option for bird-watchers and nature lovers is to rent a kayak for paddling around on the lagoon and mangrove side of the island. No admission is charged to visit either of these reserves.

Caye Caulker's leeward shoreline is also a great place to find local marine wildlife. **Seahorses** gather at a small "ranch" next to the Iguana Reef Inn, while **large tarpon** can be found off a dock on Purnell's Property at the end of Lind's Coral Street.

There is also **Koko King** (www.facebook.com/KOKOKingCayeCaulker), a day resort that opened on Caye Caulker in 2017 just north of the split. This party place is run by the folks at **Raggamuffin Tours,** and was an instant hit, which isn't too surprising given that not much changes on Caye Caulker, and rarely anything of this magnitude. For only BZ$10 guests can catch a boat ride every half-hour from just south of the Split on the leeward side to a palapa-topped dock, at the other end of which is a sandy beach peppered with lounge chairs, swings, hammocks, a pool, bar, and restaurant. The beach is wide and free of sea grass, more than doubling the swimmable area of Caye Caulker.

EXCURSIONS ON THE MAINLAND

Several tour operators on Caye Caulker offer excursions to all of the major attractions and destinations around the country, including Altun Ha, Lamanai, Xunantunich, Mountain Pine Ridge, and Tikal. You can also go cave tubing in the Caves Branch region. Most of these tours involve a flight or two in a small charter plane.

The most popular and economical tours are to the Mayan ruins of Altun Ha or Lamanai, or a spa package and lunch at Belize Boutique Resort and Spa (formerly Maruba). Various operators offer a combined trip visiting both Altun Ha and the resort. These trips begin with a short boat ride to the mainland, followed by a minibus ride to the selected attraction. Prices for these trips run BZ$140 to BZ$240, although the spa treatments are extra.

Any hotel or tour operator on the island can help you arrange any number of these tours. In most cases, these trips are subcontracted out to an operator based either in Belize City or on Ambergris Caye.

> **About the Water**
>
> Much of the water on Caye Caulker is collected rainwater. While it's usually safe to drink, and most locals are used to it, I advise visitors to stick to bottled water.

For detailed descriptions of these various destinations and attractions, see the respective regional chapters throughout this book. In addition to the dive and watersports tour operators listed above, **Tsunami Adventures** (www.tsunami adventures.com; ℂ **226-0462**) is a good, all-purpose operator with an extensive list of offerings on and under the water, and all around the cayes and mainland, too.

Shopping

In terms of shopping, you'll be amazed by the number of small gift shops and makeshift souvenir stands lining the few streets here. As on Ambergris Caye, much of the shopping on Caye Caulker is typical tourist fare. Mostly what you'll be able to buy are T-shirts and jewelry made by local artisans.

A good art gallery on the island is **Caribbean Colors Art Cafe (© 605-9242)**, which features some interesting original artwork and hand-painted silk by artist Lee Vanderwalker.

As I recommend elsewhere in this book, please avoid buying black coral jewelry. Black coral is extremely beautiful, but as with every endangered resource, increased demand just leads to increased harvesting of a slow-growing coral. The same goes for anything tortoiseshell, which exploits the hawksbill sea turtle.

Where to Stay

Accommodations on Caye Caulker have improved over the years, but there are still no resorts or real luxury options. In my opinion, this adds to the charm of the place. Budget and midrange lodging options are abundant, and some of these are quite comfortable.

If you plan on staying for any period of time, you should look into renting a small cottage, condo, or apartment. As of this writing, Airbnb.com has some 50 offerings on Caye Caulker, HomeAway.com has the same, as do the other online rental companies. If you'd like the personalized service of a local operation, contact **Caye Caulker Rentals ★** (www.cayecaulkerrentals.com; © 630-1008). Rates begin around BZ$140 per night through them, although during the high season rates go up and longer stays are often required. Another option is the fully equipped efficiency units at **Caye Caulker Condos** (www.cayecaulkercondos.com; © 226-0072), which rent for between BZ$160 and BZ$270 per night.

EXPENSIVE

CayeReef Condos ★★★   Fronting the ocean toward the north end of the caye, the two-bedroom, two-bathroom condo units here are extremely comfortable, with cushy beds and fully-equipped kitchens. Every unit comes with an ocean-facing balcony and is decorated with bright Caribbean colors and very nice original local artwork. The rooftop pool, Jacuzzi, and lounge area is a highlight. Cleaning is only once weekly, but that frequency can be increased for a BZ$30 daily fee. Hot water is solar-heated (good shower pressure, too), and the owners are consciously trying to be sustainable. Speaking of those owners: They go out of their way to assist guests, giving the type of service one usually gets in a resort, not a condo development.

Front St. www.cayereef.com. © **226-0382,** or 610-0240. 6 units. BZ$336 condo; BZ$408 penthouse. Rates slightly higher during peak weeks; lower during the off season. **Amenities:** Jacuzzi; outdoor pool; Wi-Fi (free).

Iguana Reef ★★★   The closest thing to a resort hotel on Caye Caulker, Iguana Reef has one of the nicest beaches on the caye, a large and comfortable sandy area for lounging, with a pier leading off it to a nice swimming spot. Set on the lagoon, or back side of the island, Iguana Reef is blissfully serene, but not too far from the action of town. The hotel has a very inviting pool, with a little lazy river attached. As for the rooms, they won't win style awards (think: tile floors, wicker furnishings, local art) but they're very spacious and all come with air-conditioning, a stocked minibar, and a programmable safe. The deluxe units have a sitting area and a semiprivate veranda. This is also arguably the best spot on the island to catch a sunset.

Back St. www.iguanareefinn.com. © **226-0213.** 15 units. BZ$358 double; BZ$978 penthouse. Rates include continental breakfast. Rates slightly higher during peak weeks; lower during the off season. **Amenities:** Restaurant; bar; free bike and kayak use; outdoor pool; Wi-Fi (free).

MODERATE

In addition to the places listed below, **Popeye's Beach Resort** (www.popeyes beachresort.com; © **226-0032**) is another good option in this price range, with air-conditioned rooms and an oceanfront setting.

Seaside Cabanas ★★   This hotel is built in a horseshoe around a small rectangular pool, with a broad wooden deck around it. All the rooms, none of which are actually cabanas, are very clean and painted in lively yellows and reds. Rooms 1-4 come with private rooftop lounge areas with hammocks strung under an open-air thatch roof and a hot tub. These are by far my favorite rooms, but I also like no. 6, a second-floor unit with a small private balcony. They've also recently-added an 18th unit, a two-level suite that is ideal for honeymooners, yet doesn't cost a whole lot more than the other rooms. There's no restaurant here, but they have a lively bar and an excellent in-house tour operation.

Front St. www.seasidecabanas.com. © **226-0498.** 18 units. BZ$258–BZ$378 double. Rates slightly higher during peak weeks; lower during the off season. No children 9 and under allowed. **Amenities:** Bar; bike rental; outdoor pool; Wi-Fi (free).

INEXPENSIVE

There are literally scores of budget options on Caye Caulker. I list my favorite and the most dependable options below. In addition to these, **Yuma's House Belize** (www.yumashousebelize.com; © **206-0019**) is a solid pick. Formerly known as Tina's Backpacker's Hostel, it offers clean, basic rooms with an oceanfront location and a very lively, hostel-like atmosphere.

Caye Caulker Plaza Hotel ★   What this three-story hotel in the center of Caye Caulker lacks in visual pizzazz it makes up for in location relative to price and level of service: They staff their front desk 24 hours a day, a rarity in Belize but especially in sleepy Caye Caulker. Save for a few photos of wildlife concentrated in the downstairs lobby, there aren't really any local touches to the Plaza Hotel. Despite the rather plain decor, the rooms are spacious, clean, and comfortable enough, with in-room safes and mini-fridges, and air-conditioning. There is also a nice rooftop terrace that guests can use to look out over the sea or watch the sunrise to the west.

At the corner of Avenida Langosta and Calle del Sol. www.cayecaulkerplazahotel.com. © **226-0780.** 30 units. BZ$170–$210 double. Rates lower during the off season. **Amenities:** 24-hour front desk; Wi-Fi (free).

De Real Macaw ★   If you're looking for peace and quiet, or a good nights' sleep, look elsewhere. De Real Macaw is located across from a string of makeshift artisan stalls and street-side restaurants on Front Street, so it can get loud. And if you get the wrong room, the bed can be uncomfortably hard (ask to move if that happens). Still the welcome is friendly, and price reasonable for these parts. The hotel is its own little compound, around a central sandy garden area, with a few tall shade trees hung with hammocks. The two beachfront rooms are the best rooms here, though the vendors block most of the beach views. But all are very clean and well kept, with tile floors, tiny television sets, and a front porch or balcony. Most of the rooms come with air-conditioning, but you'll pay a little more for it. The two-bedroom "condo" and separate beach house both come with a full kitchen, and these folks also rent out fully furnished apartments on a weekly basis, located a little bit away.

Front St., north of Front Bridge. www.derealmacaw.biz. © **226-0459.** 10 units. BZ$100–BZ$110 double with no A/C; BZ$120–BZ$140 double with A/C; BZ$240–BZ$260 condo or beach house. Rates lower in the off season. **Amenities:** In-room TVs; Wi-Fi (free).

Maxhapan Cabanas ★★★   The best budget lodgings on the island, guests stay in yellow wooden cottages set on raised stilts in the midst of relatively expansive grounds, just outside the "downtown" hustle and bustle. It's a peaceful private oasis, with lots of nice extras like two free bottles of water each day and free loaner bikes. Yes, everything is plain looking here, but kept immaculate. There's a communal bar area, as well as a two-story open-air structure meant for chilling out. The only thing missing is a view of the sea. The owner, Louise, is almost always on hand, providing attentive, warm, and personalized service. A true value (hence our three-star rating)!

Just south of town on Center St. maxhapan04@hotmail.com. © **226-0118.** 3 units. BZ$142 double. **Amenities:** Free bike and snorkel gear use; Wi-Fi (free).

Tree Tops Guest House ★★   Second best among the budget lodgings, Tree Tops is just off the ocean in the heart of town and set in a converted three-story home. Rooms are very clean and spacious, if nondescript. There are four rooms located on the ground floor. Two of these share a common bathroom down the hall, but each has a vanity sink in the room itself. However, the best rooms here are the two top-floor suites. Each of these comes with a king bed and private balcony. The Sunset Suite is the best of these, with the largest balcony and views to both the lagoon and the ocean. If you opt for one of the standard rooms, however, you can still enjoy the view from the rooftop lounge area, which features several hammocks hung under a shade roof. *One warning:* The Wi-Fi here is not reliable.

On the waterfront south of Front Bridge. www.treetopsbelize.com. © **226-6135.** 6 units (4 with private bathroom). BZ$144 double with shared bathroom; BZ$186–BZ$250 double with private bathroom. **Amenities:** Bicycle rentals; Wi-Fi (free).

Where to Dine

In addition to the places listed below, if you're hanging out by the Split, you'll probably want to stop in at the **Lazy Lizard** (© **226-0636**), a so-called "sunny place for shady people" serving cold drinks and a menu of local dishes, sandwiches, and burgers. And be sure to stop in at the **Lighthouse Ice Cream Parlour** on Front Street for a cone or a scoop of some fresh, homemade ice cream.

MODERATE

Il Pellicano ★★★ ITALIAN   This Italian restaurant is the place to go for ambiance in Caye Caulker. With a lush walkway, ornate wooden gate, and candlelit walkways, it feels like stepping into Italy. The menu is primarily pastas and pizzas, a fairly robust selection even when compared with Belize's other Italian restaurants. I recommend trying the salsiccia pizza for that real Italian experience, or the fish of the day in a spicy tomato sauce to keep things a little more Belizean. The dinner menu changes somewhat regularly, while the dessert switches daily. They are not open for lunch.

On Pasero St., the back side of the island. www.ilpellicano.bz. © **226-0660.** Main courses BZ$25–BZ$45. Tues–Sun 5:30–9:30pm.

Hibisca (formerly Habanero's) ★★★ INTERNATIONAL   Called Habanero's until 2018, Hibisca is a Caye Caulker classic. The food is extremely memorable and varied, from homemade pastas and Thai coconut curries to Brazilian pork or spicy fajitas made of beef, chicken, or jerk pork. I like to start things off with the Creole Voodoo Cakes, pan-sautéed seafood cakes served with a spicy dipping sauce. The nightly specials tend to be inventive takes on whatever fresh fish and seafood has been caught that day. Heavy wooden tables are spread across the pleasant, open-air, wraparound veranda of this raised-stilt wooden home. There's also indoor seating, but you'll really want to try to grab one of the outdoor spots. Margaritas and sangria are served by the pitcher, and there's a pretty good wine list for Caye Caulker. Most people find the food extremely memorable but noticeably expensive. Two downsides to dining here: It's a bit pricey and the bathrooms need a serious upgrade.

Calle del Sol at Hicaco St. © **626-4911.** Reservations recommended. Main courses BZ$34–BZ$60. Fri–Wed 6pm–midnight.

Rainbow Grill & Bar ★ SEAFOOD/INTERNATIONAL   Built over the water near the center of town, you'll dine to the sound of water lapping against the pilings below your feet. A dozen or so wooden tables with plastic chairs are set around the screened-in restaurant. The screen comes in handy, especially when the bugs are biting. Try to grab a table by the outer railing, closest to the water. Chicken, fish, conch, shrimp, and lobster are all offered in a variety of preparations from simply grilled or fried to served with sauces ranging from lemon-ginger to Cajun. All are very well-prepared and tasty. The lunch menu is much simpler and less expensive. I particularly like the conch fajitas.

Over the water on Front St., near the center of town. © **226-0281.** Reservations recommended during the high season. Main courses lunch BZ$8–BZ$24, dinner BZ$12–BZ$44. Daily 10:30am–9:30pm.

INEXPENSIVE

In addition to the places listed below, there are several simple local restaurants serving fresh fish, seafood, and Belizean standards at very economical rates.

The best of these are **Marin's Restaurant & Bar** (☏ 226-0104) and **Erro-lyn's House of Fry Jacks** (no phone), both located on Middle Street, near the center of town. My favorite of these local joints is **Rose's Grill & Bar** (☏ 226-0407), located on the side street, right next to Hibisca. Their display of the day's catches makes for a fun, interactive dining experience.

For tasty pizzas, try Southside Pizza (☏ 633-3887), an expat-run joint in a small building on Pasero Street.

The best cheap eats on Caye Caulker are the various outdoor grills that set up nightly all along Front Street, offering chicken, shrimp, beef, and lobster (in season) at very reasonable rates.

Amor y Café ★★ BREAKFAST This quaint breakfast joint is known for its freshly baked brownies, banana bread, and whole-wheat breads. These mainstays are served alongside strong coffee, cappuccino, and fresh-fruit smoothies. You can also get eggs cooked to order or a hefty sandwich. The best thing about Amor y Café, though, is that its few tables are set on an open-air deck overlooking Front Street, so you get to watch Caye Caulker as it slowly wakes up and gets going.

Front St., near the center of town. ☏ 610-2397. Reservations not accepted. Main courses BZ$5–BZ$15. Daily 6am–2pm.

Glenda's Café ★ BELIZEAN/MEXICAN This humble establishment is one of Caye Caulker's longest-standing traditions and most popular spots. The menu is written on a chalkboard on your left as you walk up to the open window into Glenda's house. Order here, and the meal will be brought to your table. They specialize in simple Mexican fare, including burritos and rice and beans. Breakfasts feature eggs and johnnycakes, but the star attractions here are the fresh cinnamon rolls and freshly squeezed orange juice. There are only a few wooden tables with either plastic lawn chairs or folding metal card chairs; the best ones are on the small screened-in porch. Come early for breakfast if you want a decent seat.

In back of Atlantic Bank. ☏ 226-0148. Main courses BZ$1–BZ$12. No credit cards. Mon–Fri 7am–3pm.

Wish Willy's ★★ FUSION/SEAFOOD Serving breakfast, lunch, and dinner out of his home's kitchen, Belizean-by-way-of-Chicago chef Maurice Moore has built a reputation for serving excellent fare in a relaxed open-air yard. Tables are long picnic-style affairs that you'll often have to share with others. There's no set menu, but it is always built around the freshest ingredients available, simply grilled, or served with an Asian-fusion flare. Conch may come stir-fried in a teriyaki sauce, or in more traditional Belizean-style fritters. And while there are set opening hours, these may be reduced if Maurice's mood or stamina flag.

On the north end of the island, lagoon side. www.wish-willy.com. ☏ 660-7194. Main courses BZ$15–BZ$25. No credit cards. Daily 7am–9pm (although opening hours may vary according to Maurice's stamina).

Caye Caulker After Dark

For evening entertainment, you can stargaze, go for a night dive, or have a drink in one of the island's handful of bars. Periodically, one of the bars will crank up the music, and *voilà*—a disco. In general, the scene is so small that most folks will congregate at one or two bars. Which one or two bars are happening might shift from night to night; ask a local or two, and you'll certainly be directed to the current hot spot. My favorite bar is the open-air **I&I Reggae Bar ★** (© 633-3126), which features rustic wooden plank swings for most of its seating. The bar itself takes up the second and third floors of this thatch-roofed wooden structure and is located on a cross street on the southern end of town. Right in the center of town on Front Street, the **Barrier Reef Sports Bar & Grill** (© 226-0077) has a good crowd most nights, with everything from trivia contests to sporting events to live music. The newer **Bondi Bar & Bistro** (© 226-0610) brings a hip element to Caye Caulker's nighttime scene with movie and DJ nights.

THE OUTER ATOLLS ★★★

40–80km (25–50 miles) E of Belize City

Roughly due east, out beyond the barrier reef, lie two of Belize's three open-ocean atolls, Turneffe Atoll and Lighthouse Reef Atoll. The reef and island rings of tranquility, in the midst of the Caribbean Sea, are stunning and pristine places. The outer island atolls are popular destinations for day trips out from Belize City, Ambergris Caye, and Caye Caulker. However, if you really want to experience their unique charms, you should stay at one of the few

---

A small caye TO SEE

Between Belize City and the popular tourist destinations of Caye Caulker and Ambergris Caye lie scores of small islands and cayes. Of these, one is of interest to travelers, **St. George's Caye ★★**.

St. George's is the closest resort caye to Belize City, just 14km (8⅔ miles) offshore. This tiny island played a crucial role in the country's history. From 1650 to 1784, St. George's was the first capital city for the early Baymen colonists, and it was also the site and namesake of the pivotal 1798 sea battle between the Baymen and a hostile Spanish fleet. Today, it is mostly a getaway for a handful of wealthy Belizeans who have vacation cottages on the caye. However, there is one excellent hotel here. **St. George's**

Caye Resort ★★ (www.belizeisland paradise.com; © 800/813-8498 in the U.S. and Canada) is a collection of individual wooden cabins built either facing the sea or on stilts out over the lagoon. The small resort has a pretty pool and extensive tour and activity options, as well as complimentary kayaks and Hobie Cats for guests. This is also a primo base for scuba diving, with a dedicated dive shop and excellent operation. You'll feel as if you have the island to yourself, although if you explore, you'll find there's a Belize Army base here. On one end of the island there's a small but excellent private **aquarium ★** (© 662-2170; daily 11am–5pm; BZ$6) that gives visitors a good look into the local marine life.

small lodges located right on the edge of one of them, or on one of the live-aboard dive boats that ply these waters.

Getting There & Departing

These are remote and isolated destinations. Aside from the lodges, which all offer their own transportation, there is no regularly scheduled transportation out here. However, private water taxis and charter flights can be arranged.

BY PLANE   The only airstrip located on these outer atolls is the private airstrip of the Lighthouse Reef Resort on Big Northern Caye.

BY BOAT   Turneffe Island Atoll is a 1½- to 2-hour boat ride from Belize City. The lodges listed below provide their own transportation to and from Belize City as part of their vacation packages.

BY HELICOPTER   The quickest and easiest way to get out to these atolls is by helicopter. **Astrum Helicopters** (www.astrumhelicopters.com; © **888/278-7864** in the U.S. and Canada, or 222-5100 in Belize) will take you out here for BZ$2,500 in a helicopter that will hold four passengers, and BZ$5,000 in a six-passenger bird.

Exploring the Atolls

Unlike Pacific Ocean atolls, which are often the crater rings of extinct volcanoes, these atolls were formed over millions of years by a combination of plate tectonics, rising water levels following the last ice age, and millennia of mid-ocean coral growth. Many of the atoll walls drop off steeply for more than a thousand feet, while in the central lagoons the water depths average only 3 to 12m (10–40 ft.).

Most folks come out here to do one of two things: fish or dive. Some do both. Both activities are truly world-class. In broad strokes, fishermen should head to Turneffe Island Atoll, while dedicated and serious divers would probably want to choose Lighthouse Reef Atoll, although there's great diving to be had off Turneffe.

TURNEFFE ISLAND ATOLL ★★

This is the largest of Belize's three ocean atolls, and the largest in the Caribbean Sea. Both the diving and the fishing here are excellent, but the fishing gets a slight edge. The extensive mangrove and saltwater flats are perfect territory for stalking permit, bonefish, snook, and tarpon. Most fishing is done with fly rods, either wading in the flats or from a poled skiff.

Turneffe Island Atoll also boasts scores of world-class wall, coral, and sponge gardens, and drift dive sites. Most of these sites are located around the southern tip of the atoll. Perhaps the most famous dive site here is **The Elbow ★★★**, a jutting coral point with steep drop-offs, huge sponges, and ample fish life. Another popular site is **Rendezvous Point ★★**, which features several grottoes that divers can swim in and out of, and there's a small modern wreck, the *Sayonara,* sitting in about 9.1m (30 ft.) of water.

LIGHTHOUSE REEF ATOLL ★★

Boasting nearly 80km (50 miles) of wall and reef diving, including some of the best and most coveted dive sites in all the Caribbean, this is a true scuba-diving mecca. The waters of this atoll, the farthest one from shore, are incredibly clear and pristine. The central lagoon of this atoll is some 48km (30 miles) long and around 13km (8 miles) wide at its widest point. In the center, you'll find the world-famous **Blue Hole ★★**, a perfectly round mid-atoll sinkhole that plunges straight down to a depth of more than 122m (400 ft.). You'll see postcards, photos, and T-shirts all over town showing off aerial views of this perfectly round hole in the ocean. Nearly 305m (1,000 ft.) across, the Blue Hole's eroded limestone karst walls and stalactite formations make this a unique and justifiably popular dive site. However, some of the wall and coral garden dives around the outer edges of the atoll are even better. Of these, **Half Moon Caye Wall ★★★** and **North Long Caye Wall ★★★** are consistently considered some of the best clear-water coral wall dives in the world.

Toward the southeastern edge of the atoll is **Half Moon Caye National Monument ★★**, a combined island and marine reserve. Half Moon Caye itself is the principal nesting ground for the beautiful and odd-looking red-footed booby. These birds are always here in massive numbers. The island is also a prime nesting site for both hawksbill and loggerhead turtles. **The Belize Audubon Society** (www.belizeaudubon.org; ✆ **223-5004**) has constructed a small visitor center here, and a wonderful viewing platform near the center of the island. They also allow overnight camping with prior arrangement. The admission fee is BZ$20 for Half Moon Caye National Monument and BZ$60 for entrance to the Blue Hole National Monument.

Water conditions here are amazingly consistent, with an average water temperature of around 80°F (27°C), while visibility on the outer atoll walls and reefs easily averages more than 30m (100 ft.).

If you want to stay here as part of a guided tour, I highly recommend **Island Expeditions ★★** (www.islandexpeditions.com; ✆ **800/667-1630**), which runs weeklong adventure excursions here based out of a private tent-camp on Half Moon Caye.

Where to Stay & Dine on Turneffe Island Atoll

EXPENSIVE

Turneffe Flats ★★★   Reserve well in advance because this dedicated flat-water fly-fishing (and snorkeling/scuba diving) resort is hugely popular, and not that large at just 12 rooms. We know of guests who return here once a year, eager to catch a stockpile of bonefish, permit, and tarpon . . . and to enjoy Turneffe Flats' renowned hospitality. Digs are simple, yet luxurious, with rooms that are all beachfront and housed in a couple of long, low buildings raised off the sandy ground just a bit on wooden pilings. Every room comes with one queen bed and one twin bed and large bathrooms. All are set off a common shared veranda. The villas have a living room and satellite television, as well. Meals are made from scratch (including all the breads and pastries) and served family-style in the main lodge or, weather permitting, outdoors on an open deck off the lodge. Guests go out daily on excursions, with those who choose to snorkel and dive being put in the care of Abel, an unusually talented nature guide who will identify a wide variety of critters in the course of a tour, and then discuss them with a storyteller's flair. Those who choose to fish are taken to grounds where no other anglers seem to go (surprising, since the fishing is so good in these parts). Packages are weeklong affairs, running Saturday to Saturday.

Blackbird Caye, Turneffe Island Atoll. www.tflats.com. © **888/512-8812** in the U.S. or Canada, or 220-4046 in Belize. 14 units. BZ$5,580 per person per week dive package; BZ$8,780 per person per week fishing package. Rates are based on double occupancy and include all meals, round-trip boat transportation from Belize City, and guided daily diving or fishing; drinks, gear rental, and national park entrance fees are extra. Combination packages are available, and rates are lower in the off season. **Amenities:** Restaurant; bar; pool; gym; kayaks; full-service dive and tackle shops; Wi-Fi (free, in Lodge Building).

Turneffe Island Lodge ★★★ Located on a tiny private caye at the southern tip of the Turneffe Island Atoll, this is the swankiest outfit on the outer atolls by a hair. It even features a small outdoor oceanfront pool. You can either stay in one of the well-appointed deluxe or superior rooms, or opt for an upgrade to one of their ten private villas. One of my favorite features of these villas is the private outdoor shower. All rooms come with brightly varnished wood floors, wooden wainscoting and ceilings, and plenty of windows to take advantage of the ample sea breezes. The high-quality beds look like four posters from the cunning way the mosquito netting is draped. The lodge has some excellent beaches and several long piers built out into the ocean with thatch-roofed open-air hammock huts built at the end. Both the fishing and the dive operations here are excellent, and the cooking in the in-house restaurant is so good that many guests purchase a copy of the chef's cookbook (for sale on-site). If the resort is full, most would-be guests are also happy at Turneffe Flats. The resorts are roughly equivalent in terms of creature comforts and expertly-guided fishing, snorkeling, and diving.

Little Caye Bokel, Turneffe Island Atoll. www.turnefferesort.com. © **800/874-0118** in the U.S. and Canada, or 532-2990 in Belize. 22 units. BZ$6,780 per person per week dive package; BZ$8,780 per person per week fishing package. Rates are based on double occupancy and include all meals, round-trip boat transportation from Belize City, and guided daily diving or fishing; drinks and gear rental are extra. Combination packages are available. Rates lower in the off season. **Amenities:** Restaurant; bar; full-service dive and tackle shops; small outdoor pool.

SOUTHERN BELIZE

S outhern Belize has only two small cities, **Dangriga** and **Punta Gorda,** and one popular beach village, **Placencia.** This was once the least developed region of Belize, but that's changed dramatically. Placencia is one of the hottest and fastest-growing destinations in the country. And the tiny Garífuna settlement of **Hopkins Village** has also become a trendy destination all its own. Both Placencia and Hopkins Village offer some of the longest and finest sand beaches to be found in the country.

Southern Belize is made up of the Stann Creek and Toledo districts. It is home to the **Cockscomb Basin Wildlife Sanctuary,** a major breeding ground and reserve for the New World's largest cat, the jaguar, as well as several other lesser-known and virtually unexplored forest reserves. It is here you'll find Belize's highest mountain, **Victoria Peak,** which stands at 1,122m (3,681 ft.).

Offshore are some of Belize's most beautiful cayes and its most remote atoll, **Glover's Reef Atoll ★★**. The cayes and barrier reef down here are as spectacular as those found farther north, yet far less developed and crowded. You can literally have an island to yourself in this region. Much of the offshore and underwater wonders are protected in reserves, such as the **Southwater Caye Marine Reserve, Glover's Marine Reserve, Sapodilla Cayes Marine Reserve,** and **Laughing Bird Caye National Park ★★**.

As historically the least developed and colonized region in Belize, the southern zone still maintains ongoing and healthy communities of traditional Mayan and Garífuna peoples. This is one of the few places on the planet where you can comfortably spend a few days in a traditional Mayan or Garífuna village and see how nice it can feel to step away from the 21st century for a bit.

DANGRIGA

116km (72 miles) S of Belize City; 103km (64 miles) SE of Belmopan; 77km (48 miles) N of Placencia

Dangriga, which means "sweet water" in the Garífuna language, was originally called Stann Creek, and you may still hear it referred to as such. The name Stann Creek comes from the Creole version

Southern Belize

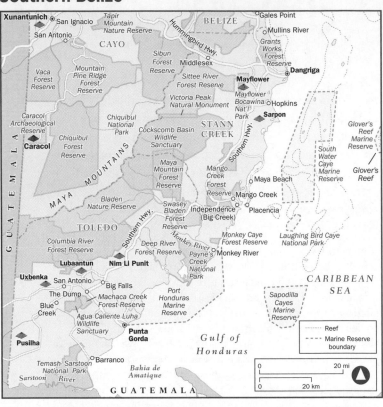

of "Standing Creek," a description of the river's slow-moving waters. As the capital of the Stann Creek District, which is one of the main citrus-growing regions of Belize, Dangriga is an important and vibrant agricultural and fishing community. However, despite its size and almost urban feel, it lacks the seaminess that characterizes Belize City. The town fronts right on the Caribbean and has several waterfront parks, which are surrounded by simple yet attractive residential neighborhoods.

Still, Dangriga is of little interest to travelers. There are no good beaches and few good hotels, and the town can feel stiflingly hot and desolate on most days. Most travelers head farther south to Hopkins Village, Placencia, or Punta Gorda, or out to one of the nearby offshore cayes. Dangriga is the main maritime transportation hub for trips out to Tobacco Caye, South Water Caye, and Glover's Reef Atoll. (See "What to See & Do," below, for more details.)

Dangriga is the largest city in southern Belize and the seat of the country's Garífuna culture. The Garífunas are a proud and independent people, who have managed to maintain their unique language and culture, which dates to the 16th-century intermingling of free Africans and Carib Indians. The only

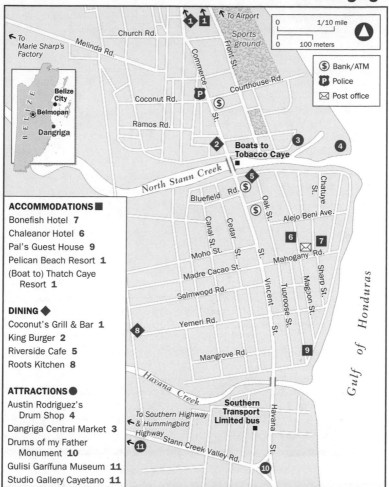

ACCOMMODATIONS ■
Bonefish Hotel **7**
Chaleanor Hotel **6**
Pal's Guest House **9**
Pelican Beach Resort **1**
(Boat to) Thatch Caye Resort **1**

DINING ◆
Coconut's Grill & Bar **1**
King Burger **2**
Riverside Cafe **5**
Roots Kitchen **8**

ATTRACTIONS ●
Austin Rodriguez's Drum Shop **4**
Dangriga Central Market **3**
Drums of my Father Monument **10**
Gulisi Garífuna Museum **11**
Studio Gallery Cayetano **11**

8

SOUTHERN BELIZE | Dangriga

time Dangriga becomes a major tourist attraction is around Garífuna Settlement Day.

Essentials
GETTING THERE & DEPARTING
BY PLANE   There are numerous flights into and out of little Dangriga Airport (DGA) from Belize City. **Maya Island Air** (www.mayaislandair.com; ℂ **223-1140,** or 223-1146 in Belize City) has 10 flights daily between the Philip S. W. Goldson International Airport and Dangriga. The first flight leaves at 8:10am and the last flight is at 5pm. Flight time is 15 minutes; the fare is BZ$143 each way. Maya Island Air also has daily flights from Belize

THE garífuna

Throughout the 18th century, escaped and shipwrecked slaves intermarried and blended in with the native Carib Indian populations on several islands in the Lesser Antilles, but predominantly on St. Vincent. The West Africans were a mixed lot, including members of the Fon, Yoruba, Ewe, and Nago tribes. Over the years, the West African and indigenous elements blended into a new people, known first as Black Caribs and today as Garífuna or Garinagu. The Garífuna have their own language, traditions, history, and rituals, all of which blend elements of the group's two primary cultural sources. African-style drumming with complex rhythmic patterns and call-and-response singing accompany ritual possession ceremonies spoken in a language whose entomological roots are predominantly Arawak.

The Black Caribs were fierce warriors and frequently fought the larger colonial powers to maintain their freedom and independence. In 1797, despite the celebrated leadership of Joseph Chatoyer, the Garífuna were soundly defeated by the British forces, who subsequently shipped several thousand of the survivors off to exile on the island of Roatan, in then British Honduras. The Garífuna began migrating and eventually settled along the entire coast of what is present-day Honduras, Nicaragua, Guatemala, and Belize.

The Garífuna reached Belize by 1802. Since the British colonial presence was concentrated in the north, the Garífuna chose to settle in the southern parts of Belize, particularly the Stann Creek and Toledo districts. During the early part of their settlement in Belize, the Garífuna were kept at arm's length by the colonial Baymen, who were still slave owners and feared the influence of this independent free black community. Nevertheless, on November 19, 1832, the Garífuna were officially recognized as members of Belizean society and permitted to participate in the public meetings. For nearly 2 centuries now, the Garífuna have lived quiet lives of subsistence farming, fishing, and light trading with their neighbors, while steadfastly maintaining their language, heritage, and traditions.

The principal Garífuna settlements in Belize include Punta Gorda, Seine Bight, Hopkins Village, Barranco, and Dangriga, the community's unofficial capital. Each year on November 19 (and for several days around the 19th), these communities, and in particular Dangriga, come alive in a riotous celebration of the Garífuna settlement and acceptance in Belize.

City's Municipal Airport as well as San Pedro, each with stops to pick up passengers at the international airport. Maya Island Air flights from Dangriga to Belize City leave between 7:20am and 4:40pm. Most of these flights stop first at the international airport and continue on to Municipal Airport.

Tropic Air (www.tropicair.com; ✆ **800/422-3435** in the U.S. or Canada, 226-2012 or 226-2626 in Belize) has seven direct flights daily between Philip S. W. Goldson International Airport and Dangriga, with the first flight leaving at 9:40am and the last flight at 5pm. The fare is BZ$192.50 each way. They also have five daily flights between Municipal Airport and Dangriga, leaving at 8:00 and 10:30am, and at 12:30, 2:30, and 4:30pm. The fare is BZ$135 each way. Tropic Air flights depart Dangriga for both of Belize City's airports daily between 7:20am and 4:40pm. Flight time is typically 15 minutes, but double when there is an intermediate stop.

On both airlines, flights are sometimes added during the high season or suspended during the low season, so check in advance.

BY CAR From Belize City, head west on Cemetery Road, which becomes the George Price Highway (formerly the Western Highway). Take this all the way to Belmopan, where you will connect with the Hummingbird Highway heading south. Ten kilometers (6 miles) before Dangriga, the Hummingbird Highway connects with the Southern Highway. Follow the signs into Dangriga; you'll be entering from the south end of town.

> ### Welcome
>
> As you enter Dangriga, you'll come to a traffic circle. Be sure to take a moment to check out the **Drums of My Father** monument here, a larger-than-life bronze casting of three ceremonial *dügü* drums and the maraca-like shaker, or *sísira*. This simple sculpture lets you know right away that you are entering the heartland of Garífuna society and culture.

Alternatively, you can take the unpaved Manatee Road (aka Coastal Highway or The Shortcut), which turns off the George Price Highway just past the Belize Zoo, at around Mile Marker 30. The Manatee Road passes by the entrance road to the small Creole village of Gales Point and rejoins the Hummingbird Highway about 14km (8½ miles) outside of Dangriga. This route is shorter as the crow flies, but in worse shape physically, so the going is slower. Either route should take around 2 to 2½ hours from Belize City.

BY BUS **James Bus Line** (✆ **664-2185,** or 631-1959) and the other bus services have regular service throughout the day between Belize City and Dangriga, roughly every half-hour between 6:30am and 5:30pm from either the main bus terminal on West Collet Canal Street (National Transport) or the nearby Shell gas station on Cemetery Road (James). The fare is BZ$16. The ride takes about 3 hours.

Note: Most of the buses in Belize look very similar, but not all take commercial passengers, as they are charter buses for workers going between cities. If a bus doesn't stop for you, that's probably why.

BY BOAT There are no regularly scheduled boats from Belize City to Dangriga, but aside from flying, water is the most direct means of covering the 58km (36 miles) between the two cities. You may be able to charter a boat by asking around the docks in Belize City. Expect to pay from BZ$400 to BZ$600 for a boat that can carry four to eight passengers.

GETTING AROUND

There are no official car-rental agencies, but if you really search, you might be able to find an enterprising local willing to rent you a vehicle. If this is absolutely necessary, your best bet is to have your hotel try to arrange this for you.

For a taxi in Dangriga, call **Star Line Taxi Service** (✆ **621-9956**) or **Tzul's Taxi Service** (✆ **522-2438**).

IF YOU COME TO A fork in the road, TAKE BOTH

Given the unique sights offered by the two possible routes down to Dangriga, you might want to consider taking one route on your way south and the other on your way back. The **Hummingbird Highway** passes through some of Belize's most picturesque countryside. The road weaves through jungle mountains and crosses clear streams and small rivers. Admire the forest-covered karst hillsides to the west as you wind your way through mostly uninhabited country. The **Manatee Road** is a gravel affair, passing through the forests, lowland swamps, and mangroves that border Belize's large southern lagoon. Still, this route is not for the faint of heart. In the rainy season it can get quite muddy and slick, while in the dry season the dirt can form a hard, jarring washboard and dust can be a problem. In some places you'll have to cross single-lane, rail-less wooden plank bridges that give some drivers vertigo, even though they're not very high. It's also more popular for heavy trucks, which can be daunting given their size.

Boats to Tobacco Caye leave from the Gumagurugu River or North Stann Creek in front of the Riverside Café, just below the bridge. The going rate is around BZ$30 to BZ$50 per person one-way. Most of the boats hold between 8 and 10 people, and they leave whenever they have at least half that many passengers ready, between 9am and 1pm. If you already have a group together, you can hire one privately and set a definite return-trip pickup time.

ORIENTATION

The main street through Dangriga is called St. Vincent Street south of the main bridge over North Stann Creek, and Commerce Street north of it. Most of the town's businesses and attractions lie within a few blocks of this bridge in either direction. The airstrip is on the north end of town, near the Pelican Beach Resort.

FAST FACTS   For the **police,** dial ℭ **911,** or 522-2022; for the **fire department,** call ℭ **522-2091.** The **Dangriga Hospital** (ℭ **522-2078**) is located on Courthouse Road, 4 blocks north and 2 blocks east of the main bridge. The **post office** (ℭ **522-2035**) is in the southern section of town next to the Bonefish Hotel.

Both of the principal banks in town are on St. Vincent Street: **Belize Bank,** 24 St. Vincent St. (ℭ **522-2903,** or 522-2904), and **Scotiabank,** 10 St. Vincent St. (ℭ **522-2031,** or 522-2005).

What to See & Do

The main activity in Dangriga is a slow walk up and down the main north–south thoroughfare. If you tire of watching the endless procession of people and listening to the colorful mix of English, Creole, and Garífuna, head a block or two over toward the sea and cop a seat in one of the town's oceanfront parks. If you're looking for a more active adventure, you'll have to head out of Dangriga, but your options are plentiful.

The only true attraction in the area is the quaint little **Gulisi Garífuna Museum** ★ (© **669-0639,** or 542-2700). Although small, this is worth a visit. You'll find interpretive displays of Garífuna history, culture, and daily life, spread around several rooms here. Three separate documentaries are shown continually on televisions in the different rooms. There's a gift shop, as well as paintings by prominent Garífuna artists such as Benjamin Nicholas and Pen Cayetano. The museum is located 1.6km (1 mile) west of town, on the road out to the Hummingbird Highway. It's open Monday through Saturday from 8am to 5pm. Admission is BZ$10.

If you're staying in Dangriga for any period of time, you may also want to visit the relatively nearby attractions, including Guanacaste National Park, Blue Hole National Park, Caves Branch, Hopkins Village, and Cockscomb Basin Wildlife Sanctuary. For more information on the first three attractions, see chapter 10. For details about the rest, see below.

If your hotel can't arrange things for you, contact **C & G Tours and Charters** (© **522-3641**) to set up any number of tours and activities around Dangriga.

FISHING   The fishing is excellent out of Dangriga. Most folks head to the flats in search of bonefish, permit, and tarpon. Closer to shore and near the river mouths you can find snook, and beyond the barrier reef lie marlin, sailfish, tuna, wahoo, and dorado. Ask at your hotel, around the docks, or at the **Pelican Beach Resort** (© **522-2044**). Expect to pay between BZ$800 and BZ$2,400 per day for a full day for several anglers aboard a modern sportfishing boat. Alternatively, you can line up a lower-tech outing around the docks for around BZ$100 to BZ$400 for a half-day.

KAYAKING   You can rent a kayak for paddling around the waters just offshore from the folks at **Island Expeditions** ★★ (www.belizekayaking.com; © **800/667-1630**). The rates are BZ$70 per day for a single kayak, and BZ$110 for a tandem.

SNORKELING & SCUBA DIVING   Dangriga is the jumping-off point for some wonderful small cayes situated right on the edge of the barrier reef, as well as Glover's Reef Atoll. Most of the hotels in town can arrange for a day trip of snorkeling or scuba diving at Tobacco Caye, South Water Caye, or one of the cayes composing Glover's Reef Atoll. Expect to pay from BZ$160 to BZ$240 per person for a full-day snorkel trip out to the reef, including lunch and transportation. Add an extra BZ$120 to BZ$180 if you plan to scuba dive.

ATTRACTIONS ON THE HUMMINGBIRD HIGHWAY

Located just off the highway in the tiny settlement of Pomona Village is one of the most important and renowned factories in all of Belize, **Marie Sharp's,** maker of Belize's favorite hot sauce, appearing all over dining tables country wide (and beyond). After seeing it in almost every restaurant and hotel, it's fun to go straight to the source. The factory is small and simple, and depending on the time of year and demand, they may be making any number of their various hot sauces, jams, and chutneys. At the end of the tour, you'll have the chance to sample the products. It's best to call in advance to arrange a tour (www.mariesharps.bz; © **532-2087**). If you're lucky, you'll get to meet Marie herself. The tour is free, but you'll want to bring some money to stock up on the sauces.

Tucked a few miles off the highway is **Five Blues Lake National Park ★**. The main feature of this park is a large cenote, whose various hues of blue originally gave the park its name. However, in July 2006, the cenote suddenly and rather inexplicably drained almost completely. By early 2008, the lake had recovered about 75% of its original level, and much of its former beauty. All around the park are forested lands and distinct karst hill formations, with a series of trails leading through them. The park is run by the folks from the local community of Saint Margaret's Village. The park and small village are located on Lagoon Road, just off the Hummingbird Highway around Mile Marker 32. There are about 4.8km (3 miles) of well-marked trails in the park. You can also take a refreshing dip in the lake, or rent a canoe for a leisurely paddle. Admission is BZ$10. Some simple accommodations and restaurants are also available in Saint Margaret's Village.

GALES POINT & THE MANATEES

Gales Point is a small Creole fishing village about 40km (25 miles) north of Dangriga. It is a peaceful little village where you can get in tune with one of Belize's traditional cultures and its slower pace of life. The village stretches along a narrow peninsula that juts into the large brackish **Southern Lagoon,** which is also called Manatee Lagoon because the manatees that inhabit the water of the lagoon bring most people to Gales Point in the first place. Ask at the Manatee Lodge (see below) or around the village, and for BZ$60 to

---

On the Road

As you drive the Hummingbird Highway, there are two interesting phenomena to be aware of. Locals swear a local mountain formation looks like a sleeping giant. There are several good views of the "sleeping giant," which is best seen just slightly left of dead ahead as you drive south from Belize City, especially around the Sibun River bridge. Even more mystical and illusive—I've only been able to make it work when a local was showing me—is the "antigravity" spot. Stop your car on the gentle hill around Mile Marker 26 and put it in neutral. Locals claim it is ancient earth energy that makes vehicles roll seemingly uphill. It's probably an optical illusion, but it's fun.

BZ$100 you can hire a small boat to take you out to where the manatees usually feed. The boats generally will hold up to eight people, so the more people you can line up, the less it will cost each of you. You can also ask around in the village about renting a canoe to paddle yourself out to where the manatees feed. I prefer this option, although be sure to get a lightweight modern canoe, as the traditional carved tree-trunk dugout canoes are a bear to paddle. Canoe rentals should run you around BZ$12 to BZ$20 for a half-day. Swimming with the manatees is not allowed, and for good reason: The contact is potentially dangerous for manatees and humans alike, and it's best to just enjoy a pleasant sighting of these gentle water mammals. Boat propellers are doing enough damage as it is. In addition to the manatees, this is one of the locations in Belize where several species of sea turtle come to lay their eggs. Look out for them on the sandy beaches on either side of the Manatee River throughout the summer, taking special care not to walk on any buried nests.

Gales Point is one of several villages in Belize to have a community-based ecotourism homestay program (© **209-8031** for the community phone line). Rooms in local villagers' homes are very basic and often do not have running water or flush toilets. The rates run around BZ$10 to BZ$16 per person.

By far the best lodgings in Gales Point are found at the **Manatee Lodge** ★ (www.manateelodge.com; © **877/462-6283** in the U.S. and Canada, or 532-2400 in Belize), a tidy little hotel with a fabulous location at the very end of the peninsula. If you decide to eat at any place other than the Manatee Lodge, check out **Gentle's Cool Spot** (© **603-5526**).

To drive here from Dangriga, head out of town to the Hummingbird Highway toward Belize City. At the village of Melinda, you'll see the turnoff for Manatee Road and Gales Point.

To get here by bus from Dangriga, you will have to take a Belize City–bound bus using the Manatee Road. These buses do not always enter the village of Gales Point. Ask in advance; if the bus doesn't enter the village, you will have to hike or hitchhike the final 2.4km (1½ miles) out onto the peninsula. From Belize City, you can take one of the Dangriga-bound buses using the Manatee Road. Again, ask in advance whether the bus enters Gales Point village.

Shopping

As the cultural seat of the Garífuna culture, Dangriga is a great place to pick up, or just admire, local arts and crafts.

Studio Gallery Cayetano at 3 Aranda Crescent (www.cayetano.de; © **628-6807**) is the best place to explore paintings, murals, and thread arts reflecting the Garífuna journey. You will likely meet the legendary artists Pen and Ingrid Cayetano, who are each a wealth of information about art and Belizean history. The gallery is open every day from 9am to 5pm, and costs BZ$5 to enter.

If the beat really gets to you, you can buy a handmade wooden drum directly from **Austin Rodríguez** (© **502-3752**), southeast of the Dangriga

garífuna SETTLEMENT DAY

Each year on November 19, Garífuna Settlement Day is celebrated in Dangriga, with Garífunas coming from around Belize and as far away as Guatemala, Honduras, Nicaragua, and New York. The celebration is a riot of street music and colorful parades. Eating, drinking, and dancing go on well into the night. The Garífuna have their own traditional music, which is based on wooden drums and choral singing. The rhythms and songs have strong African roots, and have given birth to a hybrid pop music called Punta Rock, which is probably the country's most popular music and dance form. If you plan to partake in the festivities, be sure to book far in advance, as every hotel room in Dangriga and the nearby towns and villages sells out early. For more information, contact the **National Garífuna Council of Belize** (www.ngcbelize.org; ✆ **669-0639,** or 610-1489).

Tip: Garífuna Settlement Day isn't the only opportunity to experience the full color and vitality of traditional Garífuna culture. At the end of the Christmas and New Year season, on the weekend closest to January 6, the local Garífuna community takes to the streets to enjoy the Wanaragua or John Kunnu dancers. Wearing masks, elaborate costumes, colorful headdresses topped with macaw feathers, and vibrating arrangements of shells and vedas, Wanaragua or John Kunnu dance troupes parade through the streets of Dangriga, accompanied by the beat of traditional drummers.

Central Market, by the water. Drums vary in size and cost between BZ$80 and BZ$300.

Finally, **Mercy Sabal,** 22 Magoon St. (✆ **604-6731**), has become quite famous for her handcrafted Garífuna dolls. These small dolls are predominantly of female figures in traditional dress, and cost between BZ$30 and BZ$100.

Where to Stay
MODERATE

Bonefish Hotel ★   Located a block from the water and across the street from a small park, the Bonefish is an acceptable midrange option right in the heart of Dangriga. The carpeted guest rooms are generally quite large and clean. The second-floor bar and restaurant has a view of the ocean, and serves good local fare and fresh seafood at reasonable rates. This hotel is owned and run by the same folks who have the Blue Marlin Lodge (p. 182) on South Water Caye, and is primarily used as an overnight stop for guests heading out to their island resort.

15 Mahogany St. www.bluemarlinlodge.com. ✆ **800/798-1558** in the U.S., or 522-2243. 7 units. BZ$178.50–BZ$199 double. Rates include taxes and service charge. Free parking. **Amenities:** Restaurant; bar; Wi-Fi (free).

Pelican Beach Resort—Dangriga ★★   By far the most upscale option right in Dangriga (although that's not necessarily saying much), the resort is nicely spread out and well-maintained. The rooms range in price, location, and amenities. The best rooms have second-floor ocean views with wonderful balconies, and I think they're worth the splurge. The beach here isn't very nice, but there are plenty of palm trees, lounge chairs, and hammocks spread around, as well as a long dock out into the sea, which is your best bet for swimming, and also where the boat pickup for **Thatch Caye Resort** (p. 184) is. It's situated right next to the Dangriga airstrip, ideal for early flights. There's a small gift shop featuring Garífuna crafts, Belizean books, and popular wildlife photography. The restaurant serves excellent Belizean and Garífuna meals at reasonable rates. A variety of fishing, diving, and inland tours is available, and Pelican Beach also operates a sister cottage resort out on South Water Caye. Quite logically it's called Pelican Beach—South Water Caye (p. 183).

North end. www.pelicanbeachbelize.com. (℘ **522-2044.** 18 units. From BZ$270 double. Free parking. **Amenities:** Restaurant; bar; Wi-Fi (free).

INEXPENSIVE

Chaleanor Hotel ★   There are few frills to be found at this inexpensive hotel, but as far as budget options go, the Chaleanor Hotel is a pretty good deal. Privacy, service, and location are delivered at hostel prices, with an added bonus of free fruit and coffee in the lobby. Rooms are located on three floors, with beds that are a little stiff, but daily housekeeping service keeps them clean, at least. The rooftop is a communal area with hammocks, tables, and a lovely breeze. The five economy rooms share bathroom and shower facilities, which can vary in level of cleanliness depending on how busy the hotel is. Staff are helpful and familial, and while they do offer 24-hour front desk service, it's not as consistent as you would find at a larger, more formal hotel. Still, this is a solid budget option right in the center of town.

35 Magoon St. www.chaleanorhotel.bz. (℘ **522-2587.** 18 units. BZ$55–BZ$165 double. Free parking. **Amenities:** Wi-Fi (free).

Pal's Guest House ★   This budget hotel is down at the south end of town, just off the water, near the mouth of Havana Creek. It's clean and quiet, although the years and constant sea breeze have taken their toll. If you decide to stay here, choose one of the second-floor beachfront rooms in a separate building, which have air-conditioning and small private balconies overlooking the sea. The owner, Augustine Flores, is friendly, knowledgeable, and an active member of the local Garífuna community.

86 Magoon St. www.palsbelize.net. (℘ **522-2095.** 16 units. BZ$80–BZ$120 double. Free parking. **Amenities:** Tour desk; Wi-Fi (free).

Where to Dine

When you're in Dangriga, be sure to sample some of the local Garífuna cooking. One staple you'll find at many restaurants is a bread made from cassava, also known as yuca. The best place in town to look for traditional Garífuna cooking is the down-home **Roots Kitchen** (℘ **601-2519**) on the north side of Havana Creek, at the corner of Ecumenical Drive and Yemery Road. Be sure to try the *hudut*, a dish featuring fresh fish cooked in coconut milk, accompanied by pieces of plantain and cassava.

Up and down the main street through town—St. Vincent Street and Commerce Street—you'll find numerous very basic restaurants. In addition to the restaurants listed below, **King Burger,** 135 Commerce St. (© **608-7918**), which is not affiliated with the Burger King fast-food chain, is a local favorite serving simple Belizean meals heavy on the grease. There are also several very basic Chinese restaurants along the main street.

MODERATE

Coconut's Grill & Bar ★ BELIZEAN   Located at the Pelican Beach Resort, this is easily the best restaurant in Dangriga. The dinner menu features spicy curry, served with fish, shrimp, or chicken, as well as thick pork chops in a fruit glaze. You can also get a real porterhouse steak and several pasta dishes. For lunch there are burgers, sandwiches, wraps, quesadillas, fajitas, and nachos. Or you can opt for a salad or more traditional Belizean rice and beans accompanied by fish or chicken. The best seating is on the open-air patio facing the ocean, although there's also an indoor dining room for those looking for air-conditioning.

At the Pelican Beach Resort, north end of Dangriga. © **522-2044.** Reservations not necessary. Main courses BZ$18–BZ$48. Daily 7am–10pm.

INEXPENSIVE

Riverside Café ★ BELIZEAN   This simple cafe and bar is funky and perennially run-down looking. Still, it's popular with the local boatmen and one of the best places to get travel information in Dangriga. It opens early and serves food throughout the day. You can get a full meal of fried chicken, beans, and rice for BZ$8. Breakfasts are also hearty and inexpensive. Come here to ask about rides to one of the nearby cayes, to set up a tour around the region, and to pick up brochures from the wall-mounted racks. You'll find the cafe just east of St. Vincent Street on the south side of North Stann Creek.

S. Riverside Dr. © **661-6390.** Reservations not accepted. Main courses BZ$8–BZ$20. Mon–Sat 6am–9pm; Sun 6am–3pm.

Dangriga After Dark

There's not much happening in Dangriga after dark. Your best bets would be to head to the **Pelican Beach Resort** (see "Where to Stay," above) or the nearby **Island Breeze Bar & Grill** (© **502-3087**), which sometimes has a DJ.

Beyond Dangriga: Offshore Cayes & Glover's Reef Atoll ★★

The Tobacco Caye range of mangrove cayes lies just 16km (10 miles) east of Dangriga. A little farther south sits South Water Caye. Beyond the barrier reef and farther out to sea is Glover's Reef Atoll.

Tobacco Caye ★★ itself is just 2 hectares (5 acres) large, with about five different lodging options set more or less side by side. You can walk from one end of the caye to the other in about 3 minutes, and that's at a leisurely pace.

South Water Caye ★★★ is a little bit larger than Tobacco, but you can still walk from one end to the other in about 5 minutes. Nevertheless, the vibe here is slightly more spacious and luxurious than that on Tobacco Caye, although there's not anything approaching real luxury here, either.

Located just a stone's throw from the south end of South Water Caye, the **Smithsonian Institute of Marine Research** occupies all of the tiny Carrie Bow Caye. Your lodge can make arrangements to visit the caye, meet with resident scientists, and use their beach, which is one of the sandiest in the area.

The largest caye in the area, **Man-O-War Caye ★★**, is a bird sanctuary and major nesting site for the magnificent frigate, or man-o-war. A tour to the caye is an impressive sight, with hundreds of these large seabirds roosting on and circling above the tiny caye. As part of their mating ritual, the males inflate a huge red sack on their throats to attract a mate. In addition to the frigates, the island is home to a large community of brown boobies.

Coco Plum Caye is another isolated and tiny caye in this area, with one small resort that features a handful of individual wooden bungalows spread around the small, sandy island. If you want to stay here, contact **Coco Plum Island Resort ★** (www.cocoplumcay.com; ✆ **800/763-7360** in the U.S., or 522-2611 in Belize).

A visit to snorkel, dive, or stay out on these cayes usually involves passing through, or staying within, the **South Water Caye Marine Reserve,** which includes Tobacco Caye, Carrie Bow Caye, Coco Plum Caye, and Man-O-War Caye. Admission to the reserve costs BZ$10 per person per day. This fee will be collected by your hotel, boat taxi driver, or tour operator.

To the east of these cayes, and beyond the barrier reef, lies **Glover Reef Atoll ★★★**, a stunning natural coral formation featuring an oval-shaped central lagoon nearly 35km (22 miles) long. Named after the British pirate John Glover, the steep-walled reefs here offer some of the best wall diving anywhere in the Caribbean. The entire atoll is also a marine reserve, and in 1996 it was declared a World Heritage Site by the United Nations. Inside the usually calm lagoon, patch reefs are a wonderland for snorkelers.

Finally, fishing for bonefish, permit, and tarpon is excellent throughout this area. Hire **Belize Sport Fishing Charters** (www.belizesportfishingcharters. com; ✆ **502-3434**), an expert, local outfitter. Costs run about BZ$1,000 for a full day of reef fishing.

GETTING THERE

Boats to the outlying cayes leave from the south shore of the Gumagurugu River or North Stann Creek in front of the Riverside Café, just down from the bridge. The going rate is around BZ$30 to BZ$50 per person one-way. Most of the boats hold between 8 and 10 people, and they leave whenever they get enough people to make the trip worth it. If you already have a group together, you can hire one privately and set a definite return-trip pickup time. To rent a whole boat, the going rate is from BZ$400 to BZ$600 round-trip for up to 10 people to Tobacco Caye. The ride takes around 30 to 40 minutes to Tobacco Caye, depending on how fast a boat you book. Add on about 20 to 40 minutes and between BZ$100 to BZ$200 for either South Water Caye or Glover's Reef Atoll.

Paddle to Your Own Drummer

The folks at **Island Expeditions** ★★ (www.belizekayaking.com; ℂ **800/667-1630** in the U.S. and Canada) offer sea kayak rental and logistical support for those looking to explore the barrier reef and its many small cayes by kayak. This option is generally for serious paddlers, but can be tailored to suit all needs and abilities. The basic rate is BZ$70 per day and BZ$420 per week for a single kayak, and BZ$110 per day and BZ$700 weekly for a double kayak. Camping gear rental, food supplies, boat transfers to the outer cayes, and other types of logistical assistance can all be added on. And you can combine some independent paddle and camping time with one of their organized tours to Glover's Reef Atoll (see below).

Note: You really should have a reservation before heading out to one of the lodges on these cayes, as there are very limited options and they fill up fast during high season. Be sure to arrange your transportation when booking a room.

WHERE TO STAY & DINE ON THE OUTER CAYES

All of the options listed below are self-contained lodges and resorts, meaning you will be taking all of your meals at your hotel; all offer fishing, diving, and multiday adventure packages.

In addition to the lodges listed below, **Blue Marlin Lodge** (www.bluemarlin lodge.com; ℂ **800/798-1558** in the U.S., or 522-2243 in Belize) is a semiupscale outfit on South Water Caye specializing in dive and fishing packages.

For the more adventurous traveler, **Island Expeditions** ★★ (www.island expeditions.com; ℂ **800/667-1630** in the U.S. and Canada, or 522-3328 in Belize) and **Slickrock Adventures** ★★ (www.slickrock.com; ℂ **800/390-5715** toll-free in the U.S. and Canada, or 435/259-4225 in the U.S.) operate multiday kayak and dive tours to small camps and lodges on private, isolated cayes of Glover's Reef Atoll.

Glover's Atoll Resort ★   Cold showers, composting toilets, no power—these are the realities of a vacation at this rustic lodge, where some camp, some stay in dorm rooms, and others choose simple, rustic cabins with private bathrooms and kitchen facilities. So while this is not the place to stay if you want your creature comforts and Wi-Fi, the serenity of this place is wonderful, and we think the wooden cabins built on stilts over the ocean are pretty sweet. For campers, Glover's Atoll offers large, semipermanent tents, or you can pitch your own. And while they do serve meals, some of the guests actually pack in and cook their own food at the resort's communal kitchen. In addition to what you pack in, fresh fish, lobster, and conch can be purchased on the island, as can drinking water and fresh bread. Coconuts are free! Most visitors here come as part of the resort's weeklong package, which includes transportation. A meal package will run around BZ$72 per day. Located on the private North East Caye.

Glover's Reef Atoll. www.glovers.com.bz. ℂ **532-2916.** 11 units. BZ$298 per week camping; BZ$398 per week in dorm room; BZ$498–BZ$698 per person per week in private cabin. Rates include round-trip transportation from Sittee River Village or Dangriga and all taxes. **Amenities:** Restaurant; watersports equipment rental.

Isla Marisol Resort ★★   Isla Marisol offers the plushest accommodations and best dive operation out on Glover's Reef Atoll. A series of raised stilt bungalows are set on the sand under shade trees facing the water. Each comes with a fan and swamp cooler, as well as a small balcony for lazing around on between dives or activities. But the choice digs here are the large reef houses, located on the back side of this tiny island. These are large two-bedroom, two-bathroom wooden houses, also on raised stilts, with expansive wraparound balconies and kitchenettes. After dinner in the on-site restaurant, guests tend to congregate at the large bar built on a pier out over the water.

Southwest Caye, Glover's Reef Atoll. www.islamarisolresort.com. © **888/623-5403** in the U.S. and Canada, or 610-4204 in Belize. 14 units. BZ$3,050–BZ$3,450 per person per week, double occupancy. Rates include round-trip transportation from Dangriga, all meals, several daily dive outings, and taxes. **Amenities:** Restaurant; bar; full-service dive shop; small spa; watersports equipment rental; Wi-Fi (free).

Pelican Beach Resort—South Water Caye ★★   Operated by the folks at the Pelican Beach Resort in Dangriga (see above), this isolated island getaway is one of the best-run little resorts on these little cayes. It's a serene and friendly place to visit, with coral reefs within swimming distance from the sandy beach (ideal for snorkeling). We especially like the individual wooden cottages here. Set on raised stilts by the water's edge, they vary in size somewhat, but all are very cozy and charming, often painted robin's egg blue, with similarly colorful bedding. Best is the Heron's Hideaway which has a delightful private balcony set amid and surrounded by mangroves. Standard rooms are housed on the second floor of a converted colonial-era convent. Each comes with one double bed, two single beds, and a half-bathroom. A couple of communal showers are located on the ground level. The relatively small price difference makes it very worthwhile to book one of the cabins. Note that all of the electricity at the resort comes from solar panels, so there's no air-conditioning, and you won't be able to operate some electronic equipment (like a blow dryer).

South Water Caye. www.southwatercaye.com. © **522-2044.** 13 units (5 with shared shower). BZ$810 double room; BZ$920 double cottage. Rates include 3 meals daily and taxes. **Amenities:** Restaurant; free watercraft usage; Wi-Fi (limited).

Reef's End Lodge ★   Occupying the southern tip of Tobacco Caye, this rustic lodge is geared toward students, groups, and budget travelers. Rooms are Spartan, most located in a two-story converted house. The private cabins are a better bet and not significantly more expensive; however, these also feel rather bare and rustic, although they do have air-conditioning. The best is the You and Me Cabana, which has more contemporary decor, tile floors, and loads of space. The nicest feature here is the restaurant, which is set on stilts, with a deck and some docks out over the water. Reef's End runs the only dive operation on the island.

Tobacco Caye. www.reefsendlodge.com. © **672-8363.** 7 units. BZ$858 double room for 3 nights; BZ$990 double cabin for 3 nights; BZ$1,122 honeymoon suite for 3 nights. **Amenities:** Restaurant; dive operation; Wi-Fi (free).

Thatch Caye Resort ★★★ This boutique resort was built with love, care, and real concern for sustainable development. Accommodations are in spacious individual cabins and casitas and a more modern family villa with a penthouse suite. The cabanas are smaller, built over the water, and feature thatch roofs and wonderful oceanfront balconies. The large casitas' best feature is their huge, covered rooftop patios, with a couple of hammocks strung up under a high thatch shade structure on top. The family villa is three connected structures and is ideal for families or groups of friends. Solar and wind power are used to power the joint, although a backup generator kicks in when necessary, or if guests demand air-conditioning. The Coco Lounge, where breakfast is served, is a swell place to socialize with other guests, but it's also easy to find privacy throughout the island. **Royal Belize** (www.royalbelize.com; ℂ **800/348-0546**) is their more luxurious sister resort that offers a true private island experience, as it's exclusive to just 14 guests. Between the two, the vast majority of visitors to Belize will be more likely to spend time at Thatch Caye.

Thatch Caye. www.thatchcayebelize.com. ℂ **800/435-3145** in the U.S. and Canada, or 532-2414 in Belize. 10 units. BZ$494–$890 per day. Rates include 3 meals daily, and round-trip transportation from Dangriga Airport. **Amenities:** Restaurant; bar; free kayak use; Wi-Fi in communal lounge.

Tobacco Caye Paradise ★★★ At the northern end of Tobacco Caye is this collection of cute-as-kittens, wooden cabins, set right at the edge of the ocean. Each has a small private veranda that, in most cases, juts out over the water. While not luxurious, they feature everything you need for a pleasant stay: bright furnishings, a hammock, and a simple floor fan. Their location and general vibe are exactly the image one would conjure up of a Caribbean private island paradise: palm trees, colorful cabanas, and turquoise water as far as the eye can see. There are also five other rooms in a building slightly inland. These are certainly acceptable, but nowhere near as nice as the cabins.

Tobacco Caye. www.tobaccocaye.com. ℂ **800/667-1630** or 604/894-2312 in U.S., 532-2101 in Belize. 6 units. BZ$160 double. Rates include 3 meals daily and taxes. **Amenities:** Restaurant; Wi-Fi (BZ$10 daily fee).

En Route South: Where the Wildcats Roam

Weighing up to 91kg (200 lb.) and measuring more than 1.8m (6 ft.) from nose to tip of tail, jaguars are king of the New World jungle. Nocturnal predators, jaguars hunt peccaries (wild piglike animals), deer, and other small mammals. The **Cockscomb Basin Wildlife Sanctuary ★★**, established in 1990 as the world's first jaguar reserve, covers nearly 388 sq. km (150 sq. miles) of rugged forested mountains and has the greatest density of jaguars in the world. It is part of the even larger Cockscomb Basin Forest Reserve, which was created in 1984.

The forests within the preserve are home to other wildcats as well, including pumas, ocelots, and margays, all of which are very elusive, so don't get your hopes of seeing them too high. Few people do, but a good guide may be able to find you some tracks. Other mammals that you might spot if you're lucky include otters, coati-mundi, tayra, kinkajous, deer, peccaries, anteaters, and armadillos.

The largest land mammal native to Central America, Baird's tapir, is also resident. Locally known as a "mountain cow," the tapir is the national animal of Belize. A tapir can weigh up to 272kg (600 lb.) and is related to the horse, although its protruding upper lip is more like an elephant's trunk.

Much more easily spotted in the dense vegetation surrounding the preserve's trails are nearly 300 species of birds, including the scarlet macaw, the keel-billed toucan, the king vulture, and the great curassow.

Trails inside the park range from gentle and short to quite arduous and long. Many offer wonderful views of the Cockscomb Mountains and lush forested valleys. There are quite a few waterfalls and swimming holes. During the dry season, you can even climb Victoria Peak, which, at 1,122m (3,681 ft.), is the country's highest mountain. This trip takes several days and requires a permit and local guide. For more information, contact the **Belize Audubon Society** (www.belizeaudubon.org; *C* **223-5004,** 223-4987, or 223-4988). Admission to the park is BZ$10.

Caution should be exercised when visiting the preserve. In addition to jaguars, which can be dangerous, there are poisonous snakes, including the deadly fer-de-lance. Always wear shoes, preferably boots, when hiking the trails here. Don't ever place your hand somewhere without first inspecting the area.

The Belize Audubon Society co-manages this park, and even offers a few private cabins and some dormitory sleeping options inside the sanctuary. Rates run between BZ$20 and BZ$30 per person for dormitory-style accommodations, or BZ$120 for one of the cabins, which can sleep up to six persons. Alternatively, you can stay down near the information center near the highway at the **Tutzil Nah Cottages** (www.mayacenter.com; *C* **636-4750**) in private double or single rooms with either a shared or private bath for a few dollars more.

Cockscomb Basin Wildlife Sanctuary is located 9.7km (6 miles) inland from the Southern Highway, some 32km (20 miles) south of Dangriga. The turnoff and entrance to the sanctuary are at the roadside village of Maya Center. This is where you'll find the sanctuary's information center, and where you'll pay your BZ$10 entrance fee. This is also a good place to check out some of the art and craft works at the neighboring shop run by the Maya Center Women's Group and to hook up with a local guide. Any bus heading south to Placencia and Punta Gorda will drop you off at the entrance. From here you'll have to hike the 9.7km (6 miles) or hire a local taxi for around BZ$30 round-trip.

A Nearby Back-Bush Nature Lodge

Nestled at the foot of the Maya Mountains is a little ecolodge, **Bocawina Rainforest Resort** (formerly Mama Noot's) ★ (www.bocawina.com;

© **671-554**). It's located in the heart of the **Mayflower Bocawina National Park,** and offers a collection of comfortable rooms. The park protects the small and barely excavated Mayflower Mayan ruins, as well as vast expanses of tropical forests. There's excellent hiking and bird-watching on miles of trails leaving from the resort, including a couple of wonderful waterfalls. All of the electricity is provided by an inventive mix of solar, hydro, and wind generators. A pure mountain spring provides the water. Multiday packages with transportation provided from Dangriga are the preferred means of visiting this little lodge.

HOPKINS VILLAGE & SITTEE RIVER VILLAGE ★★★

140km (87 miles) S of Belize City; 127km (79 miles) SE of Belmopan; 53km (33 miles) N of Placencia

Hopkins Village is a midsize Garífuna community located on a pretty stretch of white-sand beach, 24km (15 miles) south of Dangriga. It is a picturesque village with colorfully painted raised clapboard houses. It is also my preferred destination for getting a true taste of this unique culture. If you stick around long enough, you may be able to learn a bit about traditional Garífuna lifestyles. Fishing is still the main pursuit of many of the villagers, although tourism is rapidly becoming the main source of employment and income.

Hopkins Village is set on a long, narrow, curving swath of beach, which, in addition to Placencia, is one of the few true beaches in the country. This white-sand beach is usually quite calm and good for swimming. In recent years, several beach and dive resorts have opened just south of the village, while in the village itself you'll find a hodgepodge of budget lodgings and simple restaurants. Sittee River Village is a few miles south of Hopkins and a mile or so inland, on the banks of the gently flowing Sittee River. It's a tiny little town, but it does have a hotel or two. Fishermen like the quiet riverside setting and access to both fresh- and saltwater angling.

Essentials

GETTING THERE & DEPARTING

BY PLANE   The closest airport to Hopkins Village is in Dangriga. See "Dangriga," earlier in this chapter, for flight details. A taxi from Dangriga to Hopkins or Sittee River Village should cost BZ$80 to BZ$100 for up to four people. For a taxi in Dangriga, call **Star Line Taxi Service** (© **621-9956**).

BY CAR   From Belize City, head west on Cemetery Road, which becomes the George Price (Western) Highway. Take this all the way to Belmopan, where you will connect with the Hummingbird Highway heading south. Ten kilometers (6¼ miles) before Dangriga, the Hummingbird Highway connects with the Southern Highway. Take the Southern Highway toward Placencia and Punta Gorda. About 13km (8 miles) south of this junction, you'll see signs for the entrance to Hopkins Village. From here, it's 6.4km (4 miles) on a graded gravel road. A few miles farther south on the Southern Highway is the entrance to Sittee River Village; however, you can also enter at Hopkins and head south from there along the coast, as it's really just a small loop.

BY BUS Only a couple of the buses each day from Dangriga south make the loop through Hopkins Village and Sittee River. The ride takes between 25 and 35 minutes to Hopkins Village, with Sittee River Village just a few miles farther on the route. The fare is BZ$6 each way. Be sure to ask before you get on the bus if it will drop you off in the village. If not, you will be let off on the Southern Highway, at the entrance to Hopkins, but still some 6.4km (4 miles) away. If this is the case, you will hopefully have arranged pickup with your hotel in advance. Otherwise, you'll have to hitchhike into town. The buses heading back to Dangriga or to points south can be caught in either Hopkins or Sittee River, or better yet, from the Southern Highway. See "Essentials" on p. 195 for details on bus travel between Dangriga and Belize City, and between Dangriga and points south.

GETTING AROUND

Hopkins Village itself is very small, and you can easily walk the entire town. If you're staying south of town or in Sittee River Village, or want to explore, a bicycle is the preferred means of transportation. Most of the hotels will either lend you a bike or rent you one for a few dollars per day.

There are no official taxi services, but if you ask around town or at your hotel, you should be able to hire someone for small trips or excursions. There are also a number of freelance guides in the area who have vehicles and may be willing to provide transportation.

ORIENTATION

The access road from the Southern Highway heads right into the heart of Hopkins Village. If you continued straight, you'd be in the Caribbean Sea. The village itself spreads out for a few hundred yards in either direction. Heading south you'll come to the larger resorts listed below. At the turnoff and entrance to Almond Beach Resort & Jaguar Reef Lodge, the road heads back toward the highway, passing through Sittee River Village. *Note:* It's only a 15- to 20-minute walk from the village to any of the resorts to the south, with the exception of Kanantik, which is farther away.

FAST FACTS Both Hopkins and Sittee River villages are tiny, and there are no banks or major stores or services like hospitals, though there is an ATM. You can also get gas at the little marina in Hopkins.

What to See & Do

This is a very isolated and underdeveloped area. All of the resorts listed below specialize in scuba diving, snorkeling, and, to a lesser extent, fishing. All of them also have a long list of tour options to attractions such as Cockscomb Basin Wildlife Sanctuary, Sittee River canoeing, Blue Hole National Park, the Mayflower Mayan ruins, and cultural tours of Dangriga. If you're staying at one of the lodgings in either of the villages, you'll find numerous local operators offering snorkeling, scuba, and fishing outings, as well as all the above-mentioned tours.

If you really want to get a taste of the local culture, sign up for traditional Garífuna drumming and dancing classes at the **Lebeha Drumming Center** ★ (www.lebeha.com; ☎ 665-9305), which is located on the northern edge of the village.

SNORKELING & DIVING

Snorkeling and scuba diving are stellar all along the Belize Barrier Reef. The Tobacco Caye range lies just offshore from Hopkins Village, a simple 30- to 40-minute boat ride away, with numerous snorkeling and dive sites. Moreover, the location makes these dive resorts excellent jumping-off points for trips to Glover's Reef Atoll and even Turneffe and Lighthouse Reef atolls. All of the resorts listed below offer multiday dive packages, which are the way to go for serious divers, though we particularly recommend Hamanasi. They also all offer certification classes and advanced open-water courses. If you're not staying at one of the dedicated dive resorts, your best bet is to arrange to dive with them, as their equipment and dive masters are generally top-notch, and the price savings of going with a less active operator just aren't worth it. If you're feeling adventurous, for snorkeling excursions, ask around the village and head out with a local boat captain or tour guide. The lower cost and cultural richness might just make up for a slow boat, leaky mask, and loose-fitting fins.

FISHING

There's excellent bonefishing in the inland and barrier reef flats in this area. Anglers can also go for tarpon, permit, and snook, or head offshore for bigger game. Experienced guides can help you track any of the above fish, which you can stalk using traditional casting and trolling techniques, or try catching with a saltwater fly rod and reel. Most of the major lodges and resorts here offer fishing packages and excursions. Well-equipped sport-fishing outings cost between BZ$1,000 and BZ$3,000 per day, depending on the size of the boat, number of anglers, and distance traveled. Alternatively, you can ask around Hopkins Village to line up a more low-tech outing for around BZ$100 to BZ$400 for a half-day.

LIGHT UP THE NIGHT

One of the highlights, quite literally, of this area is the **nocturnal bioluminescence river tour** in Anderson's Lagoon, just south of Hopkins. **Happy Go Luckie Tours** ★★★ (www.hgltours.com; ☎ 635-0967) offers this phenomenal experience where guests can witness the animals that come awake in the night before entering the mystical world of glowing plankton. The dark water turns a shocking blue when disturbed by the boat cutting through it, making for one of the most memorable Belize activities I've ever taken part in. Cost is BZ$60 per person if three or more people take the tour. If you only have two aboard, the price rises to BZ$90 each. Tours run from January to June to avoid rainy nights. The glow is at its most intense when the moon is full.

Shopping
GARIMAYA GIFT SHOP

Hopkins is not a shopping destination by any means, but the recent addition of **Garimaya Gift Shop** (✆ 666-7970) to the community is a decent outlet for Mayan and Garífuna handicrafts such as blankets, wood carvings, and paintings. Look for it by the curve on Sittee River Road.

Where to Stay

There's a host of lodging options in this area, ranging from simple budget and backpacker hotels in Hopkins Village to upscale dive resorts on the beaches to the south. Beyond what you see here, search such websites as Airbnb.com and HomeAway.com for options.

EXPENSIVE

In addition to the places listed below, **Belizean Dreams** (www.belizean dreams.com; ✆ 522-2400, or 800/456-7150 from the U.S.) is a condo-resort project on the south end of Hopkins Village, featuring a series of large and luxurious fully equipped condo units spread around a grassy lawn and pool area fronting the beach.

Hamanasi Adventure and Dive Resort ★★★ Superb service, breathtakingly beautiful grounds, darn good food, and a well-curated menu of offered tours all combine to make Hamansi one of the finest resorts in Belize. Diving is the main focus here, and the hotel has an excellent operation. But they also offer daily snorkeling, nature hikes, canoe trips, and other inland adventures. Guests have a choice of two types of lodgings and both are delightful, with artistic tile and woodworking touches in all rooms; most have high ceilings. Those who choose beachfront rooms are housed in a couple of ocean-facing two-story buildings—ask for a second-floor room for the improved view and privacy of your balcony. There is also a series of "treehouses": spacious individual bungalows set on stilts 3.7m (12 ft.) high in the midst of the hotel's tiny coastal forest, just a few yards behind the main operation. While these don't have an ocean view, they do offer a lush sense of tropical isolation. Hamanasi means "almond" in the local Garífuna language, and you'll see plenty of the namesake *hamans* trees growing around the grounds.

Hopkins Village. www.hamanasi.com. ✆ **844/235-4930** in the U.S., or 520-7073 in Belize. 28 units. BZ$836–BZ$1,450 double. Rates include continental breakfast, taxes, and service charge. Rates lower in the off season. **Amenities:** Restaurant; bar; bike rental; full-service dive operation; outdoor pool; room service; all rooms smoke-free; Wi-Fi (free).

Jaguar Reef Lodge & Spa and Almond Beach Resort & Spa ★★ These two resorts were once one, and are still owned by the same company. They're right next to each other and even share amenities, like the heated pool with a swim-up Tiki bar, so either one you pick will bring the benefits of both. Each has spacious, tastefully decorated rooms, with Jaguar taking a more clean-cut modern approach and Almond sticking with an airy, island vibe. The room rates are comparable until you get to the large suites at Almond Beach, the largest of which has five bedrooms. In 2017, outdoor hot tubs were added to the beachfront villas. In addition to the on-site activities and services, there's a small, full-service spa shared by both resorts. If you just want to hang around the lodge, hammocks and Adirondack chairs are set under the shade of palm trees along the lodge's white-sand beach. There's complimentary use of sea kayaks, Hobie Cats, bicycles, and snorkel gear. A second, smaller fresh-water pool is on the Jaguar side.

Hopkins Village. www.vivabelize.com/jaguar-reef and www.vivabelize.com/almond-beach. © **888/822-2448** in the U.S. and Canada. 25 units in Almond Beach, 20 units in Jaguar Reef. BZ$600–BZ$700 double; BZ$898–BZ$998 suite. Rates lower in the off season, slightly higher during peak weeks. **Amenities:** Restaurant; bar; free bike and kayak use; full-service dive operation; 2 outdoor pools; small spa; watersports equipment rental; Wi-Fi (free).

Kanantik Reef & Jungle Resort ★★

Except for the purchase of a bottle of wine or some top-shelf liquor, little falls outside the all-inclusive price you pay at this swank resort. That includes more than you'll get at other similar resorts like all tours, scuba diving and dive equipment, and fishing gear. The rooms are backed by some 1,300 acres of jungle. All are handsome hexagonal, thatch-roof cabins, set either right in front of the ocean or slightly back in flowering gardens. Each is capacious and features sapodilla wood floors, driftwood beds, a walk-in closet, and showers built of smooth river stones. The owner is Italian, so there's usually an excellent chef on hand serving a mix of local, Italian, and other international cuisine in the large, high-pitched dining room. *Note:* It *is* possible to bypass the all-inclusive plan, which may make sense if you don't plan on doing serious diving or fishing, or eating three meals a day.

Southern Hwy., Mile 18.2, south of Hopkins Village. www.kanantik.com. © **877/759-8834** in the U.S., or 533-7048 in Belize. 25 units. BZ$804 per person double occupancy. Rates include all meals, local drinks and soft drinks, taxes, tips, and activities. Kanantik is located 29km (18 miles) south of Dangriga, accessed by a graded gravel road that connects with the Southern Hwy. They also have their own private airstrip, and charter flights directly to the resort can be arranged. **Amenities:** Restaurant; bar; free bike and kayak use; full-service dive operation; midsize outdoor pool w/unheated Jacuzzi; watersports equipment; Wi-Fi (free).

INEXPENSIVE

In addition to the places listed below, there are literally a score (or more) of simple guesthouses and small inns. Some are run by a local renting a spare room, while others are converted houses. Most inns charge around BZ$20 to BZ$30 per person. If you have the time, it might be worth your while to check out a couple before deciding where to stay.

Hopkins Inn ★★

Located right on the beach, near the center of the village, this little hotel offers clean and comfortable individual cabins that have benefited from recent renovation. The cabins are all tiled, and feature wood-paneled, pitched roofs. Each has a small front porch. The two units closest to the water have the best views of the sea, but the others are larger and still have good views. A simple continental breakfast is served on your private veranda, and a host of restaurants are within easy walking distance. The owners are very friendly and knowledgeable, and can help arrange any number of tours. Hopkins Village. www.hopkinsinn.com. © **665-0411.** 4 units. BZ$186–BZ$261 double. Rates include continental breakfast. **Amenities:** Bike rental; laundry service; Wi-Fi (free).

Jungle Jeanie's by the Sea ★ Set on an unusually lovely swatch of beach, the individual wooden cabins here are supported by raised stilts on the sand. Most have direct views of the ocean, although one large unit with a loft is set back slightly among some trees. All have a private balcony in front, as well as a small refrigerator, microwave oven, and coffeemaker. However, aside from these amenities, the furnishings and decor are quite basic. Still, if you're looking for a comfortable cabin on the sand, just steps from the sea, this place should fit the bill. Some of the cabins are painted in bright primary colors, while others are simply varnished over natural wood. The staff here are a friendly, helpful bunch. Hopkins Village. www.junglebythesea.com. © **523-7047.** 10 units. BZ$140–BZ$280 double. Rates lower in the off season. **Amenities:** Restaurant; kayak, windsurfer, and Hobie Cat rentals; Wi-Fi (free).

Tipple Tree Beya ★★ This is an excellent, laid-back option for budget travelers. Located at the far southern end of the village, literally where the pavement ends, Tipple Tree Beya combines the isolated feel of the more expensive beach resorts here with the convenience and proximity of the in-town options. Right in front of the hotel is a pristine stretch of beachfront. There are hammocks spread on a broad shared veranda, and rustic chairs set out on the sand. The cabin has a small kitchen area, equipped with microwave oven, refrigerator, coffeemaker, and some basic utensils. Hopkins Village. www.tippletreebelize.com. © **615-7006.** 7 units; BZ$90–BZ$350 double. **Amenities:** Bike and kayak rental; Wi-Fi (free).

Where to Dine

Even if you're staying at one of the large resorts around here, it's worth heading into town to try a meal at one of the simple, locally run restaurants on the main street. Of these, **Innies Restaurant** (© **503-7333**) is a perennial favorite. All serve excellent fresh fish and seafood, and will usually have some *hudut* and other Garífuna dishes on hand. That being said, the town's restos tend to be very basic, inexpensive, and somewhat funky in decor and vibe. A similar option, which I prefer for its seafront location, is **Laruna Hati** (© **661-5753**), which is located toward the north end of the village.

For excellent grilled fish and seafood, international fare, and tasty bar food, head to the **Barracuda Bar & Grill** ★ (© **523-7259**) at the **Beaches and Dreams** hotel, at the south end of the village. And for a relaxed, European-style cafe, try **Thongs** ★ (© **662-0110**), right on the main road, near the center of the village.

Chef Rob's Gourmet Cafe ★★★ FUSION   The profile of an old red car sliced in half serves as a billboard for this little place. After working in the trenches for years as executive chef for some of the better resorts and hotels around Belize, Dutch-born chef Rob has opened his own place. Grab one of the heavy wooden tables on the open-air wood deck under dim, atmospheric lighting with flowing cotton drapes billowing in the breeze. The eclectic menu changes daily but always contains a mix of fresh seafood and quality meats prepared with fresh local ingredients and creative sauces. You might find lamb served with a balsamic vinegar and coconut milk reduction, or the daily catch expertly grilled and topped with a homemade papaya ketchup. Everything is artfully prepared by Rob in his small show kitchen. The four-course dinner is a great deal at BZ$59. During high season, lunches are sometimes served.

At Parrot Cove Lodge on Sittee River Rd. www.chefrobbelize.com. ℂ **532-7225.** Reservations recommended. Main courses BZ$40–BZ$60. Tues–Sun 5–9pm.

Driftwood Beach Bar & Pizza Shack ★ PIZZA/SEAFOOD   This place is what a laid-back beach bar and restaurant should be—good food, great prices, cold beer, and a friendly atmosphere. And everything's just steps from the sea. There's a small interior dining room, but you'll want to grab one of the outdoor tables under a thatch-roof shade structure. If you're feeling athletic, there's a beach volleyball court, which is typically active during the Saturday afternoon BBQs. If you're not feeling athletic, there's a hammock or two on hand. In addition to thin-crust pizzas, there's usually some seafood and a nightly pasta special.

On the beach, north end of Hopkins Village. www.driftwoodpizza.com. ℂ **667-4872,** or 664-6611. Reservations accepted. Main courses BZ$16–BZ$50. Thurs–Tues 11am–10pm.

Hopkins Village After Dark

Aside from the various resort hotels, there is very little in the way of nightlife here—unless you can line up a night dive. Most of the resorts, however, hire local bands and dance troupes to entertain their guests. It's worth combining a dinner at one of these places with the nightly show. On full-moon nights, the folks at **Driftwood Beach Bar & Pizza Shack** (see above) host blow-out rave parties, with a live DJ and big bonfire.

PLACENCIA ★★

241km (150 miles) S of Belize City; 161km (100 miles) SE of Belmopan; 89km (55 miles) NE of Punta Gorda

Placencia is still Belize's foremost and fastest-growing beach destination. Located at the southern tip of a long, narrow peninsula that is separated from the mainland by a similarly narrow lagoon, Placencia boasts nearly 26km (16 miles) of white sand fronting a calm turquoise sea and backed by palm trees. Placencia attracts everyone from hippy backpackers and avid naturalists to hard-core divers and upscale snowbirds. The whole peninsula is in the midst of an ongoing major boom, and development currently stretches from the

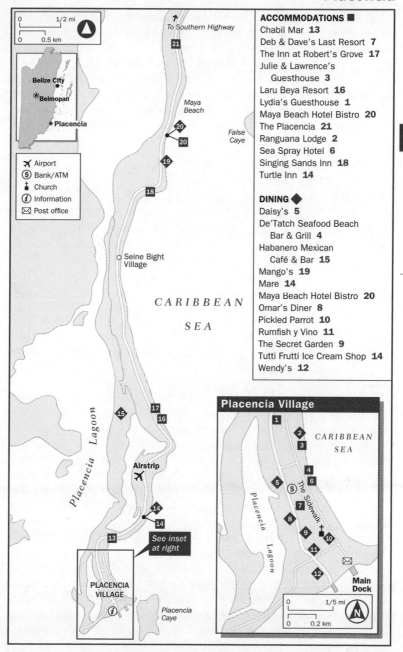

Placencia

0 —— **1/2 mi**
0 —— **0.5 km**

To Southern Highway

21

Maya Beach

False Caye

20
20

19

18

✈ Airport
$ Bank/ATM
✝ Church
ⓘ Information
✉ Post office

Belize City
⊛ Belmopan
● Placencia

○ Seine Bight Village

CARIBBEAN

SEA

Placencia Lagoon

17
16
15

Airstrip ✈

14
14

13

See inset at right

PLACENCIA VILLAGE

ⓘ

Placencia Caye

See inset at right

ACCOMMODATIONS ■
Chabil Mar **13**
Deb & Dave's Last Resort **7**
The Inn at Robert's Grove **17**
Julie & Lawrence's Guesthouse **3**
Laru Beya Resort **16**
Lydia's Guesthouse **1**
Maya Beach Hotel Bistro **20**
The Placencia **21**
Ranguana Lodge **2**
Sea Spray Hotel **6**
Singing Sands Inn **18**
Turtle Inn **14**

DINING ◆
Daisy's **5**
De'Tatch Seafood Beach Bar & Grill **4**
Habanero Mexican Café & Bar **15**
Mango's **19**
Mare **14**
Maya Beach Hotel Bistro **20**
Omar's Diner **8**
Pickled Parrot **10**
Rumfish y Vino **11**
The Secret Garden **9**
Tutti Frutti Ice Cream Shop **14**
Wendy's **12**

Placencia Village

1
2
3

CARIBBEAN SEA

4
5 $ **6**
The Sidewalk
7
8
9 ✝ **10**
11
✉
12

Placencia Lagoon

Main Dock

0 —— **1/5 mi**
0 —— **0.2 km**

N

8

SOUTHERN BELIZE | Placencia

peninsula's southern tip all the way up to Maya Beach on the northern end of the peninsula.

Placencia itself is a tiny Creole village of colorful clapboard houses mostly built on stilts. Once you settle into the slow pace and relaxed atmosphere, it's hard to move on. Placencia is *the* definition of laid-back. For years, the village's principal thoroughfare was a thin concrete sidewalk. Once listed in the *Guinness Book of World Records* as the narrowest street in the world, the sidewalk still runs through the heart of the village parallel to the sea. However, the ongoing construction and development boom have made the main road through town (called "the Back Road") actually the town's busiest thoroughfare most days.

Essentials

GETTING THERE

BY PLANE   There are numerous flights into and out of Placencia's little airport (PLJ). **Maya Island Air** (www.mayaislandair.com; © **223-1140**) has nine regularly scheduled flights daily between the Philip S. W. Goldson International Airport in Belize City and Placencia, and four additional seasonal flights. The first flight leaves at 8:10am and the last flight is at 5pm. Direct flight time is 35 minutes, though some have a layover, and a few have three, so check which flight you're booking. They also have seven daily flights between Belize City's Municipal Airport and Placencia between 8am and 4:15pm. The fare is about BZ$312 each way. Maya Island Air flights from Placencia to Belize City depart throughout the day, with the first regular flight at 6:40am and the last flight at 4:30pm. Some of these flights stop first in Dangriga, and then at the international airport, before continuing on to the Municipal Airport.

Tropic Air (www.tropicair.com; © **800/422-3435** in the U.S. or Canada, 226-2012 in Belize City, or 523-3410 in Placencia) has 10 flights daily between Philip S. W. Goldson International Airport and Placencia, with the first flight leaving at 7:45am and the last flight at 5pm. The fare is BZ$266 each way. They also have six daily flights between Municipal Airport and Placencia, leaving at 8:00, 9:50, and 10:31am, and at 12:20, 2:30, and 4:30pm. The fare is BZ$236 each way. Tropic Air flights depart Placencia for Belize City's airports daily beginning at 7:00am, with the last flight of the day at 4:20pm.

Flights to and from Punta Gorda on Maya Island Air and Tropic Air stop in Placencia to pick up and drop off passengers. On both airlines, flights are sometimes added during the high season or suspended during the low season, so check in advance. Flight time runs between 25 and 50 minutes, depending on whether there is an intermediate stop or two or three.

A big runway meant for international flights was planned, started, and then scrapped, and has since been reclaimed by nature. Old articles and forum questions about this airstrip are still lingering around online, so make sure all your flight research is for PLJ, not the runway that never was.

BY CAR   From Belize City, head west on Cemetery Road, which becomes the George Price Highway. Take this all the way to Belmopan, where you will connect with the Hummingbird Highway heading south. Ten kilometers (6¼ miles) before Dangriga, the Hummingbird Highway connects with the Southern Highway. Take the Southern Highway toward Placencia and Punta Gorda. After 37km (23 miles) on the Southern Highway, turn left onto the road to Riversdale and Placencia. From this turnoff, it's another 32km (20 miles) to Placencia. The drive from Belize City should take around 2½ to 3 hours.

BY BUS   There is frequent bus service between all major cities in Belize and Dangriga. See p. 173 for more information. Direct buses leave Dangriga for Placencia throughout the day, and the fare is BZ$10. Buses leave Placencia for Dangriga, with onward connection to Belmopan, San Ignacio, and Belize City, daily as well. If you're heading south, you'll want to get off the bus as soon as it hits the Southern Highway and flag down the next southbound bus.

However, many independent and bus travelers also reach Placencia via Independence Village and Mango Creek, using the *Hokey Pokey* **ferry** (© 523-2376). This 15-minute boat ride used to cut a lot of bumpy, dusty miles off the road trip; however, now that the road is paved, this is no longer necessary. Still, if you're heading south, this is the best way to go. The ferry fare is BZ$12. All north- and southbound bus traffic along the Southern Highway stops in Independence Village, near the ferry dock. Ferries between Placencia and Independence Village leave regularly throughout the day, with at least six trips in each direction. See p. 208 for information on buses making the run between Belize City and the southern reaches of Belize.

GETTING AROUND

Placencia Village itself is tiny, and you can walk the entire length of the sidewalk, which covers most of the village, in about 10 to 15 minutes. If you need a taxi, call **S & M Taxi** (© 602-4768) or **Peninsula Star** (© 602-4768). Fares within the village run BZ$6 for one person, and BZ$3 per person for two or more people. A trip from the airstrip to the village costs BZ$12 for one person, and BZ$6 per person for two or more people.

If you want to rent a car or golf cart while in Placencia, **Barefoot Rentals** (www.barefootservicesbelize.com; © 523-3066) is the best option, charging around BZ$100 per day for a golf cart, and between BZ$160 and BZ$180 per day for an SUV.

If you want to explore more, a scooter is a good way to get around. Several hotels and operators in the area rent scooters. Rates run around BZ$60 to BZ$80 for a half-day and BZ$100 to BZ$120 for a full day.

Bicycles are also a decent option, and will get you more exercise. The terrain is flat, although it can get hot on the main road, and there aren't really any trails or off-road options. Many hotels have bikes either free for guests or for rent. Several shops around town also rent out bicycles. A relatively modern bike in good shape should cost between BZ$20 and BZ$30 per day.

ORIENTATION

For most of the peninsula there is only one road. As the road reaches the end of the peninsula and the village of Placencia, it basically dead-ends at the Shell station and some boat docks. Just before this, a dirt spur turns right just beyond the soccer field and heads for a few hundred yards toward the lagoon. Once you've arrived, your main thoroughfare will hopefully be the beach and the sidewalk, which run parallel to each other starting near the docks and heading north.

Hotels and resorts are spread all along the length of the Placencia peninsula. To make it easier to understand where a hotel or resort is, the peninsula is broken up into three broad sections: Maya Beach, Seine Bight, and Placencia Village. Maya Beach is the northernmost section of the peninsula, and the hotels and resorts here are quite spread out, with few other services or businesses. More or less anchoring the center of the peninsula is the tiny Garífuna village of Seine Bight. Just to the north and south of Seine Bight village are several other isolated resorts. Down at the southern end of the peninsula is Placencia Village itself.

The very helpful **Placencia Information Center** (www.placencia.com; ℂ 523-4045) is located toward the end of the road in a tiny mini-mall just across from the soccer field.

FAST FACTS   For the local **police,** dial ℂ **911,** or 503-3142; you can also reach the newly formed **tourist police** at ℂ **503-3181.** If you need any medical attention, the **Placencia Medical Services** (ℂ **622-7648**) is located in the center of the village.

There's a **Scotiabank** (ℂ **523-3277**) on the main road near the center of the village, as well as an **Atlantic Bank** (ℂ **523-3431**). Scotiabank has an ATM that accepts international cards. **Placencia Pharmacy** (ℂ **523-3346**) is in the center of the village. The **post office** is located above the Fishermen's Co-op, near the start of the sidewalk.

There are a couple of gas stations in Placencia. You'll find the Shell station where the road hits the end of the peninsula in the heart of the village. There's also a Texaco station at the Inn at Robert's Grove Marina.

Connectivity isn't much of an issue here, as you'll be hard-pressed to find a hotel or restaurant in the area that doesn't offer free Wi-Fi.

Fun On & Off the Beach

You just can't help slowing down and relaxing in Placencia. Sit back, sip a seaweed shake, and forget your cares. Nobody ever seems to get up early (except maybe the fishermen), and most people spend their days camped in the sand reading books and eating seafood. The beach, although narrow in places, is arguably the best in Belize. You can walk for miles and see hardly a soul. Still, if you need more activity and adventure, there's a host of options.

WATERSPORTS EXCURSIONS

SNORKELING & SCUBA DIVING   There's often decent snorkeling right off the beach, especially if you head north a mile or so. The water's clear and

Gentle Giants

From late March to early July—especially just before, during, and after the full moons—the waters offshore from Placencia are a world-renowned place to spot and dive with mammoth **whale sharks** *(rhincodon typus)*, the largest fish in the sea. Whale sharks can reach lengths of up to 12m (40 ft.) and weigh in at more than 20 tons. It's about a 30-minute boat ride to Gladden Spit, an offshore, deepwater site where tens of thousands of cubera snapper come to spawn right around the full moons. No dummies, the whale sharks come to feed on the nutrient-rich snapper spawn. And not only whale sharks. During these peak feeding periods, you are also likely to see dolphins, bull sharks, and sea turtles, as well as the massive schools of snapper. *Note:* Even during peak periods, whale shark sightings on these dives are far from guaranteed. If you sign up for one of these dives, you must be very prepared for the possibility that you'll see little more than some snapper and jack.

you'll see plenty of fish and bottom life in the sea grass and along the sand bottom.

One of the more popular snorkel excursions is to the nearby **Laughing Bird Caye** (www.laughingbird.org; ✆ 523-3565). Located just a few miles offshore from Placencia, Laughing Bird Caye is a national park. It's a tiny little island measuring roughly 11×107m (35×350 ft.). Because the area surrounding the island is protected, the wildlife is allowed to live naturally without being picked off, so the snorkeling is excellent. Many tour operators take folks here and then serve a picnic lunch on the beach or head to nearby **Little Water Caye.**

However, if you're serious about diving or snorkeling, you'll want to get out to the **barrier reef** and its dozens of little offshore cayes. It's between 16 and 40km (10–25 miles) out to the reef here, making it a relatively quick and easy boat ride. Diving here is as spectacular as at other more popular dive destinations in Belize, and you'll often have far fewer fellow divers around.

Most of the larger resorts have their own dive operations, and these tend to be some of the better operations on the peninsula. There is also a handful of independent operators in the village servicing folks at the rest of the hotels. If you're not staying at a hotel with a dedicated dive operation, check in with the folks at **Seahorse Dive Shop ★** (www.belizescuba.com; ✆ 523-3166).

A snorkeling trip should cost between BZ$60 and BZ$160, depending on the distance traveled and whether lunch is included. Rates for scuba diving run between BZ$120 and BZ$300 for a two-tank dive, also depending on the length of the journey to the dive site and whether gear and lunch are included. Equipment rental should cost from BZ$15 to BZ$30 for a snorkeler, and BZ$30 to BZ$60 for a scuba diver.

FISHING The Placencia area has some of the best fishing in the country, and that includes excellent bonefishing in flats in this area. Anglers can also go for tarpon, permit, and snook, or head offshore for bigger game, including grouper, yellowfin tuna, king mackerel, wahoo, mahi-mahi, and the occasional sail or marlin. Most of the hotels and resorts on the peninsula offer fishing packages and excursions. Well-equipped sport-fishing outings run between BZ$1,200 and BZ$3,000 per day, depending on the size of the boat, number of anglers, and distance traveled. However, you can hire a smaller open-air skiff perfectly suited for fly-casting for bonefish, permit, or tarpon for between BZ$400 and BZ$1,000 per day. We particularly recommend the team at **Tarpon Caye Lodge** ★ (www.tarponcaye.com; ℂ **1/833-827-7661,** or 523-3323); these are some of the more experienced fishing guides in town, specializing in fishing for permit and tarpon. They run a small fishing lodge on the remote Tarpon Caye. You can also try **Trip 'N Travel** (www.tripntravel. bz; ℂ **660-7189**), another long-standing local operation with well-regarded guides.

KAYAKING Several hotels and tour operators in town rent out sea kayaks. The waters just off the beach are usually calm and perfect for kayaking. However, the lagoon is probably a better choice, offering more interesting mangrove terrain and excellent bird-watching opportunities.

Rates for kayak rental run around BZ$10 to BZ$20 per hour, or BZ$60 to BZ$80 for a full day. A guided tour of the mangroves or a combined snorkeling and kayak tour offshore should cost between BZ$80 and BZ$150 per person.

If you're looking for a guided tour, the best kayak operator in Placencia is **Toadal Adventure** ★ (ℂ **523-3207**). These folks offer several different multiday kayaking trips, both out on the ocean and on inland rivers. Custom trips can also be designed.

SAILING The crystal-clear waters, calm seas, and isolated islands surrounding Placencia make this an excellent place to go out for a sail. Your options range from crewed yachts and bareboat charters for multiday adventures to day cruises and sunset sails.

The Moorings ★ (www.moorings.com; ℂ **800/416-0820** in the U.S. and Canada) is a large-scale charter company with its Belizean operations based out of Placencia. Options include monohulls, catamarans, and trimarans of varying sizes. Given the shallow draft, increased interior space, and reduced drag, a multihull is your best bet. All of the boats are well-equipped and seaworthy. Rates for a weeklong charter run between BZ$4,000 and BZ$18,000, depending on the size of the boat and whether you charter it bareboat or with a crew.

GUIDED DAY TRIPS

While the ocean and outlying cayes are the focus of most activities and tours in Placencia, there are a host of other options. The most popular of these include tours to Cockscomb Basin Wildlife Sanctuary (see "Dangriga," earlier in this chapter), the Mayan ruins of Lubaantun and Nim Li Punit (see "Punta Gorda & the Toledo District," later in this chapter), and up the Monkey River. Day trips can run between BZ$100 and BZ$300 per person, depending on the distance traveled and the number of activities offered or sites visited. Almost every tour agency in town offers these trips, or ask at your hotel for a recommended guide or operator.

Monkey River ★   Perhaps the most popular "inland" trip offered out of Placencia is up the Monkey River, and most of it is actually on the water, anyway. Located about a half-hour boat ride down the coast and through the mangroves, the Monkey River area is rich in wildlife. If you're lucky, you might spot a manatee on your way down. Once traveling up the Monkey River, you should keep your eyes peeled for crocodiles, green iguana, wild deer, howler monkeys, and the occasional boa constrictor. In addition, you're likely to see scores of bird species. These tours can be done entirely in a motor launch or may allow you to kayak on the Monkey River portion; I recommend the latter. Most tours include lunch in the quaint little Creole fishing village of Monkey River itself, as well as a short hike through a forest trail. Monkey River trips cost between BZ$90 and BZ$120 per person.

SPAS & BODY WORK

Most of the big resorts, such as Turtle Inn and The Inn at Robert's Grove, have their own spas, which you may be able to book even if you're not a guest there. Alternatively, there are a couple of day spas right in the village. The **Secret Garden Day Spa** (www.secretgardenplacencia.com; ✆ 523-3420) is located behind Wallen's Market near the center of the village, while **Siripohn's Thai Massage & Oriental Spa** (www.thaimassagebelize.com; ✆ 620-8718) is located in the Placencia Village Square, next to the Tutti Frutti Ice Cream Parlor. An hour-long massage should cost you between BZ$140 and BZ$200.

Sidewalk Fair

Most days, the Placencia sidewalk is a lazy affair. However, on the second weekend of February, it comes alive with the annual **Placencia Sidewalk Arts Festival.** Local artists show their wares, and restaurants set up outdoor booths. There are also games, events, and raffles. For more information, contact the **Placencia Information Center** (www.placencia.com; ✆ 523-4045).

Shopping

Simple souvenir shops are abundant in Placencia. Located right on the main road near the Scotiabank, the **Beach Bazaar** ★ (✆ 523-3113) is the best of the bunch. It has a selection of traditional souvenirs, as well as some higher-end ceramic, wood, and metal artworks.

If you're looking for some finer art, stop in at **Art 'N Soul** (© 503-3088), which is on the sidewalk about 91m (300 ft.) north of the pier and features paintings and prints by local artists. While farther north, in Seine Bight, you should definitely stop in at **Lola's Art Gallery ★** (© 523-3342), which features the colorful acrylic paintings of owner Lola Delgado, which come in a wide range of sizes and prices.

Tip: Be on the lookout for locally produced organic chocolate. Marketed under the brand name **Goss** (www.goss-chocolate.com), these milk and dark-chocolate bars are sold at stores around town. If you don't pick up any here, they are also on sale at the international airport.

Where to Stay

There is a host of accommodations options in and around Placencia. In general, the town's budget hotels and guesthouses are located in the village proper, either just off the sidewalk or around the soccer field. As you head north to the broader and more isolated beaches, prices tend to rise.

EXPENSIVE

Chabil Mar ★★★   Ready to be pampered? The staff at Chabil Mar have hospitality down to a fine-tuned art. They have a way of making every guest feel special . . . and like they're having the best vacation of their lives. How does this play out? In many ways, but I was most impressed that meals are not only scrumptious, but can be served anywhere on the resort—the pier, poolside, on your deck, you name it. The food is brought with a smile and some fresh flowers. Set right on the beach, Chabil Mar is a collection of mostly two-bedroom, two-bathroom condo units in a series of two-story buildings with blue roofs spread around lushly planted, gated grounds, toward the southern end of the Placencia peninsula. All digs feature Mexican-clay tile floors and lively, tropical decor, though the resort as a whole has an Italian villa feel with flowering vines wrapping around white columns. Most rooms have spacious private balconies or verandas, and all come with full kitchens featuring granite countertops. A long dock leads out to a large deck area covered with a thatch-roofed shade structure, and there are two midsize pools to choose from, plus 400 feet of private white-sand beach. Relative to other luxury resorts, it's quite close to town, giving guests more restaurant and activity options.

Placencia Village, on the beach just north of the center of the village. www.chabilmar villas.com. © **866/417-2377** in the U.S., or 523-3606 in Belize. 21 units. BZ$820–BZ$1,210 double. **Amenities:** Restaurant; bar; free bike and kayak use; free evening shuttle service to/from town; on-site golf cart rental; concierge; 2 outdoor pools; room service; all rooms smoke-free; Wi-Fi (free).

Laru Beya Resort ★★   This resort offers roomy, bright, and comfortable rooms and condo units (the beds are high quality) on an idyllic patch of Placencia's pristine white beach. Guests have the choice of one-bedroom rooms, or one-, two-, and three-bedroom condo units but the better rooms are higher up (they have swell ocean views). The penthouse suites come with their own rooftop Jacuzzis. Kayaks, Hobie Cats, and bicycles are available free for guests, and there's even a small miniature golf course, which is a hit with the kids.

Placencia, on the beach north of the airstrip. www.larubeya.com. ℗ **800/890-8010** the U.S. and Canada, or 523-3476 in Belize. 30 units. From BZ$340 double; BZ$780 2-bedroom condo; BZ$1,040 3-bedroom condo. Rates lower in the off season; higher during peak weeks. **Amenities:** Restaurant; bar; free bike, windsurfer, and Hobie Cat use; outdoor pool; mini-golf course; Wi-Fi (free).

Singing Sands Inn ★★ Despite its sandy name, what makes this resort stand out is its landscaping: Singing Sands has the most lush gardens and grounds in the area. It's a small resort, with just six individual thatch-roofed wooden cabins set in a row perpendicular to the beach, with cabin nos. 1 and 2 closest to the ocean. You'll still get something of an ocean view from cabin nos. 3, 4, and 5, while no. 6 is set amid the flowers and foliage. Each has new hardwood floors, a small porch with a couple of chairs, and handmade local and Guatemalan decor. In addition to the cabins, there are four larger, fully equipped apartments with kitchenettes. On-site also: a midsize outdoor pool, a large open-air deck area facing the ocean, and a long dock built out into the sea with a shaded palapa at the end of it. The restaurant here is quite good, with oceanfront open-air seating either under the stars or protected by a thatch roof.

Maya Beach. www.singingsands.com. ℗ **440/579-3386** in the U.S. and Canada, or 533-3022 in Belize. 12 units. BZ$220–BZ$550 double. Rates lower in the off season. **Amenities:** Restaurant; bike and kayak rental; pool; smoke-free rooms; Wi-Fi (free).

The Placencia ★ This large resort and condo project dwarfs everything else on the peninsula. Its multilevel pool, with a swim-up bar and separate children's section, is the largest in the country. Rooms and apartments feature marble floors throughout and a minimalist, contemporary decor that some will find handsome, others a bit cold. That being said, most of the master bedrooms come with Jacuzzi tubs, and some of the rooms have lovely ocean views (try for a second- or third-floor unit with a sea-facing balcony). The resort sits on an excellent long stretch of white-sand beach, with the requisite wooden dock jutting out into the sea, featuring a bar, some chaise longues, hammocks, and a swimming ladder on the end of it. As high-end as it is, The Placencia feels more like something plucked out of the U.S. than Belizean by nature, so look elsewhere if you're wanting a more authentic accommodation. Also, despite their website advertising things like a golf course and shooting range, these exist only as concepts.

Maya Beach. www.theplacencia.com. ℗ **533-4117.** 92 units. BZ$394–BZ$656 double; BZ$458–BZ$588 2-bedroom villa. Rates higher during peak weeks. **Amenities:** 4 restaurants; 3 bars; tennis courts; babysitting; free bike and kayak use; concierge; full-service dive shop; large outdoor pool; room service; small spa; Wi-Fi (free).

Robert's Grove ★★ Though it's a bit dated in spots, this boutique resort has a lot to recommend it including two good restaurants, three pools, an in-house spa, professional dive and fishing operations, and a tennis court. In the rooms, rustic red-tile floors, Guatemalan textiles, and Mexican ceramic accents abound, and all come with a private balcony, hung with a hammock. If you're traveling with family, know that suites, and newly constructed villas, come with fully equipped kitchenettes, and all have a large living room and a large balcony. Guests also enjoy unlimited free use of the hotel's sea kayaks, windsurfers, Hobie Cat sailboats, tennis court, and bicycles, as well as free airport transfers. Because the hotel owns and manages two small private islands, Ranagua Caye and Robert's Caye, guests can take a day trip to these tiny offshore cayes, or spend a night or two in a simple yet comfortable cabin.

Placencia, on the beach north of the airstrip. www.robertsgrove.com. (℮ **800/565-9757** in the U.S., or 523-3565 in Belize. 72 units. BZ$400–BZ$430 double; BZ$530–BZ$920 suite. Rates lower in the off season; higher during peak weeks. **Amenities:** 2 restaurants; 3 bars; lounge; babysitting; concierge; full-service dive shop; exercise room; 3 outdoor pools; room service; small spa; lit tennis court; free watersports equipment and bike use; Wi-Fi (free).

Turtle Inn ★★★ This is filmmaker-turned-hotelier Francis Ford Coppola's poshest property in Central America, and that's saying something (as all his hotels are luxe). All guests stay in roomy one- or two-bedroom private villas here, each of which has a large living room and a spacious bathroom that lets out onto a private interior rock garden, with its own open-air shower. Tons of beautiful woodwork and a heavy dose of Indonesian decor and furnishings dominate the rooms. The front desk can be contacted via an in-room "Shell-phone," made from a conch shell, which is as amusing as it is functional and serves as a great reminder that you're in the hotel of a creative legend. All the villas are set on the sand just steps from the beach, but not all have ocean views (so ask to move if that's important to you). For those really splashing out, the Coppola Pavilion is a two-bedroom unit set on the beach a little off the main resort, with its own pool and a kitchen, wine cellar, and steam bath/shower in each of the two bathrooms. Finishing off the amenities here is a small spa and a full-service dive operation across the street on the lagoon side of the peninsula, as well as their private island, Coral Caye, a quick 25-minute boat ride away.

Placencia Village, on the beach north of the center of the village. www.turtleinn.com. (℮ **866/356-5881** in the U.S., or 824-4912 central reservation number in Belize, or 523-3150 at the hotel. 25 units. BZ$700–BZ$960 1-bedroom double; BZ$1,080–BZ$1,350 2-bedroom double; BZ$4,158 Coppola Pavilion. Rates include continental breakfast. Rates lower in the off season; higher during peak weeks. **Amenities:** 4 restaurants; 2 bars; gelato shop; babysitting; free bike and kayak use; concierge; full-service dive shop; 2 outdoor pools; room service; watersports equipment rental; Wi-Fi (free).

MODERATE

In addition to the places mentioned below, The Maya Beach Hotel (www.mayabeachhotel.com; (℮ **627-4718**) offers five clean, cozy beachfront rooms and a cool pool, and is home to **Maya Beach Hotel Bistro** (see below), one of the best restaurants on the peninsula.

Ranguana Lodge ★★　In this price range, it's impossible to do better than the Ranguana. All of the cabins are just steps from the ocean, are clean and cozy, and all come with a private balcony or porch area. They're also darn cute, painted a blinding pure white, with trim in colors from a Crayola box. In the two older cabins, nearly everything is made of hardwood—walls, floors, ceilings, even the louvered windows. These rooms feature a full kitchenette. The three oceanfront cabins are right in front of the sea and have air-conditioning; however, they are a little smaller and have a little less character. The only real downside to staying here is occasional noise from a next door bar.

Placencia Village, on the beach in the center of the village. www.ranguanabelize.com. ℂ **523-3112.** 5 units. BZ$160–BZ$250 double. Rates include taxes. **Amenities:** Beach; Wi-Fi (free).

INEXPENSIVE

If the places listed below are full, you can simply walk around the village and see what's available, or head to either **Julia & Lawrence's Guesthouse** (www.juliascabanas.com; ℂ **503-3478**) or **Deb and Dave's Last Resort** (debanddave@btl.net; ℂ **523-3207**), both located just off the sidewalk toward the center of the village.

Lydia's Guesthouse ★★　One of the longest-running and most popular budget options in Placencia, and it's fitting that this classic two-story converted home survived Hurricane Iris. You'll find a convivial hostel-like atmosphere—travelers from around the world make up the guest list. There's even a good ocean view from the shared balcony on the second floor, a real steal in this price range. Rooms are simple and clean, although a few can be a bit cramped. The twelve-room house has six shared bathrooms (four of which have showers), which are kept immaculate. The four cabanas and one apartment have their own bathrooms. Guests have free use of the kitchen that takes up the ground floor of the amiable Lydia Villanueva's private home next door.

Placencia Village, toward the northern end of the sidewalk. www.lydiasguesthouse. com. ℂ **523-3117.** 17 units. BZ$40–BZ$60 double. **Amenities:** Communal kitchen; Wi-Fi (free).

Sea Spray Hotel ★　Rooms and prices vary substantially in this perennial budget and backpacker favorite. Most rooms are in a two-story building built perpendicular to the sea. The four deluxe rooms are in a separate two-story building fronting the sea, and these come with televisions and kitchenettes, as well as comfortable private oceanview balconies. There's also a separate, fully equipped beachfront cabana, although I think the deluxe rooms are a better and more comfortable choice. The economy rooms are a bit cramped and dark. The attached De'Tatch Seafood Beach Bar & Grill serves hearty local fare at very reasonable prices, and also has an Internet cafe. As at Lydia's (above), the vibe is hostel, even though there are no communal sleeping areas.

Placencia Village, on the beach toward the middle of the sidewalk. www.seasprayhotel. com. ℂ **523-3148.** 21 units. BZ$66–BZ$170 double. **Amenities:** Restaurant; Wi-Fi (free, in public areas).

Where to Dine

In addition to the places mentioned below, the restaurant at **The Inn at Robert's Grove** (℃ 523-3565) is consistently top-notch. On the other end of the spectrum, **Wendy's** (not the chain; ℃ 523-3335) is a popular, low-key spot serving excellent Belizean, Mexican, and international fare, located on the main road, at the southern end of town, almost by the pier.

Finally, as you wander around town in the heat of the day, be sure to stop in at **Tutti Frutti Ice Cream Shop** for fresh, homemade ice cream or gelato. Tutti Frutti is on the main road in the Placencia Village Square shopping center, across from the soccer field. **Daisy's,** located on the main road near the center of town, also serves fresh homemade ice cream, as well as breakfast, lunch, and dinner. Tutti Frutti is the place to go if you've got just ice cream on the mind, since it's their specialty.

There are also several grocery stores in the village, in case you want to put together a picnic lunch.

EXPENSIVE

Mare ★★★ ITALIAN/SEAFOOD   Subdued lighting, tables adorned with candles and flowers, and a view out to the sea—the director behind the Godfather movies (Francis Ford Coppola, the owner of the resort Mare is in) knows how to set the scene for a romantic dinner. The restaurant is also darn nice for lunch, thanks to the expertly prepared Italian fare and warm service. I like to start things off with the *insalata de pesce,* which features fresh red snapper smoked on the premises. In addition to nightly specials, there are delicious thin-crust wood-oven pizzas, a selection of pastas, and whole, locally caught fish are roasted in the wood oven (lobster tails get the same treatment in season). Most of the herbs and vegetables served are grown right here at the hotel's organic garden. The wine list features fine vino from Francis Ford Coppola's own vineyard.

At Turtle Inn, on the beach north of the center of the village. www.turtleinn.com. ℃ **523-3244.** Reservations recommended. Main courses BZ$40–BZ$92. Daily 11am–3pm and 6:30–9pm.

Maya Beach Hotel Bistro ★★★ FUSION/SEAFOOD   Lobster bread pudding. Plantain gnocchi. Prosciutto-wrapped grouper. These are just a few of the dazzling, inventive dishes served up at this beachfront restaurant. It has the finest food in Placencia, and arguably, in Belize. Signature main dishes here include the cacao-dusted pork chop served on a risotto cake, and the nut-encrusted fresh catch served with a curried watermelon reduction. The coconut ribs are also excellent. All of this is served in an open-walled, simple dining room overlooking the ocean, which makes sense. When you are offering food this scintillating, you don't need fancy decor to make a statement.

At Maya Beach Hotel, on Maya Beach. www.mayabeachhotel.com. ℃ **520-8040.** Reservations recommended. Main courses BZ$24–BZ$58. Tues–Sun 7am–9pm.

MODERATE

In addition to the places listed below, **Mango's** (www.mangosbelize.com; © 600-2040) is a lively beachside bar and restaurant up in Maya Beach. The bar food here runs from burgers and shrimp po' boy sandwiches to burritos and quesadillas.

De'Tatch Seafood Beach Bar & Grill ★ BELIZEAN/SEAFOOD   This funky and friendly open-air beachfront joint is one of the most popular spots in town. Traditional Belizean breakfasts here are hearty and inexpensive. You can get excellent seafood or shrimp burritos or tacos for lunch, and a selection of tasty meat, poultry, and seafood offerings for dinner. I like the seafood gumbo and Belikin-battered conch steak. The second-floor open-air deck can get hot in the daytime, but it is especially nice on starry nights.

Placencia Village, on the ocean just off the Sea Spray Hotel toward the center of the village. © **503-3385.** Reservations not accepted. Breakfast and lunch main courses BZ$12–BZ$32; dinner main courses BZ$24–BZ$72; lobster BZ$64–BZ$100. Daily 7am–10pm.

Habanero Mexican Café & Bar ★ MEXICAN   Set on the lagoon side of the peninsula beside the marina at Robert's Grove, this restaurant serves a mix of Tex-Mex and traditional Mexican fare. When the bugs aren't biting, you'll want to grab a table outdoors on the deck overlooking the water. This is also a great spot to catch the sunset. When the bugs *are* biting, you can seek refuge in the screened-in main dining room. My favorite dishes here are the carnitas tacos and the shrimp chimichanga. For those looking for a fiesta, sangria and margaritas are available by the pitcher.

At the marina across from The Inn at Robert's Grove, north of the airstrip. © **523-3565.** Reservations recommended. Main courses BZ$14–BZ$52. Daily for dinner.

Rumfish y Vino ★★ SEAFOOD/FUSION   On a breezy balcony in the center of town, Rumfish y Vino offers a a wide-ranging menu of food from across the Americas (most prominently Mexico, Peru, and the U.S.). Most days that includes succulent conch fritters, homemade fish pâté, and Jamaican jerk pork chops. On the comfort food front there's a gourmet mac 'n' cheese and primo fish tacos. The wine list here is unique for Belize, featuring a broad selection of Italian and California wines that they import themselves; there are also several local beers on tap.

Placencia Village Sq., on the main road, across from soccer field. www.rumfishyvino. com. © **523-3293.** Reservations recommended. Main courses BZ$22–BZ$38. Daily 2pm–midnight.

INEXPENSIVE

Omar's Diner ★ BELIZEAN/MEXICAN   There's no assembly-line production, Styrofoam wrappings, or U.S.-style short-order cook here. Which means that the speed of service won't be up to American diner norms. So get on Belize time and enjoy this long-standing restaurant, which consistently serves hearty, tasty local fare at great prices. Best on the menu is the fresh fish or shrimp in the Belizean creole, Cajun, or curry sauces—Omar isn't afraid to spice up his cooking. There's a homey, welcoming vibe to the whole operation, which is located streetside on the main road. If there's no free table, you'll probably be able to take a seat with another fellow diner who has room.

Placencia Village, on the main road in the center of the village. ℂ **523-4094.** Breakfast and lunch main courses BZ$5–BZ$14; dinner main courses BZ$10–BZ$24; lobster BZ$30–BZ$40. Daily 7am–10pm.

Pickled Parrot ★ INTERNATIONAL   The chillest hangout in Placencia, this palapa-roofed pub is owned by a gregarious former New Jersey resident who knows what the expat community (and visitors) want. He serves up quality bar food—pizzas, burgers, subs, and burritos—and some more elevated fare at night (mango-rum glazed chicken, lobster curry, and the like), and lets his friendly dogs roam the resto, to the delight of all. One of the best deals in town is the daily BZ$10 lunch special. This open-air sand-floored joint can get rowdy, especially after folks have downed a few rounds of Parrot Piss, the bar's signature mixed drink. *Note:* Thursdays are trivia night.

Placencia Village. ℂ **636-7068.** Reservations not accepted. Main courses BZ$10–BZ$30; pizzas BZ$34–BZ$44. Wed–Mon 11am–midnight.

The Secret Garden ★ INTERNATIONAL/COFFEE HOUSE   The name of this quiet and cozy little spot is appropriate. Reached over a small yellow bridge, the Secret Garden has a few outdoor tables on a wood deck in, yes, a shady garden. A few more tables are located on a covered veranda, and a couple more are inside the small restaurant. Dinner choices change regularly, but might feature fresh grilled red snapper with a roasted red pepper sauce or some spicy shrimp "Diablo" served over linguine. There's always fresh fish, conch, and lobster in season, and even some vegan options.

Placencia Village, behind Wallen's Market. www.secretgardenplacencia.com. ℂ **523-3617.** Breakfast main courses BZ$8–BZ$14; dinner main courses BZ$25–BZ$45. Tues–Sat 7:30–11am and 5–9pm.

Placencia After Dark

Placencia is a quiet and remote beach destination, which is why my favorite late-night activity here is simply taking a stroll on the beach and stargazing. Still, there are a few bars in the village, and some of the larger resort hotels have lively nightlife scenes.

Two of the most popular spots in town are neighboring establishments, the **Barefoot Beach Bar** ★ (ℂ **523-3515**) and the **Tipsy Tuna Sports Bar** (ℂ **523-3089**); I prefer the relaxed vibe and outdoor setting of the Barefoot Beach Bar, while the Tipsy Tuna is more of a late-night place, with pool tables and regular live music and karaoke. You'll also often find a lively scene at the **Pickled Parrot** (see above).

PUNTA GORDA & THE TOLEDO DISTRICT ★

330km (205 miles) S of Belize City; 161km (100 miles) S of Dangriga

Punta Gorda, or simply "P.G.," is Belize's southernmost town. This is the end of the road and feels a bit like the end of the world. P.G. is a quiet place with clean, paved streets, few cars, lush vegetation, and a very slow pace. Although it is right on the Caribbean, there is no beach to speak of, and the water just off town is rather uninviting. However, there are several wonderful offshore cayes within easy reach that have excellent beaches and serve as bases for equally excellent snorkeling, scuba diving, and fishing. Inland from P.G., the surrounding scenery is as verdant as you'll find anywhere in Belize (due to nearly 508cm [200 in.] of rain a year). The surrounding Toledo District is home to various Mayan ruins and numerous villages that are still peopled by Kekchi and Mopan Maya Indians, who have been migrating here from Guatemala over the past century.

Settled by Garífunas in 1823, Punta Gorda was accessible only by boat for decades, and even though the Southern Highway is now paved and easily connects the town with points north, there's still a sense of this being a distant frontier. As the administrative center for the Toledo District, Punta Gorda has an active market and bus services to the many surrounding Mayan and Garífuna villages, although connections are not very frequent. Most travelers do little more than pass through Punta Gorda on their way to or from Guatemala by way of the Puerto Barrios ferry. However, there is plenty to keep the adventurous traveler busy for several days, including fishing, scuba diving, rainforest hiking, and bird-watching.

Essentials
GETTING THERE & DEPARTING
BY PLANE   There are several daily flights into and out of Punta Gorda's little airport (PND). **Maya Island Air** (www.mayaislandair.com; ✆ 223-1140) has four flights daily between Belize City and Punta Gorda. These flights leave from the Municipal Airport at 8am and at 2:30 and 4:15pm. Most of these flights stop 15 minutes later at the Philip S. W. Goldson International Airport to pick up passengers. The fare is BZ$350 each way from Municipal Airport, and BZ$410 each way from the international airport. When you're ready to leave, Maya Island Air flights from Punta Gorda to Belize City depart at 6:30 and 9:30am, and at 4pm. Most of these flights stop first in Placencia and Dangriga, and then at the international airport, before continuing on to Municipal Airport.

Tropic Air (www.tropicair.com; ✆ 800/422-3435 in the U.S. or Canada, 226-2012 in Belize City, or 722-2008 in Punta Gorda) has five daily flights from Philip S. W. Goldson International Airport to Punta Gorda at 7:45 and

10:45am, and at 12:45, 2:45, and 4:45pm. These flights stop 15 minutes later at the Municipal Airport to pick up passengers. The fare is BZ$319 each way from the Municipal Airport, and BZ$366.50 each way from the international airport. Tropic Air flights depart Punta Gorda for Belize City's airports daily at 6:40, 9:20, and 11:40am, and at 1:40 and 4pm.

Flight times run between 55 minutes and 1 hour and 20 minutes, depending on the number of stops, since most flights to and from Punta Gorda on Maya Island Air and Tropic Air stop in Placencia and Dangriga to pick up and drop off passengers. On both airlines, flights are sometimes added during the high season or suspended during the low season, so check in advance.

BY CAR   It is a long way to Punta Gorda. However, the Southern Highway, which starts just outside of Dangriga, is paved the entire 161km (100 miles) to Punta Gorda, where it ends. Coming from Belize City, head first to Belmopan and turn south on the Hummingbird Highway. Just before Dangriga, the Hummingbird Highway connects with the Southern Highway, which takes you all the way to Punta Gorda. Alternatively, you can take the Manatee Road turnoff just past the Belize Zoo, although the Manatee Road is a washboard dirt-and-gravel road for most of its length. See "By Car" in "Essentials" on p. 173 for more information. It should take between 4 and 5 hours to drive between Belize City and Punta Gorda.

BY BUS   **James Bus Line** (© **664-2185** or 631-1959 in Belize City, or 662-8189 in Punta Gorda) has regular service throughout the day between Belize City and Punta Gorda. Buses leave at irregular intervals between 4:30am and 5pm, with at least 15 buses making the run throughout the day. In Belize City, the buses leave from nearby the Shell gas station on Cemetery Road. It's worth getting an express bus, which should take only a little more than 5 hours. However, there are far more frequent nonexpress buses. On these, the trip takes 6 hours or more. In some cases, you may have to change buses in Belmopan or Dangriga. The one-way fare is BZ$24.

Departing buses begin running at 3am, with the last bus leaving at 4pm. All buses, even the express buses, stop in Belmopan, Dangriga, and Independence. However, the express buses are not supposed to stop along the route to pick up and drop off passengers at intermediary points.

BY BOAT   Several boats run daily between Punta Gorda and Puerto Barrios, Guatemala. If there's enough demand, the boats may stop in Livingston, Guatemala, as well. Expect to pay between BZ$30 and BZ$40 per person. The boats leave from the main pier in Punta Gorda. **Requena's Charter Service,** 12 Front St. (watertaxi@btl.net; © **722-2070**), is one of the more dependable operators. When the seas are calm, the crossing takes about 1 hour. Departures for Guatemala tend to leave between 8:30 and 9am, although there are often afternoon departures as well. The boats tend to return from Puerto Barrios between 2 and 4pm. You'll have to pay the BZ$37.50 in exit taxes. *Note:* When coming and going, be sure to get your passport stamped at the immigration office just up from the dock.

Punta Gorda

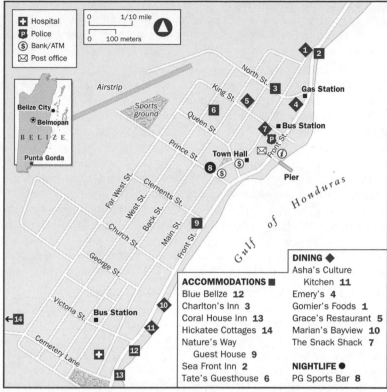

Hospital
Police
Bank/ATM
Post office

0   1/10 mile
0   100 meters

Airstrip

Belize City
Belmopan
B E L I Z E
Punta Gorda

North St.

King St.

Gas Station

Sports ground

Queen St.

Bus Station

Prince St.

Town Hall

Pier

Far West St.
West St.
Clements St.
Back St.
Main St.
Church St.
Front St.

George St.

Gulf of Honduras

Victoria St.   Bus Station

Cemetery Lane

ACCOMMODATIONS ■
Blue Belize **12**
Charlton's Inn **3**
Coral House Inn **13**
Hickatee Cottages **14**
Nature's Way
   Guest House **9**
Sea Front Inn **2**
Tate's Guesthouse **6**

DINING ◆
Asha's Culture
   Kitchen **11**
Emery's **4**
Gomier's Foods **1**
Grace's Restaurant **5**
Marian's Bayview **10**
The Snack Shack **7**

NIGHTLIFE ●
PG Sports Bar **8**

GETTING AROUND

Punta Gorda is a very small and compact town, and you should be able to get around primarily on foot. If you're just too hot or tired, or you're heading farther afield, have your hotel call a cab, or call **Galvez's Taxi Travel & Tour Service** (𝄐 **722-2402**) or the **Roots & Herbs Taxi Service** (𝄐 **722-2834**).

Another option for getting around is to rent a bike. Ask at your hotel, and they should be able to help you find one for rent.

ORIENTATION

Punta Gorda is a small coastal town, and the road into town runs right along the water before angling a bit inland. There's a tiny triangular park at the center of the town. On one side is the Civic Center, or Town Hall. On one corner is a cute little clock tower, and the Belize Bank anchors another corner. Still, much of the town's activity is water based, and many of the most important businesses, hotels, restaurants, and government offices are located on Front Street, which runs along the waterfront. The town's main pier is off the center of Front Street. On the western edge of town, only 6 blocks from the water, is P.G.'s airstrip.

The **Belize Tourism Industry Association** (✆ **227-1144**), in conjunction with local hotels and tourism operators, runs a well-staffed and helpful information center on Front Street just north of the main pier. This is a good place to come to find current transportation schedules, book a tour, or arrange a homestay.

FAST FACTS   For the local **police**, dial ✆ **911,** or 722-2022, and for the **fire department,** call ✆ **722-2032.** If you need medical attention, go to the **Punta Gorda Hospital** on Main Street, toward the southern end of town (✆ **722-2026**). The **post office** (✆ **722-2087**) is on Front Street across from the main pier. **Belize Bank,** 30 Main St. (✆ **722-2324**), can handle most of your banking needs.

There's a **Texaco** gas station (✆ **722-2926**) out toward the northern end of Front Street and a Shell station out by "The Dump." Finally, if your hotel can't or won't do it for you, take your dirty clothes to **Punta Gorda Laundry Services,** on Main Street across from the Belize Bank, which charges around BZ$15 per load.

Malaria isn't particularly prevalent in Belize, but the Toledo District is the most likely place where you would contract it. Make sure to protect yourself against this and other mosquito-borne illnesses with long sleeves and pants, bug spray, and prophylactic medication.

What to See & Do

There's very little in the way of attractions right in town. A stroll through Punta Gorda is the best way to enjoy the Caribbean atmosphere. If you get a little antsy at such a slow pace, there are plenty of cultural wonders and natural adventures within easy reach of Punta Gorda. There are a host of tour operators and guides in P.G. Your hotel and the information center listed in "Essentials," above, can probably hook you up with a good guide or adventure operator. Alternatively, you can check in with the folks at **Tide Tours ★** (www.tidetours.org; ✆ **722-2129**), a local ecotourism initiative that integrates environmentally and socially aware practices with their wide range of tour and adventure options.

REACHING THESE ATTRACTIONS   Most of the villages and attractions discussed below (such as Nim Li Punit) are located along the highway and have regular bus service every day. Buses to and from the other villages and attractions generally run at least once daily. Buses tend to leave for the villages from Punta Gorda between

Celebrating the Sweet

Each year in late May, P.G. pulls out all the stops for the **Toledo Cacao Fest** (www.facebook.com/belizechocolate festival). The festival, which runs over a weekend, includes a wide range of events and activities, including live concerts, fireworks, cacao farm tours, and of course plenty of opportunities to taste all sorts of dishes and creations made from or with cacao and chocolate. See the above website for exact dates.

noon and 2pm, depending on which village or destination you are traveling to. These buses all leave from the market area in front of the Civic Center along Queen Street.

The time of departure from the villages to P.G. varies but is usually early in the morning, sometimes right around dawn. There's often only one bus per day, but some villages have two or more daily buses. Ask in P.G., or in the actual village, as schedules are subject to change. Fares run around BZ$2 to BZ$8 per person each way.

Another alternative is to hire a taxi or go on an organized trip. Ask at your hotel or the information center, and you should be able to set up a trip. You can usually hire a car and driver/guide for BZ$180 to BZ$360 per day. This price will usually cover a group of four.

The truly adventurous might want to tour this area by mountain bike. You can reach most of the above sites and villages in an athletic couple of hours of riding. Leave early to avoid the oppressive midday heat, and expect slow going and lots of mud in the rainy season.

MAYAN RUINS

None of Belize's southern ruins are as spectacular or actively restored as the more famous sites in the northern and western parts of the country. Still, the ancient Maya did have substantial cities and trading posts all up and down the Belizean coast, and several impressive reminders can be found near Punta Gorda. Travelers interested in the ongoing Mayan tradition will find themselves in a region of numerous small Kekchi and Mopan Maya villages, many of which have taken tentative steps to enter the tourism industry with homestay programs or basic guesthouses.

Lubaantun ★   The largest of the nearby Mayan ruins is **Lubaantun.** The name, which means "Place of the Fallen Stones" in Yucatec Maya, was given to the site in 1924 and it was descriptive of the state of the buildings at that time. This Late Classic Maya ruin is unusual in that the structures were built using a technique of cut-and-fitted limestone blocks rather than the usual rock-and-mortar construction technique used elsewhere by the Mayans. Set on a high ridge, the site features five plazas and two ball courts. The highest temple here rises just 15m (50 ft.) or so, and it's still mostly in ruins, with trees growing out of the rubble. Although largely unexcavated, the ancient city's center has been well cleared, and the surviving architecture and urban outline give a good sense of the former glory of this Mayan ceremonial center.

Lubaantun is perhaps most famous as the site where a crystal skull was allegedly discovered by a young Canadian woman in 1926. There's much debate as to the origin and age of the skull, which some say was planted as a surprise present for Anna Mitchell-Hedges, who just happened to discover the carved skull on her 16th birthday while accompanying her father, who just happened to be leading the archaeological expedition. Others claim that the skull was a plant that had actually been purchased in London by Mitchell-Hedges. There are also claims that the crystal skull is the work of extraterrestrials, and that it has shown remarkable healing powers. The skull is currently kept in a vault in Canada.

About 32km (20 miles) northwest from Punta Gorda, about 11km (7 miles) from the well-marked turnoff on the highway near Big Falls, and 1.6km (1 mile) from the small Mayan village of San Pedro Columbia. Admission BZ$10.

Nim Li Punit ★ Nim Li Punit, meaning "Big Hat" in Kekchi Mayan, features 26 steles, including the largest Maya carved stele in Belize, measuring almost 9m (30 ft.) tall. This stele bears the depiction of a local ruler wearing a large, broad diadem, or "big hat," hence the name of the site. Discovered only in 1976, Nim Li Punit is a relatively small site, with four compact plazas and one very well-preserved ball court, with a stone marker in its center. One of the plazas served as an astronomical observation area, with a platform and stone markings indicating the point where the sun rises on the equinoxes. There are three Royal tombs that have been discovered and partially excavated, and you can peer down into two of them. However, overall, very little excavation or restoration has been undertaken. Nonetheless, the eight carved steles, and in particular, stele 14, make this a worthwhile stop. The best-preserved steles, including stele 14, are currently housed at the small museum and visitor center at the entrance to the site.

Nim Li Punit is set on a high hilltop, and on a clear day, you have a great view over the flat southern plains, all the way to the Caribbean Sea. It is believed that this Late Classic city had close ties to Copan, Honduras. If you can visit only one of the Mayan sites in southern Belize, I recommend Nim Li Punit over Lubaantun.

About 3.2km (2 miles) off the Southern Highway, near the village of Indian Creek, 40km (25 miles) north of Punta Gorda. A dirt road leads from the highway to a parking area near the visitor center. Admission BZ$10.

Other minor ruins in the area include **Uxbenka** near Santa Cruz and **Pusilha** near Aguacate.

PLACES FOR A DIP

Mayan culture, past and present, may be the main attraction of Punta Gorda, but it also boasts plenty of natural attractions. In the forested hills south of San Antonio is one of the most beautiful swimming holes in all of Belize. Flowing out of a cave in a limestone mountain, the aptly named **Blue Creek** ★★ is a cool stream with striking deep turquoise water. Lush rainforest shades the creek, creating an idyllic place to spend an afternoon. You can cool off by swimming up into the mouth of the cave from which the stream flows. Blue Creek is also known locally as Ho Keb Ha, which means "the place where the water flows from." During the dry season, you can actually hike about 8km (5 miles) through the cave to an aboveground exit. The village of Blue Creek is reached from a turnoff about 2.4km (1½ miles) east of San Antonio. From here it's another 4km (2½ miles) south on a rough dirt road. The creek runs right through the little village, but the best swimming holes and the cave source of the creek are about a 10- to 15-minute hike upstream.

Just off the Southern Highway, near the village of Big Falls, there is a natural **hot spring** that's billed as the only such hot spring in Belize. You can have a refreshing swim in the river at the falls and then warm your muscles in the hot spring. This is a popular spot for locals on weekends.

There are also some attractive small waterfalls near the village of San Antonio, with inviting pools for a refreshing dip.

WATERSPORTS

The fishing, scuba diving, and snorkeling to be had off Punta Gorda are world-class. Kayaking on the ocean or up the Moho River is also excellent. Most tour operators and hotels in town can offer or line up a snorkel, dive, or fishing expedition to the very underexplored Sapodilla Cayes.

If you want to do an extended dive trip, or some volunteer work in marine conservation, contact **Reef Conservation International ★** (www.reefci.com; ✆ 513/334-9393 from the U.S.). The organization has cabins and campsites, as well as research and dive facilities on the idyllic Frank's Caye, which is part of the Sapodilla Marine Park.

For fishing, I recommend you check in with **Dan Castellanos** at Blue Belize (see below) or with **Garbutt's Fishing Services** (✆ 722-0070). Both know the waters and fishing grounds around here, and can guide you in pursuit of tarpon, bonefish, and permit.

A BOTANICAL GARDEN

The **Toledo Botanical Arboretum ★** (✆ 722-2470) is a sustainable farm and botanical garden project that accepts day visitors. In addition to a broad variety of ornamental flowers and orchids, tropical palms and bromeliads, they grow more than 100 varieties of tropical fruit, and something is always ripe for a just-picked treat. The Toledo Botanical Arboretum is close to both the Kekchi Maya village of San Pedro Columbia and the Lubaantun ruins. A 2-hour guided tour of the facility costs around BZ$10. Visits and transportation should be arranged in advance.

Deer Dance

The Mopan Maya village of San Antonio is the site of the Deer Dance, a 9-day traditional Mayan cultural celebration that takes place in late August and early September. Although this traditional cultural ceremony coincides with a Catholic religious holiday, the Feast of San Luis, its roots are traditional Maya.

STAYING IN A MAYAN VILLAGE

Many people who make it as far as Punta Gorda are interested in learning more about Mayan village life. Though the ruins were abandoned centuries ago, Maya Indians still live in this region. The villages of the Toledo District are populated by two main groups of Maya Indians, the Kekchi and the Mopan, who have different languages and agricultural practices. The Mopan are upland farmers, while the Kekchi farm the lowlands. Both groups are thought to have migrated into southern Belize from Guatemala less than 100 years ago. Four decades of political violence and genocide in neighboring Guatemala have bolstered this migration.

San Antonio, the largest Mopan Maya village, is in a beautiful setting on top of a hill, with an old stone church in the center of the village. Steep streets wind through the village, dotted with both clapboard houses and traditional Mayan thatched huts. In addition to the Deer Dance, the nearby village of San Pedro is known for its annual festival on June 13 in honor of that village's patron saint. This festival includes masked dances and other Mayan rites mixed with more traditional Catholic themes and celebrations. Beyond San Antonio and San Pedro, there is a host of even smaller and more remote traditional Mayan villages.

The Maya Village Homestay Network (demdatsdoin@btl.net; ☎ 722-2470) provides accommodations directly with families in the Mayan villages. There's a BZ$10 registration fee for any stay, and then accommodations cost BZ$20 per person per night, and meals are BZ$8 per person per meal. These fees are paid directly to your host family. Accommodations during a homestay can range from a hammock to a simple bed, and almost all families have some sort of bathroom or latrine. Currently, the villages involved in the homestay program include Aguacate, Na Luum Ca, and San José.

If you opt for this program, you can expect plenty of close contact with the local villagers. You will be eating what the locals eat, which in most cases means plenty of beans and tortillas, as well as the occasional chicken soup or meat dish. One of the highlights for many guests is participating in the cooking chores and learning the simple art of tortilla making.

STAYING WITH A GARÍFUNA FAMILY

Those seeking a unique Caribbean cultural experience can also look into staying with a local Garífuna family. Just 18km (11 miles) south of Punta Gorda lies the small Garífuna village of Barranco. With a little more than 100 residents, Barranco is a quintessential quiet Garífuna village. However, this is the hometown of one of Belize's most famous and beloved musicians, Andy Palacio (p. 30), and the town's little House of Culture is a mini-museum to the history, traditions, and culture of the Garífuna people of this area. Although the road to Barranco is usually passable during the dry season, it's best to get there by boat. Ask around at the Punta Gorda pier whether there's any regular ferry service. If not, you should be able to hire a ride for about BZ$80 to BZ$120 per boat.

Shopping

Wednesday and Saturday are market days around the small market square in front of the Civic Center and along the waterfront. This is a great time and place to find local and Guatemalan handicrafts, as well as fresh fruit and produce. If the outdoor market isn't happening, you can find most of the same items at the **Fajina Craft Center ★**, on Front Street next to the post office (☎ 722-2470), which is a cooperative of Mayan women from the area. There's also **Maya Bags** right near the airstrip (☎ 917/697-2203), which sells a plethora of different bag types handmade by 90 Mayan women from eight nearby villages.

Where to Stay

Located on a bend in the Moho River, about a 20-minute drive outside P.G., the **Cotton Tree Lodge** ★ (www.cottontreelodge.com; 𝄢 **212/529-8622** in the U.S. and Canada, or 670-0557 in Belize) offers almost a dozen large, individual wood and thatch bungalows.

EXPENSIVE

Copal Tree Lodge ★★★   Formerly called Machaca, then Belcampo, the new and improved Copal Tree Lodge is set in the midst of a pristine 12,000-acre nature reserve and offers stellar personalized service, high design cabins, excellent cuisine, and a raft of adventures. It is the most luxurious option in the Toledo area and one of the top hotels in the country. Guests often spend their entire stay just exploring the grounds here, which allows for scintillating birding, visits to the Lodge's organic farm, cacao groves, a sugar cane plantation, and its chocolate- and rum-making facilities, and challenging fishing. Fly-fishing for world-class permit is the principal game, although tarpon, bonefish, and snook can also be tackled. A tramway connects the lodge to the river below, where there's a lovely dock and bar area. The 16 large individual bungalows, jungle suites, and family villa are set on a high hillside of rich forest above the Río Grande. Each features a huge shower made of smooth river stone, and has two showerheads (some rooms also have a bathtub on the porch for jungle bathing). Screened-in porches for enjoying the views without bugs are another welcome feature, as are the high-ceilinged rooms, sleek contemporary décor, and tremendously plush beds. The kidney-shaped pool has a broad and inviting stone deck area around it, and it's also set on one of the highest points on the property, giving it excellent views all around. A renowned chef comes in for a week per month from California to set the menus, based on what's freshest at the on-site organic farm (the food is superb).

Punta Gorda. www.copaltreelodge.com. 𝄢 **722-0050,** or 844/238-0216 from the U.S. 16 units. From BZ$600 double. Rates include breakfast, afternoon tea, on-site activities, and all taxes. Fishing and all-inclusive package rates are also available. **Amenities:** Restaurant; bar; lounge; concierge; outdoor pool; small luxurious spa; Wi-Fi (free).

The Lodge at Big Falls ★★   Another extremely special place, this handsome nature lodge caters to ecotourists and those looking to explore the nearby Mayan ruins and villages. It's set on the banks of the Río Grande, just outside the village of Big Falls, and its gardens are verdant and well maintained. Six thatch cabanas and two hardwood ones all overlook the river and feature high thatched ceilings, large windows providing plenty of cross-ventilation, and cool rustic tile floors. The thatch cabanas come with a large covered veranda equipped with a hammock for lazing away and watching the river flow. Named after birds, my favorite cabins are Trogon, Aracari, and Tiger Heron, the closest ones to the river. Although there's electricity here, at night the light is provided by kerosene lanterns. There's a good-size outdoor pool on the broad lawn outside the main lodge, and a host of tour options is available, including lazy inner tube floats on the river right here. While the food at the on-site restaurant is a bit pricey, it is tasty and quite hearty, so you can save a bit by skipping appetizers.

Near the village of Big Falls, 29km (18 miles) north of Punta Gorda. www.thelodgeat bigfalls.com. ✆ **732-4444,** or 610-0126. 9 units. BZ$320–BZ$440 double. **Amenities:** Restaurant; bar; kayak and mountain bike rentals; outdoor pool; Wi-Fi (free, in main areas).

MODERATE

In addition to the places listed below, **Beya Suites** (www.beyasuites.com; ✆ 722-2956) is a small hotel with well-equipped, tidy rooms; an on-site restaurant; and a rooftop patio, located just across from the bay, just north of town.

Blue Belize Guesthouse ★★   Located on a peaceful seafront street, the Blue Belize Guesthouse is wonderfully convenient and within walking distance of Punta Gorda's restaurants and bars. Rooms are found in two neighboring houses connected by an elevated wooden walkway and stairs. All are cheery, immaculately kept, with contemporary decor and lots of natural light. My favorites are those on the second floor of the newer building. These share a huge wraparound veranda. Staff here run an excellent tour operation, and Dan Castellanos, one of the owners, is considered one of the area's top fishing guides. An excellent breakfast is included in the nightly rate.

139 Front St. www.bluebelize.com. ✆ **722-2678.** 6 units. BZ$170–BZ$340 double. Rates include continental breakfast. **Amenities:** Kitchenette; Wi-Fi (free).

Coral House Inn ★★   This homey bed-and-breakfast is my favorite option right in P.G. The rooms are simple but pleasant affairs, with firm beds, and orchid colored walls and bedspreads. They're all on the second floor, with a large shared balcony overlooking the sea. There's a refreshing lap pool set at an angle off the main building, and an artsy open-air cement door leading to a lawn and gardens that run off to the sea. The gardens also provide innovative wastewater treatment. The owners are a cheerful and helpful couple, and they provide free bicycles for use during your stay and oversee an honor bar on-site. These folks also rent out a separate, private little cottage. The hotel borders the town cemetery, so consider yourself forewarned if that spooks you.

151 Main St. www.coralhouseinn.com. ✆ **722-2878.** 6 units plus 2 apartments. BZ$220–BZ$290 double. Rates include continental breakfast. **Amenities:** Bar; lounge; pool; free bike use; Wi-Fi (free).

Hickatee Cottages ★★★   This cozy retreat is my favorite moderately-priced lodging right outside of town. This small collection of rooms is set under tall trees among flowering gardens. It's located just a mile or so from downtown, but you'll feel a world apart nonetheless. All the rooms are quite spacious, with varnished wood floors, furniture made by Belizean

Mennonites, a separate sitting area, and a front veranda strung with a hammock. The suite comes with a flatscreen television and DVD player. There's no regular programming, but the hotel has a DVD lending library. A small creek runs through the property, and guests can hike trails through thick forest and brush from the cottages. The bird-watching is excellent, and you're very likely to see, or at least hear, howler monkeys. If the heat of the day gets to you, there's a small but refreshing plunge pool.

Ex-Serviceman Rd. www.hickatee.com. © **662-4475.** 6 units. BZ$190–BZ$290 double. Rates include continental breakfast and round-trip transfer to P.G. airport or bus station. **Amenities:** Restaurant; bar; small plunge pool; Wi-Fi (free, in common areas).

INEXPENSIVE

Punta Gorda has a host of budget lodgings. In addition to the place listed below, you could check out **Charlton's Inn,** 9 Main St. (www.charltonsinn.com; © **722-2197**), or **Tate's Guesthouse,** 34 José María Núñez St. (© **722-0147**).

And, for an ecolodge experience at rather budget prices, check out **Sun Creek Lodge** (© **604-2124**), a delightful collection of individual cabins, at Mile 14 on the Southern Highway.

Nature's Way Guest House ★ Located 3 blocks south of the central park and across the street from the water, Nature's Way is a longtime favorite of budget travelers. There's a variety of room, bathroom, and bed configurations, from bunk beds to a mix of twins and matrimonials. Still, everything is quite basic and rustic. Even though most rooms do not have private bathrooms, everything is kept tidy, and the shared bathrooms are large and clean. A plentiful breakfast is served, and the hotel is close to downtown and other dining options for other meals. The guesthouse is operated by an American named William "Chet" Schmidt, who moved down here some 40 years ago to promote sustainable agricultural and tourism practices.

65 Front St., Punta Gorda. © **702-2119.** 6 units (1 with private bathroom). BZ$30–BZ$60 double. No credit cards. **Amenities:** Wi-fi (free, in public areas).

Where to Dine

Dining options are far from extensive in Punta Gorda. In addition to the restaurants listed below, check out **Grace's Restaurant,** at the corner of Main and King streets (© **702-2414**), for good local fare.

Out a little bit north of town, just across from and facing the bay, **Waluco's Restaurant** (© **702-2119**) is a good place for fish, pasta, or rotisserie chicken. The open-air restaurant has a great view and a friendly, casual vibe. And even a bit beyond Waluco's, you'll find the **Mangrove Inn ★** (© **623-0497**), which serves a limited nightly menu in an intimate setting with personalized service.

Asha's Culture Kitchen ★★ SEAFOOD Come for the sustainably caught seafood, stay for live music, or the exceptional view from the restaurant's vantage point fully out over the water. Chef Ashton Martin, who is not a knock-off British sports car but an eco-friendly purveyor of Creole recipes, changes the menu daily. Depending on when you visit you might sample fried conch, a snapper filet, or one of their refreshing fruit shakes. Keen eyes may spot dolphins, manatees, and even seahorses, from the outdoor deck.

74 Front St. ℭ **722-2742.** Main courses BZ$15–BZ$33. No credit cards. Wed–Mon noon–9pm.

Emery's ★ BELIZEAN   This is a good bet for straightforward, fresh, local cuisine. I prefer the tables in a large, open-air, thatch-roof structure off the small wooden building that has the kitchen, bar, and small screened-in dining area. This large dining area has half-walls of bamboo and a series of floor fans cooling things off. There's a chalkboard menu with the standard fare and daily specials. Offerings range from stew chicken and pork to whole fried snapper and snook filets. Everything is well-prepared, and the prices are right.

North St. ℭ **702-2929.** Main courses BZ$8–BZ$30. No credit cards. Daily 8am–10pm.

Gomier's Foods ★★ BELIZEAN/VEGETARIAN   Attention vegan and vegetarian travelers: You won't be relegated to side dishes here. Owner Gomier not only makes a slew of plant-based dishes, many of them are created from his backyard garden. That includes the tofu that Gomier makes from his homegrown soybeans from scratch. It comes stir-fried in a scrumptious coconut curry. The vegetarian lasagna is also highly recommended. There are also fish dishes, other vegetarian entrees, and wine and beer on the menu, but no meat. Gromier's is a colorful, casual spot that's predominantly a one-man show, so the hours listed below are somewhat optimistic. Be sure to check first whether this place is open before heading over.

At the corner of Vernon and Front sts. ℭ **722-2990.** Main courses BZ$8–BZ$20. No credit cards. Tues–Sat 8am–2pm and 6–9pm.

Marian's Bayview ★ INDIAN/BELIZEAN   For years, Marian made a name for herself selling authentic East Indian food out of a simple stall at the small market in downtown Punta Gorda. She's got her own digs now, and you can sit at a table and enjoy your meal. Granted, the tables are rather rickety, the chairs are plastic, and the third-floor dining area has an unfinished feel to it, with bare cement on the floors and some of the walls. Still, the food is delicious. Every day, Marian makes a limited menu that usually includes a mix of Indian and Belizean fare, and a mix of seafood and meat options.

At the corner of Vernon and Front sts. ℭ **722-0129.** Main courses BZ$8–BZ$18. Mon–Wed and Fri–Sat 11am–2pm and 6–10pm; Thu 11am–2pm; Sun noon–2pm and 6–10pm.

The Snack Shack ★★ INTERNATIONAL   Breakfast, a light lunch, a cool drink on a hot day? This little open-air spot works for all of that. Heavy wooden tables are spread around a wooden deck surrounded by heliconia and red ginger flowers, and large tree-trunk columns support the corrugated tin roof. Fans keep the enterprise relatively cool. In addition to burritos, which are their specialty, you can get a range of fresh-baked goodies. For lunch there is a selection of filling salads, as well as burgers, chicken sandwiches, tuna melts, and BLTs. But what keeps people coming back is the chatty, warm welcome here. You'll feel like a local in no time.

On Main St., between King and Queen sts. © **620-3499.** Main courses BZ$5–BZ$15. Mon–Fri 7am–3pm; Sat 7am–noon.

Punta Gorda After Dark

Overall, Punta Gorda's a pretty quiet town. The most dependable spot for any action is the **PG Sports Bar** (© **722-2329**), which only very occasionally has sporting events on the tube. Instead, this is really an all-purpose nightspot with occasional live bands, DJs, and karaoke nights. It's located on Main Street at the southern edge of the little central park. The view from **Asha's Culture Kitchen** (see above) looking out towards Guatemala can't be beat, and live music and DJ nights are regularly on the docket. Finally, you can try heading out north of town to **Waluco's** (see above), where there are occasionally live music jam sessions, a local Punta Rock band, or a Garífuna drumming outfit.

NORTHERN BELIZE

With few exceptions, Northern Belize is overlooked by most tourists who fly into the country and head quickly to the cayes, the Cayo District, the southern beaches, or the Mayan Mountains. Even those who enter by land from Mexico frequently make a beeline to Belize City and bypass this region. Still, northern Belize has its charms, not least of which is its undiscovered and undeveloped feel. It's here that you'll find some of the country's larger biological reserves, including the **Crooked Tree Wildlife Sanctuary,** the **Shipstern Nature Reserve,** and the **Río Bravo Conservation Area.** With more than 430 species of birds and 250 species of orchids, this region should be especially attractive to naturalists.

The region was also an important and strategic part of the Mayan Empire, and ancient ruins abound. Most notably, it is here that you will find the **Altun Ha** and **Lamanai** ruins, two of the country's most popular and important Mayan sites. Lesser sites such as **Cuello, Cerros, Santa Rita,** and **Noh Mul** are also possible stops for true aficionados. Finally, northern Belize is home to three unique and isolated lodges: **Belize Boutique Resort and Spa, Chan Chich Lodge,** and **Lamanai Outpost Lodge,** all of which are described in detail in this chapter.

For our purposes, "Northern Belize" refers to the northern section of the Belize District, as well as the entire Orange Walk and Corozal districts, a roughly 7,250 sq. km area (2,800 sq. miles). The land here is largely low-lying savanna, with massive sugar cane, citrus, soybean, and pineapple plantations set amid large swaths of forests, swamps, lagoons, and slow, steamy jungle rivers that wind their way to a mangrove-lined coast. There are also many marijuana farms hidden among the more traditional agriculture, so it's advised to stay on well-traveled roads. Belize's Philip Goldson Highway, known as the Northern Highway until 2012 and still often referred to as such, runs from Belize City to the Mexican border, a little more than 156km (95 miles) away. The road is paved, although rough in certain patches, with little scenery worth mentioning. Small villages and stores pop up every so often, but there are only

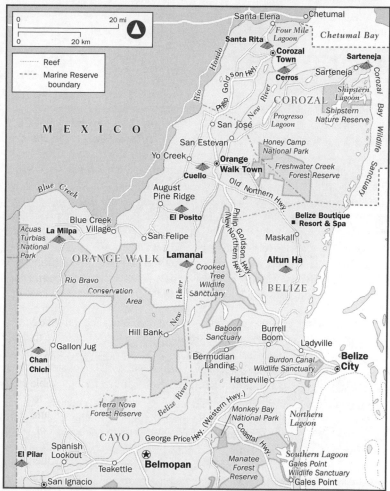

two cities of any note along the way: **Orange Walk Town** and **Corozal Town.** Of these, only sleepy Corozal, with its seaside setting and proximity to the Mexican border and Shipstern Wildlife Reserve, is a destination with much appeal to travelers. Orange Walk, for its part, serves mainly as a gateway to the Lamanai ruins and the Río Bravo Conservation Area. Locals may refer to it as "Sugar City" in reference to the thriving sugar industry in the area.

Much of this area was originally settled by immigrants fleeing southern Mexico's Yucatán peninsula during the Caste Wars of the mid–19th century, making Spanish a common first language and Mexican traditions more prevalent here than anywhere else in Belize. However, it is also the region with the largest concentration of Mennonite communities. Members of this somewhat radical Christian order have thrived in this farming area. You can't miss the Mennonites in their distinctive, heavy, home-sewn garb and horse-drawn carriages.

ALONG THE OLD NORTHERN HIGHWAY

The Philip Goldson Highway, formerly named the Northern Highway, but still often called that, runs from Belize City to the Mexican border town of Chetumal. It's a newer paved road, so don't get it confused with the Old Northern Highway, which was, as the name suggests, the original road north, and is so full of potholes and gravel that it was easier to build a new one. A section of the Old Northern Highway still exists as an offshoot of the Philip Goldson Highway so people can get to one major attraction and one unique resort, which are accessible only by taking this route. Aside from these two places, there's not much else along this highway, save for a few tiny communities and the occasional roadside restaurant or bar. To get here, take Freetown Road out of Belize City to connect with the Philip Goldson Highway. The turnoff to the Old Northern Highway is to the right just past Sand Hill; watch for signs for Altun Ha and Belize Boutique Resort and Spa.

Altun Ha ★

Altun Ha is a small, well-preserved Mayan ruin. Only a few of the most imposing temples, tombs, and pyramids have been uncovered and rebuilt; hundreds more lie under the jungle foliage. You'll be able to see the two large central plazas surrounded by midsize pyramids and mounds, as well as the beginnings of the excavation of residential areas. While nowhere near as extensive as some other sites, Altun Ha offers admirable quality and detail of excavation and restoration, allowing for great visibility into what the site would've looked like in its prime. Sections of different structures have been left in various states of repair and restoration, giving visitors a sense of the process involved. Moreover, while the climb to the top of the tallest pyramids here is rather easy by Mayan standards, the views are still wonderful. The site was named after the village in which it's situated—Rockstone Pond, the literal Mayan translation meaning "stone water." At the back of the site, behind Plaza B, is the namesake pond. Archaeologists theorize that the pond is an example of a pre-Columbian waterworks project and a demonstration of the ingenuity of Mayan engineering.

Despite its somewhat diminutive size, Altun Ha was a major trade and ceremonial center. In its prime, during the Classic Period, Altun Ha supported a population of about 10,000. Many jade, pearl, and obsidian artifacts have been discovered here, including the unique jade-head sculpture of **Kinich Ahau** (the Mayan sun god), the largest well-carved jade from the Mayan era. Today, it's kept in a bank vault in Belmopan, out of public view, although you can see

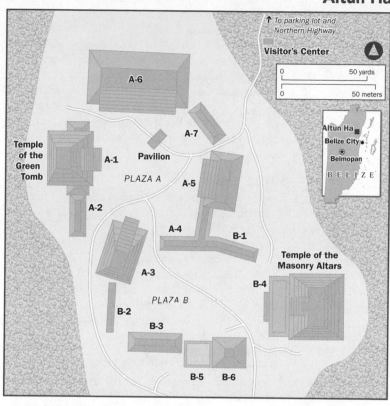

To parking lot and
Northern Highway

Visitor's Center

0 — 50 yards
0 — 50 meters

A-6

A-7

Temple
of the
Green
Tomb

A-1   Pavilion

PLAZA A

A-5

A-2

A-4

B-1

A-3

Temple of the
Masonry Altars

B-4

PLAZA B

B-2

B-3

B-5   B-6

Altun Ha
Belize City
Belmopan
BELIZE

a replica at the onsite museum, which is near the pond (the jade is also pictured on most of the country's paper money). Some of the pieces found here show a direct link to the great Mexican city of Teotihuacán.

The largest (though not the tallest) temple here is the **Temple of the Masonry Altars,** which fronts Plaza B. It has been well-restored, and the pathway to the top is well-maintained and even features handrails. However, if you're fairly fit and not acrophobic, I recommend you climb the almost entirely unrestored **Temple A-6,** which is truly the tallest building at Altun Ha. A climb to the top of Temple A-6 affords an excellent panorama of the entire site. Be careful climbing down; the Mayans were a society run by priests and holy men, not lawyers. A more litigious society would have never permitted the construction of such steep and treacherous stairways.

The site is open daily from 8am to 5pm. Admission is BZ$10 for adults. The ticket booth is past all the vendors, if you want to make a beeline. There is no public transportation to Altun Ha, so you'll need to take a tour, a taxi, your own wheels, or hitchhike. If you're driving, Altun Ha is located about

48km (30 miles) north of Belize City on the Philip Goldson Highway. Once you're on the Old Northern Highway, it's 18km (11 miles) to the Altun Ha road. From the highway, it's another bumpy 3.6km (2¼ miles) to the ruins, which are well-marked on the left side of the road.

Half-day tours to Altun Ha from Belize City cost between BZ$80 and BZ$200. Full-day tours can be combined with visits to Crooked Tree Wildlife Sanctuary (see "En Route North: Crooked Tree Wildlife Sanctuary," below) or the Community Baboon Sanctuary (see "What to See & Do" in chapter 6), and should run between BZ$200 and BZ$350. Many of the tours include lunch and an optional spa treatment at Belize Boutique Resort and Spa. Note that Altun Ha is a popular stop for cruise ship guests, who typically visit mid-week and can crowd the ruin while there.

An Isolated Jungle Spa

Belize Boutique Resort and Spa ★★   Decadent, sensual, and exotic are words often used to describe this boutique resort, and for good reason. The whole place is an imaginative jungle fantasy where health and happiness are the primary goals. (The name was very recently changed from Maruba Resort and Spa, so you may hear people refer to it by that name.)

The accommodations are a collection of uniquely designed and decorated rooms and private villas, set in a patch of densely planted gardens and forest, where kinkajous and frogs can be heard at night. Artistic touches abound, many seen in the eclectic mix of pieces and building techniques from Africa, Asia, the Caribbean, the Middle East, and, of course, Belize. This is also the only place in Belize where you'll spot a Tesla, which belongs to the owner. If you want a full-on luxe experience, choose one of the bungalows. The standard rooms and suites are certainly up to snuff, but it's hard to beat the in-room Jacuzzis that the bungalows have.

There are two outdoor pools here, as well as a separate hot mineral pool. The spa facilities and services are relaxing and expertly done. The Mood Mud Massage is their signature offering, and I highly recommend it—don't forget to have your picture taken at the end. The food at the restaurant here is scrumptious, featuring a creative mix of international and fusion cuisine.

Belize Boutique Resort is popular with day-trippers from the cayes and Belize City, as well as cruise-ship passengers, so sudden crowds are not unusual here. Luckily, one of the pools is reserved for hotel guests, and once the day tours clear out, you'll have the place to yourself. In addition to the spa treatments, a host of tours, activities, and adventures are offered. If you're in the mood for some serious imbibing, don't miss a taste of their home-brewed Viper Rum and Scorpion Stinger.

Old Northern Hwy., Mile Marker 40½, Maskall Village. www.belizeresortandspa.com. ⓒ **800/627-8227** in the U.S., or 225-5555 in Belize. 17 units. BZ$460 double; BZ$540 junior suite; BZ$850 suite or bungalow. **Amenities:** Restaurant; bar; lounge; 2 outdoor pools; spa; anti-mosquito coils in rooms; Wi-Fi (free, at the mineral pool).

EN ROUTE NORTH: CROOKED TREE WILDLIFE SANCTUARY ★

53km (33 miles) NW of Belize City

Crooked Tree Wildlife Sanctuary is a swampy lowland that is home to more than 260 resident species of birds and serves as a resting spot for scores of migratory species. During a visit here, you are sure to spot any number of water birds, including kites, hawks, ducks, grebes, pelicans, ospreys, egrets, and herons. However, the preserve was established primarily to protect Belize's main nesting site of the endangered jabiru stork, the largest bird in the Western Hemisphere. The jabirus arrive every November and pass the winter in these warm lowland climes. The jabiru is an impressive bird, standing nearly 1.5m (5 ft.) tall, with a wingspan that can reach up to 3.7m (12 ft.).

Crooked Tree has also become known as an excellent place to spot other endangered wildlife. Crocodiles, iguanas, coati-mundi, and howler monkeys are all frequently sighted, as well as the endangered Hicatee turtle. There are six major lagoons here connected by a series of creeks, rivers, and wetlands, essentially making the sanctuary an island.

The small Creole village of Crooked Tree is the gateway to this wildlife sanctuary. The village is reputed to be some 300 years old, which makes it one of the oldest ongoing settlements in Belize. If you poke around, in addition to the sanctuary's visitor center, you'll find the church, the school, the soccer field, a noticeably British cricket pitch, a few general stores, and a couple of simple guest houses.

The best way to explore the preserve is by dugout canoe, though boardwalk hiking is available, too. Head to the green visitor center at the end of the causeway to pay the BZ$8 admission fee and to hire a guide who will paddle you around in a dugout for a few hours, or rent a canoe on your own. You can also rent a canoe from the Bird's Eye View Lodge for BZ$30 for the day. The going rate for a guide is around BZ$20 to BZ$30, but the price goes up when you add in a canoe or a horseback ride. The Crooked Tree Wildlife Sanctuary was set up and is still administered by the **Belize Audubon Society** (www.belizeaudubon.org; ✆ **223-5004**). The sanctuary accepts visitors all day, but birds are best sought in the early morning, and serious birders should plan to visit during the dry season when birds are grouping around the smaller water sources.

> ## Going Nuts
>
> Crooked Tree is also home to a thriving cashew industry. Each year during the first weekend of May, Crooked Tree village hosts its annual Cashew Festival, where you can sample raw and roasted nuts and taste some cashew wine, cashew jelly, and a whole plethora of dishes cooked around or including the local nut.

If you'd like to spend the night, a simple bed can be found for BZ$80 to BZ$100 a night at **Tillett's Village Lodge** (www.tillettvillage.com; ✆ **671-7100**), a legacy of Sam Tillett, one of the country's great naturalists. For a more comfortable lodge right on the edge of a lagoon, check out the **Bird's Eye View Lodge** ★ (www.birdseyeviewbelize.com; © **225-7027**), where a double costs between BZ$200 and BZ$300 during the high season.

Crooked Tree is located 53km (33 miles) northwest of Belize City. If you are driving, head up the Philip Goldson Highway and watch for the turnoff to Crooked Tree. From the turnoff, it's another 4.8km (3 miles) on a well-graded dirt road.

Jex & Sons (© **225-7017**) direct buses leave for Crooked Tree Village Monday through Saturday from a bus terminal on Regent Street West and West Canal Street in Belize City at 10:50am and from a terminal at the Save-U Plaza at the corner of the highway and Central American Boulevard at 5:15pm. The bus to Belize City leaves Crooked Tree at 6:30am. The fare is BZ$7 each way. Alternatively, you can take any bus heading to Orange Walk Town, Corozal, or the northern border and ask to be dropped off at Crooked Tree Junction. From here you'll have to walk, hitchhike, or get really lucky and find a cab patrolling around (drivers are unlikely to come pick you up out here). If you're staying at a hotel in the village, they will usually pick you up.

Half-day tours to Crooked Tree from Belize City or the northern cayes cost between BZ$100 and BZ$200. A full-day trip combining Crooked Tree and Altun Ha, including transportation, guide, and lunch, should cost between BZ$200 and BZ$310.

ORANGE WALK TOWN

89km (55 miles) N of Belize City; 50km (31 miles) S of Corozal

Between Belize City and Corozal Town, the only settlement of any size is Orange Walk Town, a bustling agricultural and business community with a population of some 18,000. This is the heart of Belize's sugar cane industry, and some locals still call the town "Sugar City." Originally called Holpatin by the ancient Maya, the town's riverside location has ensured its status as a trade center for more than 2,000 years. The town's current name comes from the many citrus groves once planted alongside the New River here. Orange Walk Town's residents are a very heterogeneous mix of mestizos, Mayans, Chinese, and Black Creoles. There's not too much of interest to travelers in the town, but this is the gateway to several of the surrounding attractions of note, including the Lamanai ruins and the Río Bravo Conservation Area to the west.

> **What's in a Name?**
>
> "Orange walk" is the Creole term for "orange orchard" or "orange grove," just as "sugar walk" would be the Creole version of "sugar plantation."

Essentials

GETTING THERE & DEPARTING

BY PLANE   Just southwest of Orange Walk town is the asphalt Tower Hill airstrip which has two daily flights between the municipal airport in Belize

Orange Walk Town

ACCOMMODATIONS ■

D*Victoria Hotel **6**
Hotel De La Fuente **3**
Mestizo Riverside Cabins **7**
St. Christopher's Hotel **2**

DINING ◆

Nahil Mayab Restaurant **5**
Cocina Sabor **8**

ATTRACTIONS ●

Banquitas House
of Culture **1**
La Inmaculada Church **4**

City for BZ$288. Some days there are also flights between Orange Walk and San Pedro/Caye Caulker starting at BZ$70.

BY CAR   Orange Walk is on the Philip Goldson Highway about 89km (55 miles) from Belize City. Take Freetown Road out of Belize City to connect with the Philip Goldson Highway. The highway is also known in this area as the Belize-Corozal Road, and Queen Victoria Avenue right in the heart of town. After passing through the small downtown section of Orange Walk Town, the highway continues north to Corozal.

There's a tollbooth where the Philip Goldson Highway crosses the New River a few miles south of Orange Walk Town. The fee is BZ$1 per car.

BY BUS   Buses (© **227-2255** in Belize City, or 302-2858 in Orange Walk Town) leave throughout the day, roughly every half-hour between 5:30am and 7:30pm. Morning buses leave from the main bus terminal on West Collet Canal Street. Catch any bus going to Corozal Town or Chetumal. The Orange Walk Town bus station is right on the Philip Goldson Highway in the center of town near Town Hall. You can pick up a return bus here to Belize City, or continue onward to Corozal. The best place to catch the bus to Sarteneja is from the bus stop outside the Banquitas House of Culture on Main Street; it costs BZ$10. Buses can be either direct or local, and they vary in age and comfort. You'll pay more for a comfortable direct or express bus. The fare is BZ$5 to BZ$8 between Belize City and Orange Walk Town, and BZ$6 to BZ$10 between Orange Walk Town and Corozal Town.

GETTING AROUND
Orange Walk is pretty compact, and the city center is just a few blocks wide in either direction. Still, a few taxis can be had around town. If you can't flag one down, call ℂ **322-2050,** or head to the little park across from Town Hall.

ORIENTATION
The Philip Goldson Highway runs right through the heart of Orange Walk Town. However, there is also a bypass that skirts the city proper, for those in a rush to get to Corozal or Sarteneja. Several gas stations are located on the outskirts of either end of town. As you're traveling north, the New River and "downtown" district will be to your right, while the Town Hall and Sports Ground are on the highway, on your left.

mennonites IN BELIZE

Mennonites are a Protestant branch of the 16th-century Anabaptist movement, which also gave birth to the Amish and Hutterites. Believing that the New Testament is the sole word of God and that children should not be baptized, the Mennonites also believe that true Christians should not hold political or public office or serve in the military. Modern Mennonites are somewhat split as to the use of electricity and the internal combustion engine.

Mennonites get their name from Menno Simons, a Dutch Catholic priest who converted to Anabaptism and went on to lead the budding movement. From the start, the Anabaptists were severely persecuted and repeatedly forced into exile. Mennonites first migrated to Belize from Mexico in 1958. While the initial wave of immigrants was small, the Mennonites quickly settled in, buying large tracts of land and establishing very successful dairy farming and agricultural enterprises. The early Mennonite settlers were successful in negotiating certain strategic concessions and guarantees from the government, including that of

religious freedom and exemption from military service and some forms of taxation. This has enabled the Mennonite community to be politically influential without getting involved in governance firsthand.

While there are Mennonites throughout Belize, the Orange Walk District and northern Belize have one of the highest concentrations in the country, with large communities in Shipyard, Blue Creek Village, Little Belize, and Spanish Lookout. There is variation between the communities, where some are more progressive and others are more conservative, but even so most Mennonites collectively speak an archaic form of German. They are easily recognized, with their fair skin and blond hair, especially when they're traveling in their low-riding, horse-drawn carriages. The women often wear puffy cloth bonnets and simple cotton dresses, while the men sport broad-rimmed straw hats, dark jeans, and distinctive full beards with no mustache. It is considered rude to photograph them without first asking permission.

FAST FACTS If you need to call the **police**, dial ✆ **911** or 322-2022; for the **fire department**, dial ✆ **322-2090**; and for medical emergencies, call the **Northern Regional Hospital** at ✆ **322-2072**.

There's a **Belize Bank** (✆ **322-2019**) at the corner of Main and Market streets, and a **Scotiabank** (✆ **322-0866**) down the block on the corner of Main Street and Park Street. The **post office** (✆ **322-2345**) is located on the highway and Arthur Street, across from the Town Council.

Seeing the Sights

If you're staying in Orange Walk Town, you might want to visit the **Banquitas House of Culture,** at Main Street and Banquitas Plaza (✆ **322-0517**), which is set just off the river on some expansive and manicured grounds. The House of Culture itself features a small collection of artifacts and historic displays from the Mayan, logging, and colonial eras. There's also a small amphitheater here that very occasionally may have live music, theater, or dance. In the center of town, you'll find **La Inmaculada Church** (✆ **322-2043**), one of the few colonial Spanish churches in the country.

Two of the most popular tours out of Orange Walk Town are to **Crooked Tree Wildlife Sanctuary** (see "En Route North: Crooked Tree Wildlife Sanctuary," earlier in this chapter) and the **Lamanai ruins** (see "The Submerged Crocodile: Lamanai," below).

Fun Fact
The original Mayan name for the New River, Dzuilhuinicob, translates roughly as "River of Strange People."

If you're looking for some nearby outdoor adventure and a refreshing dip, head to **Honey Camp Lagoon,** which features an unlikely sandy beach ringed by palm trees next to a spring-fed freshwater swimming hole. Honey Camp Lagoon is located about a 20-minute drive south from Orange Walk Town, via the Old Northern Highway, and there are signs indicating how to get there.

If your hotel can't hook you up and you want a local guide for any of the aforementioned tours or trips to any of the nearby ruins or up to Lamanai (see below), call **J. Avila & Sons River Tours,** 42 Riverside St. (✆ **322-3068**), or **Jungle River Tours ★**, 20 Lovers Lane (✆ **302-2293**), which is run by the very personable and knowledgeable Wilfrido Novelo.

A COUPLE OF MINOR MAYAN SITES NEARBY

CUELLO This small site is located just more than 4.8km (3 miles) from Orange Walk Town, near the **Cuello Rum Distillery** where everyone's favorite, Caribbean Rum, is made. It is named after the family that owns the land and distillery, and permission to visit the site must be obtained in advance. While very small and little excavated, Cuello is nonetheless one of the oldest-known Mayan sites in Belize, showing evidence of occupation as far back as 2600 B.C., in the early Pre-Classic Period.

There are two main plazas on the site, surrounded by small temples and ceremonial structures. Very little has been excavated and restored so far.

Evidence exists that this minor ceremonial city was razed on more than one occasion during distinct warring periods.

You can obtain permission to visit Cuello by stopping at the rum distillery at the entrance to the site, or by calling in advance (© **322-2183**). If you ask, you will probably be able to get a quick tour of the distillery as well. You might also be able to arrange for a guided tour by asking around Orange Walk Town. To get here, take the San Antonio Road out of Orange Walk Town toward Yo Creek.

NOH MUL   Noh Mul means "great mound," and this site boasts the largest Mayan structure in the Orange Walk District. Noh Mul was active in two distinct periods, the late Pre-Classic era from around 350 B.C. to A.D. 250, and during the late Classic era from A.D. 600 to 900. At the time, it was a major ceremonial center and supported a massive residential community that extended for nearly 21 sq. km (8 sq. miles). One of the more interesting features here is the fact that the two major ceremonial plazas are connected by a raised walkway, or *sacbe*. Crude excavation techniques, pillaging, and local agriculture have combined to limit the amount of restoration and conservation in evidence at Noh Mul.

Noh Mul is located about 1.6km (1 mile) west of the small village of San Pablo, which itself is about 14km (8⅔ miles) north of Orange Walk Town. Any nonexpress bus running the northern line to Corozal and Chetumal can drop you off at San Pablo. However, your best bet for visiting Noh Mul is to try to arrange a tour in advance in Orange Walk Town or Belize City. You should have permission to visit Noh Mul; to get permission in San Pablo, check in with **Estevan Itzab** (no phone), whose house is located across from the water tower in the heart of the village. There are no facilities on-site, so bring some food and water with you.

Where to Stay & Dine

There are few good dining options in Orange Walk Town. Your best bet is **Nahil Mayab Restaurant ★** (www.nahilmayab.com; © **322-0831**), on the corner of Santa Ana and Guadalupe streets behind the Shell station, a surprisingly upscale all-purpose restaurant and bar serving a range of Latin American dishes and Caribbean classics. The best seats here are located in a pretty garden patio, though the air-conditioning keeps the main dining area cool on hot days. The restaurant is closed for dinner on Monday, and for the entirety of Sunday. Another good option is **Cocina Sabor** (© **322-3482**), a mostly-locals restaurant that serves up solid Belizean cuisine and fanciful cocktails that get the party going on weekend nights. It's in southern Orange Walk near L&R Liquor, on the highway.

INEXPENSIVE

D*Victoria Hotel ★   For years, this was the hotel of choice in Orange Walk Town, but I much prefer the two newer options: Hotel De La Fuente (see below) and St. Christopher's Hotel (also see below). You'll still find spacious, clean rooms here and a swimming pool, but the decor is definitely dated, and the hotel sits right on the side of a dreary section of the Northern Highway. Every room features air-conditioning and a fan; a price bump gets you an in-room fridge. The restaurant serves decent Belizean and Chinese food at reasonable prices. Between the raucous bar here on weekends and the everyday street noise, this is not exactly a quiet spot.

40 Belize-Corozal Rd. www.dvictoriabelize.com. © **322-2518.** 31 units. BZ$70–BZ$150 double. Rates include taxes. **Amenities:** Restaurant; bar; small outdoor pool; room service; Wi-Fi (free, in lobby).

Hotel De La Fuente ★★   This is easily the best hotel option in Orange Walk Town. Located just north of the St. Christopher, Hotel De La Fuente offers more amenities, and a soupçon more style, than any other hotel in town. Even the budget rooms here feature televisions, air-conditioning, free Wi-Fi, minifridges, and in-room coffeemakers. The pricier rooms are larger and come with a kitchenette. All are painted a fresh white, and have clean white tile floors, and dignified dark wood four poster beds. For a more immersive experience in nature, consider the owners' new **El Gran Mestizo Riverside Cabins** (www.elgranmestizo.bz, © **322-2290**) which has 18 rooms starting at BZ$160 and overlooks the river.

14 Main St. www.hoteldelafuente.bz. © **322-2290.** 22 units. BZ$80–BZ$170 double. **Amenities:** Smoke-free; bicycles available; Wi-Fi (free).

St. Christopher's Hotel ★   Named after the patron saint of world wanderers, this is a dependable option in Orange Walk Town. The rooms and bathrooms are roomy, clean, and comfortable, and the hotel is on a quiet street, just up from the New River. Most of the accommodations here have air-conditioning, although a few less expensive rooms come with just fans.

10 Main St. www.stchristophershotelbze.com. © **302-1064,** or 322-2420. 23 units. BZ$80–BZ$140 double; Wi-Fi (free).

THE SUBMERGED CROCODILE: LAMANAI ★★

Lamanai is one of the more interesting and picturesque Maya ruins to visit in Belize. Set on the edge of the New River Lagoon, it is one of the largest Maya sites in Belize and features three large pyramids, a couple of residential areas, restored steles, and open plazas, as well as a small and unique ball court that featured a large round stone set flush in its center. In addition, nearby are the ruins of two churches built by the Spanish during the 16th century; just off these ruins are the rusting remains of an abandoned sugar mill, which was set up and settled by U.S. Confederate soldiers who chose exile after the Civil War.

Lamanai was occupied continuously from around 1500 B.C. until the Spanish arrived in the 16th century, and it supported non-Maya populations into the 19th century. Because it was still occupied by the Maya when the Spanish arrived, Lamanai is one of the few sites to retain its traditional name. Lamanai translates as "submerged crocodile" in Mayan; one of the principal rulers here was Lord Smoking Shell, who claimed he was the descendant of the spirit of a crocodile. Numerous crocodile images have been found in the steles, carvings, and pottery here. And there are still plenty of live crocs in the lagoon.

Lamanai was an important and powerful Pre-Classic trading city. As at Altun Ha, relics here can be traced to various cities throughout the early Mayan, Aztec, and Olmec worlds. It's a steep and scary climb to the top of the **High Temple,** but the view over the treetops and the lagoon is well worth it. The site's most striking feature just may be the **Mask Temple,** which features a series of 3.7m-high (12-ft.) stone-and-mortar faces set into its sides. One of these faces is well-restored and shows a distinct Olmec influence.

While many of the temples and ruins here have been cleared and restored to varying degrees, they are still surrounded by dense rainforest. The trails leading between temples offer excellent bird- and wildlife-watching opportunities.

There's a modern visitor center and museum here. The collection, though small, is quite interesting as it shows chronologically the distinct styles and influences present over the long history at Lamanai.

Lamanai is open daily from 8am to 5pm. Admission is BZ$10. Although you can drive or fly here, the most common and scenic way to reach Lamanai is via boat up the New River. A host of different boats leave from docks just south of Orange Walk. The trip on the river is an hour of naturalist heaven as you cruise between narrow and densely forested banks and alongside flooded marshes and wetlands. Eventually, the river opens onto the New River Lagoon, with the ancient Mayan city perched strategically atop some small limestone cliffs.

Most of the year it's possible to drive to Lamanai if you have a four-wheel-drive vehicle. During the heavy part of the rainy season, the road may become impassable. To drive here, take the Philip Goldson Highway into Orange Walk Town. Turn left near the center of town onto San Antonio Road. Follow signs to Yo Creek and San Felipe. There's an intersection at San Felipe; follow the signs to Indian Church and Lamanai. The total distance from Orange Walk Town is just about 48km (30 miles), but it will take you at least an hour to drive there on the rough dirt road. There's also a small airstrip in the neighboring village of Indian Church, and charter flights can be arranged through Lamanai Outpost Lodge.

Take Your Time

With the rise in cruise-ship traffic, many of the new operators run massive speedboats between Orange Walk and Lamanai. Not only are these noisier and more impersonal, but they also remove almost all the opportunity to enjoy the bird- and wildlife-viewing along the way. Be sure to try to book a smaller, slightly slower boat—you'll enjoy the trip much more.

While most folks either go on a guided tour or have a reservation at the Lamanai Outpost Lodge (see below), you can drive yourself to the boat docks, just south of the Toll Hill Bridge over the New River a few miles before Orange Walk, and pick up a boat there. Expect to pay around BZ$70 to BZ$80 per person for a boat to take you upriver to the ruins and back. The boats tend to leave for Lamanai between 8 and 10am, returning between 2 and 5pm. Many are booked in advance by large tour groups, although it's almost always possible

Lamanai

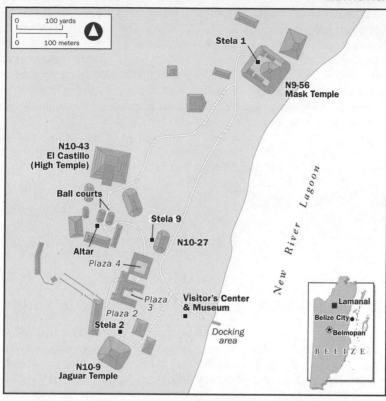

0 — 100 yards
0 — 100 meters

Stela 1

N9-56
Mask Temple

N10-43
El Castillo
(High Temple)

Ball courts

Stela 9

N10-27

Altar

Plaza 4

Plaza 3

Plaza 2

Stela 2

Visitor's Center
& Museum

Docking
area

New River Lagoon

N10-9
Jaguar Temple

Lamanai
Belize City
Belmopan
BELIZE

to find a few spaces available with a boat departing in short order. Parking is safe near the docks, and the boat companies will usually watch your car for free or a nominal fee. If you want to set up the trip in advance, I recommend you book with **Jungle River Tours** ★, 20 Lovers Lane (✆ **302-2293**).

A Neighboring Nature Lodge

Lamanai Outpost Lodge ★★ Transportation from the airport is included in many packages here, and it ends with an hour-long boat ride up the river, setting the stage for this nature-rich experience. Even before you get to the hotel, the touring begins, with an onboard guide pointing out critters on the river. Set on a gentle hillside on the banks of the New River, and surrounded by dense jungle, Lamanai Outpost feels extremely remote, but is in reality just about a mile from the Lamanai ruins, and many of the other area attractions you've come here to see (it's so close to the ruins, that many guests visit them several times, to see them in different lights of day). Rooms here are large and made of heavy local hardwoods, with high thatch roofs. Save for two cabanas with air-conditioning, a ceiling fan is all you have—and all you will need—to cool things off. All have a private or semiprivate balcony or veranda, most of which come with a hammock all ready for your afternoon siesta. While all the rooms are similar in comfort and design, you'll want to ask for a riverfront room to be able to catch the sunrise from your front porch. A wide range of tours and activities is available here, and the guides are excellent. Don't miss the airboat ride with George: It may be one of Belize's most adrenaline pumping adventures (and you get cocktails!). Also highly recommended are the nighttime owl spotting walks. Down by the river there's a swimming and sunbathing dock. There are also canoes here that guests can take out on the New River at any time.

Indian Church Village, on the New River. www.lamanai.com. © **954/636-1107** in the U.S., or 235-2441 in Belize. 17 units. BZ$556–BZ$1,000 double. Multiday and all-inclusive packages available. **Amenities:** Restaurant; bar; lounge; smoke-free; Wi-Fi (free).

GOING WEST

The far western section of Orange Walk District is a wild area of virgin forest, remote farmlands, and underexplored Mayan ruins. It is also home to one of the country's premier and most unique nature lodges, Chan Chich Lodge.

Río Bravo Conservation Area ★

Administered by the nonprofit **Programme for Belize,** this 105,218-hectare (260,000-acre) tract is a mix of virgin forest, sustainable-yield managed forest, and recovering reforestation areas. The goal of the project is to combine sustainable management techniques with educational and tourism uses in a model that can prove the practical benefits of forest preservation and conservation. The land is home to nearly 400 bird species and more than 200 species of tropical trees. It also supports a healthy population of most of the new-world cat species, and is one of the best areas in the Americas for spotting a jaguar—although these sightings are far from common or easy to come by.

LA MILPA ★

Located inside the Río Bravo Conservation Area, La Milpa is the third-largest Mayan site in Belize, behind Caracol and Lamanai. Enshrouded in jungle and just barely beginning to be excavated, La Milpa is a great site for budding archaeologists and those looking for a sense of what it must have been like to discover and begin uncovering an ancient Mayan city. Set on a high ridge, La Milpa was once a great ceremonial city. So far, at least one **Great Plaza,** numerous smaller plazas and courtyards, and two ball courts have been uncovered. The main plaza is one of the largest such public spaces yet discovered in the Mayan world. Polychrome pottery from various periods as well as numerous carved steles have been uncovered. In 1996, excavation of a royal tomb here revealed a male skeleton buried with an elaborate and beautiful jeweled necklace. Ongoing archaeological research is being led by Boston University, in conjunction with the National Geographic Society and Programme for Belize.

A visit to La Milpa ruins is usually combined with a stay at **La Milpa Field Station** (see below), although it is possible to do it as a day trip from Orange Walk or on your way driving to or from Chan Chich Lodge. In any event, you will need permission and a reserved guide arranged in advance by calling the **Programme for Belize** (www.pfbelize.org; ℂ **227-5616**).

Where to Stay

INSIDE RIO BRAVO

La Milpa Field Station ★   Run by the Programme for Belize, this simple lodge is located in the heart of the wild Río Bravo Conservation Area and just 4.8km (3 miles) from La Milpa ruins. It is a working biological and archaeological field station that also offers rooms, meals, and tours for travelers, students, and volunteers. The private thatch-roof cabins, while still relatively rustic, feature private bathrooms and a sense of being at a more typical nature lodge. For their part, the dormitory rooms and shared bathrooms are kept quite clean, and would certainly please even the most discerning backpacker or budget traveler. The dorm rooms and shared bathrooms use solar power and high-tech composting toilets. Guided tours are always available, and educational packages, sometimes including fieldwork, are often offered.

La Milpa section of Río Bravo Conservation Area, Orange Walk district. www.pfbelize. org. ℂ **227-5616.** 8 double-room cabins, 30 dormitory beds. BZ$175 per person for cabins; BZ$162 per person for dormitories. Rates, based on double occupancy, include taxes and 2 guided tours daily. Meals are BZ$65 each. **Amenities:** Restaurant; lounge; Wi-Fi (free).

RUINS OF YOUR OWN

Chan Chich Lodge ★★   Set in the central plaza of a small Mayan ceremonial city, Chan Chich is one of the most unusual jungle lodges in Mesoamerica. The low hills that surround 14 individual bungalows are all unexcavated pyramids and temples. It's so remote that it's safe enough to leave your door unlocked, which takes some getting used to. The rooms feature high-pitched thatch roofs and wraparound wooden decks, and are all big, clean, and quite comfortable. Most come with two queen beds made up with heavy comforters and lots of pillows, plus essential mosquito nets. The deluxe bungalows are slightly larger, especially in the bathroom area, and feature king-size beds and Japanese-style decor. There's also a luxurious two-bedroom villa, with its own Jacuzzi, expansive living areas and air-conditioning, well suited for families.

Behind one of the overgrown temple mounds, there's a screened-in pool and Jacuzzi area with its own bar. Some 14km (8.65 miles) of well-groomed trails lead off from the central plaza, and a host of guided tours and hikes is available. Wildlife viewing here is excellent, with more than 350 bird species identified nearby. The lodge hosts nighttime safaris that contribute to the many annual jaguar sightings. They are committed to the big cat's success, among other sustainability endeavors, so Chan Chich hosts and supports jaguar researchers as they place camera traps in the area. Guests spend their time

barry bowen, **BELIKIN BEER, COCA-COLA & CHAN CHICH**

Building a modern nature lodge in the central plaza of an ancient Mayan ceremonial city is bound to be controversial. Some see it as a desecration and outrage. However, most recognize that the construction and operation of Chan Chich Lodge has served as an important safeguard against looters, and a strong tool for raising awareness and money to support conservation and excavation efforts.

First discovered in 1938 by J. Eric Thompson, the site was originally named Kaxil Uinic, before being renamed by Barry Bowen in 1987. Bowen, owner of the Belikin Beer company and exclusive distributor for Coca-Cola in Belize, bought more than 303,514 hectares (750,000 acres) of land (about one-sixth of the country) in the western Orange Walk District in 1984. When Bowen and his workers rediscovered Chan Chich,

the site had been severely looted, and many of the mounds and temples showed signs of active looting trenches.

Chan Chich sits on some 101,171 hectares (250,000 acres) of private reserve and is bordered to the north by the 106,028 hectares (262,000 acres) of the Río Bravo Conservation Area. Since Bowen bought the land, a total hunting ban has been enacted, and if these protected lands are connected to the Kalakmul Reserve in Mexico and the Maya Biosphere Reserve in Guatemala, they may one day form a major Mesoamerican environmental and archaeological megareserve spanning three countries.

In February 2010, Bowen was killed, when the small plane he was piloting crashed just before landing in San Pedro. His children remain very active in the community.

horseback riding, visiting nearby agricultural communities, or canoeing and swimming at Laguna Verde. Day trips to Lamanai, La Milpa, and other Mayan sites can also be arranged. The food is excellent, which is lucky, since there are no other options.

Gallon Jug, Orange Walk District. www.chanchich.com. (©) **800/343-8009** in the U.S., or 223-4419 in Belize. 14 units. BZ$780–BZ$900 double; BZ$1,790 villa. Rates lower in the off season. A meal package will run you an extra BZ$140 per day. Multiday all-inclusive packages are available. You can either drive here or take a charter flight to nearby Gallon Jug; if you choose the charter, Chan Chich can arrange the flight and pick you up at the airport. If you choose to drive, it takes about 4 hr. from Belize City, much of it on dirt roads, so a 4-wheel-drive vehicle is recommended. If you are driving here, you will need permission to pass through the Programme for Belize's lands; call the lodge in advance to arrange this. **Amenities:** Restaurant; bar; lounge; Jacuzzi; small pool; Wi-Fi (free, in bar and restaurant area).

COROZAL TOWN

13km (8 miles) N of Belize City; 50km (31 miles) N of Orange Walk Town; 13km (8 miles) S of the Mexican border

Corozal is a quiet seaside town, located just south of the Río Hondo (Hondo River), which forms the border between Mexico and Belize. Set on a

Corozal Town

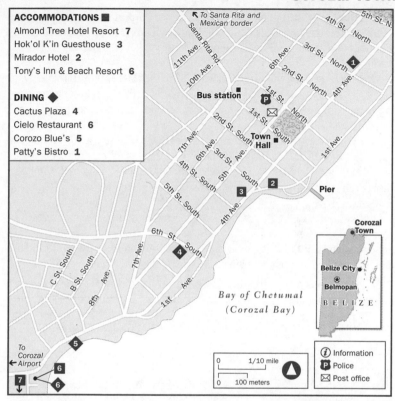

↖ To Santa Rita and Mexican border

ACCOMMODATIONS ■
Almond Tree Hotel Resort **7**
Hok'ol K'in Guesthouse **3**
Mirador Hotel **2**
Tony's Inn & Beach Resort **6**

DINING ◆
Cactus Plaza **4**
Cielo Restaurant **6**
Corozo Blue's **5**
Patty's Bistro **1**

Bus station
Town Hall
Pier

Bay of Chetumal (Corozal Bay)

To Corozal Airport

Corozal Town

Belize City
Belmopan
B E L I Z E

0 — 1/10 mile
0 — 100 meters

ⓘ Information
🅿 Police
✉ Post office

crystal-clear bay, Corozal was an important point on the early Mayan trading routes, and the evidence remains in the ruins of **Cerros** and **Santa Rita.** During the mid-1800s, the modern town was settled with a large population of refugees from Mexico's Caste War. In 1955, Hurricane Janet paid a visit and left few of the town's wooden buildings standing. The rebuilding relied heavily on cement and cinderblock construction. Today, Corozal is home to a growing expatriate community. While not part of the traditional tourist circuit, Corozal Town makes a good base for fishing excursions in the calm bay; bird- and wildlife-viewing tours into nearby **Shipstern Nature Reserve;** shopping trips to neighboring **Chetumal, Mexico;** and explorations of the aforementioned Mayan ruins. Visitors to Corozal often flock to the Commercial Free Zone, with shopping centers and casinos located just on the Belizean side of the Mexico-Belize border. *Note:* If you go, you will have to pay exit costs since you are technically leaving the country.

Essentials

GETTING THERE & DEPARTING

BY PLANE   Most flights to and from Corozal Airport connect through San Pedro Airport on Ambergris Caye. There are numerous flights connecting San Pedro to both of Belize City's airports, as well as other destinations around the country.

Maya Island Air (www.mayaairways.com; © **223-1140** in Belize City, or 422-2333 in Corozal) has daily flights between Corozal and San Pedro, leaving San Pedro at 7 and 10am and at 2 and 4:30pm, and returning at 7:30 and 10:30am and at 2:30 and 5pm.

Tropic Air (www.tropicair.com; © **800/422-3435** in the U.S. or Canada, 226-2012 in Belize City, or 422-0356 in Corozal) has direct flights between San Pedro and Corozal, leaving every 2 hours between 7am and 5pm. The flights return to San Pedro following a similar schedule between 7:30am and 5:30pm.

On both airlines, the flight duration is 25 minutes, and the fare is BZ$150 each way.

See chapters 6 and 7 for more information on flights between San Pedro and Belize City, and other destinations around the country.

BY CAR   Corozal Town is the last town on the Philip Goldson Highway before you reach the Mexican border. Take Freetown Road out of Belize City to connect with the Philip Goldson Highway. If you're driving in from Mexico, you'll reach a fork in the road 4.8km (3 miles) from the border; bear left and follow the signs to reach Corozal Town.

BY BUS   Buses (© **227-2255** in Belize City, or 402-3034 in Corozal) leave Belize City for Corozal and the Mexican border throughout the day, roughly every half-hour between 5:30am and 7:30pm from the main terminal on West Collet Canal Street. Catch any bus going to Corozal Town or Chetumal. The Corozal Town bus station is located 2 blocks west of the small central plaza and Town Hall. You can pick up a return bus here to Belize City, or onward to the Mexican border and Chetumal. The fare is BZ$16 to BZ$20 between Belize City and Corozal Town, BZ$6 to BZ$10 between Orange Walk Town and Corozal Town, and around BZ$6 between Chetumal and Corozal Town.

BY BOAT   The *Thunderbolt* (© **610-4475** in San Pedro, or 422-0026) has two daily boats running between San Pedro on Ambergris Caye (on the leeward side behind the soccer field) and Corozal (from the big municipal pier). The boats leave each destination at 7am and 3pm and cross paths about midway. The trip takes around 2 hours, and a stop in Sarteneja can be made upon request. Fare is BZ$50 one-way and BZ$90 roundtrip.

GETTING AROUND

Corozal Town is very compact, and it's easy to walk anywhere in the entire downtown and waterfront areas. However, if it's just too hot, you're too tired, or you're heading farther afield, you can have your hotel call a taxi. Or try **Corozal Bus Terminal Taxi Union** (✆ 422-3194) or **Corozal Taxi Association** (✆ 422-2035). If it's lunchtime you may be hard-pressed to find a ride without spending a little extra.

If you're looking to rent a car up here, contact Mr. Angel Riverol at **Corozal Car Rentals** (www.corozalcars.com; ✆ 422-3339).

ORIENTATION

Corozal is located right on a beautiful section of Corozal Bay (on the Mexican side of the border it's called Chetumal Bay). The town is laid out more or less in a grid, with avenues running roughly north–south and streets running east–west. The avenues run up numerically in order beginning with the waterfront 1st Avenue. The streets run in parallel but separate numerical order north and south from the town's central plaza, so that 3rd Street North and 3rd Street South are two distinct roads, one located 3 blocks north of the central plaza, the other 3 blocks south. The Philip Goldson Highway from Belize City and Orange Walk enters the town from the south. If you bear right and stay close to the water, you will be on 1st Avenue. If you bear left, you will be on 7th Avenue, the town's busiest thoroughfare, which skirts the western edge of downtown before passing the bus terminal and continuing on to Chetumal and the Mexican border.

The **post office** (✆ 422-2462) and Town Hall front the small central plaza. Most banks and businesses are within a 2-block radius in either direction.

FAST FACTS If you need to call the **police,** dial ✆ **911,** or 422-2202; for the **fire department,** dial ✆ **422-2105;** and for medical emergencies, call the **Corozal Community Hospital** at ✆ **402-3909,** and ✆ **422-2076** will get you an ambulance.

There are several banks in Corozal Town: **Atlantic Bank,** 3rd Street North (✆ 422-3473); **Scotiabank,** 1st Street South (✆ 422-2322); and **Belize Bank,** 1st Street North (✆ 422-2087). All these change U.S. dollars, Belize dollars, and Mexican pesos, as well as provide cash advances on your credit card.

If your hotel doesn't have a tour desk or good connections, and you want to visit any of the sites mentioned below or take an organized tour in this region, call **Belize VIP Transfer & Tours** (www.belizetransfers.com; ✆ 422-2725).

What to See & Do

There isn't much to see or do in Corozal Town. It's mostly just a stopping point for weary travelers. However, it sits on the shores of a pretty, quiet bay with amazing turquoise-blue water that is officially the **Bay of Chetumal,** but locally dubbed **Corozal Bay.** If you want to split hairs, the small bay just off Corozal Town could be considered a separate entity from the larger Bay of Chetumal that it sits in. The beaches are nothing to write home about, but the water is beautiful and a haven for manatees.

If you've just come from Mexico, you can take a day or two to walk around town and marvel at the difference between Mexican culture and Belizean culture. The countries are so close and yet worlds apart. Belize is truly a Caribbean country, with frame houses built on high stilts to provide coolness, protection from floods, and shade for sitting.

The heart of Corozal Town is the small plaza between 1st Street North and 1st Street South and 4th and 5th avenues. This is a good place to grab a bench and watch the locals go about their daily business. However, if you want a really inviting park bench, I recommend heading a couple of blocks east to tiny parks and public lands you'll find all along the bayfront.

MAYAN RUINS

If you haven't yet had your fill of Mayan ruins, there are a couple to visit in the area. If you look across the water from the shore in Corozal Town, you can see **Cerros** or **Cerro Maya** on the far side of the Bay of Chetumal. "Cerro" means hill in Spanish, and the site is that little bump in the forest you can see across the bay. (Up close it seems much larger.) Cerros was an important coastal trading center during the late Pre-Classic Period. Some of the remains of this city are now under the waters of the bay, but there's still a 21m-tall (69-ft.) **pyramid** built right on the water's edge that you can climb for a wonderful view of the bay. Ask around town to find someone willing to take you by boat to the ruins. Or you can drive, by heading out of town to the south and catching the free ferry across the New River; this will connect you with the road to Cerros.

Right on the outskirts of town, you'll find some of the remains of another ancient city many believe was the Mayan trading center of **Chactemal (Chetumal)**. It is currently called **Santa Rita.** Corozal Town is actually built on the ruins of Santa Rita, which was an important late Post-Classic Mayan town and was still occupied at the time of the Spanish Conquest. The only excavated building is a small temple across the street from the Coca-Cola bottling plant. To reach it, head north past the bus station and about a kilometer (⅔ mile) later, at the sharp curve to the right, take the road straight ahead that leads up a hill. You'll see the building 1 block over to the right.

TWO NEARBY NATURE RESERVES

Bird-watchers and naturalists will want to visit the nearby **Shipstern Nature Reserve** ★ (www.visitshipstern.com). The reserve's 8,903 hectares (22,000 acres) protect a variety of distinct ecosystems and a wealth of flora and fauna. Managed by the Corozal Sustainable Future Initiative (www.csfi.bz), Shipstern Nature Reserve is home to more than 250 bird species, and its mangroves, lagoons, and flat wetlands are excellent bird-watching sites. The massive network of lagoons and wetlands is home to manatees and Morelet's crocodiles. The reserve also has lowland tropical dry forest unique to Belize, as well as a butterfly breeding project. You'll get a good look at much of it by climbing the observation tower; best viewing times are sunrise and sunset. The reserve is open daily from 8am to 5pm, and guided tours can be arranged onsite. It is possible to spend the night in some simple accommodations; rates are around BZ$40 for a dorm bed and BZ$98 for a double room. A basic restaurant offers meals between BZ$20 and BZ$40, plus there's a bar.

Tip: The wetlands here are a major insect breeding ground. This is a bonanza for the birds and bats, but you'll want to bring along plenty of insect repellent, and probably lightweight long-sleeved shirts and pants.

Five kilometers (3.1 miles) beyond Shipstern Nature Reserve, on the edge of the peninsula, lies the tiny lobster and fishing community of **Sarteneja.** In Sarteneja, the best place to stay is **Fernando's Seaside Guesthouse** (www. fernandosseaside.com; © **423-2085**) for BZ$100 a night, including air-conditioning and Wi-Fi. Fernando is an excellent guide, and he can arrange everything from fishing or snorkeling trips to Mayan ruin excursions and night tours of the Shipstern Nature Reserve.

To drive to Shipstern Nature Reserve and Sarteneja, you used to have to first drive down to Orange Walk Town and take the Sarteneja Highway through San Estevan and Little Belize. There is now another route that cuts some time and distance off this trip. Heading south out of Corozal, stick close to the bay. Just outside of Corozal, take the small barge ferry over the New River, which then connects to the roads to Copper Bank, Progresso, Shipstern, and on to Sarteneja.

Several buses daily connect Shipstern Nature Reserve and Sarteneja to Orange Walk, Corozal Town, Chetumal, and Belize City. Alternatively, you can hitch a ride on the *Thunderbolt* (see "By Boat" under "Essentials," above) heading to San Pedro, or hire a boat on the docks in Corozal for around BZ$160. The price is for the entire boat, and most boats can carry as many as 10 passengers.

The **Bacalar Chico National Park & Marine Reserve** lies about an hour's boat ride away from Corozal Town. This is a great spot for snorkeling and wildlife viewing. Ask around town or at the docks; you should be able to hire a boat for around BZ$240 to BZ$300, and the snorkeling equipment and a bag lunch will probably run an extra BZ$30 to BZ$50 per person. More people get here from San Pedro than Corozal. For more information on Bacalar Chico National Park & Marine Reserve, see chapter 7.

Where to Stay
MODERATE

Tony's Inn & Beach Resort ★★ By far the most impressive hotel in Corozal, this waterfront spot has long been the lodging and meeting place of choice in town. The rooms are all housed in a two-story L-shaped building and feature clean tile floors, one king bed or two double beds, a small sitting area, and a 27-inch TV. The second-floor rooms are all nonsmoking and have a shared veranda overlooking a grassy garden area. There's a sandy area by the water's edge here that can sort of be considered a beach, although the best swimming is off the end of the private pier. Its **Cielo Restaurant ★** (see below)

CROSSING INTO mexico

While Corozal Town is a sleepy little burg with a village feel to it, Chetumal, its nearby Mexican neighbor, is a small, bustling border city with a lively shopping and nightlife scene. Chetumal is also the gateway to the beaches and Mayan ruins of the Yucatán Peninsula.

Chetumal is the capital of Quintana Roo, the Mexican state that makes up much of the Yucatán Peninsula, and is home to the resort towns of Cancún, Cozumel, Playa del Carmen, and Isla Mujeres, as well as the Mayan sites of Tulúm and Cobá.

Most Belizeans come to Chetumal to take advantage of the town's "free zone," an area with scores of duty-free shops, modern multiplex cinemas, restaurants, and a couple of casinos. You can also visit the **Museo de la Cultura Maya ★**, Avenida de los Héroes, between avenidas Colón and Ghandi (**℃ 983/832-6838**), which offers a much more extensive museum representation of Mayan history, art, and archaeology than you will find anywhere in Belize. The museum is open Tuesday through Sunday from 9am to 7pm (it stays open 1 hr. later Fri–Sat). Admission is around US$4.

Just 40km (25 miles) north of Chetumal lies the beautiful **Bacalar Lagoon.** This natural area is also known as Las Lagunas de los Siete Colores (The Lagoons of Seven Colors) and is a good place to have lunch and admire the views.

Frequent buses run between Corozal and Chetumal. The ride takes about 1 hour, including the formalities of the border crossing. The actual border is at the Belizean city of Santa Elena on the Hondo River, 13km (8 miles) north of Corozal Town. You don't need a visa in advance, but you will have to pay BZ$40 in departure fees. The bus fare runs around BZ$12 one-way.

Alternatively, you can head to Chetumal by boat, a quick 10-minute hop away. If you depart Belize by boat, your departure fee is still BZ$40.

Tip: Your best bet for changing money from U.S. or Belize dollars into Mexican pesos are the money-changers on the Belize side. Alternatively, there's widespread compatibility between ATMs in Chetumal and other Mexican destinations and most PLUS and Cirrus debit and credit cards.

serves breakfast, lunch, and dinner in a beautiful, open-air building designed by a local architect.

Bayshore Dr., Corozal Town. www.tonysinn.com. **℃ 442-2055.** 24 units. BZ$190–BZ$250 double, with lower rates in the off season. **Amenities:** Restaurant; bar; room service; Wi-Fi (free).

Almond Tree Hotel Resort ★★   Located right on the water, toward the southern end of Bayshore Drive, sometimes referred to as "Gringo Lane," this small hotel is cozy, very friendly, and beloved by man and well, other critters. The owners have two dogs and have earned the trust of a coati-mundi, who greets guests as enthusiastically as the canines. Rooms aren't glamorous, but they're very comfortable with good beds, Mexican-tile floors, and high ceilings (all are on the second floor, which might be a difficulty for people with mobility impairments). Half of them come with televisions, and two feature fridges. The Almond Tree's pool is set amid verdant gardens, with orchids trailing off tree branches. There's also the semblance of a beach with lounge chairs. It is not within walking distance of downtown, so many guests opt to rent a bike. Bob and Lynn, the owners, are expert at making guests feel like family.

Bayshore Dr., Corozal District. www.almondtreeresort.com. ✆ **628-9224.** 10 units. BZ$210–BZ$378 double. **Amenities:** Restaurant; outdoor pool; smoke-free rooms; Wi-Fi (free).

INEXPENSIVE

Hok'ol K'in Guesthouse ★　There are a handful of budget hotels right in Corozal Town, but this is the best of the bunch. Rooms are located in a two-story building located right across the street from the bay and its little seaside promenade. They're simple and most are a bit cramped, but everything's kept sparkling clean. Those on the second floor have small private balconies, most with pretty sea views. Some of the rooms have air-conditioning, although you'll pay a little more for it. The restaurant here serves good American and Belizean fare at very reasonable prices.

89 4th Ave., Corozal Town. www.corozal.net. ✆ **442-3329.** 11 units. BZ$104–BZ$120 double. **Amenities:** Restaurant; Wi-Fi (free).

Mirador Hotel ★　With its commanding location, fronting Corozal Bay in the heart of Corozal Town, this imposing four-story concrete building (with a curved facade) looks a bit out of place. Inside, though, it is not all that different from the other hotels in town, and in some ways it's a little better. Rooms are spotless, if simply appointed. About half of the rooms face town, so be sure to request an oceanview or cornerview room (not only will they have better views, they'll also be quieter). The best feature here is the large rooftop terrace, with a covered area hung with a couple of hammocks. The hotel's restaurant serves local and Chinese fare.

2nd St. S. and 4th Ave., Corozal Town. www.mirador.bz. ✆ **442-0189.** 24 units. BZ$70–BZ$90 double; BZ$100–BZ$118 double with A/C. **Amenities:** Restaurant; room service; Wi-Fi (free).

Where to Dine

In addition to the places listed below, **June's Kitchen** (3rd St. S, ✆ **422-2559**) has an inexpensive Belizean breakfast characterized by large helpings of fresh food, with no skimping on the fruit. Since Miss June's home-restaurant can only seat a few people, her husband does delivery by bike.

MODERATE

Cielo Restaurant ★ BELIZEAN/INTERNATIONAL　This open-air joint is the principal restaurant and bar at Tony's Inn & Beach Resort and was remodeled in November 2017. It has a lovely setting on the water's edge under a vaulted roof. Most of the seating is in the main room, but my favorite tables on a warm starry night are located on an uncovered little wooden deck built right over the water. Start things off with some deep-dish nachos or seafood au gratin. The burger, and beef fajitas, are the most popular items here, but if you want something more upscale, try a steak or pasta dish. There's also always plenty of fresh seafood and shrimp served in a variety of sauces.

At Tony's Inn & Beach Resort (p. 241), Corozal Bay Rd. ℂ **422-2055.** Main courses BZ$20–BZ$50. Daily 11am–11pm.

Corozo Blue's ★★ PIZZA   Wood-fired pizzas in a friendly, bayside environment, what could be better? Sure, they have Belizean dishes, burgers, and other dishes as well, but it's the nicely charred pizza that gets people talking. Corozo's is on the South End of Corozal, near Tony's and Almond Tree, but people come from all over to dine here. As a bonus Corozo Blue's does delivery, a rare treat to find anywhere in Belize, though the outdoor seating makes it an inviting place to eat.

South End. www.facebook.com/CoroBlues. ℂ **422-0090.** Main courses BZ$15–BZ$30. Sun–Thurs 10am–1am; Fri–Sat 10am–2am.

INEXPENSIVE

Cactus Plaza ★ MEXICAN   Serving basic Mexican fare in a pleasant open-air setting, this is perennially one of the most popular restaurants in Corozal Town. The menu here is simple: Get some tacos, tostados, or *salbutes* (a disk of fried cornmeal, somewhat thicker than a traditional tortilla, usually topped with some shredded chicken, refried beans, or a cabbage salad), and maybe a side of rice and beans. My favorite seats are on the canvas-shaded rooftop patio, although you can also grab a seat at the small counter or at heavy tables on the ground floor. This hard-to-miss place was once the happening nightlife spot in town, but is now best as an eatery.

6 6th St. S. ℂ **422-0394.** Reservations not accepted. Main courses BZ$3–BZ$20. Tues–Sun 11:30am–10pm.

Patty's Bistro ★★ BELIZEAN/INTERNATIONAL   This quaint little joint is a local favorite for lunch, but it's also open for dinner and does a brisk business in takeout as well. The menu here ranges from Belizean staples such as stew chicken and *escabeche* (a local chicken soup) to coconut curry shrimp and chicken mole. Brave souls might start things off with the cow-foot soup, but I prefer the shrimp and conch ceviche. There are daily chalkboard specials. The air-conditioned dining room features yellow and salmon painted walls, kitschy art, and tables with tablecloths covered in plastic and set with Mexican or Guatemalan place mats.

13 4th Ave. ℂ **402-0174.** Reservations not accepted. Main courses BZ$8–BZ$20. Daily 11am–9pm.

Corozal Town After Dark

Corozal Town is a pretty quiet place. Continue on to Mexico, or your next destination in Belize, for more of a party scene. But if you want to meet some locals, fellow travelers, or expatriates, you'll find them hanging at such bars as **Tony's Inn & Beach Resort** (p. 241) or any of the new places popping up along the southern waterfront, such as the **Woodhouse Bistro** on 1st Avenue (✆ **636-0209**). On Friday and Saturday nights, you can also try the bar at **Corozo Blue's** (see above) or **Scotty's Bar and Grill** (41 1st Ave.), which hosts live music and karaoke nights.

If you're in the mood to try your luck, head north of town to the free zone and hit the tables at the **Princess Casino** (✆ **423-7652**) or the **Las Vegas Hotel and Casino** (✆ **423-7600**), the self-proclaimed largest of its kind in Central America.

9

NORTHERN BELIZE | Corozal Town

CAYO DISTRICT & WESTERN BELIZE

Western Belize, from the capital city of Belmopan to the Guatemalan border, is a land of rolling hills, dense jungles, abundant waterfalls, clear rivers, extensive caves, and numerous Maya ruins. This region was the heart of the Belizean Maya world, with the major ruins of **Caracol, Xunantunich,** and **El Pilar,** as well as lesser sites such as **Cahal Pech.** At the height of the Classic Maya Period, there were more residents in this area than in all of modern Belize.

Today, the area around Belmopan and extending throughout the Cayo District is the center of Belize's ecotourism industry. There are a host of national parks and protected areas, including the **Guanacaste** and **St. Herman's Blue Hole national parks,** the **Mountain Pine Ridge Forest Reserve,** and the **Chiquibil National Park.** The pine forests and rainforests here are great for hiking and bird-watching; the rivers are excellent for canoeing, kayaking, and inner tubing; and the dirt roads are perfect for horseback riding and mountain biking.

The cave systems of the Cayo District were sacred to the ancient Maya, and many of them are open for exploration by budding and experienced spelunkers alike. Some of the more popular underground attractions include **Actun Tunichil Muknal, Barton Creek Cave, Chechem Ha, Crystal Cave,** and the **Río Frío Cave.** Of particular interest is the **Caves Branch River,** which provides the unique opportunity to float on an inner tube, kayak, or canoe through a series of caves.

The George Price Highway (once known as the Western Highway, and still referred to as such by locals) runs through the heart of the Cayo District all the way to the Guatemalan border and serves as the gateway to side trips into Guatemala's Petén Province and the majestic Mayan ruins of **Tikal** (see chapter 11).

BELMOPAN

84km (52 miles) W of Belize City; 32km (20 miles) E of San Ignacio; 161km (100 miles) NW of Placencia

Belmopan is a rather desultorily planned city and the official capital of Belize. After Hurricane Hattie devastated Belize City in

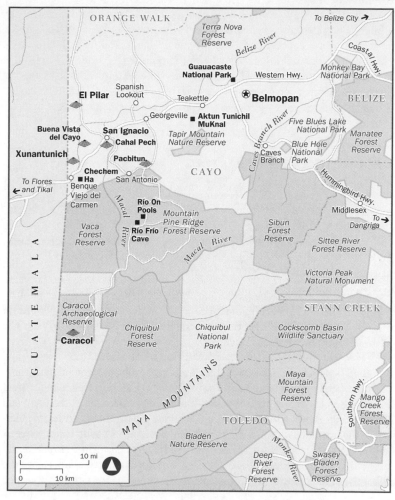

ORANGE WALK

Terra Nova
Forest
Reserve

Belize River

To Belize City ➚

Coastal Hwy.

Guauacaste
National Park

Western Hwy.

Monkey Bay
National Park

El Pilar

Spanish
Lookout

Teakettle

⊛ **Belmopan**

BELIZE

Georgeville ■ **Aktun Tunichil
MuKnal**

**Buena Vista
del Cayo**

San Ignacio
Cahal Pech

Tapir Mountain
Nature Reserve

Caves Branch River

Five Blues Lake
National Park

Xunantunich

Pacbitun

Blue Hole
Caves National
Branch Park

Manatee
Forest
Reserve

Chechem
■ **Ha**

San Antonio

CAYO

Hummingbird Hwy.

To Flores
← and Tikal

Benque
Viejo del
Carmen

Macal River

**Río On
Pools**

Mountain
Pine Ridge
Forest Reserve

Middlesex

To →
Dangriga

Vaca
Forest
Reserve

**Río Frío
Cave**

Macal River

Sibun
Forest
Reserve

Sittee River
Forest Reserve

Victoria Peak
Natural Monument

G U A T E M A L A

Caracol
Archaeological
Reserve

Caracol

Chiquibul
Forest
Reserve

Chiquibul
National
Park

STANN CREEK

Cockscomb Basin
Wildlife Sanctuary

Maya
Mountain
Forest
Reserve

Southern Hwy.

Mango
Creek
Forest
Reserve

M A Y A   M O U N T A I N S

TOLEDO

Bladen
Nature Reserve

Monkey River

Deep
River
Forest
Reserve

Swasey
Bladen
Forest
Reserve

0 ____ 10 mi
0 ____ 10 km

10

1961—not the first time a storm leveled or flooded the city—government officials figured enough was enough and decided to move the country's capital safely inland. A host of government buildings, including the National Assembly and the U.S. embassy, are laid out according to a master plan, surrounded by residential areas, with everything connected by a ring road. Although it's not the most popular place to live, residential and commercial developments have sprung up over the past few years and the city is seeing a little more activity. Still, many government workers prefer to make the daily commute from either Belize City or San Ignacio—both are easy rides on well-paved roads, speed bumps notwithstanding.

Unless you are coming to Belize on government business, you will probably miss Belmopan entirely. However, if you are traveling cross country, particularly by bus, you will at least pass through it. If you get into town late at night, don't despair—there are a few decent hotels and then you can make an early onward connection in the morning. The area around Belmopan is chock-full of natural wonders, including **Guanacaste National Park**—the country's smallest—and **St. Herman's Blue Hole National Park,** as well as the **Caves Branch River** and its network of hollowed-out limestone caves. There are also several very comfortable and interesting nature lodges in close proximity to Belmopan.

Essentials

GETTING THERE & DEPARTING

BY PLANE   Flying into Belmopan is generally unnecessary since the drive is so easy and quick. If you have your reasons, here is how to get to Belmopan via **Tropic Air** (www.tropicair.com; ℂ **800/422-3435** in the U.S. or Canada, or 226-2012 in Belize): Twice daily flights to Belmopan's small airport (BCV) from the international airport at 11:45am and 2:45pm, costing BZ$188.50. Flights leave from San Pedro three times a day at 8 and 11am and at 2pm and will run you BZ$255.

BY CAR   From Belize City, take Cemetery Road to the George Price Highway. At Mile 50 you'll see the well-marked turnoff for the Hummingbird Highway and Belmopan. Turn left here and follow signs to the entrance to Belmopan, about 3.2km (2 miles) beyond the turnoff. It should take about an hour to drive from Belize City to Belmopan.

BY BUS   Belmopan has very frequent bus service from Belize City. Nearly all buses heading west and south from Belize City stop in Belmopan. Buses to Belmopan leave roughly every half-hour from the main bus station on West Collet Canal Street between 5am and 9:30pm. Return buses to Belize City leave the main bus station in Belmopan about every half-hour between 4:15am and 8:45pm. The fare each way is BZ$6. The trip takes 1½ hours. From Belmopan, there are also frequent onward connections to Dangriga, Placencia, Punta Gorda, and other points south, as well as to San Ignacio, Benque Viejo, and the Guatemalan border.

GETTING AROUND

Belmopan is an extremely compact little city. You can easily walk to most places around the central hub. If you need a taxi, there are always taxis near the bus station and central market. Alternatively, you can call **Elvi's Taxi Service** (ℂ **802-3732**) or **Market Square Taxi Service** (ℂ **822-0371**). A taxi ride anywhere in town should cost around BZ$6 to BZ$10.

ORIENTATION

Belmopan is a planned city with a ring road and broad streets. The city itself is located just off the Hummingbird (Southern) Highway, 3.2km (2 miles) south of the George Price Highway. The bus station and small central market

Belmopan

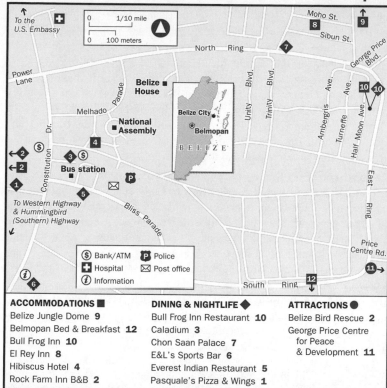

ACCOMMODATIONS ■	DINING & NIGHTLIFE ◆	ATTRACTIONS ●
Belize Jungle Dome **9**	Bull Frog Inn Restaurant **10**	Belize Bird Rescue **2**
Belmopan Bed & Breakfast **12**	Caladium **3**	George Price Centre
Bull Frog Inn **10**	Chon Saan Palace **7**	for Peace
El Rey Inn **8**	E&L's Sports Bar **6**	& Development **11**
Hibiscus Hotel **4**	Everest Indian Restaurant **5**	
Rock Farm Inn B&B **2**	Pasquale's Pizza & Wings **1**	

area are the heart of the town, and you will hit them soon after heading in off the highway. Within a 2-block radius, you'll find a couple of banks, two gas stations, and a few small strip malls. At the center of the city's radius, just off the market and bus station, is Independence Plaza, which houses the post office and prime minister's office. Sidewalks cut through Independence Plaza in various directions, making most of downtown Belmopan easily accessible by foot.

FAST FACTS   All of the principal banks in town, **Atlantic Bank,** Garden City Plaza (℃ **822-0693**), **Scotiabank,** Ring Road (℃ **822-1412**), and **Belize Bank,** 60 Market Sq. (℃ **822-2341**), are located close to the central market and bus station.

For the **police,** dial ℃ **911,** or 822-2220; for the **fire department,** dial ℃ **822-2311.** The **Belmopan Hospital** (℃ **822-2263**) is located on Constitution Drive, a block north of its intersection with the North Ring Road.

The **Market Square Drug Store** (℃ **822-0045**) is a well-stocked pharmacy located just off the Market Square.

What to See & Do

Perhaps the biggest attraction close to Belmopan is the **Belize Zoo,** Western Highway, Mile Marker 29. For more information on visiting the zoo, see p. 107 in the Belize City chapter. A recent addition to the area that animal lovers will enjoy is **Belize Bird Rescue,** 3 miles west of Belmopan on Roaring River Drive, off the George Price Highway (p. 254).

If you're spending any time in Belmopan, it pays to see if anything is happening at the **George Price Centre for Peace & Development** (www.gpc belize.com; ✆ **822-1054**). Primarily geared toward providing the local community with a library, classes, computer facilities, and meeting facilities, this place often hosts traveling art and museum exhibits, as well as movie showings, concerts, dance recitals, and theater performances.

Caves Branch River Cave System ★★★

The Caves Branch River is a gently flowing body of water coming down off the Mountain Pine Ridge. It really should be called a creek in most places. However, what makes the Caves Branch River unique is the fact that it flows in and out of a series of long limestone caves that are easily navigable on inner tubes and in kayaks.

There are two major entry points along the river for visits to the Caves Branch caves: One is at **Ian Anderson's Caves Branch** jungle lodge (p. 258), and the other is **Nohoch Che'en Caves Branch Archeological Reserve,** which was once a lodge called Jaguar Paw, and is still referred to by that name. In general terms, travelers looking for more adventurous and extensive trips into the caves should head to Ian Anderson's place; those seeking a gentler tour into the underworld or who sign up for a guided excursion out of any of the country's major tourist centers will inevitably be doing the tour out of the Nohoch Ch'en entrance, which is where the cruise ship passengers flock when they're in town.

Because of this, most visitors go directly through Nohoch Che'en. There's a decently sized parking area about a kilometer (⅔ mile) downriver from

The Underworld

The ancient Maya believed that caves were a mystical portal between the world of the living and the underworld of spirits and the dead. From their earliest days, there is evidence that the Mayans made extensive use of caves for ritual purposes, as well as for more mundane and rudimentary things such as keeping dry, storing grains, and gathering water. They called this mystical realm **Xibalba.**

Belize is literally riddled with caves. In almost every explored cave to date, some evidence of use by the Mayans has been uncovered. Fire pits, campsites, burial mounds, and ritual altars have all been found. Numerous pieces of pottery and abundant bones and artifacts have also been encountered. Belize offers many unique and easily accessible opportunities to explore this fascinating world on foot, by kayak or canoe, or by floating on an inner tube. Don't miss it.

Caves Branch: For the Most Enjoyable Experience

The Caves Branch River cave system is a very popular tourist attraction, and it can get crowded at times, especially at Nohoch Che'en and the public entrance. When the cruise ship groups are in the caves, it's downright overcrowded. Whatever tour operator you use, try to time it so that you avoid other large groups if possible (ask the operator for advice). Or do the tour with Ian Anderson's Caves Branch outfit, so you are assured of avoiding the crowds. Also, wear plenty of insect repellent, as the mosquitoes can be fierce here (only on the hike—once you're in the caves there are none).

Nohoch Che'en and a host of operators running the tubing tour from here, plus changing rooms, souvenir stands, and a few lunch tables. You will be supplied with a headlamp on a helmet (GoPro mounting helmets sometimes available), an inner tube, and plenty of information about how the caves were held sacred by the Mayans. Bring hardy water shoes or else you'll have to rent some, and most of the options are Crocs. There's an easy 30-minute hike upstream to a dock where you get to enter the river. If your group is small enough, I recommend you coordinate and all shut off your headlamps for a period of time. It's quite a spooky sensation to be floating in total darkness, wondering where the walls and ceilings are and whether you'll ever emerge into daylight again.

Most of the caves here contain Mayan pottery and artifacts, though not all guides incorporate a stop to view the artifacts into their tour. Ask when you're booking to make sure you get a tour that covers Mayan history, too.

Note that the dry season (Dec-Apr) can see depleted water levels, making tubing impossible. Similarly, too much rain in the wet season (summer months) can raise the water too high for a trip through the caves. Either of these occurrences is rare, but even so check with the company you're using a few days in advance of travel and have an alternate activity planned just in case.

Cave tubing tours cost between BZ$50 and BZ$240, depending on who you book with and what they provide. The most inexpensive way to go is to drive yourself to the parking area mentioned above and hire one of the local guides there for around BZ$30 to BZ$50. However, you'll generally get better guides, better service, and better equipment, if you go with one of the more established operators. Cave tubing without a licensed guide is against the law, so don't try and bring your own.

Actun Tunichil Muknal ★★★

Actun Tunichil Muknal means "Cave of the Crystal Sepulcher," and the site was featured in the 1993 National Geographic Explorer film *Journey Through the Underworld*. It deserves to star in even more films, we think. This is one of the most adventurous and rewarding caves you can visit in Belize. That being said, it's not for everyone. The trip involves a 45-minute hike and three shallow river crossings through dense forest to the entrance of the cave. A midsize stream flows out of the beautiful entrance. From here you wade, crawl, swim, and scramble, often up to your waist in water. There are some tight squeezes, not great for the claustrophobic. Inside, you'll come to several ceremonial and sacrificial chambers. Fourteen skeletons and burial sites have been found inside here, as well as numerous pieces of pottery and ceramic shards. There are even two rare slate steles, believed to have been used by Mayan religious and political leaders for ritual bloodletting ceremonies. Many of the skulls, skeletons, and pieces of pottery have been encased in calcium, creating an eerie effect, while others are very well maintained, making it hard to imagine that they are more than a thousand years old. Moreover, given its remote location and relatively recent discovery, Actun Tunichil Muknal has been spared much of the serious looting that has plagued many other Mayan cave sites; as you're going through you'll be in awe that what's in front of you is still in the cave and not in a museum. (It's the reason you'll be asked to take off your shoes at one point, so wear socks. They don't want visitors to accidentally break those precious relics) Only licensed guides can take visitors into this cave. Most hotels and tour agencies in the Cayo District can arrange these tours.

Note: You will get wet on this trip. Be sure to pack a change of clothing for when you get back to your transportation.

Another Note: You cannot bring a camera inside this cave, because one guest dropped his directly onto a preserved skull, breaking it and ruining it for everyone else. This means no GoPros either.

Zipline Canopy Tour ★
Belize Zipline Adventure (www.zipline.bz; ✆ **602-8975**) has the longest zipline in the Caves Branch area and lets visitors glide along steel cables from one treetop platform to another, above and through the forest canopy. There is a total of 12 platforms through 7 runs. At its highest, you are some 61m (200 ft.) above the forest floor. The trip costs BZ$150 per person and can easily be combined with their cave tubing excursion for a full-day adventure outing at BZ$200. Throw in the **Belize Zoo** for only BZ$70 more! Whatever you pick, it will include mainland pickup, transportation, lunch, and all the involved fees.

NATIONAL PARKS
Guanacaste National Park ★, a 20-hectare (50-acre) park located where the Hummingbird Highway turns off the George Price Highway, about 3.2km (2 miles) north of Belmopan, is an excellent introduction to tropical forests. It shares a name with an area of Costa Rica, so make sure during online searches that you've got the right country. The park is named for a huge old guanacaste (or tubroos) tree that is found within the park. Guanacaste trees were traditionally preferred for building dugout canoes, but this particular tree, which is about 100 years old, was spared the boat builders' ax because it has a crooked and divided trunk that makes it unacceptable for canoe building. More than 35 species of epiphytes (plants that grow on other plants), including orchids,

bromeliads, ferns, mosses, lichens, and philodendrons, cover its trunk and branches.

There are nearly 3.2km (2 miles) of well-marked and well-maintained trails in the park, with several benches for sitting and observing wildlife. The park is bordered on the west by Roaring Creek and on the north by the Belize River. Among the animals you might see are more than 120 species of birds, large iguanas, armadillos, kinkajous, deer, agoutis (large rodents that are a favorite game meat in Belize), and jaguarundis (small jungle cats). Bring along a bathing suit in case you want to take a refreshing dip in the Belize River. This park is administered by the **Belize Audubon Society** (www. belizeaudubon.org; © **223-5004**) and is open daily from 8am to 4:30pm. Admission is BZ$5.

The Belize Audubon Society runs a Christmas Bird Count in the park between December 14 and January 5, which is a swell way to meet bird-loving locals as well as contribute to the Belize Audubon Society's understanding of their birds. Check the events page on their site for more info.

The Maya Mountains are primarily limestone and laced with caves, which is why this region of Belize is also known as Caves Branch. About 19km (12 miles) south of Belmopan on the Hummingbird Highway, you'll find **St. Herman's Blue Hole National Park ★★**, which is not the same entity as the more famous Blue Hole in the sea (check that one out on p. 167), and will likely be referred to just as Blue Hole National Park. The first signs you see of the park will be the parking area, visitor center, and trail entrance to **St. Herman's Cave,** a less than .8km (.5-mile) hike from the road to one of the largest and most easily accessible caves in Belize. You'll need a good flashlight and sturdy shoes to explore this undeveloped .8km-long (½-mile) cave.

The principal entrance to St. Herman's Blue Hole National Park is just a hop down the Hummingbird Highway from the visitor center, with a separate parking lot. The park gets its name from a crystal-clear pool, or cenote, formed in a collapsed cavern. There's a small information center, then a short, well-marked trail that leads to the main attraction here. Dense jungle surrounds a small, natural pool of deep turquoise. A limestone cliff rises up from the edge of the pool on two sides. The water flows for only about 30m (100 ft.) on the surface before disappearing into a cave and flowing on underground to the Sibun River. This is a great place for a quick dip on a hot day because the water is refreshingly cool and clear, and there is a cement platform where you can leave your towel, clothes, and belongings in plain sight. It can get crowded here on weekends, but early in the morning during the week, you may have the place almost to yourself. You can clearly see fish swimming around the edges of the Blue Hole. A 2.4km (1.5-mile) trail connects the Blue Hole pool with St. Herman's Cave. This trail passes through lush and beautiful primary and secondary tropical forests that are rich in flora and fauna. More than 200 species of birds have been recorded here. Be sure to wear plenty of insect repellent or long-sleeved clothing, as the mosquitoes can be fierce. *Tip:* If you're interested in only the pool, be sure to continue on the Hummingbird Highway, and don't park at the St. Herman's Cave entrance.

The entire park, which is administered by the **Belize Audubon Society** (www.belizeaudubon.org; ℗ **223-5004**), is open daily from 8am to 4:30pm, and admission is BZ$8. A self-guided trail map and a brochure about the park are available at the small visitor center. And if the park ranger is available, he'll usually throw in a brief guided tour for free.

Extreme adventurers should check out the **Crystal Cave** (or Mountain Cow Cave per the locals) here. This cave system goes on for miles and features striking geological structures and formations, Mayan relics, and some calcified skeletons. Guided tours through **Maya Walk** on Burns Avenue in San Ignacio (www.mayawalk.com; ℗ **824-3070**) start with a 50-minute jungle hike before entering the dry cave for a rigorous 7-hour exploration, and cost BZ$220.

A PRIVATE PARK & EDUCATIONAL CENTER

Located just inland from Mile Marker 31 on the Western Highway is **Monkey Bay Wildlife Sanctuary** (www.monkeybaybelize.com; ℗ **820-3032**), a private reserve and environmental education center comprising some 433 hectares (1,070 acres) of varied natural habitat. There's a visitor center, and a range of tours is offered. Monkey Bay specializes in hosting student groups, but anyone can visit for the day, or even stay in on-site accommodations ranging from somewhat plush private rooms to a dormitory-style bunkhouse to camping. Excluding the cabins, showers are cold water only, and the bathrooms are outdoor latrines. The cabins have bathrooms en suite. Tours include guided hikes, bird-watching expeditions, cave explorations, and canoe outings on the Sibun River. With the addition of the neighboring 911-hectare (2,250-acre) **Monkey Bay Nature Reserve,** this is a very large protected area, with more than 250 recorded bird species.

While walk-ins can often be accommodated, it's best to contact them in advance before coming for any tour or stay. Rates run around BZ$24 per person for camping; tents can be rented for BZ$10.50. It costs BZ$60 per person for a dorm bunk and shared bathroom, BZ$84 for a private field station room, and between BZ$192 and BZ$240 for the deluxe cabins. Two of them even have air-conditioning. Meals cost between BZ$24 and BZ$30 and are served buffet style.

A BIRD SANCTUARY

On a farm just beyond Belmopan is **Belize Bird Rescue** (www.belizebird rescue.org; ℗ **610-0400**), where up to 200 birds at a time—mostly parrots, but a few raptors, owls, and others—are rehabilitated either for release back into the wild or for a life in captivity, should they have injuries or behavioral problems that prevent successful release. Many of the birds are rescued from the illegal pet trade, sometimes directly from the hands of poachers. The organization offers free tours (though donations are highly encouraged); tours must be arranged by e-mailing or calling ahead of time. The owners also run an on-site lodge called **Rock Farm Inn B&B** (see below) which helps the organization stay afloat. Visiting is an ethical way to see some of Belize's most beautiful birds, in particular the yellow-headed amazon, while supporting a beloved non-profit.

GOLF

Belize's only public mainland golf course is located on the outskirts of Belmopan. The **Roaring River Golf Course** near Camalote Village (www.belizegolfcourses.com; ✆ **820-2031**) is a par-64, 9-hole executive course featuring natural jungle elements like native trees, iguanas running around, and over 120 different bird species. The water traps sometimes have crocodiles in them, so be as careful as you would around any other murky water. Greens fees run BZ$50 for 18 holes and BZ$35 for 9. The course is open every day of the year from dawn to dusk, and your best option for hitting the links (unless you're already a member of the ultra-exclusive course on Caye Chapel). Grab a bite or a drink at The Meating Place by making a reservation in advance, or at the clubhouse.

SHOPPING

Located just a mile or so outside of Belmopan, on the way to Belize City, **Art Box** ★★ (www.artboxbz.com; ✆ **822-2233**) is an excellent gift shop spread over two adroitly decorated floors, with an extensive collection of souvenirs, art and craft works, T-shirts, books, hot sauces, and other assorted Belizean-made gift items. There's also a pleasant coffee shop on the premises, with free Wi-Fi to go along with your cappuccino or latte.

Where to Stay

In addition to the places listed below, there are five well-equipped individual cabins at the **Roaring River Golf Course** (www.belizegolfcourses.com; ✆ **820-2031**) on the outskirts of Belmopan. All come with air-conditioning and a riverview private patio and run BZ$350 per night.

IN BELMOPAN
Moderate

Belize Jungle Dome ★★★   You know you want to stay at a place called the "Jungle Dome." The reality won't disappoint. Though it's within walking distance to town, the property is right on the edge of the jungle and feels like it's far off the beaten path. Along with the jungly setting, the big perk here is that instead of simply booking visitors' tours with outside companies (as many lodges do), the Jungle Dome's expert and entertaining staff lead all of the well-executed excursions, to Mayan ruins, caves—the works. The six large rooms are darn nice, too, painted in sherbet colors, with colorful quilts and works of local art on the walls. They surround a pool where cocktails are served (extra cost) come evening, and all the guests gather to compare adventures. Three meals a day are also offered (for between BZ$24 and BZ$44 each). All in all, it's a wonderfully social place to stay.

Mile 47, George Price Hwy. www.belizejungledome.com. ✆ **628-3425.** 6 units. BZ$250 in winter; BZ$200 in summer. **Amenities:** Restaurant; pool; bike rental; guided tours; air-conditioning; Wi-Fi (free).

Bull Frog Inn ★   Popular with business travelers, this motel is situated near pretty much every business one would travel for. Rooms are spacious and come with one king bed or two queen beds, air-conditioning, and in-room Wi-Fi. They also have a small private balcony with a wrought-iron railing overlooking a little patch of grass and the ring road. The restaurant here is one of the more dependable in town, and the bar can actually get hopping.

25 Half Moon Ave. ℭ **822-3425.** www.bullfroginn.com. 25 units. BZ$185 double. **Amenities:** Restaurant; room service; mini-fridges in the rooms; Wi-Fi (free).

INEXPENSIVE

In addition to the places listed below, you could also try the **Belmopan Bed & Breakfast** (www.belmopanbedandbreakfast.com; ℭ **822-0176**), which is located at 8 Trio St. and rents two neat rooms in a residential home with a swimming pool. Rates run around BZ$110 for a double, including taxes, and free Wi-Fi. Air conditioning is available for BZ$14 extra.

El Rey Inn ★   If you're looking for a clean, inexpensive place to spend the night, try this small hotel located in a residential neighborhood just off North Ring Road. The rooms are fairly basic, but the rates are some of the best in Belmopan. This little hotel has a simple restaurant serving reasonably priced meals; staff can arrange a host of tours. El Rey Inn is about a 10-minute hike or a short taxi ride from the bus station. These folks also have a sister property, **Hibiscus Hotel** (www.hibiscusbelize.com; ℭ **822-0400**), closer to the center of town, government offices, and bus station, with rooms that feature air-conditioning and televisions, but at rates more than double El Rey's for half as many rooms. A compelling reason for spending the extra money on Hibiscus is that 50% of hotel profits go to the **Belize Bird Rescue,** but if cost is your limiting factor, stick with El Rey.

23 Moho St. www.elreyhotel.com. ℭ **822-3438.** 12 units. BZ$70–BZ$130 double. **Amenities:** Restaurant; laundry services; Wi-Fi (free).

Rock Farm Inn B&B ★★★   Many consider a stay at Rock Farm Inn a highlight of their trip to Belize. Set on a lush, 52-acre nature reserve known as the Belize Bird Rescue (see above), a stay here allows guests to get up-close-and-personal with some of the country's loveliest wildlife. At guests' sides are Nikki and Jerry, the charming, erudite British expats who run the sanctuary. They are superb hosts, eager to share their knowledge of the country, and good cooks, too. For a reasonable fee, guests can add in a hearty breakfast, dinner, and/or beer and wine on the porch. Rooms are clean and comfortable, with options ranging from a compact double to a two-bedroom cottage. This is a rare opportunity to see behind the scenes of wildlife conservation, while supporting it. *Note:* Because of all the birds, things can get loud here. Stay elsewhere if you're sensitive to noise.

Roaring River Dr. www.rockfarmbelize.com. ℭ **610-0400.** 6 units. BZ$90–BZ$131 double. **Amenities:** Meals (extra cost); Wi-Fi (free).

Where to Dine

In addition to the places listed below, Belmopan now has a branch of the ever-popular and ever-expanding local Chinese franchise, **Chon Saan Palace,** 7069 George Price Blvd. (✆ **822-3388**), where you can get a host of well-prepared Cantonese and Szechuan favorites. The restaurant at the **Bullfrog Inn,** 25 Half Moon Ave. (✆ **822-2111**), which serves a mix of local and international cuisine, is another of the better restaurants in the city proper. While just outside of town, the restaurant at **Roaring River Golf Course** on Roaring River Drive off the George Price Highway (www.belizegolfcourses.com; ✆ **664-5441**) garners praise for its tender steaks. And do look through the hotel listings in this chapter, as many serve excellent meals and are open to the general public.

Budget travelers and those looking for some local flavor should grab a meal from the vendors and stalls at the central market. This is not an option for those with delicate digestive tracts, with the exception of **Everest Indian Restaurant** (✆ **600-8850**), where owner Raj prepares fantastic, large-portioned Indian dishes while charming his guests. (He also keeps a spic-and-span kitchen). His stall isn't easy to find: It's across from the market proper at the end of a row of other food stalls. Look for a sandwich board that says "Everest."

A couple of other options lie just outside of the city, about 26km (16 miles) east along the Western Highway at Mile Marker 32, where you'll find a pair of popular roadside restaurants and bars: **Cheers** (✆ **822-8014**) and **Amigos** (✆ **802-8000**). Both are large and lively spots serving local fare, grilled meats, seafood, and typical bar food such as nachos and burgers.

Pasquale's Pizza & Wings ★ PIZZA/INTERNATIONAL   I like the casual vibe of this local fave. The best tables are those on an open-air wooden deck. These are picnic tables with vinyl tops stapled in place. The menu features a range of pizzas, pastas, and submarine sandwiches, as well as the namesake wings, which come in spicy and mild variations. If you want something more substantial, try the chicken cacciatore or vodka shrimp.

Corner of Forest Dr. and Slim Lane. www.pasquales.wordpress.com. ✆ **822-4663.** BZ$12–BZ$25. Mon–Sat 11am–9pm; Sun noon–9pm.

Caladium ★★ BELIZEAN   Also in the Market Square adjacent to the bus station, this restaurant has been around since 1984. They serve up Caribbean favorites like conch soup, rice and beans with chicken, and BBQ pork ribs. The service is friendly, and the restaurant air-conditioned. Plus, the convenience of the location is ideal.

Market Sq. ✆ **822-2754.** Main courses BZ$10–BZ$25. Mon–Tues 7:30am–8pm; Wed–Fri 7:30am–10pm; Sat 7:30am–7pm.

Belmopan After Dark

The most happening spot in town is the **E&L's Sports Bar** (✆ **610-2455**), located just off the Hummingbird Highway to the south. The **Bullfrog Inn** (see above) is another of the city's more popular watering holes, and they frequently have raucous karaoke nights. The restaurants out on the George Price Highway mentioned above are another good bet for an evening out.

Lodges Near Belmopan

While Belmopan itself is of little interest to most travelers, several of the country's best and most interesting nature lodges are located within close proximity to the capital city. All of the places below have their unique charms.

Ian Anderson's Caves Branch ★★ Once you've stayed at Ian Anderson's you'll get an e-mail from them once a month . . . for the rest of your life. That's the downside to booking here. But there are many, many upsides, not the least of which are the proprietary tours that are offered *only* by this resort on land they own (including an extraordinary spelunking adventure during which participants climb several waterfalls). You'll have to stay here to try those, and that trumps any e-mail concerns. Originally a rustic camp for hard-core adventure travelers, Ian Anderson's has become an upscale destination hotel, and one that's beloved by families: Many of the suites and rooms have bunk beds, along with luxe queen- and king-size beds (often in two separate rooms). Set on the banks of the Caves Branch River amid dense forest, the resort offers five categories of lodgings, the most swanky of which are the jungle suites and bungalows. Set on a hill looking out into the tree canopy, they have large, screened-in verandas, and a beautiful shower with a big (screened) window opening up to the forest. A 3-night minimum stay is required, and most book a package that includes activities and meals. The resort sits in the middle of a massive private nature reserve; it's actively involved in local conservation programs.

Hummingbird Hwy., Mile Marker 41½. www.cavesbranch.com. ℂ **610-23451.** 29 units. BZ$338 double cabana; BZ$422–BZ$588 double suite or bungalow. **Amenities:** Restaurant; bar; Jacuzzi; two-tier pool; smoke-free rooms; botanical garden; Wi-Fi (free, in Main Lodge, turned off at dinner).

Pook's Hill Lodge ★★ This isolated jungle resort is set on the grounds of an actual Mayan ruin in the midst of a lush forest and a 121-hectare (300-acre) private reserve, a stone's throw from the famed cave Actun Tunichil Muknal (p. 251). That proximity gives Pook Hill's guests a huge advantage: They can usually tour the caves a good hour earlier than the *hoi polloi*, seeing them before the crowds descend. Beyond the ATM cave, Pook's Hill offers complimentary on-site activities that you won't find at all resorts, including guided birding in the morning, night walks, jungle hikes, and tours of their resident Mayan site. It's just off the ancient central plaza where guests lodge in individual, thatched-roof dwellings. Those highest up the hill have the best views of the surrounding forest, but they're a little bit smaller and slightly less luxurious than the units a little lower down. My favorite cabin is Kinka-jou, which is tiled with river stones. Two cabins are located below the main lodge and across a small creek; they are built on raised stilts 3.7m (12 ft.) above the ground and have large decks that are great for bird-watching. The open-air lounge and bar is lit by kerosene lanterns at night and buzzes with hummingbirds during the day. The vibe is relaxed, and perfect for meeting fellow wilderness travelers, but bring plenty of bug spray: This is a true jungle lodge.

George Price Hwy., Mile Marker 52½. www.pookshilllodge.com. © **832-2017.** 11 units. BZ$476 double. Rates lower in the off season. Turn south off George Price Hwy. at Mile Marker 52½ at Teakettle Village. Follow signs on the dirt roads 9.7km (6 miles) until you reach the lodge. **Amenities:** Restaurant; bar; complimentary guided tours; laundry service; Wi-Fi (free).

Dream Valley Belize ★ It's not as luxurious as the lodges we've touched on above, but Dream Valley is also not as expensive. And it shares with the others a stunning jungle setting, which you can enjoy from one of the many hammocks strung around the property. In the rooms the emphasis is on wood, wood, and more polished wood, which gives digs a rustic feel. Each is spacious and spic-and-span, and 10 of them are right on the Belize River. The owner's suite is particularly enticing with an en suite Jacuzzi built into the floor surrounded by large open-air windows. As per usual, the staff can arrange a variety of tours. Meals cost extra, but some take the adventure package, which covers both food and activities.

Young Gyal Rd. off the George Price Hwy., Teakettle Village. www.dreamvalleybelize. com. © **665-1000.** 15 units. BZ$286 double. **Amenities:** Restaurant; spa; large outdoor pool; smoke-free rooms; Wi-Fi (free, in public area).

SAN IGNACIO ★★

116km (72 miles) W of Belize City; 32km (20 miles) W of Belmopan; 13km (8 miles) E of the Guatemalan border

In the foothills of the mountains close to the Guatemalan border lie the sister towns of Santa Elena and San Ignacio, which are set on either side of the beautiful Macal River. For all intents and purposes, San Ignacio is the more important town, both in general terms and particularly for travelers. Just north of town, the Macal and Mopan rivers converge to form the Belize River. San Ignacio is the business and administrative center for the Cayo District, a region of cattle ranches and dense forests, of clear rivers and Mayan ruins. It is also the second-largest metropolitan center in the country. Still, you won't find any urban blight here. If you've come from Guatemala, you'll sense immediately that you are now in a Caribbean country. If you've come up from the coast, you might be surprised by how cool it can get up here in the mountains. Despite the similarity in the sound of their names, the Cayo District and the cayes are worlds apart. While the cayes cater to those looking for fun in the sun, Cayo caters to those interested in nature, outdoor adventures, and Mayan ruins. This area makes a great first stop in Belize; you can get in a lot of activity before heading to the beach to relax.

> **For Short**
>
> The name "Cayo" is used to refer to both the Cayo District and the city of San Ignacio.

Essentials

GETTING THERE & DEPARTING

BY PLANE   Once a simple jungle airstrip, San Ignacio now has developed something more like a proper airport (CYD) in recent years, though it's not terribly close to town. Two flights head here from Belize City every day at 11:45am and 2:45pm for BZ$166.50 per passenger. Three flights leave from San Pedro daily at 8 and 11am, and 2pm for BZ$310, and these have layovers. If you take a taxi from the airport or water taxi terminal, expect to pay BZ$200 or more. Unless you're incredibly pressed for time, it's better to drive to San Ignacio from the international airport, and it's worth the experience: In just over an hour and a half, you'll witness how the landscape shifts from flat savannah to mountainous jungle.

BY CAR   Take the George Price (aka Western) Highway from Belize City. It's a straight shot all the way to San Ignacio, with plenty of "sleeping policemen" or speed bumps along the way. You'll come to the small town of Santa Elena first. Across the Macal River lies San Ignacio. Both cities have big colorful signs indicating which town you're in. If you're heading to San Ignacio and points west, a well-marked detour will lead you through the town of Santa Elena to a Bailey bridge that enters San Ignacio toward the north end of town. The more prominent and impressive Hawkesworth Bridge is solely for traffic heading east out of San Ignacio toward Santa Elena, Belmopan, and Belize City.

BY BUS   San Ignacio has very frequent bus service from Belize City. Buses to San Ignacio leave roughly every half-hour from the main bus station on West Collet Canal Street between 5am and 9:30pm. Return buses to Belize City leave the main bus station in San Ignacio roughly every half-hour between 4am and 6pm. The fare is BZ$10. The trip takes 2½ hours. Most of the western-bound buses continue on beyond San Ignacio to Benque Viejo and the Guatemalan border.

GETTING AROUND

The downtown center of San Ignacio is quite compact and easily navigated by foot. If you want to visit any of the major attractions listed below, you'll probably have to find transportation. Frequent buses (see above) will take you to the entrances to most of the hotels listed below on Benque Viejo Road, as well as within walking distance of the Xunantunich ruins. Infrequent buses (ask around town or at the bus station; ✆ **824-3360**) do service the Mountain Pine Ridge area. However, if you don't have your own vehicle, you will probably need to take some taxis or go on organized tours.

As in the rest of Belize, roads are minimal, and almost everything can be found on or just off the Western Highway, or the road through Mountain Pine Ridge. Numerous buses ply the main road between Belmopan and San Ignacio, continuing on to the border town of Benque Viejo del Carmen. If you want to drive yourself, particularly anywhere off the main highway, a four-wheel-drive vehicle is recommended.

San Ignacio

Bank/ATM
Hospital
Police
Post office

To Parrot's Nest,
Bullet Tree, El Pilar,
& Cohune Palms

ACCOMMODATIONS ■
Casa Blanca Guest House **10**
Hi-Et **5**
Ka'ana Resort **14**
Martha's Guest House **8**
Midas Tropical Resort **2**
The Old House Hostel **12**
San Ignacio Resort Hotel **13**

NIGHTLIFE ●
Belize Soul Project **12**
Hode's Place Bar & Grill **2**
Princess Casino **13**

To Xunantunich,
Benque Viejo del Carmen
& Guatemalan border

DINING ◆
Erva's **4**
Eva's Restaurant & Bar **7**
Guava Limb Café **1**
Hode's Place Bar & Grill **2**
The Ice Cream Shoppe **3**
Ko-Ox Han-Nah **11**
La Ceiba **14**
Maxim's Chinese
　Restaurant **6**
Pop's Restaurant **9**
Running W Steakhouse
　& Restaurant **13**

You can rent a car from **Cayo Rentals** (www.cayoautorentals.com; ☏ **824-2222**) or **Matus Car Rental** (www.matuscarrental.com; ☏ **824-2005**). A small four-wheel-drive vehicle here should run you around BZ$100 to BZ$240 per day.

If you need a cab, call the **Cayo Taxi Association** (☏ **824-2196**). Taxi fares around the Cayo District should run you as follows: BZ$6 to BZ$10 around town, BZ$20 between San Ignacio and Bullet Tree Falls, and BZ$50 between San Ignacio and Chaa Creek or duPlooy's. Collective taxis run regularly between downtown San Ignacio and the border at Benque Viejo; the fare is BZ$8 per person. If you are in San Ignacio, taxis, with their green license plates, can be found at the end of the walking street Burns Avenue in front of Courts furniture store. Negotiating on price is expected.

ORIENTATION

San Ignacio is on the banks of the Macal River, on the western side of an old metal bridge across from its sister city of Santa Elena. Across the single-lane Hawkesworth Bridge (the only suspension bridge in Belize) is a traffic circle and a Shell gas station. Downtown San Ignacio is to the north on Burns Avenue, and the San Ignacio Hotel is located south up a steep hill on Buena Vista Road, past the police station. Most of the hotels and restaurants in town are on or within a block of Burns Avenue. The road to Benque Viejo del Carmen, Xunantunich ruins, and the Guatemalan border branches off Buena Vista Road. This is actually a continuation of the George Price Highway.

FAST FACTS There are several banks located right in the heart of downtown San Ignacio: **Atlantic Bank,** at Burns Avenue and Columbus Park (© **824-2347**); **Scotiabank,** at Burns Avenue and Riverside Street (© **824-4190**); and **Belize Bank,** 16 Burns Ave. (© **824-2031**).

To reach the **police,** dial © **911,** or 824-2022; for the **fire department,** dial © **824-2095.** The **San Ignacio Hospital** is located on Simpson Street, on the western side of town (© **824-2066**). The **post office** (© **824-2049**) is located on Hudson Street, near the corner of Waight's Avenue.

The succinctly named **The Pharmacy** (© **824-2510**) is located on West Street. If you need eyeglass repair or help, head to the **Hoy Eye Center,** 4 Far West St. (© **824-4101**). If you need laundry done and your hotel doesn't offer the service or charges too much, you can drop off your dirty clothes at **Rainforest Haven Inn,** 2 Victoria St. (© **674-1984**), for same-day service at about BZ$12 per load.

What to See & Do

The Cayo District is Belize's prime inland tourist destination. There's a lot to see and do in this area, from visiting Mayan ruins and caves to engaging in a broad range of adventure activities. In addition to the tours, activities, and attractions listed below, all of the listings in the Mountain Pine Ridge section (later in this chapter) and in the Belmopan section (earlier in this chapter) are easily accessible from San Ignacio.

Some of the tours, activities, and attractions listed below can be done on your own, but others will require a guide or adventure tour operator. Almost all hotels in the area either have their own tour operations or can arrange to hook you up with a reputable local operator. In addition, there are several long-standing tour agencies based in San Ignacio. Some of the best of these are **Cayo Adventure Tours** (www.cayoadventure.com; © **824-3246**), **Pacz Tours ★★** (www.pacztours.net; © **824-2477,** or 824-0536), and **Yute Expeditions ★** (www.inlandbelize.com; © **824-2076**). All these companies offer virtually all of the options listed in this chapter and more, including multiday tours, treks, and adventures.

Serious bird-watchers might want to sign up for a tour with **Birding in Belize ★** (www.birdinginbelize.com; © **824-2772**). The birding culture of the country is centered in this area, so there is a wealth of expert guides. Many of the hotels and lodges have birding tours on their properties as well.

Note: ATVing has become a popular outdoor activity in the last year or so, but the cars tear up the land and disturb wildlife, so I cannot recommend any tour operators until the environmental impact has been significantly reduced.

A lot of what follows counts as serious adventures. If you'd like to mix that with some spa time, head to the **Spa at Chaa Creek** ★★ (www.chaacreek. com; (© **834-4010**). A wide range of treatments is offered, including a hydrating manicure, a variety of facials, and a range of full-body massage treatments. Full-day and multiday spa packages are available. The spa is set on a high hill above the Chaa Creek lodge (p. 275) with soft breezes rolling in to open-air sitting areas; equipment and facilities are top-notch. It's usually open daily 8am to 4pm.

MAYAN RUINS

The Cayo District is in the heart of the Mayan highlands, with several major ruins and cave systems used by the ancient residents of this region. The most impressive are **Xunantunich** ★★★ (on Benque Viejo Rd.), **El Pilar** ★★ (near Bullet Tree Falls Village), and **Caracol** ★★ (deep in the Mountain Pine Ridge area; see "Mountain Pine Ridge & Caracol," later in this chapter), but true Maya-philes can keep busy visiting a host of sites in this area. Close by, in Guatemala, lies **Tikal** ★★★, arguably the best excavated and most impressive of the Mayan cities in Mesoamerica. See chapter 11 for complete coverage.

Cahal Pech ★   High on a hill to the southwest of downtown San Ignacio are the Mayan ruins of **Cahal Pech.** Although compact, there are actually seven plazas here, as well as numerous residences, temples, and a couple of ball courts. Formerly the home of Mayan royals, the restoration of this site created a bit of controversy in town. Parts of the ruins were restored to an approximation of the way they were supposed to have looked when they were first built, which is more polished and modern-looking than most people like their ruins. However, the setting is beautiful, with tall old trees shading the site's main plaza and pyramid. *Tip:* Be sure to climb the small B4 pyramid, on your left near the entrance to the site. Though diminutive, it offers excellent views of the Macal River.

The name Cahal Pech means the "Place of Ticks," thanks to the presence of the bloodsuckers back in the 1950s when the site was surrounded by pasture instead of the city you see now. The ticks are mostly gone today, and in Belize they do not carry Lyme disease. The ruins date back to between A.D. 650 and 900, though many think that the site was used prior to this time as well.

At the entrance, you'll find a small museum that displays a collection of artifacts recovered from the site and provides insight into the Cahal Pech social structure. It also has a small model of the old city, as well as a skeleton recovered from one of the graves here.

Guides can be hired on-site but it's also a site that's easy to explore without one. To reach Cahal Pech, walk or drive up toward the **San Ignacio Resort Hotel** (p. 269), continuing around the curve for a few hundred yards until you pass the soccer field. Turn left here and climb the hill toward the ruins. The entrance to the ruins is beyond the **Cahal Pech Village Resort** (p. 270).

Admission to museum and ruins BZ$10. Daily 6am–6pm.

Chechem Ha ★ This ancient Mayan burial cave was discovered by accident when a local hunter, Antonio Morales, went chasing after his errant dog. When the cave was explored, a cache of Mayan artifacts, including many large, fully preserved pots, was discovered. Archaeologists estimate the relics could have been placed here more than 2,000 years ago. This cave is one of only two in the area with an elaborate altar used for ceremonial purposes by the religious and ruling classes.

The cave is located 16km (10 miles) south of Benque Viejo, on a dirt road that is recommended only for four-wheel-drive vehicles. Chechem Ha, which means "Cave of Poisonwood Water," is privately owned by the Morales family, and admission is allowed only with a prearranged guided tour. Almost every hotel and tour agency in the area can arrange a visit for you as well, though they tend to charge a little bit more for their efforts.

Getting to the cave entrance requires a reasonable degree of physical fitness, so skip this one if a 40-minute uphill hike is not for you. The nearby Chechem Ha Falls make a refreshing spot to wash and cool off after clambering around inside the caves. Also close to Chechem Ha is **Vaca Falls,** a beautiful and remote waterfall that's often combined with a visit to the cave, though it's a destination in its own right. This cave is less popular than others in the area, so it's a safe bet if you want to avoid crowds while spelunking.

http://chechemhacave.weebly.com. ✆ **667-4714.** Tour BZ$100 for one person, BZ$50 for every person thereafter.

Xunantunich ★★★ Everyone has trouble pronouncing it (say "Shoe-nahn-too-*neetch*"). But that shouldn't stop you from going to Xunantunich, an impressive, well-excavated, and easily accessible Mayan site. The name translates as "Maiden of the Rocks." The main pyramid here (and the second tallest in Belize) is **El Castillo,** which rises to 39m (128 ft.) and is clearly visible from the highway as you approach. It's a steep climb, but the view from the top is amazing—don't miss it. You'll be able to make out the twin border towns of Benque Viejo, Belize, and Melchor de Menchos, Guatemala. On the east side of the pyramid, near the top, is a remarkably well-preserved stucco frieze.

Down below in the temple forecourt, archaeologists found three magnificent steles portraying rulers of the region. These have been moved to the protection of the small on-site museum, yet the years and ravages of weather have made most of the carvings difficult to decipher. Xunantunich was a thriving Mayan city about the same time as Altun Ha, in the Classic Period from about A.D. 600 to 900.

The visitor center at the entrance contains a helpful scale model of the old city, as well as a replica of the original frieze. Xunantunich is located 10km (6¼ miles) past San Ignacio on the road to Benque Viejo. To reach the ruins, you must cross the Mopan River aboard a tiny hand-cranked car-ferry in the village of San José Succotz at no cost. Colorfully dressed women can be seen washing clothes in the river as you are cranked across by the ferryman. After crossing the river, it is a mile-long, uphill walk to the ruins. If you've got your

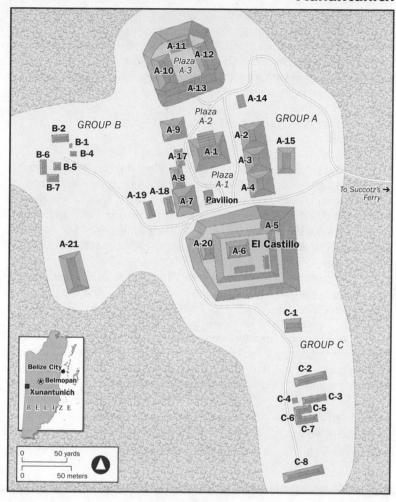

B-2, B-1, GROUP B, B-6, B-4, B-5, B-7, A-11, A-12, Plaza A-3, A-10, A-13, A-14, A-9, Plaza A-2, GROUP A, A-2, A-15, A-17, A-1, A-3, A-8, Plaza A-1, A-4, A-19, A-18, A-7, Pavilion, To Succotz's Ferry, A-5, A-21, A-20, A-6, El Castillo, C-1, GROUP C, C-2, C-4, C-3, C-5, C-6, C-7, C-8

Belize City, Belmopan, Xunantunich, BELIZE

0 50 yards / 0 50 meters

own vehicle, you can take it across on the ferry and drive right to the ruins. To get here by bus, take any bus bound for Benque Viejo and get off in San José Succotz. You'll see a small line of makeshift souvenir stands lining the road, just beside the ferry crossing. **Hanna Stables** (www.hannastables.com; © **661-1536**) also offers a 4-hour tour for BZ$144 from their property in San José Succotz for those who want to explore Mayan history by horseback.

Admission BZ$10. Daily 8am–4pm.

RIVER TOURS

For much of Belize's history, its rivers were the main highways. The Maya used them for trading, and British loggers used them to move mahogany and logwood. Which is why it's fascinating to explore the Cayo District's two rivers—the Macal and Mopan—by canoe, kayak, and inner tube. Throughout most of the year, the waters in these rivers are easily navigable both up- and downstream. However, during the rainy season, things can change drastically—and fast. I've heard of a few flash floods, and even one story of water nearly reaching the road on the Hawkesworth Bridge.

Still, for the most part, trips are leisurely, with plenty of places to stop for a quick swim or land excursion. During the rainy season (July–Sept), whitewater kayaking is available, although it's not very consistent. Inflatable kayaks are a much more common and dependable option, not requiring nearly as much technical proficiency or water.

Most tours put in upstream on the Macal River somewhere around Chaa Creek (p. 275) or duPlooy's (p. 274) and then float leisurely downstream. The trip can take anywhere from 1 to 3 hours, depending on how much time you spend paddling, floating, or stopping to hike or swim. All the local riverside hotels offer this service, as well as a host of operators in San Ignacio. For its part, the Mopan River is more easily accessible in many ways, because Benque Viejo Road borders it in many places. The Mopan is well-suited for inflatable kayaks and inner tubes.

In addition to most of the tour operators listed on p. 262, **David's Adventure Tours** (www.davidsadventuretours.com; © **804-3674**) offers primo float tours.

Both of Cayo's principal rivers are great for swimming. On the Macal River you can join the locals right in town, where the river is treated as a free laundry, car wash, horse and dog wash, and swimming hole. However, you'll do better to head upstream. The farther upstream you head, the more isolated and clear the swimming holes become.

Another alternative is to head downriver about 2.4km (1½ miles) to a spot called **Branch Mouth,** where the different-colored waters of the Macal and Mopan rivers converge. Branch Mouth is a favorite picnic spot, with shady old trees clinging to the riverbanks. There's even a rope swing from one of the trees. The road is dusty, so you'll be especially happy to go for a swim here.

River Race

While it's still possible to navigate the Belize River all the way to Belize City—the Macal and Mopan rivers join and become the Belize River—this is not generally something tourists get to do. Still, each year in early March, scores of three-person canoe teams undertake the long 290km (180-mile) paddle from San Ignacio to Belize City in the **Ruta Maya Belize River Challenge.** Teams gather in San Ignacio below the Hawkesworth Bridge in the first week of March, and thousands of people line the banks of the river for the start. The finish line, fittingly enough, is the Swing Bridge in Belize City. It takes between 3 and 4 days to complete the course, with the teams scheduled to arrive in Belize City on or around Baron Bliss Day. Read more about it on their website, www.larutamaya.bz.

Farther upstream, on both the Macal and Mopan rivers, are numerous swimming holes.

UP CLOSE WITH WILDLIFE

Chaa Creek Natural History Centre and Blue Morpho Butterfly Farm ★★

The Chaa Creek Lodge (p. 275) property is right in the heart of the jungle, and the shaded canopy is the perfect place for blue morpho butterflies to breed. Although the metallic blue butterflies are easy to spot in the wild, the farm is your best shot at getting close enough to them for a picture. Naturalists lead tours inside a screened-in building, where blue morphos fly around, land on people, and pose for photos. They don't look like anything special with their wings closed, but if the sun is shining they'll spread their wings and you can glimpse their beauty. There are other butterfly species as well, from pupae form to fully grown, plus the Natural History Centre which has a library and animals in jars on display.

www.chaacreek.com. *℃* **834-4010**. Admission BZ$10, or BZ$20 when combined with the **Rainforest Medicine Trail** (see below) tour, also on the lodge's property. Daily 8am–5pm, with 50-minute tours hourly, the last at 4pm.

Green Iguana Conservation Project ★★

The Green Iguana Conservation project) is a very popular attraction at the **San Ignacio Resort Hotel** (see below) where guests get hands-on time with iguanas, an overhunted reptile. Visitors can touch and feed the iguanas, some of which were born there and will be released into the wild (most are residents that must stay in captivity for medical reasons). You can pose with them, but wear long sleeves to protect your skin from their sharp claws.

www.sanignaciobelize.com/belize-iguana-project. *℃* **824-2034**. Admission BZ$18 per person. Reservations not required. Daily 8am–4pm, hourly tours.

OTHER ADVENTURE ACTIVITIES & NATURAL WONDERS

Belize Botanic Gardens ★★

Located next to duPlooy's (p. 274) and run by the same family, the Belize Botanic Gardens is a collection of local and imported tropical fauna spread across 45 acres. They have an excellent mix of fruit trees, palms, bromeliads, and bamboos, all well laid out whether you are taking a self-guided or guided tour. The orchid house is not to be missed, with its beautiful collection of over 100 orchid species and a palm exhibit. Ken duPlooy was an ornithologist, so be sure to keep your eyes open for the beautiful birds in the area.

www.belizebotanic.org. *℃* **824-3101**. Admission BZ$15, guided tours BZ$15 extra. For BZ$70 guests get entry and a shuttle pickup in San Ignacio. Daily 7am–5pm, guided tours 7:30am–3pm.

Barton Creek Cave ★

This is one of the area's more relaxing caves to explore, and not nearly as crowded as some of the others. The trip is conducted entirely by canoe, and while there are a few tight squeezes and areas with low ceilings, in general you won't get as wet (you'll stay dry, in fact) or claustrophobic here as you will at many of the other caves in Belize. Located beside a small Mennonite community, Barton Creek is navigable for nearly a

San Ignacio

If you enjoy horseback riding, there's some wonderful terrain in this area. The region is known for its horsemanship: It's common to see people riding horses as transportation, and skilled riding guides are easy to come by. Rides can be combined with visits to jungle waterfalls and swimming holes, as well as nearby Mayan ruins. Most of the hotels in the area offer horseback riding tours.

Mountain Equestrian Trails (www.met belize.com; ℰ **669-1124**) has one of the better stables and horse-riding operations in the Cayo District. It was built around providing a top-notch horse riding experience, whereas elsewhere it's clear that horses were not the priority. These are the best-trained horses I've come across in Cayo, and the guides are knowledgeable and helpful about riding, ideal for new and experienced riders alike.

mile inside the cave. Along the way, by the light of headlamps and strong flashlights, you'll see wonderful natural formations, a large gallery, and numerous Mayan artifacts, including several skeletons, believed to be the remains of ritual sacrifices.

There's a BZ$10 fee to visit the site, but that doesn't include the canoe trip or transportation. If you drive there yourself, you can hire a canoe that holds two passengers, plus the guide, for around BZ$40 to BZ$50. Tours out of San Ignacio average around BZ$120 to BZ$150 per person, including the entrance fee. Barton Creek Cave is located several miles down a bumpy side road off the Pine Ridge Road, about 6.4km (4 miles) from the George Price Highway.

The Rainforest Medicine Trail ★ Located directly between Chaa Creek and the Macal River Jungle Camp, this is the former Ix Chel Farm, which was set up by Dr. Rosita Arvigo and Dr. Greg Shropshire. Dr. Arvigo studied traditional herbal medicine with Don Elijio Panti, a local Mayan medicine man and a folk hero in Belize. Panti died in February 1996 at the estimated age of 104. Here on the farm, they built a trail through the forest to share with visitors the fascinating medicinal values of many of the tropical forest's plants.

The farm boasts a small gift shop that features local crafts, T-shirts, and several relevant books, including a couple by Arvigo. You'll also find Ix Chel's line of herbal concentrates, salves, and teas called Rainforest Remedies.

Self-guided visits to the Medicine Trail, along with a tour of Chaa Creek's **Natural History Centre and Blue Morpho Butterfly Farm** (see above), cost BZ$20. You can easily spend 3 hours visiting all three attractions.

ℰ **834-4010** for reservations. Self-guided tours BZ$20 each, guided tours of just the Medicine Trail BZ$20.

Shopping

Orange Gift Shop & Gallery (www.orangegifts.com; ℰ **824-3296**) is the best-stocked gift shop in this region and can be found about 11km (7 miles)

10

San Ignacio

CAYO DISTRICT & W. BELIZE

east of San Ignacio at Mile Marker 60 on the George Price Highway. However, I find the prices a bit high. Similar goods can be found less expensively at other shops that are within walking distance of accommodations in town, such as **Arts & Crafts of Central America,** 24 Burns Ave. (© **824-2253**). **Bakabush Books** (© **608-0324**) at the corner of Bullet Tree Road and Far West Street is a brand-new addition to the neighborhood and is likely the best selection of books in Belize, which is notorious for not having many books for sale.

I especially love perusing the **San Ignacio Market** (no phone), where farmers, traders, and vendors gather to sell jewelry, art, traditional medicines, and heaps of fresh fruit and veggies across from the main soccer stadium, on the banks of the Macal River. It's open daily from 5am to 6pm, but Saturday is the busiest and best time to visit.

Throughout Belize, and especially in Cayo, you will see slate carvings of Mayan hieroglyphs. If you're in the area, it's worth a visit to one of the sources, the **García Sisters ★★**. This family of artisans runs an interesting little museum-cum-craft shop (p. 284). It's located outside of San Antonio village on the road to Mountain Pine Ridge (see "Mountain Pine Ridge & Caracol," later in this chapter, for more information).

Where to Stay

EXPENSIVE

Ka'ana Resort ★★★   A honeymoon-worthy spot, this boutique hotel pulls off the neat trick of being chic, luxurious, *and* highly authentic to its roots. All rooms are individually decorated, with unique art and furniture produced within a 65km (40-mile) radius of the hotel. For those celebrating special occasions we recommend the larger, private casitas over the guest rooms. Hidden away in the lush gardens of the resort, they feature small decks in both the front and the back, hammocks, and bathrooms with a wall of glass tiles in the large showers, letting in natural light. If that isn't cushy enough, go for a villa—each has its own private pool (the resort also has an infinity pool set above a waterfall). In addition to the excellent restaurant here (p. 272), they have a well-stocked wine cellar and cigar bar. All of this pampering is extended to the offered tours—not only are they expertly executed, but the staff take photos and videos so that guests can enjoy their time gadget-free. Ka'ana is a member of the Small Luxury Hotels of the World group. It's located about 3km (2 miles) southwest of downtown San Ignacio, on the road out to Benque Viejo.

Mile 69¼ on the road to Benque Viejo, Cayo District. www.kaanabelize.com. © **305/735-2553** in the U.S. and Canada, or 820-3350 at the hotel. 15 units. BZ$675 double; BZ$900 casita. **Amenities:** Restaurant; bar; lounge; concierge; wedding services; outdoor pool; room service; airport shuttle; small spa; gift shop; Wi-Fi (free).

San Ignacio Resort Hotel ★★   This is easily the most comfortable and luxurious option in the town proper (Ka'ana is outside town). Set on a high ridge above the Macal River, the freshly renovated rooms are all spacious, with a touch of old world charm: four-poster beds (in some), wrought iron railings, high ceilings. Three of the suites boast Jacuzzis. Queen Elizabeth II stayed in room 131 when she visited, which is why that room, and the others with a hillside view, are called the Regal rooms. In addition to the pool, there are jungle trails, the **Green Iguana Conservation Project** (p. 267), and a medicinal plant trail. Staff, as at other resorts, will help arrange for all sorts of adventures. There's one lighted tennis court, and an excellent restaurant and bar with great views from its terrace. The lobby bar and lounge and neighboring casino are equally popular with locals and guests.

18 Buena Vista St., San Ignacio, Cayo District. www.sanignaciobelize.com. ℂ **800/822-3274** in the U.S., or 824-2125. 26 units. BZ$480 double; BZ$480 Regal suite; BZ$1,120 master suite. Rates slightly lower in the off season. **Amenities:** 2 restaurants; bar; lounge; casino; concierge; midsize outdoor pool; room service; small full-service spa; lit tennis court; Wi-Fi (free).

MODERATE

In addition to the places listed below, **The Rolson Hotel** (ℂ **824-2730**) offers clean, business class–style rooms with televisions, air-conditioning, and free Wi-Fi.

Cahal Pech Village Resort ★★   Set on a hillside on the outskirts of town, the resort has a wonderful view of San Ignacio and is just a stone's throw from the Cahal Pech ruins. Accommodations can be had either in the main building or in one of the thatched-roof individual cabanas, and while we prefer the latter (love their screened-in porches), they do require a bit of tramping up and down that hill. The rooms in the main building also have larger bathrooms, though some are in need of renovation (so ask to be moved if the furnishings seem a bit old). That being said, all accommodations are clean, spacious, and feature carved Mayan wall hangings and colorful Guatemalan bedspreads. There's a large, open-air restaurant on the second floor of the main building, where guests gather for meals and to trade travel tales, and a two-tiered midsize outdoor pool set on a high spot near the main building with a great view over the town and valley. Service is unusually caring and professional here. A pterodactyl statue overlooks the pool—we have no idea why.

Cahal Pech Hill. www.cahalpech.com. ℂ **824-3740.** 56 units. BZ$180 double; BZ$228–BZ$274 family cabanas and suites. **Amenities:** Restaurant; bar; lounge; mountain bike rental; tour desk; outdoor pool; Wi-Fi (free).

Martha's Guest House ★   This cozy guesthouse is located in the heart of San Ignacio, above a popular little restaurant. The vibe here is somewhere between that of a homestay and a youth hostel. All the rooms are immaculate. The more expensive rooms are larger and have minifridges and coffeemakers. There are also a couple of common lounge and balcony areas, where guests can hang out and read a book or chat. The fourth-floor First Lady suite is huge, and it features a large balcony with wonderful views of the town. It also comes with its own kitchenette, making it a good option for families. These folks also have a separate option a few blocks away that they are calling The Inn at Martha's, with fully equipped studio apartments.

10 West St., San Ignacio, Cayo District. www.marthasbelize.com. © **804-3647.** 10 units. BZ$120 double; BZ$140–BZ$160 suite. **Amenities:** Restaurant; bar; tour desk; Wi-Fi (free).

INEXPENSIVE

San Ignacio is a very popular budget travel destination, and there are plenty of affordable options in town. During the high season, advance reservations are highly recommended. At other times, backpackers might prefer to arrive in town early enough to visit a few places, and see which place gives the best bang for the buck. Of the backpacker-geared options, my favorite is **The Old House Hostel,** 3 Buena Vista St. (http://hostelbelize.weebly.com; © **623-1342**). It's a great place to make friends with fellow travelers and younger locals. I've also enjoyed the private rooms at **Hi-Et,** 12 West St. (thehiet@yahoo.com; © **824-2828**), with its hostel-like vibe and playful name.

Casa Blanca Guest House ★   As the name suggests, this centrally-located hotel is white, but it's the pink trim that makes it stand out among the hubbub of Burns Avenue. The rooms are all located on the second floor of a building set in the heart of the city's commercial core. The compact rooms all come with a television, ceiling fan, private bathroom, and air-conditioning, although you'll have to pay more for the A/C. There's a large common sitting area and a communal kitchen where you're always likely to bump into fellow travelers. There's also a small common balcony overlooking the hustle and bustle of Burns Avenue.

10 Burns Ave., San Ignacio, Cayo District. www.casablancaguesthouse.com. © **824-2080.** 9 units. BZ$70 double with fan; BZ$100 double with A/C. **Amenities:** Wi-Fi (free).

Midas Tropical Resort ★★   Is this San Ignacio or Las Vegas? Whoever designed the pool would like guests to think the latter. It features LED lights changing the color of the water, plus a hidden grotto that requires swimming underwater to enter. This is presumably where people go to make out, so enter at your own risk. The rest of the resort is all Belize, though, with Mayan-style cottages (thatched roofs, screen walls), plus wooden cabins on raised stilts and corrugated roofs. There are also basic rooms in the main building (clean and comfortable, though the water isn't always reliable). Some digs have air-conditioning and televisions, though you'll pay more for those perks. All have ceiling fans, and with the large, breeze-catching windows, most find they don't need the A/C. The Macal River is only a stroll away down a grassy lane, and you can spend the day lounging on the little beach on the riverbank. We also have to tip our hats to the staff who are an unusually friendly, helpful group.

To reach Midas, walk north out of town on Savannah St., which is 1 block east of Burns Ave. The hotel is about .8km (½ mile) from the center of town. www.midasbelize.com. © **824-3172.** BZ$94–BZ$172 double; BZ$282 king deluxe. 13 units. **Amenities:** Restaurant; big pool; pool bar; Wi-Fi (free).

Where to Dine

In addition to the places listed below, **Maxim's Chinese Restaurant,** 23 Far West St. (℗ **824-2283**), is a local's favorite. You might also want to take the adventure of finding **Sanny's Grill,** 23rd Street (℗ **664-9083**), which is tucked away in a residential neighborhood and serves excellent seafood and grilled meats. For inexpensive eats in a large outdoor setting, you can try **Hode's Place Bar & Grill** (www.hodesplace.com; ℗ **804-2522**), located out on the northern end of town. They are also one of the only places in town that do delivery. **The Ice Cream Shoppe** at 24 West St. (℗ **615-6160**) serves up excellent scoops, with Belize-specific flavors, like soursop, a fruit found only in the tropics of Latin America. They serve standard flavors too, plus milkshakes that are expensive but totally worth it.

EXPENSIVE

La Ceiba ★★★ BELIZEAN/FUSION   This resort restaurant should not be missed if you're staying in the region. The kitchen combines contemporary techniques with local ingredients, many harvested from the organic gardens on-site. Especially remarkable are the creative interpretations of Belizean classics, which often show up as daily specials and might feature a version of the seafood stew *Sere,* or a jazzed-up stew of beans and rice. A favorite is the local pork sausage served in *Dukunu*—a roasted corn tamale recipe that dates to Mayan times—accompanied by a chipotle, guava, and tomato chutney. The wine selection here is excellent, well-priced, and expertly stored. The ambiance is also exceptional, with a cozy fire pit and dazzling outdoor lighting.

At Ka'ana resort, Mile Marker 69¼ on the road to Benque Viejo. ℗ **820-3350.** Reservations recommended. Main courses BZ$35–BZ$80. Daily 6:15am–3pm and 6–10pm.

Running W Steak House & Restaurant ★★ STEAKHOUSE/BELIZEAN   Located in the San Ignacio Resort Hotel, this restaurant is affiliated with Belize's largest beef and cattle operation, its namesake. Which means that all the beef dishes are winners, though I'm partial to the grass-fed ribeye. The restaurant also serves up seafood, chicken, and other dishes with the same attention to quality as their beef. Belizean standards will cost you more here than at a local joint, but the taste reflects the quality of the ingredients. From Friday through Sunday sushi is served, and live music is often played in the dining room, which is large and comfortable, with plenty of varnished wood and air-conditioning to keep it cool. A few wrought-iron tables line an outdoor patio and make a great place to have lunch with a jungle view or dinner under the stars.

18 Buena Vista St., in the San Ignacio Resort Hotel. ℗ **824-2034.** Reservations recommended. Main courses BZ$40–BZ$75. Daily 7am–11pm.

MODERATE

Guava Limb Café ★★★ INTERNATIONAL   In a verdant garden, lit by candles, diners relax, sometimes canoodle (it *is* a romantic setting) and dine on some of the best food in Belize. Don't be put off by the fact that the menu runs the gamut from Indonesian dishes to Mediterranean classics like falafel and hummus, in addition to Italian, American, Chinese, and Caribbean options. What's served is expertly prepared and handsomely plated. And hearty! Portions here tend to be oversized, so don't be shy about asking to share: The genial staff willingly divide entrees onto two plates for diners.

79 Burns Ave. www.guavalimb.com. © **824-4837.** Main courses BZ$20–BZ$45. Tues–Sat 11am–10pm; Sun 11am–5pm.

Ko-Ox Han-Nah ★ INDIAN/PAN-ASIAN This place is also known simply as Hannah's, though we like the Mayan name which translates roughly to "let's go eat." Don't be put off by the humble decor, with simple furniture and half walls with steel grating substituting for windows. The menu is massive, with a host of curries, vindaloos, and other Indian staples, mixed with a hefty dose of Chinese and Thai cuisine. Heck, you can even get burgers, burritos, Belizean fare, and big breakfasts here. Still, I recommend you come for the Indian cooking. The chef here is not shy to spice things up. The vindaloos and other fiery dishes can blow your head off if you're not accustomed to authentic cooking. This is a great restaurant for vegetarians, with ample options to choose from.

5 Burns Ave. © **824-3014.** Main courses BZ$16–BZ$48. Daily 6am–9pm.

INEXPENSIVE

Pop's Restaurant ★★★ BELIZEAN Everyone loves Pop's—it's the most popular breakfast spot in the area. The fry jacks are made perfectly, the breakfast burrito is the beginning to a great day, and the atmosphere fosters conversation among strangers. It's frequented by locals, repeat travelers, and lucky guests who stumble into the small restaurant on Far West Street. Try the cheese and Chaya omelet for a more Belizean breakfast (Chaya essentially being a tropical spinach) or dive into any of the American options on the menu.

At Far West and Waight sts. www.pops-restaurant.com. © **824-3366.** Main courses BZ$6–BZ$20. Daily 6:30am–3pm.

Erva's ★★ BELIZEAN/MEXICAN There are scores of places in San Ignacio serving local cuisine, but Erva's is a long-standing favorite. Erva is an excellent cook and congenial hostess. In addition to traditional Belizean and Mexican standards, you can get pizza and some seafood dishes here. Still, it's the stew chicken and rice and beans that brings folks in the door—and keeps them (and me) coming back for more. Erva's is located on the ground floor of the Pacz Hotel, a few blocks away from the center of town.

4 Far West St. © **824-2821.** Main courses BZ$12–BZ$28. Mon–Sat 7am–10pm.

Eva's Restaurant & Bar ★ BELIZEAN/INTERNATIONAL Eva's is ideally located for people-watching, with tables right on the edge of the pedestrian walkway. On offer are hearty and well-prepared Belizean and Mexican standards. The *escabeche,* a traditional soup or stew, is top-notch, as are the stew beans and rice. The service is a little slow, but they have free, reliable Wi-Fi.

22 Burns Ave. ℰ **804-2267.** Main courses BZ$6–BZ$18. Daily 6:30am–9pm.

San Ignacio After Dark

Recently, and inexplicably, all the reliable nightlife spots of San Ignacio went out of business making this into a very sleepy town. The younger generation is doing their best to bring the party back with the **Belize Soul Project** (ℰ **653-1855**), a twice-weekly live music event beneath The Old House Hostel during which alcohol is served. Check it out Wednesday and Friday from 6 to 11pm. Also, on the north end of town, **Hode's Place Bar & Grill** (ℰ **804-2522**) is a massive spot that is very popular with locals. They have a tiny casino, as well as a large video arcade, and a pool and foosball tables.

If you're the gambling type, you'll want to head to the **Princess Casino,** 18 Buena Vista Ave. (ℰ **824-4047**), which is located next to the San Ignacio Resort Hotel and stays open as late as 5am. I'd definitely choose this one over the very little casino at **Hode's Place** (above).

Nearby Lodges & Retreats

ON THE ROAD TO BENQUE VIEJO & THE GUATEMALAN BORDER

While San Ignacio is the regional hub and does make a good base for side trips, the real attractions in western Belize are up the rivers and in the forests. Within a few miles of San Ignacio are several lodges set somewhat off the beaten path, where you can canoe down clear rivers past 1.2m (4-ft.) iguanas sunning themselves on the rocks, ride horses to Mayan ruins, hike jungle trails, and spot scores of beautiful birds and, occasionally, other wild animals. Out on the road to Caracol and Mountain Pine Ridge, there are more of these lodges. Except for the true budget traveler, I highly recommend that you stay at one of the lodges listed below while you're in the area. A few of the lodges can be reached by public bus from San Ignacio, though you may have up to a 20-minute walk after getting off the bus, so consider taking a taxi or arranging pickup in town. Self-driving is also possible, but know that the roads are in heavy disrepair. All the lodges offer a wide range of active adventures and tours to all the principal sites in the area.

Expensive

duPlooy's ★   This family-run lodge overlooks the Macal River, with jungle-covered limestone cliffs opposite. This stunning location, combined with personalized attention, makes duPlooy's one of Cayo's more popular jungle lodges. My favorite rooms are the spacious bungalows, which come with a king-size bed, futon couch, and large wooden veranda. Another option is the Belize River House, two separate multiroom suites that can be rented separately, or as one huge unit sleeping up to 14 people. The lodge's open-air bar features a spacious deck overlooking the river. There's a beach on the river, as well as several trails through the forest. One of the nicest features here is an elevated walkway running at the level of the forest canopy, which connects much of the complex and also juts out into the forest, offering wonderful opportunities for bird-watching. The neighboring **Belize Botanic Gardens** ★★ provides even more bird-watching opportunities, in addition to an abundance of tropical flora. They also offer horseback riding, canoeing, tubing, and can arrange any tour you're interested in.

Off the road to Benque Viejo, Cayo District. www.duplooys.com. © **824-3101.** 19 units. BZ$410 double; BZ$460 bungalows. Rates include continental breakfast and unlimited entrance to the Belize Botanic Gardens. To get here, head out of town on the road to Benque Viejo; the turnoff for duPlooy's is the same as that for Chaa Creek, and it is well marked. DuPlooy's is a bit farther on the same dirt road, but be sure to take the right fork and follow the signs. **Amenities:** Restaurant; bar; lounge; small spa; Wi-Fi (free).

The Lodge at Chaa Creek ★★★   Located on a high, steep bank over the Macal River, this is one of the top hotels in the country. It's easy to see why once on the property. All the thatched-roof cottages are artistically decorated with local and Guatemalan textiles and handicrafts. Each comes with a quiet porch or balcony area set amid the flowering gardens, where provided hammocks can be hung. My favorite rooms are the large treetop suites, which feature a queen bed, a sunken living-room area, and a wraparound deck fitted with a sunken Jacuzzi. Budget travelers can stay in the camp casitas for BZ$130 a night, and even though they lack the luxury of the main buildings, they're right in the heart of the jungle and all the wild animals that come with it (and the budget rate includes breakfast and dinner). The lodge has a lovely full-service spa, and a host of on-site attractions, including a natural history museum, a blue morpho farm, a medicinal plant trail, and a beautiful pool. Canoes and mountain bikes are available, and horseback rides can always be arranged. Mick and Lucy Fleming, who originally began farming this land in 1977, are the engaging hosts, and much of the food served in the restaurant is organically grown on the hotel's own farm. In 2017 Chaa Creek received the prestigious World Legacy Award from National Geographic for their accomplishments in sustainable ecotourism.

Off the road to Benque Viejo, Cayo District. www.chaacreek.com. © **877/709-8708** in the U.S. and Canada, or 824-2037 reservations office in Belize, or 820-4010 at the

Los Finados

On November 2, the residents of Benque Viejo del Carmen celebrate **Los Finados,** a local version of El Día de los Muertos (The Day of the Dead), or All Souls' Day. Families visit the local cemetery, where graves are spruced up and adorned with flowers and votive candles. Many families set up a makeshift altar for their dead at home or on the front lawn. *Bollos* are prepared from cornmeal dough stuffed with chicken and a local purple bean, the *ixpelon.* Local children make jack-o'-lanterns out of hollowed-out squash or even grapefruit. At night the cemetery is alight with the flicker from hundreds of candles.

lodge. 37 units. BZ$778 double; BZ$1,118–BZ$1,278 suite or villa. Rates include breakfast. To reach Chaa Creek, drive 8km (5 miles) west from San Ignacio and watch for the sign on your left. It's another couple of miles down a rough dirt road from the main highway. **Amenities:** Restaurant; bar; lounge; bike rental; concierge; large outdoor pool; smoke-free rooms; small well-equipped spa; Wi-Fi (free).

Moderate
Black Rock Jungle River Lodge ★★
So, you *really* want to get away from it all? Well, this is the place. The setting, on a high bluff overlooking the Macal River, 6 miles down a bumpy dirt road off the main highway, is one of the most stunning/majestic/awe-inspiring in the area. The individual cabins here don't quite match that level of pulchritude (what could?) but are quite nice, with high-pitched ceilings and big windows. The pricier ones feature large private balconies and fabulous views of the river and/or canyon cliffs. Meals are served at large communal tables in the large open-air dining room and main lodge area, which also has a fabulous view of the river below and forests all around. Much of the fresh produce is organically grown on-site, and electricity is provided by a combination of solar and hydro power sources. Swimming and inner tubing on the river from the lodge are excellent. So why two rather than three stars? While the service is top-notch, there is a good bit of nickel and diming here (like charging for coffee refills at meals).

Off the road to Benque Viejo, Cayo District. www.blackrocklodge.com. © **834-4038** reservations office, or 820-3929 at the lodge. 20 units. BZ$280–BZ$310 double; BZ$370–BZ$430 deluxe. Rates lower in the off season; higher during peak periods. If you're driving, take the turnoff for Chaa Creek and duPlooy's, and then follow the signs to Black Rock. **Amenities:** Restaurant; bar; pool; Wi-Fi (free).

Clarissa Falls Resort ★★
Situated on a 324-hectare (800-acre) working cattle ranch, this modest resort boasts a range of accommodations from deluxe suites to individual cabins to campsites. The thatched-roof cabins are fairly basic, with cement floors, bamboo walls, simple beds, and little else. Suites are a step up and are nicely done, featuring a full kitchen and dining area. But it's unlikely you'll want to cook: The open-air restaurant here serves excellent Belizean and Mexican cuisine for very reasonable prices, and sits atop a small Mayan ruin. Owner Chena Gálvez is extremely personable (she makes guests feel like family), and staff members can help arrange boats and inner tube rentals for use on property; horseback riding is also available. If you'd like to just visit for the day, you can swim in the river and picnic for BZ$2, which is a very popular activity on weekends (if you crave peace and tranquility, visit on a weekday). Contrary to the name, there is no waterfall on the property, but there is a little babbling rapid in the river that is pleasant to listen to.

Benque Viejo Rd., Mile Marker 70½. www.clarissafallsresort.com. © **668-6979.** 12 units. BZ$150 double; BZ$350 suite; BZ$15 per person to camp. Clarissa Falls Resort is about 1.6km (1 mile) down a dirt road, off the highway about 6km (4 miles) west of San Ignacio. The bus to Benque Viejo will drop you at the turnoff. Free parking. **Amenities:** Restaurant; bar; Wi-Fi (free).

Inexpensive

Macal River Jungle Camp ★   Run by the folks at Chaa Creek, this deluxe campsite is a top choice for those who want to be close to nature but don't need a lot of frills. The spacious tent units are all set on raised platforms among the forest trees. Each comes with two to four single beds, as well as a couple of kerosene lanterns. There's a small sitting area or front porch, with an oil lamp and a couple of chairs. Meals are served in a central, open, thatched-roof structure, which also has some hammocks for hanging out. The communal bathroom and shower areas are clean and well-maintained. The river is down a short path from the campsite; Rainforest Medicine Trail and Chaa Creek are nearby. Guests at the tent camp can rent canoes, head over for meals a la carte, or sign up for tours offered at Chaa Creek.

Off the road to Benque Viejo, Cayo District. www.chaacreek.com. ℂ **877/709-8708** in the U.S. and Canada, or 824-2037 reservations office in Belize, or 820-4010 at the lodge. 10 tents. BZ$110 per person. Rates include breakfast and dinner. Rates slightly lower during the off season. **Amenities:** Restaurant; no Wi-Fi or electricity.

The Trek Stop ★   This rustic little outpost is geared toward backpackers and adventure travelers. The accommodations here are spread around a broad garden and backed by dense forest, and they range from campsites to simple cabins to a couple of newer cabins with private bathrooms. Most of the wooden cabins are quite small, but they do come with a private little front porch, where you can sit and read. Guests can either eat at the little restaurant here or cook their own food in the communal kitchen. A wide range of tours and activities is offered, and inner tubing on the Mopan River is one of their specialties. They even have a 9-hole Frisbee golf course—claimed to be the only one in Belize. This place is very close to the ferry over to Xunantunich. The Trek Stop is located next to the Tropical Wings Nature Center, just off the main road about 9.7km (6 miles) west of San Ignacio.

Benque Viejo Rd., Mile Marker 71½, San José Succotz, Cayo District. www.thetrekstop. com. ℂ **660-7895.** 10 units (8 with shared bathroom). BZ$80–BZ$150 double cabin with shared bathroom; BZ$14 per person camping. **Amenities:** Restaurant; mountain-bike rental; Wi-Fi (free).

ON THE ROAD TO BULLET TREE FALLS

El Pilar ★★ (www.marc.ucsb.edu; ℂ **824-3612**) was discovered in the 1970s, but real excavation and exploration didn't begin for another 20 years, and in fact it's still in its nascent stages. The site sits on a high hill some 274m (900 ft.) above the Mopan River and is one of the largest Mayan settlements in Belize. Some say it even rivals Caracol. This ancient ceremonial city featured more than 25 known plazas and covered some 40 hectares (100 acres), straddling the Belize and Guatemala border. The site is quite large, but most visitors concentrate on Xaman Pilar (North Pilar) and Nohol Pilar (South Pilar). Pilar Poniente (West Pilar) is in Guatemala, a little less than a mile away. There are several well-marked and well-maintained trails throughout the site. While you can explore El Pilar by yourself—you can even download a very informative trail map from the above website—I still recommend hiring a local guide. Plan on spending at least 3 hours here, though you could easily spend a full day or two exploring this site. The sunsets from Plaza Ixim looking west to Pilar Poniente and the forested hills of Guatemala are spectacular.

El Pilar is located about 19km (12 miles) north of San Ignacio, past the village of Bullet Tree Falls. In addition to driving your own vehicle, several tour agencies in San Ignacio offer horseback or mountain-bike tours out to El Pilar.

Where to Stay in Bullet Tree Falls

To get to the hotel mentioned below, take Waight's Avenue west out of the center of San Ignacio. This turns into Bullet Tree Falls Road. Follow the flow of traffic to the village of Bullet Tree Falls. The whole trip is just more than 2 miles. If you arrange it in advance, the hotel will provide pickup, or a taxi should cost you around BZ$25.

Parrot Nest Lodge ★★ One of our favorite budget lodgings in Belize, the Parrot Nest is a quirky, friendly place run by an expat family who clearly love their adopted home and are expert in the art of hospitality. Each evening they run an informal "salon" in the common area, and guests gather, grab a drink from the honor bar, discuss their days, and admire the small menagerie of exotic pets that live on the property (including a possum). The hotel features some of the more unique rooms in the Cayo District, and yes, some are "nest"-like. Set on a 2-hectare (5-acre) tropical plant farm on the banks of the Mopan River, two of the resort's rustic cabins are set high above the ground on stilts, amongst the branches of a huge guanacaste tree. Four of the units have private bathrooms, but the shared showers and toilets are kept immaculate. As for the decor: Think summer camp and you won't be disappointed. The furnishings are pretty basic but most guests don't mind, especially at these reasonable prices. Upon request, owners Theo and Marcus serve delicious dinners and breakfasts (extra charge). They arrange an array of activities for guests. You can also take an inner tube right from the lodge and spend some time floating on the river, for free (staff will pick you up down the river).

Bullet Tree Falls, Cayo District. www.parrot-nest.com. © **669-6068.** 9 units (5 with shared bathroom). BZ$110–BZ$162 double. Parking available. **Amenities:** Restaurant; mountain-bike rental; tubing; Wi-Fi (free).

MOUNTAIN PINE RIDGE & CARACOL ★★

111km (69 miles) W of Belize City

South of San Ignacio and the George Price Highway, and east of the Macal River, lies the Mountain Pine Ridge region of Belize. Few people think of pine trees when thinking about the tropics, but you'll see plenty of them in these rugged mountains. This area is a natural wonderland of spectacular waterfalls,

Mountain Pine Ridge

ACCOMMODATIONS ■
Black Rock Jungle
  River Lodge **5**
Blancaneaux Lodge **16**
Chaa Creek **2**
Crystal Paradise Resort **4**
duPlooy's **6**
Gaia River Lodge **14**
Hidden Valley Inn **17**
Macal River Jungle Camp **2**
Mountain Equestrian Trails **12**
Mystic River Resort **7**
Pine Ridge Lodge **15**
Table Rock **3**
The Trek Stop **1**

**ATTRACTIONS
AND SHOPPING ●**
Barton Creek Cave **9**
Belize Botanical Gardens **6**
Calico Jack's Village **10**
Caracol **21**
Five Sisters Falls **13**
Hidden Valley Falls **20**
Magaña Zaac Tunich
  Art Gallery **11**
Rio Frio Cave **19**
Rio on Pools **18**
Tanah Mayan Art Museum **8**

wild orchids, parrots, keel-billed toucans, and other exotic flora and fauna. **Mountain Pine Ridge Forest Reserve, Hidden Valley Falls** (also called Thousand Foot Falls), **Five Sisters Falls,** and the **Río on Pools** and **Río Frío Caves** are all located in this area.

Continuing through the Mountain Pine Ridge, you'll eventually come to **Caracol,** which is the largest of the Belizean Mayan ruins. Caracol was a major Classic Mayan center, rivaling and frequently battling nearby Tikal. Excavation is still in its infancy here, but the site is nonetheless impressive. At nearly 42m (138 ft.), the main pyramid at Caracol remains the tallest man-made structure in Belize.

Pine beetle infestations and forest fires have periodically ravaged the forests of the Mountain Pine Ridge reserve, leaving broad swaths totally barren for miles. However, the forests here tend to recover well, and quickly. Still, it's surprising to watch the landscape shift so quickly from dense jungle to young, sparse woods.

Essentials
GETTING THERE & DEPARTING
BY PLANE   The nearest airport to this region is in San Ignacio. Although it gets no regularly scheduled commuter traffic, there is a private airstrip at Blancaneaux Lodge (p. 284) and Hidden Valley Inn (p. 285) for charter flights to those hotels. These can be arranged with **Javier's Flying Service** (www.javiersflyingservice.com; ℓ **824-0460**), and with **Tropic Air** (www.tropicair.com; ℓ **226-2626**). That being said, we don't think the cost is worth it. Driving is an easy and convenient way to get most anywhere in the country.

BY CAR   If you're driving to the Mountain Pine Ridge area from Belize City along the George Price Highway, the first turnoff is at Georgeville, around Mile Marker 61. This is the quickest route if you're going deep into the Mountain Pine Ridge area and to Caracol. There's another turnoff in the town of Santa Elena that will take you through Cristo Rey and San Antonio villages, as well as to some of the lodges listed below. Whichever of these routes you take, the roads merge around Mile Marker 10, where you will come to the entrance to the Mountain Pine Ridge Forest Reserve. The guard will ask you where you are going, and whether you have a reservation, but there is no fee to enter the reserve.

These roads can get pretty muddy and slick in the wet season and are bumpy and rugged in the dry season, so I recommend you have a four-wheel-drive vehicle, if nothing else for the extra clearance it will provide. Even though the distances seem relatively slight in terms of mileage, the going can be slow, so allow plenty of driving time if you plan on visiting this area.

Tip: The difference in time and distance between these two turnoffs is negligible, as they meet up about 14km (8⅔ miles) in from the Western Highway (19km [12 miles] if you're coming via Cristo Rey Village and San Antonio Village).

BY BUS   There is no regular direct bus service to the Mountain Pine Ridge area from Belize City.

GETTING AROUND
Your best bet for getting around this area is to have your own vehicle. Short of that, you can rely on your hotel or organized tours. Taxis can be called from San Ignacio and Santa Elena. For a cab, call **Cayo Taxi Association** at ℓ **824-2196.** A cab from San Ignacio to any of the hotels in this area costs around BZ$80 to BZ$120, and a cab from Philip S. W. Goldson International Airport in Belize City to a hotel in this area costs between BZ$250 and BZ$300.

ORIENTATION
Once the two entrance roads join up, there is basically one "major" road leading through the Mountain Pine Forest Reserve and on out to the Caracol ruins. This rough dirt road is alternatively known as the Pine Ridge Road or the Chiquibil Road. Caracol, the Río On Pools, Río Frío Cave, and Five Sisters Falls are located either right on or just off this road. Various spurs and assorted

lesser roads head off toward some of the other attractions and destinations listed below. Everything is fairly well-marked and signposted.

There are no major settlements in this area. The only town of any size and note is San Antonio Village, a quaint little Maya village. This is where the cement portion of the road ends.

What to See & Do

The easiest way to visit Mountain Pine Ridge and its many attractions is on a guided tour out of San Ignacio or one of the nearby lodges. These tours average between BZ$60 and BZ$120 per person for a half-day tour of Mountain Pine Ridge and a visit to one of the waterfalls, and about BZ$180 to BZ$300 for a full-day guided trip to Caracol with lunch. If you're staying in Mountain Pine Ridge, just arrange the tour with your hotel. If you're in San Ignacio, check in with **Pacz Tours ★★** (www.pacztours.net; ℂ **824-0536**) or **Yute Expeditions ★** (www.inlandbelize.com; ℂ **824-2076**).

HORSEBACK RIDING   The terrain here is wonderful for horseback riding. Most horseback tours will take you to one or more of the major attractions in this area, or at least to some quiet swimming hole or isolated waterfall. Most of the hotels out here offer horseback riding tours. Alternatively, you can contact the folks at **Mountain Equestrian Trails** (www.metbelize.com; ℂ **669-1124**), who have one of the better stables and horse-riding operations in the Cayo District. A half-day trip including lunch costs BZ$136 per person; a full-day trip costs BZ$186.

ZIPLINE CANOPY & CAVE TOURS ★   The folks at **Calico Jack's Village** (www.calicojacksvillage.com; ℂ **820-4078**) have opened up a multiadventure sport attraction in the hills and forests just outside the village of El Progresso. The main attraction here is a zipline canopy tour, in which you use a climbing harness and pulley system to glide along steel cables from one treetop platform to another. There are three ziplining options, from four to nine runs, and one night tour for the truly bold. Their longest run is 884m (2,900 feet) long. The trips range between BZ$80 and BZ$176 per person. While here you can also take a guided tour of one of their on-site caves or hike their jungle trails. Combination packages with lunch are available, and they have a few on-site villas for BZ$150 for those looking to stay.

WILL NATURAL WONDERS NEVER CEASE?

WATERFALLS   Waterfalls are abundant in this region. Perhaps my favorite are the falls found at the **Río On Pools ★★**. This is a series of falls and pools somewhat reminiscent of Ocho Ríos in Jamaica. There's a little entrance hut and parking lot when you enter the area. From here, some concrete steps lead straight down a hill to the base of the falls. Many of the rocks among the pools are perfect for sunbathing. This place can get crowded on weekends, when locals come for family picnics and getaways. The Río on Pools are located at around Mile Marker 18½ of the Pine Ridge Road. There is no entrance fee.

You can also visit the **Five Sisters Falls ★★**, a lovely series of cascading falls that divides into five distinct side-by-side cascades just above the riverside beach and bar area of the Gaia River Lodge (aka Five Sisters Lodge) (p. 287). If you are not staying at the lodge, you may visit the falls for BZ$10. It's 290 steps, almost straight down, to the water and the base of the falls. Luckily, you don't have to hoof it, unless you want to, since they have a little funicular. For an extra charge of BZ$8, the funicular will take you to and from the base of the falls, where the hotel has a little beach area and several natural swimming holes. There are some nature trails you can hike, and a small snack bar, restrooms, and changing facilities. You'll even find a wonderful open-air thatch palapa on the banks of the river strung with hammocks—a compelling spot for an afternoon siesta.

RÍO FRÍO CAVE   This high, vaulted cave is about 183m (600 ft.) long and open at both ends, with a lazy creek flowing through it. There's a path leading through the cave, and several hiking trails run through the forests surrounding it. This is a good cave for those who might normally find the thought of spelunking too claustrophobic for comfort. The views looking out from within the cave are gorgeous. Along the neighboring trails you will find other caves that you can venture into. However, be careful and be sure to have a good flashlight. To reach the Río Frío Cave, drive the Pine Ridge Road to Douglas Da Silva Village at about Mile Marker 24. Do not follow the turnoff for Caracol, but head into the little village. Here you will see signs for the turnoff to the cave. The cave is about 1.6km (1 mile) outside the village. There's a small parking area very close to the mouth of the cave and a couple of picnic tables and benches along the river. No admission is charged to visit here. *Important:* Ask at the Douglas de Silva forestry station along the way if a Belize Defence Forces escort is required at the time, if bandit activity is prevalent.

CARACOL ★★

Caracol (www.caracol.org) is the largest known Mayan archaeological site in Belize, and one of the great Mayan city-states of the Classic era (A.D. 250–950). At one point, Caracol supported a population of more than 150,000. Caracol, which means "shell" in Spanish, gets its name from the large number of snail shells found here during early explorations. So far three main plazas with numerous structures and two ball courts have been excavated.

Caracol has revealed a wealth of informative carved glyphs that have allowed archaeologists to fill in much of the history of this once powerful city-state. Glyphs here

Sky Scraper

The largest pyramid at Caracol, **Caana** or "Sky Palace," stands some 42m (138 ft.) high, and is the tallest Maya building in Belize, and still the tallest man-made structure in the country (the Radisson Fort George in Belize City is the only modern structure that even comes close).

Caracol

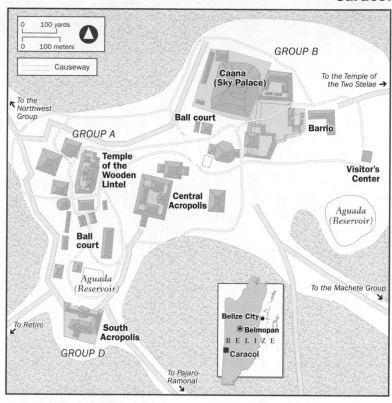

claim Caracol defeats rivals Tikal in A.D. 562 and Naranjo in 631. One of the earliest temples here was built in A.D. 70, and the Caracol royal family has been officially chronicled since 331. The last recorded date on a glyph is 859, and archaeologists conclude that by 1050 Caracol had been completely abandoned.

Caracol is located deep within the Chiquibil Forest Reserve. The ruins are not nearly as well-cleared or excavated as Tikal or Xunantunich. However, this is part of the site's charm. There is great bird-watching and the chance to see other wild fauna out here. Moreover, the area has been declared the **Caracol Archaeological Reserve,** and excavation and restoration are ongoing. A visit to Caracol is often combined with a stop at the Río on Pools or one or more of the other attractions in the Mountain Pine Ridge area.

Caracol is open daily from 8am to 4pm; admission is BZ$15. There's a small visitor center at the entrance, and a guide can sometimes be hired here, although most visitors come with their own guide as part of an organized tour. Caracol is about 80km (50 miles) along a dirt road from the George Price Highway. Actually, the final 16km (10 miles) into the park are paved. Plan on the drive taking about 2 hours, a little more if the road is in bad shape, which it usually is.

Note: Visitors have been robbed in this area, since witnesses are hard to come by. This is also a hotspot of conflict between the Belize Defence Forces and Guatemalans encroaching to poach animals, or hunt for Xate palm. These incidents have been few and far between but it's wise to take precautions when traveling on your own in this area. Stop at the Douglas de Silva forestry station along the way to get a Belize Defence Forces escort.

Shopping

If you're in the area, be sure to stop at the **Tanah Mayan Art Museum** ★ (𝒞 **669-4023;** daily 7am–7pm), run by the García sisters, some of the premier artisans working in carved slate. While it's a stretch to call their little shop and showroom a museum, you will find a nice collection of the García sisters' carvings, as well as other Maya artifacts and handicrafts. This place is located at about Mile Marker 8 of the Cristo Rey Road, about a mile before you reach the village of San Antonio. On the other side of the village, you should stop at the **Magaña Zaac Tunich Art Gallery** (no phone), which carries a range of local craftworks and specializes in woodcarvings.

Where to Stay & Dine
EXPENSIVE

Blancaneaux Lodge ★★ Hollywood glamour Belize-style. That's the vibe at this remote ecolodge, one of film director Francis Ford Coppola's properties. It's set on a steep, pine-forested hillside, overlooking the Privassion River and a series of gentle falls (though there's a lovely pool on site, many guests prefer to dip in the river). Guests stay in individual cabanas with a large, open-air central living area, which flows into a forest- and riverview deck. It's pretty sweet. Each has palapa roofs, lots of local art on the walls, and highly colorful Guatemalan woven bedspreads and rugs. The so-called honeymoon suites get private plunge pools; most villas are two-bedroom, two-bathroom affairs. Villa 7 is Coppola's private villa whenever he visits, (though he's been spending more of his Belize time at his island resort, **Coral Caye,** p. 202), and it features some of the director's photo memorabilia, as well as a painting by his daughter, and fellow director, Sofia Coppola. You can rent it whenever he's not around, and it comes with a private plunge pool and a personal butler. If you can't afford to stay here (it's pricey), at least come by for a meal at the also expensive, but really terrific on-site restaurant.

Mountain Pine Ridge Reserve. www.blancaneaux.com. 𝒞 **800/746-3743** in the U.S., 824-4912 reservations office in Belize, or 824-3878 at the lodge. 20 units. BZ$560–BZ$1,000 double cabin; BZ$1,080–BZ$1,450 2-bedroom villa; BZ$2,800 Enchanted Cottage. Rates include continental breakfast. Rates lower in the off season; higher during peak weeks. Blancaneaux has its own airstrip, and charter flights from Belize City can be arranged. **Amenities:** Restaurant; bar; lounge; bike rental; horse stables; 2 outdoor pools; small spa; Wi-Fi (free hot spots at bar and reception, none in rooms).

Hidden Valley Inn ★★★   This isolated mountain resort has an idyllic setting on more than 2,833 hectares (7,000 acres) of private land. It's a luxury resort with the ambiance of an explorer's club, which means your fellow guests are more likely to talk about the birds they've spotted than about the stock market. The individual bungalows are all plenty roomy, and come with either one queen bed or two twin beds, as well as cool red-tile floors, high ceilings, and a working fireplace. Deluxe units feature beautiful claw-foot bathtubs and outdoor waterfall showers. The outdoor pool and Jacuzzi are surrounded by a handsome slate deck. This is the closest hotel to the Thousand Foot Falls, the tallest waterfall in Belize, a semi-strenuous 2-hour hike from the hotel. However, there are actually several other, much more easily accessible, jungle waterfalls and swimming holes right on the property, as well as 90 miles of hiking trails. This is the only place in Belize where the endangered orange-breasted falcon can reliably be spotted. The hotel hosts the conservation team for this bird, as well as jaguar researchers, as they are deeply invested in protecting their surrounding wilderness. The coffee you're served at breakfast is grown right here, as are many of the fruits and vegetables. The common area has a small library with all the field guides animal lovers could want.

Mountain Pine Ridge, Cayo District. www.hiddenvalleyinn.com. ⓒ **844/859-2227** in the U.S., or 822-3320 in Belize. 12 units. BZ$670 double; BZ$890 deluxe. Rates slightly lower in the off season; higher during peak periods. **Amenities:** Restaurant; bar; lounge; free mountain bike use; Jacuzzi; small outdoor pool; Wi-Fi (free, in main building).

Mystic River Resort ★★   Perched on a hill overlooking the Macal River, every room here is a private little cabin, with high wood ceilings, a working fireplace, a small sitting area with a divan, and a cozy, private balcony for peering through the trees to the river below. Furnishings and decor are tasteful. The small plunge "pool" is only .6m (2 ft.) deep, but features a central fountain and an adjacent shade area with chaise longues and a nearby bar, making it a popular place to hang out. Creative meals are served in the large open-air dining room.

Mile Marker 6, Cristo Rey Rd., Cayo District. www.mysticriverbelize.com. ⓒ **834-4100.** 6 units. BZ$400–BZ$478 double. Free parking. **Amenities:** Restaurant; bar; room service; free canoe use; small plunge pool; smoke-free rooms; Wi-Fi (free).

Table Rock Jungle Lodge ★★   This intimate resort is another spectacular choice in the region. As its name suggests, it's set right in the jungle, but this corner of that jungle has an orange grove to wander and tame donkeys to feed. Rooms have every comfort: airy high-pitched thatched roofs, plenty of louvered windows for ventilation, soft lines and nicely firm beds, and pretty showers built with smooth, local river stones. Two of the rooms are part of a duplex building, with small private decks off the front. But the Mot Mot cabin here is the top choice, with more space and a spacious private veranda. It's a short hike down to the Macal River, where the lodge keeps several canoes (one can paddle from here to the nearby Botanical Garden) and has built an open-air octagonal hammock hut beside a pretty patch of beach. Much of the land here is devoted to organic gardens and citrus groves, which guests are free to explore, in addition to many hiking trails. Meals in the restaurant are crafted from produce grown on-site, and while meals are pricey, portions are huge (so don't be shy about sharing if you'd like to save a bit). Service, as it is through much of Cayo, is flawless and friendly. A brand-new infinity pool was added to the property in 2018.

Mile Marker 5, Cristo Rey Rd. www.tablerockbelize.com. © **672-4040.** 10 units. BZ$350 double. Rates lower in the off season; higher during peak periods. **Amenities:** Restaurant; bar; free bike and canoe use; all rooms smoke-free; Wi-Fi (free, in dining room).

MODERATE

Mountain Equestrian Trails (MET) ★★★ Set in a very lush part of the forest, MET is one of of the best horse- and adventure-tour operators in the area, and the country for that matter. Rooms are decidedly rustic, but, for some, the kerosene lamps that light the rooms at night will be a charming adventure in life without electricity. Housed in a series of duplex buildings, all feature high thatched roofs, colorful Guatemalan bedspreads, indigenous arts and crafts on the walls, queen beds hung with mosquito netting, and plenty of windows for cross-ventilation. A large open-air palapa, The Cantina, serves as the lodge's restaurant, bar, and meeting area. While horses and horseback riding tours are the principal draw here, a whole range of tours and activities is offered. And an added bonus of staying here is getting to socialize with the owners and their family, who share stories about Belize through the decades, and often invite other members of the community by to join guests at dinner. The MET owners also helped create the private Slate Creek Preserve, a 1,214-hectare (3,000-acre) tract of land bordering the Mountain Pine Ridge Reserve, in addition to running their operation off the grid, and acting as huge support for scarlet macaw conservation efforts.

Pine Ridge Rd., Cayo District. www.metbelize.com. © **800/838-3918** in the U.S. and Canada, or 669-1124 in Belize. 10 units. BZ$250 double. Rates lower in the off season. **Amenities:** Restaurant; bar; Wi-Fi (free, in The Cantina).

Crystal Paradise Resort ★★ Beloved by birders, the Crystal Paradise is run by the Tut family, native Belizeans who provide a very warm welcome and expert birding tours (the resort features an on-site bird-watching platform built to blend in with the forest canopy). But even non-birders will enjoy this homey resort, with its thatched-roof duplex buildings, with tile floors, ceiling fans, and private verandas. The best rooms face the Macal River Valley, with superb views of the surrounding forests. A host of tours are offered, and the in-house guides—most of them family members—are excellent. The restaurant serves tasty Belizean cuisine, and there's always a convivial vibe in the open-air dining room, bar, and lounge areas. Crystal Paradise is located on the road to Mountain Pine Ridge, near the tiny Cristo Rey Village. This is one of the few Belizean family-owned resorts left in the Cayo District.

Cristo Rey Village. www.crystalparadise.com. © **615-9361.** 18 units. BZ$190 double. **Amenities:** Restaurant; bar; lounge; Wi-Fi (free).

Gaia River Lodge ★★★ Have you ever been lulled to sleep by the sounds of a waterfall (and the sight of it)? That's one of the unique perks at Gaia River Lodge (formerly the Five Sisters Lodge, and still often called by that name). The hotel is located in the heart of the Mountain Pine Ridge Reserve, about 61m (200 ft.) above its (previous) namesake Five Sisters Falls, an eye-popping and rambling series of waterfalls and swimming holes. Many of the rooms feature a spectacular view *right over* the falls. That vista may take your attention away from the digs but they're darn nice, too: individual cottages with tropical hardwood floors, thatched roofs, and beds languorously draped with mosquito netting. All feature a mix of local and Guatemalan furnishings and decor, as well as a screened-in veranda hung with a hammock. Arguably the best choice, although it's a good distance from the main lodge, is the Riverside Villa, a luxurious cabin set down by the river and falls. There are 300 stairs between the bottom and top of the falls, but Gaia recently installed a cable tram for those who can't manage the incline. Food on property is delish, with fresh fish brought in from its sister property, the **Matachica** (p. 144) on Ambergris Caye, and veggies grown in the garden. In addition to paid adventures for guests, the lodge offers first-rate, expertly led guided nature walks after dusk and first thing in the morning. *Note:* Gaia only accepts guests 16 years of age or older.

Mountain Pine Ridge. www.gaiariverlodge.com. © **820-4005,** 820-4048 for reservations. 16 units. BZ$210–BZ$230 double; BZ$300 junior suite; BZ$500 Riverside Villa. Rates include continental breakfast. Rates lower in the off season. **Amenities:** Restaurant; bar; spa; gift shop; natural swimming pools; waterfall; Wi-Fi (free, in restaurant).

Pine Ridge Lodge ★★ As we go to press, this lodge is undergoing a transformation, thanks to new ownership. Right now, most of the rooms are in duplex units, with polished concrete floors, simple wooden furniture, and local and Guatemalan crafts and textiles completing the decor. Mayan glyphs are painted on the outsides of the rooms. Light in the rooms is provided by kerosene lanterns, and the showers are heated by on-demand butane heaters. But the owners have already built one new, thatched-roof, wooden floor hut, which ups the ante here. Not that this place was bad to begin with: Its grounds are stunning, blessed with a wide variety of orchids and attracting an equally wide variety of bird species. It's right in the heart of the Mountain Pine district, close to all the major attractions. And on-site is a small creek; many of the lodgings are built to overlook the little stream. There's also a small waterfall an easy hike from the lodge. Meals, which feature organic fruits and vegetables grown on-site, are served family-style in the small screened-in dining room and bar. In the mornings the owner, at a time of your choosing, will leave cups and French Press coffee outside your door, so you can come to life before you come into the dining room.

Mountain Pine Ridge. www.pineridgelodge.com. © **606-4557.** 6 units. BZ$328 double. Rates lower in the off season. Rates include continental breakfast. No credit cards. **Amenities:** Restaurant; bar; Wi-Fi (free, in shared areas).

TIKAL & GUATEMALA'S PETÉN

B ordering Belize, Mexico, and Honduras, and occupying the entire northeastern section of Guatemala, the Petén is Guatemala's largest and least populated province. Most of the Petén is forest—thick tropical rainforest. It is a lush and wild landscape that contains some of Mesoamerica's richest archaeological treasures. In 1990, the government of Guatemala officially established the **Maya Biosphere Reserve,** a tract of 1 million hectares (2.5 million acres) that includes most of the Petén Province. Moreover, the Maya Biosphere Reserve adjoins the neighboring **Calakmul Biosphere Reserve** in Mexico and the **Río Bravo Conservation Area** in Belize, comprising a joint protected area of more than 2 million hectares (5 million acres).

The Petén Province is home to perhaps the most impressive and best preserved of the ancient Mayan ceremonial cities, **Tikal ★★★**. It also holds numerous other lesser, and less excavated, sites, many of which we have yet to find. In early 2018, scientists announced the discovery of a massive lost Mayan city using aerial mapping techniques that allowed them to see what was hiding beneath the dense jungle, adding to the mysteriously vast network of known ancient civilizations.

In addition, the area is a rich and rewarding destination for birdwatchers and ecotourists.

Given the close proximity of Tikal to the Belize border (and the long distance between Guatemala City and the Petén), it is in some ways more convenient to visit Tikal from Belize than it is from Guatemala's bigger cities. This chapter will give you all the necessary information to plan a visit to this fascinating destination, whether you want to take a quick 1-day tour of the ruins at Tikal or a multiday adventure exploring the region.

TIKAL ★★★

100km (62 miles) NW of the Belize border; 65km (40 miles) N of Flores

Tikal is one of the greatest of the surviving Classic Maya cities. It is estimated that Tikal once supported a population of about 100,000 people. Archaeologists have identified more than 3,000 structures, and in its heyday, the city probably covered as much as 65 sq. km (25 sq. miles). Tikal is far more extensively excavated than any ruins in Belize, and unlike the grand cities and excavations in Mexico, Tikal rises out of dense jungle. The pyramids here are some of the most perfect examples of ceremonial architecture in the Maya world. Standing atop Temple IV, you are high above the rainforest canopy. From this vantage point the peaks of several temples poke through the dense vegetation, a view that will look very familiar to fans of *Star Wars: A New Hope (*which was partially filmed here). Toucans and parrots fly about, and the loudest noise you'll hear is the guttural call of howler monkeys.

Tikal is within easy reach of Belize's western border, and scores of organized tour groups and independent travelers from Belize visit the site every day. Remember this is a separate country and you will need your passport to visit it, even for the day.

Essentials
GETTING THERE & DEPARTING
BY PLANE   **Tropic Air** (www.tropicair.com; ✆ **800/422-3435** in the U.S. or Canada, 226-2012 in Belize City, or 502/7926-0348 in Flores) has one daily flight to Flores Airport (FRS) from Philip S. W. Goldson International Airport in Belize City, at 4:40pm. The flight returns at 8:30am. Flight duration is 45 minutes; it costs BZ$300 to Flores, BZ$190 from Flores, or BZ$445 round-trip.

Leaving Belize, you will pay a departure tax that's included in the cost of the plane ticket. Leaving Guatemala, there is a US$33 departure tax for international flights, which is paid at the airport after checking in but before going through security. Cash and credit card are acceptable.

The airport is on the road to Tikal, about 2.4km (1½ miles) east of Santa Elena. A taxi from the airport into Santa Elena or Flores should cost you around Q25 (25 quetzales; see p. 297). Or you can take a local bus (usually an old Blue Bird school bus) for around Q1. Collective taxis and minivans to Tikal are usually waiting at the airport and charge around Q50 per person each way. You can sometimes bargain, and you can often get a slight discount if you purchase a round-trip fare right from the start. A private taxi can be hired for the drive for around Q400.

> ### Telephone Tip
>
> Guatemala's country code is **502** (Belize's is 501). Guatemala uses an eight-digit phone numbering system. Nonetheless, to avoid confusion between Belizean and Guatemalan telephone numbers, we have included the country code in the Guatemalan numbers, whereas in this section and throughout the book, we've omitted the Belizean country code in phone number listings.

BY CAR   Driving from Belize City, take the George Price (Western) Highway to San Ignacio, and continue to the border town of Benque Viejo del Carmen. From Benque, follow the signs to the border at a bridge over the Mopan River, a little more than 1.6km (1 mile) out of town.

The border crossing and formalities are very similar to those described below in "By Bus." You will be corralled by touts on the Guatemalan side offering all sorts of aid and services and demanding all sorts of fees and duties. By law you are supposed to have your tires fumigated. This should cost only a U.S. dollar or two. You should not have to pay any additional fees. Whether you are driving your own car or a rental car, be sure to have all your current registration, title, and insurance papers.

Once across the border, follow signs out of Melchor de Mencos toward Flores and Tikal. It's about a 1-hour drive to the crossroads at Ixlú, also known as El Cruce. If you are going to El Remate or Tikal, you will turn right here. If you are going to Flores or Santa Elena, you will continue straight. From

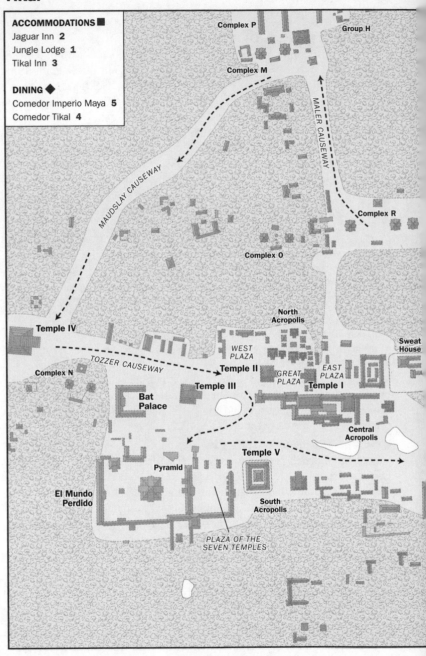

ACCOMMODATIONS ■
Jaguar Inn **2**
Jungle Lodge **1**
Tikal Inn **3**

DINING ◆
Comedor Imperio Maya **5**
Comedor Tikal **4**

Complex P

Group H

Complex M

MAUDSLAY CAUSEWAY

MALER CAUSEWAY

Complex R

Complex O

North Acropolis

Temple IV

WEST PLAZA

Sweat House

TOZZER CAUSEWAY

Complex N

Temple II

GREAT PLAZA

EAST PLAZA

Temple III

Bat Palace

Temple I

Central Acropolis

Temple V

Pyramid

El Mundo Perdido

South Acropolis

PLAZA OF THE SEVEN TEMPLES

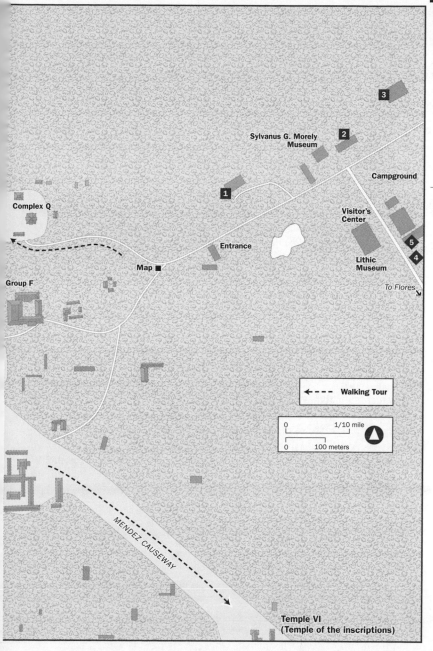

Sylvanus G. Morely
Museum

Campground

Complex Q

Visitor's
Center

Entrance

Lithic
Museum

To Flores

Map

Group F

←--- Walking Tour

0   1/10 mile
0   100 meters

MENDEZ CAUSEWAY

Temple VI
(Temple of the inscriptions)

Ixlú, it's about 25 to 30 minutes either way to Santa Elena/Flores or the ruins at Tikal. The entrance to Tikal National Park is located 18km (11 miles) south of the visitor center and true entrance to the ruins and its network of trails. Here you will have to pay the Q150 entrance fee. The entrance is open daily from 6am to 6pm. If you arrive after 3pm, tell them you plan to visit the ruins the following day, and they will stamp your ticket to that effect. If you plan to spend more than a day here staying at one of the hotels or campsites near the ruins, advise them and try to pay your entrance fee for subsequent days in advance, as sometimes they send people all the way back to the entrance gate to buy a subsequent day's ticket.

If you're traveling in a rental car, be sure that the company you rented from in Belize allows the car to cross into Guatemala. **Crystal Auto Rental** (www.crystal-belize.com; ✆ **223-1600** in Belize) does, but you'll need to get the paperwork prepared at least 2 days in advance, and your insurance will not cover you once you're over the border.

Beware: It is strongly advised that you do not travel at night. It is a sad fact that armed groups occasionally set up roadblocks along these isolated yet frequently trafficked roads.

BY BUS If you're traveling from Belize City by bus, you can take one of the private company buses to Santa Elena. From there, you'll have to get further transportation to visit Tikal. The buses leave from right in front of the Marine Terminal in downtown Belize City. The fare is around BZ$50 one-way. The trip takes around 5 to 6 hours. Several bus lines make this trip run: **Línea Dorada** (www.lineadorada.com.gt; ✆ **502/7924-8434**), **San Juan Travel** (✆ **502/5847-4738**), and **Autobuses Fuente del Norte** (✆ **502/7947-7070** to book with Grupo del Fuente in Guatemala, 223-1200 with Mundo Maya in Belize). All can be booked in Belize by **Mundo Maya Travels** (www.travelmundomaya.com; ✆ **223-1200**).

Alternatively, you can take one of the many public buses from Belize City (or from San Ignacio) to the Guatemalan border. Buses to San Ignacio leave roughly every half-hour from the main bus station on West Collet Canal Street between 5am and 8pm. Return buses to Belize City leave the main bus station in San Ignacio roughly every half-hour between 4am and 6pm. The fare is BZ$10. The trip takes 2½ hours. Most of the western-bound buses continue beyond San Ignacio to Benque Viejo and the Guatemalan border. Some of these leave you in Benque Viejo, while others go all the way to the border crossing, a little more than 1.6km (1 mile) away. There are numerous taxis at the Benque Viejo bus station that will take you to the border for BZ$8. None of them will take you across the border.

On the Belize side, you will have to fill out a departure card, have your passport stamped, and pay the departure tax of BZ$40. Just over the bridge lies the Guatemalan border town of Melchor de Mencos. When you pass through Guatemalan immigration, you will be provided with a tourist card good for up to 90 days. Theoretically this card is free. However, border formalities in Guatemala are often open to corruption, with border officials and local touts looking to glean some extra money. Moreover, Guatemalan border formalities change from time to time, and there is a long-running dispute between Guatemala and Belize (Guatemala claims that all of Belize is actually part of Guatemala, dating back to the mid–19th c.), so it always pays to check with the Guatemalan Embassy in your home country if you are certain you will be traveling there. The border crossing can take from 20 minutes to more than an hour, depending on the crowds.

Tips: Bring a pen to fill out your departure card, as they rarely have any to spare. And if you do get hit up for an unofficial border tax on the Guatemalan side, it's safer to pay it than to protest.

Once you're finished with the border formalities, it is a simple matter to find onward transportation to Tikal or Flores and Santa Elena. The least expensive means of transport is the local chicken bus; however, none of these go directly to Tikal. Instead, they head to Flores and Santa Elena, but they will drop you off at Ixlú (El Cruce), where you can flag down one of the many minivans and collective taxis going from Flores and Santa Elena to the ruins. Be forewarned that while local buses are very inexpensive (around Q3–Q8), they can be overcrowded and very slow. They stop almost constantly along the way to pick up and discharge passengers and their cargo. I recommend you take one of these buses only if you're interested more in the local color and adventure of the trip than in a speedy arrival at the ruins.

A much better bet is to take one of the collective taxis or minivans that leave right from Melchor de Mencos. Most of these wait just outside the border station and leave as soon as they fill up. Some go to Flores and Santa Elena, while others go directly to Tikal. Most charge Q80 to Q160 per person.

Finally, if there are no collective taxis or minivans available, you can hire a taxi that will carry up to six people for between Q400 and Q600.

Tip: If you are only going for the day, try to arrange a round-trip fare with your taxi or minivan driver, with a specific departure time from Tikal. Usually, it's best to leave Tikal by 4pm, so as to drive during daylight and arrive at the border with plenty of time.

BY ORGANIZED TOUR   Organized day trips leave daily for Tikal from Belize City, San Ignacio, San Pedro, Caye Caulker, and Placencia. Costs for these all-inclusive trips are approximately BZ$200 and BZ$400 by land (from Belize City, or any of the other major tourist destinations in Belize), depending on group size. Budget an additional BZ$100 to BZ$300 per person per day for multiday excursions. In Belize City, call **Discovery Expeditions** (www.discoverybelize.com; ℭ **671-0748**) or **S & L Travel and Tours** (www.sltravel belize.com; ℭ **227-7593**). In San Ignacio, you can call **Pacz Tours** ★★ (www.pacztours.net; ℭ **824-0536**) or **Yute Expeditions** ★★ (www.inland belize.com; ℭ **824-2076**).

GETTING AROUND
BY TAXI OR MINIVAN   Minivans and collective taxis leave throughout the day plying the route between Tikal and Santa Elena/Flores. Minivans and collective taxis charge between Q50 and Q60 per person each way. From

safety IN GUATEMALA

Over the past 60 years, Guatemala has had an ongoing history of political and civil violence and repression. Crime, both petty and violent, is a problem throughout Guatemala. The Guatemalan police and judiciary are underfunded, understaffed, and largely ineffectual. Decades of civil war, genocide, and paramilitary activity, in addition to historic poverty and underdevelopment, have created a dangerous climate where lawlessness is rampant. Foreign nationals—as well as everyday Guatemalans—are the targets of robberies, kidnapping, murders, and rapes. The U.S. State Department strongly cautions visitors to Guatemala and keeps a relatively up-to-date analysis of the situation at **http:// travel.state.gov**.

Luckily, the Petén District, where Tikal is located, is a largely isolated and forgotten section of eastern Guatemala. The most common attacks against tourists visiting Tikal occur on the road between the Belizean border and Flores, but they're not an everyday occurrence. Yes, taxis, local buses, and air-conditioned minivans have all been targeted. But these highway robberies tend to occur in waves, and are by far the exception and not the norm. In almost all known cases, the attacks are armed but nonviolent robberies. If you plan to visit Tikal for a few days as a side trip from Belize, it is often a good idea to find a hotel safe in Belize that will guard any

valuables you do not need with you while in Guatemala.

Still, hundreds of tourists visit Tikal and Flores every day, and the vast majority of them have no problems whatsoever. Be sure to take all necessary precautions. Never travel alone or at night and stick to the most popular and populous tourist destinations and attractions. If you are driving, stop only for people holding guns; do not try to run blockades. Common wisdom cautions against using the low-fare Guatemalan buses and tour agencies; however, high-end tour groups in fancy air-conditioned microbuses do attract the attention of organized criminal gangs. Some tour groups travel with armed guards. This may or may not increase your sense of security and your actual security, to boot. (As far as I'm concerned, the jury is out on that one.) If you are confronted with any sort of criminal attempt, do not resist, as a simple mugging can easily end up turning into murder.

The Guatemalan Tourist Institute (INGUAT) and National Police have set up a special police force, POLITUR, created to patrol tourist destinations and deal directly with tourists. You will hopefully see them present in most major tourist destinations, including Tikal and Flores. You can also call ASISTUR, a tourist assistance service of INGUAT, by dialing ⓒ **1500** from any phone in the country.

Santa Elena, you can catch a bus back to the border. A private cab from Tikal to Santa Elena/Flores will run around Q350 to Q450 each way. Between Tikal and El Remate, the fare is about Q150 to Q200.

BY CAR   There are several local car-rental agencies at the airport. Of these, a good choice is **Tabarini Rent A Car** (www.tabarini.com; ⓒ **502/2444-4200**). All rent small jeeps and SUVs. Do get a four-wheel-drive vehicle; even though you may never need the traction or off-road ability, the extra clearance will come in handy. Four-wheel-drive rates run from Q625 to Q940 per day.

Money

The Guatemalan monetary unit is the quetzal. At press time, the exchange rate was 7.34 quetzales to the U.S. dollar, and 10.26 quetzales to the British pound. If you're coming from Belize, your best bets for changing dollars into quetzales are at the border or at the numerous banks in Santa Elena and Flores (see "Flores & Santa Elena," later in this chapter). Most of the hotels and restaurants in Tikal, in fact, will exchange dollars for quetzales, although they may give you a slightly less favorable rate than you would get at a bank.

ORIENTATION

There is no village or town inside Tikal National Park. After having paid your Q150 admission at the entrance booth 18km (11 miles) south of the ruins, you will eventually come to the large central parking area and visitor center. This is where you will find the three hotels and campsite reviewed in "Where to Stay," later in this chapter, as well as the two museums and a collection of simple restaurants. The ruins themselves are about a 15- to 20-minute walk through the forest from the trail entrance here.

You'll spot a post office and telegraph office on the left as you arrive at the parking area. There is no bank or ATM here in Tikal, and most of the little restaurants and gift stands accept only quetzales. Moreover, while some of the hotels here do accept credit cards, the phone connections are spotty, and they sometimes have problems getting the authorizations. It's best to bring quetzales to pay for your entire stay. Also, be sure to bring plenty of insect repellent with you—the bugs here are rapacious.

Tikal National Park is open daily from 6am to 6pm. If you'd like to stay in the park until 8pm (for sunset and nocturnal wildlife viewing), get your admission ticket stamped at the office behind the Stelae Museum. If you arrive after 3pm, your admission is good for the following day as well. If you are staying multiple days, you must pay the admission fee each day. The best times to visit the ruins are in early morning and late afternoon, which are the least crowded and coolest times of day.

A Familiar Site

Tikal provides such a stunning and unique landscape that it was chosen for an exterior shot in George Lucas's *Star Wars: A New Hope,* as well as the site of a famous series of Nike commercials.

FAST FACTS There are no banks, medical facilities, laundromats, or other major services available at Tikal. All of these can be found in Flores and Santa Elena, some 64km (40 miles) away; see p. 312.

Exploring Tikal

Tikal, one of the largest Mayan cities ever uncovered and the most spectacular ruins in Guatemala, ranks with Mexico's Chichén Itzá in pre-Columbian splendor. However, unlike at Chichén Itzá, the ruins of Tikal are set in the middle of a vast jungle through which you must hike from temple to temple.

The many miles of trails through the park provide numerous opportunities to spot colorful birds such as toucans and parrots and such wild animals as coatimundi, spider monkeys, howler monkeys, and deer. Together, the ruins and the abundance of wildlife make a trip to Tikal an absolute must for anyone interested in Mayan history, bird-watching, or wildlife viewing.

Tikal was a massive ceremonial metropolis. So far, archaeologists have mapped about 3,000 constructions, 10,000 earlier foundations beneath surviving structures, 250 stone monuments (steles and altars), and thousands of art objects found in tombs and cached offerings. There is evidence of continuous construction at Tikal from 200 B.C. through the 9th century A.D., with some suggestion of occupation as early as 600 B.C. The Maya reached their zenith in art and architecture during the Classic Period, which began about A.D. 250 and ended abruptly about 900, when for some reason Tikal and all other major Mayan centers were abandoned. Most of the visible structures at Tikal date from the Late Classic Period, from A.D. 600 to 900.

No one's sure just what role Tikal played in the history of the Maya: Was it mostly a ceremonial center for priests, artisans, and the elite? Or was it a city of industry and commerce as well? In the 16 sq. km (6 sq. miles) of Tikal that have been mapped and excavated, only a few of the buildings were domestic structures; most were temples, palaces, ceremonial platforms, and shrines. Workers are excavating the innumerable mounds on the periphery of the mapped area and have been finding modest houses of stone and plaster with thatched roofs. Just how far these settlements extended beyond the ceremonial center and how many people lived within the domain of Tikal is still to be determined. At its height, Tikal may have covered as much as 65 sq. km (25 sq. miles).

MAKING THE MOST OF YOUR VISIT

Tikal is such an immense site that you really need several days to see it thoroughly. But you can visit many of the greatest temples and palaces in 1 day. To do it properly, as a first-time visitor, you should probably hire a guide. Guides are available at the visitor center and charge around Q80 to Q200 for a half-day tour of the ruins, depending on the size of your group and how well you negotiate. In addition, most hotels and all tour agencies in the region offer guided tours for a similar price.

A WALKING TOUR

To orient yourself, begin your tour of Tikal at the visitor center and neighboring Stelae Museum. Here you'll find some informative exhibits and relics, as well as an impressive relief map of the site. See "The Museums," below, for more information on the steles.

A full tour of Tikal will require an extensive amount of walking, as much as 9.7km (6 miles). The itinerary described here will take you to most of the major temples and plazas, and can be accomplished in about 3 to 4 hours. If your time is really limited, you should follow the signs and head straight to the Great Plaza. If you have a full day, consider this route:

Walking along the road that goes west from the museum toward the ruins, turn right at the first intersection to get to **twin complexes Q** and **R.** Seven of these twin complexes are known at Tikal, but their exact purpose is still a mystery. Each complex has two pyramids facing east and west; at the north is an unroofed enclosure entered by a vaulted doorway and containing a single stele and altar; at the south is a small palace-like structure. Of the two pyramids here, one has been restored and one has been left as it was found, and the latter will give you an idea of just how overgrown and ensconced in the jungle these structures had become.

At the end of the twin complexes is a wide road called the **Maler Causeway.** Turn right (north) onto this causeway to get to **Complex P,** another twin complex, a 15-minute walk away. Some restoration has been done at Complex P, but the most interesting points are the replicas of a stele (no. 20) and altar (no. 8) in the north enclosure. Look for the beautiful glyphs next to the carving of a warrior on the stele, all in very good condition. The altar shows a captive bound to a carved-stone altar, his hands tied behind his back—a common scene in carvings at Tikal. Both these monuments date from about A.D. 751.

From Complex P, head south on the **Maudslay Causeway** to **Complex N,** which is the site of **Temple IV, the Temple of the Two-Headed Serpent ★★★**. Finished around A.D. 740, Temple IV is the tallest structure in Tikal and is 65m (213 ft.) from the base of its platform to the top. The first glimpse you get of the temple from the Maudslay Causeway is awesome, for the temple has not been restored, and all but the temple proper (the enclosure) and its roof comb are covered in foliage. The stairway is occluded by earth and roots, but there is a system of steep stairways (actually rough-hewn wooden ladders set against the steep sides of the pyramid) to the top of the temple. The view of the setting and layout of Tikal—and all of the Great Plaza—is magnificent. From the platform of the temple, you can see in all directions and get an idea of the extent of the Petén jungle, an ocean of lush greenery. **Temple III (Temple of the Great Priest)** is in the foreground to the east; **temples I** and **II** are farther on at the Great Plaza. To the right of these are the **South Acropolis** and **Temple V.**

Temple IV, and all the other temples at Tikal, are built on this plan: A pyramid is built first, and on top of it is built a platform; the temple proper rests on this platform and is composed of one to three rooms, usually long and narrow and not for habitation but rather for priestly rites. Most temples had beautifully carved wooden lintels above the doorways. The one from Temple IV is now in the Völkerkunde Museum in Basel, Switzerland.

From Temple IV, walk east along the **Tozzer Causeway** to get to the **Great Plaza,** about a 10-minute walk. Along the way you'll pass the twin-pyramid Complex N, the **Bat Palace,** and Temple III. Take a look at the altar and stele in the complex's northern enclosure—two of the finest monuments at Tikal—and also the altar in front of Temple III, showing the head of a deity resting on a plate. By the way, the crisscross pattern shown here represents a woven mat, a symbol of authority to the Maya.

THE GREAT PLAZA ★★★

Entering the Great Plaza from the Tozzer Causeway, you'll be struck by the towering stone structure that is Temple II, seen from the back. It measures 38m (125 ft.) tall now, although it is thought to have been 43m (140 ft.) high when the roof comb was intact. Also called the Temple of the Masks, from a large face carved in the roof comb, the temple dates from about A.D. 700. Walk around this temple to enter the plaza proper.

Beat the Crowds

Tikal fills up with tour buses most days, with the hours between 10am and 2pm being the busiest period. I prefer visiting the Great Plaza either before or after the main crowds have left. Feel free to reverse the order of this walking tour if it will help you avoid the masses.

Directly across from Temple II you'll see Temple I (Temple of the Great Jaguar), the most striking structure in Tikal. Standing 44m (145 ft.) tall, the temple proper has three narrow rooms with high corbeled vaults (the Mayan "arch") and carved wooden lintels made of zapote wood, which is rot resistant. One of the lintels has been removed for preservation in the Guatemala National Museum of Archaeology and Ethnology in Guatemala City. The whole structure is made of limestone, as are most others at Tikal. It was within this pyramid that one of the richest tombs in Tikal was discovered. Believed to be the tomb of Tikal ruler Hasaw Chan K'awil, when archaeologists uncovered it in 1962, they found the former ruler's skeleton surrounded by some 180 pieces of jade, 90 bone artifacts carved with hieroglyphic inscriptions, numerous pearls, and objects in alabaster and shell. *Note:* Tourists can no longer scale temples I or III. However, those in need of serious cardio workouts will get their fill climbing some of the other temples.

The **North Acropolis** (north side of the Great Plaza) is a maze of structures from various periods covering an area of 8.5 hectares (21 acres). Standing today 9m (30 ft.) above the limestone bedrock, it contains vestiges of more than a hundred different constructions dating from 200 B.C. to A.D. 800. At the front-center of the acropolis (at the top of the stairs up from the Great Plaza) is a temple numbered **5D-33.** Although much of the 8th-century temple was destroyed during the excavations to get to the Early Classic temple (A.D. 300) underneath, it's still a fascinating building. Toward the rear of it is a tunnel leading to the stairway of the **Early Classic** temple, embellished with two 3m-high (10-ft.) plaster polychrome masks of a god—don't miss these.

Directly across the plaza from the North Acropolis is the **Central Acropolis,** which covers about 1.6 hectares (4 acres). It's a maze of courtyards and palaces on several levels, all connected by an intricate system of passageways. Some of the palaces had five floors, connected by exterior stairways, and each floor had as many as nine rooms arranged like a maze.

Before you leave the Great Plaza, be sure to examine some of the 70 beautiful steles and altars right in the plaza. You can see the full development of Mayan art in them, for they date from the Early Classic Period right through to the Late Classic Period. There are three major stylistic groups: the steles with wraparound carving on the front and sides with text on the back; those with a figure carved on the front and text in glyphs on the back; and those with a simple carved figure on the front, text in hieroglyphs on the sides, and a plain back. The oldest stele is no. 29 (now in the Tikal Museum—see "The Museums," below), dating from A.D. 292; the most recent is no. 11 in the Great Plaza, dating from A.D. 869.

If you head south from Temple II, you will come to the area known as **El Mundo Perdido (The Lost World).** This plaza contains the **Great Pyramid,** which stands 35m (115 ft.) high and is the oldest excavated building in Tikal. This pyramid is one of the most popular spots for watching the sunset. If you've timed it right, you might be able to hang out here and watch the show; otherwise, make a mental note to get your bearings and come back later, if possible. Directly east of the Great Pyramid is the **Plaza of the Seven Temples,** which dates to the Late Classic Period. Bordering this plaza on the east side is an unexcavated pyramid, and behind this is Temple V. This entire area is known as the **South Acropolis.** You can climb Temple V, but be forewarned, the climb, both up and down a very steep and rather rickety wooden stairway, is somewhat harrowing. The view from above is beautiful. However, the steep pitch of the pyramid's original stairway is almost as scary as the climb.

If you cross through the South Acropolis to the east and then turn north in the general direction of the Great Plaza, you will come to the East Plaza. From here you can walk southeast on the Mendez Causeway to **Temple VI (Temple of the Inscriptions),** which contains a nearly illegible line of hieroglyphics

SUNRISE, sunset

Tikal is a magical and mystical place. Many claim that this magic and mystique is only heightened around sunrise and sunset. Sunsets are easier to catch and a more dependable show. Sunrises tend to be more a case of the sun eventually burning through the morning mist than of any impressive orb emerging. However, afternoons can often be clear, especially during the dry season, allowing for excellent sunset viewing from the tops of the main temples here. In either case, much of the attraction can be found all around you, as the bird and animal life of the jungle are much more active around sunrise and sunset. If you're staying right at the ruins, your chances are better of catching either or both of these occasions.

If you're not staying inside the national park, minivans and collective taxis leave Flores and El Remate early enough to get you to the Tikal entrance gate at 6am when it opens. This will generally enable you to get to the top of one of the main temples by 6:30am, which is usually still early enough to catch the sun burning through the mist just over the rainforest canopy.

If you plan on staying for sunset, be absolutely positive that your return transportation will wait for you. The park officially closes at 6pm. Depending on the season, the sun will set below the treetops anywhere between 5 and 6pm, allowing just enough time to watch the spectacle and get out of the park in time.

Tip: If you're planning on catching either the sunrise or the sunset, it's a very good idea to bring along a flashlight, just in case.

that are the most extensive in Tikal. It's worth coming out this way just for the chance to spot some wild animals, which seem to be fairly common in this remote corner of the park.

THE MUSEUMS

The most formal museum here has been officially christened the **Sylvanus G. Morely Museum,** but is also known as **El Museo Tikal** or **Ceramic Museum.** This museum contains a good collection of pottery, mosaic masks, incense burners, etched bone, and steles that are chronologically displayed—beginning with Pre-Classic objects on up to Late Classic pieces. Of note are the delicate 7.6 to 13cm (3- to 5-in.) mosaic masks made of jade, turquoise, shell, and stucco. There is a beautiful cylindrical jar from about A.D. 700 depicting a male and female seated in a typical Mayan pose. The drawing is of fine quality, and the slip colors are red, brown, and black. Also on exhibit are a number of jade pendants, beads, and earplugs, as well as the famous **stele no. 31,** which has all four sides carved. On the two sides are spear throwers, each wearing a large feathered headdress and carrying a shield in his left hand; on the front is a complicated carving of an individual carrying a head in his left arm and a chair in his right. It is considered one of the finest stele examples from the Early Classic period. Another fine attraction here is the reconstruction of the tomb of Hasaw Chan K'awil, who was also known as Ah Cacao, or "Lord Chocolate." The museum is located between the Jungle Lodge and the Jaguar Inn.

The second museum is known as the **Lithic** or **Stelae Museum** and is in the large visitor center, which is on your left as you arrive at the parking area coming from Flores. This spacious display area contains a superb collection of steles from around the ruins. Just outside the front door of the museum is the scaled relief map (mentioned above) that will give you an excellent perspective on the relationships among the different ruins here at Tikal. Both museums are open daily from 9am to 5pm. A Q30 admission will get you into both.

Tip: Visit the museums only if you have extra time or a very specific interest in either the steles or the ceramic works. The ruins themselves are by far a much more interesting attraction.

---

seeing the forest FROM THE TREES

Just outside the entrance to Tikal National Park is the **Canopy Tours Tikal** (www.tikalcanopy.com; ✆ **502/7926-2411**). A series of treetop platforms is connected by heavy wire cables, allowing more adventurous travelers to zip from platform to platform via a harness-and-pulley system. Canopy Tours Tikal actually has two separate zipline tours to choose from: a somewhat slower tour for wary souls and a faster system for adrenaline junkies. They also have a series of trails and hanging suspension bridges through the thick rain forest here. This attraction is open daily from 7am to 5pm, and the cost is about Q190 per person, but shuttle transportation to or from Tikal or El Remate and the park entrance fee cost extra.

Where to Stay

There are only three hotels and a campground at the little Tikal village near the entrance to the ruins. Unless you have more than 2 days to spend exploring the region, I personally recommend staying near the ruins at least 1 night, as it allows you to enter early and stay late. It also allows you to avoid the Great Plaza and North Acropolis during the peak period of the day, when they are swarmed with day-trippers.

Although the ruins are officially open from 6am to 6pm, those staying at the site can usually finagle their way in even earlier. Better yet, those staying at the site can have their admission ticket stamped, allowing them to stay inside the park until 8pm. When the moon is full or close to full, that's enough time to catch both the sunset and the moonrise from the top of one of the temples here.

Note: Rooms are often difficult to get at the park, and making reservations is essential during the high season. However, communication with the hotels here is difficult and undependable, and many reserve all of their high-season bookings for groups and prepaid package tours. Overbooking on behalf of these hotels is also not uncommon. Demand is high, and rooms are very limited. If you're going for just a couple of nights, go with an organized tour to save yourself some hassle; if you plan to spend more time in the area or don't mind spending a night in Flores or Santa Elena if necessary, you can probably make your arrangements in Tikal.

Note: All the hotels below get their electricity from generators, and some run these generators only for limited periods throughout the day. None has air-conditioning, and even though most have fans, these fans will do you little good on a hot night when the generator isn't running.

EXPENSIVE

Jungle Lodge ★   Also known as Posada de la Selva, this is the biggest and most upscale hotel right at the park. However, that's not saying much. At times there can be a cattle-car feel to the operation, and service can be lax. The majority of the rooms are housed in duplex bungalows, with high ceilings, white-tile floors, two double beds with mosquito netting, and a ceiling fan. Each has its own little porch with a couple of chairs, which are nice places to sit and read a book or do some bird-watching. The bungalows are connected by stone paths through lush gardens. Two junior suites feature king-size beds, a large Jacuzzi-style tub (but without jets), and private patios in both the front and back of the room.

Tikal village, Petén. www.junglelodgetikal.com. ✆ **502/7861-0447.** 50 units. Q510–Q1,400. **Amenities:** Restaurant; bar; small outdoor pool; Wi-Fi (free).

Tikal Inn ★   Set back amid the trees, the Tikal Inn is the farthest hotel from the entrance to the ruins as you walk down the old airstrip. If you must stay here, the individual bungalows are best, featuring high thatched roofs, tile floors, local furniture and textiles, and rustic wood trim. The smaller rooms in the main building have cement floors. All of the rooms feel pretty Spartan, in addition to looking like nature is taking over due to lack of care. And power is only available from 6:30 to 8am and 6 to 9:30pm, so if it's a hot night you can't run a fan to keep cool. If you need to charge a phone or camera you can use the power outlets at the front desk. As at the Jungle Lodge, there's a refreshing pool. Meals are served family-style, and the food is a definite step up from the fare served at the *comedores* (restaurants) near the campground.

Tikal village, Petén. www.tikalinn.com. ✆ **502/7861-2444,** or 502/7861-2445. 25 units. Q350–Q735 double. Rate includes breakfast. **Amenities:** Restaurant; bar; small outdoor pool; room service; satellite Wi-Fi (free, in public areas).

INEXPENSIVE

Jaguar Inn ★　This is the most humble and economical of the hotels right at the park. Still, the rooms are all quite clean, spacious, and well-kept. Most come with two queen beds and a small veranda strung with a hammock. The best rooms are a couple of large second-floor affairs. However, I also like bungalow no. 10, with its king-size bed and private veranda. If you're on a tight budget, you can also camp here in one of their tents with an inflatable mattress and access to showers and bathrooms for Q100 per person. *Best perks:* electricity 24 hours per day, as well as twilight and full-moon tours which are otherwise hard to arrange.

Tikal village, Petén. www.jaguartikal.com. ✆ **502/7926-2411.** 14 units. Q535 double. **Amenities:** Restaurant; small outdoor pool; unique tours; Wi-Fi (free).

CAMPING

Just off the main parking lot at the site is a nice lawn with some trees for shade, marked and designated as the camping area. Visitors put their tents on the concrete pads here, under an open-air thatch palapa roof. The camping area has simple shared shower and toilet facilities, and a communal cooking area. The campground (no phone) charges Q50 for the privilege of putting up a tent and using the facilities. Visitors can also rent hammocks and pitch them under open-air palapas for an additional Q50. Another Q5 allows guests to store valuables in a lockbox.

Tip: If you plan on sleeping in a hammock, or even taking an afternoon siesta, you should really try to get a mosquito net that fits over the hammock. Most of the places that rent and sell hammocks in this area have these nets. Biting bugs are notoriously opportunistic, so make sure to keep it zipped up at pretty much all times.

Where to Dine

Most folks who stay near the ruins take all their meals at their hotel, and these restaurants are also available to the public. If you're looking for variety, there are several little *comedores* between the main camping area and parking lot and the gate at the beginning of the road to Flores. As you arrive at Tikal from Flores, you'll see them on the right side: **Comedor Imperio Maya, Restaurante Imperio Maya,** and **Comedor Tikal,** which is the best of the bunch. All are rustic and pleasant, and all serve hefty plates of fairly tasty food at low prices. You can get a large serving of roast chicken with rice, beans, and fresh tortillas, along with a drink, for around Q40.

Within the area of the ruins, you'll find picnic tables beneath shelters and itinerant soft-drink and candy bar peddlers. If you want to spend all day at the ruins without having to walk back to the parking area for lunch, take sandwiches. Most of the hotels here and in Flores, as well as the *comedores,* will make you a bag lunch to take into the park.

Tikal After Dark

Aside from hanging around at your hotel bar or at one of the simple *comedores,* or swinging in a hammock at the campsite, the best nighttime activity here is to visit the ruins by moonlight. Those staying near the entrance to the ruins can have their admission ticket validated to allow them to roam the park until 8pm, and in some cases even later, depending on the disposition of the guards. If the moon is waxing, full, or just beyond full, you're in for a real treat. *Tip:* Before venturing into the park at night, be sure to ask around as to the current level of safety inside the park after dark. The moonlight is less lovely when getting robbed.

EL REMATE ★★

32km (20 miles) E of Flores; 32km (20 miles) S of Tikal; 60km (37 miles) W of Melchor de Mencos

El Remate is a small village on the eastern shores of Lake Petén Itzá that is a popular spot in which to stay while visiting Tikal. It's located about midway between Flores and Tikal, which means that staying here cuts travel time between your hotel and the ruins. El Remate is much more tranquil and pristine than Flores or Santa Elena. Currently, a handful of budget lodgings can be found in the tiny village here, while more upscale options can be found on the shores of the lake heading north out of the village.

Essentials

GETTING THERE & DEPARTING

BY MINIVAN   Scheduled and independent minivans ply the route between Santa Elena/Flores and Tikal throughout the day. Any of these will drop you off in El Remate. For more information on these, see "Getting Around" on p. 295 and below. Fares from Flores to El Remate run around Q20 and Q40 per person each way.

BY CAR   El Remate is located about 1.6km (1 mile) north of Ixlú (El Cruce). The road is paved and in good shape all the way from the Belize-Guatemala border 60km (37 miles) away.

GETTING AROUND

El Remate is a tiny village, and you can easily walk anywhere in town. Some of the hotels listed below are located 1.6km (1 mile) or so north of the village, on the road that circles Lake Petén Itzá. If you're in El Remate, you'll most likely want to go to Tikal, visit Santa Elena and Flores, or explore the region.

BY TAXI   Taxis charge between Q150 and Q200 for the one-way trip between El Remate and Tikal, and around Q100 to Q150 for the trip between El Remate and Santa Elena and Flores. The higher rates are for a minivan that can hold anywhere from six to eight passengers. A taxi is your best option if you decide to explore the area around the lake. There are often taxis hanging around the small village. If not, your hotel can call one for you. Be sure to have your hotel set a fair price, or be prepared to bargain, as the first price you are quoted is almost assuredly above the going rate and subject to some negotiation.

BY MINIVAN If you don't have a car, the best way to get around is by minivan. Scheduled and unscheduled minivans ply the route between Flores and Tikal throughout the day. All of these pass through El Remate, dropping off and picking up passengers. You can get a minivan at almost any hotel in El Remate, or walk a few hundred yards out to the main road to Tikal and flag one down. The ride takes about a half-hour to either Tikal or Flores, and the one-way fare is from Q20 to Q40 per person.

What to See & Do

The village of El Remate itself is very small and provincial, with little of interest to tourists. Most people use El Remate as a base for explorations of the ruins at Tikal. However, as small lodges and isolated resorts start to pop up here, many tour and activity options will follow.

Just west of El Remate is the **Biotopo Cerro Cahuí,** a small nature reserve with some trails and good wildlife-viewing opportunities. More than 180 species of birds have been spotted in the reserve's 1,500 acres. A couple of loop trails climb uphill from the entrance and at various points offer excellent views of the lake. I recommend visiting this park with a guide, as a spate of robberies and attacks against tourists closed it for a period several years ago. The reserve is open daily from 8am to 4pm, and admission is Q40.

Watch Out for Crocs

If you're out on the lake during the daytime, scan the shoreline northwest of El Remate and try to pick out the **"Sleeping Crocodile,"** a silhouette formed by the shape of the forested hills as they descend toward the lake. If you can't pick it out, ask a local for help.

One of the most popular activities in El Remate is **renting a canoe or kayak** for paddling around on the lake. Most of the hotels in town either rent kayaks or canoes, or can arrange one for you. Rates run around Q35 per hour, or around Q120 per day.

Similarly, most of the hotels in town either rent or provide **mountain bikes** for their guests, or can arrange for their rental. The dirt road that circles Lake Petén Itzá is excellent for a mountain-bike ride. Rates are about Q60 per day.

Finally, the village of El Remate is gaining some local renown for its woodcarving, with over 70 families involved in the art in this town alone. You'll see several roadside stands set up on the route between Ixlú and El Remate, and onward to Tikal. If you ask around El Remate, you might even be able to visit one or more of the artisans.

Where to Stay & Dine

Most folks take their meals at their hotels. You'll find some simple *comedores* in the center of the village. The best of these is probably **El Muelle** (www. hotelelmuelle.com; *℅* **502/5581-8087**), which has a great view of the lake, as well as a swimming pool, which you can use if you eat here. If you're looking for something different, try the restaurant at the **Hotel Mon Ami** (www.hotel monami.com; *℅* **502/3010-0284**), which features a mix of Guatemalan, French, and Italian fare.

VERY EXPENSIVE

La Lancha Resort ★★   This is filmmaker Francis Ford Coppola's Guatemalan piece of his mini hotel chain in the Mundo Maya, and it is as creatively luxe as the others in this consortium. The main lodge has a commanding view of the lake and features a soaring, open-air, A-frame thatched roof oriented toward the view. Below the lodge is a kidney-shaped pool. A newly added funicular leads down to the shore of the lake, where guests swim, canoe, kayak, and surf the Web (as one of the thoughtful touches here, the resort added Wi-Fi coverage on the lake beach in 2017). Lodgings are all in duplex bungalows. The "lake view" units are quite spacious, while the "jungle view" rooms are more compact. All are handsome enough for a honeymoon, with brightly colored handmade blankets on the beds, sculptures and other local art work here and there, and lots of burnished wood. All feature a shared wooden veranda hung with hammocks, and you can probably figure out the view from the room names. Plans here include the addition of some independent suites with private plunge pools.

Lago Petén Itzá, Petén. www.lalancha.com. *℅* **855/670-4817** in the U.S., or 502/7928-8331 in Guatemala. 10 units. Q1,095–Q2,717 double, includes breakfast. Rates lower in the off season; higher during peak periods. **Amenities:** Restaurant; bar; room service; bike rental; free canoe use; outdoor pool; gift shop; sweat lodge; Wi-Fi (free).

MODERATE

Hotel Gringo Perdido ★★   Three kilometers (1¾ miles) north of El Remate, on the dirt road that circles Lake Petén Itzá, you'll find one of Guatemala's original jungle lodges. This little offbeat paradise is arranged along the lakeshore, with shady rustic hillside gardens, an unusually good restaurant, a quiet camping area, and rooms ranging from a rustic dormitory to some almost plush private bungalows. The whole thing seems to blend into and get swallowed up by the rainforest. The Gringo Perdido, which means "the lost American," offers good swimming in the lake, 3.2km (2 miles) of nature trails, and tranquility. They also arrange Sacred Fire Ceremonies with a Mayan Shaman, a cultural experience that is absolutely worth having.

3.2km (2 miles) west of El Remate, Petén. www.hotelgringoperdido.com. *℅* **502/5804-8639.** 13 units (2 with shared bathroom). Q735 double private room. Rates include breakfast and dinner. Q37 per person to camp, with meals extra. **Amenities:** Restaurant; Wi-Fi (free).

INEXPENSIVE

In addition to the places listed below, a few very inexpensive options, catering to the backpacker crowd, are right in El Remate. I recommend simply walking around to see which one best suits your fancy and budget. One good option is **Hotel Mon Ami** (www.hotelmonami.com; ✆ 502/3010-0284).

La Casa de Don David Hotel ★★   Rooms here are located in a series of buildings arrayed around a large and lush garden area. All are clean and simple; most have air-conditioning, though at a small extra charge. There's an open-air octagonal hammock hut for reading and resting, and you can catch a glimpse of Lake Petén from here. My favorite room is no. 13, which is a corner unit with a private hammock on its front porch. The hotel offers bicycles free for guest use. David Kuhn and his wife, Rosita, have lived in this area for more than 40 years, and they are a wealth of information and advice. David was the original *gringo perdido* of the nearby nature lodge (see above), but left there to open this delightful little place.

El Remate, Petén. www.lacasadedondavid.com. ✆ **502/75306-2190.** 13 units. Q367–Q440 double, 20% higher in peak season. Rates include 1 meal (breakfast, lunch, or dinner). **Amenities:** Restaurant; tour desk; Wi-Fi (free).

La Mansión del Pájaro Serpiente ★★   Set off the main road to Tikal, on a hillside overlooking the lake, the mansion is set in Edenic gardens. Really, they rival what you'll see in many of Central America's official botanic gardens. Guests stay in either standard or deluxe bungalows, both of which feature handsome stone and woodworking details, with local textile and crafts filling out the decor. The deluxe rooms have televisions and air-conditioning. Several rooms are quite large and should be classified as junior suites, as they also have a separate sitting area just off the bedroom. The "honeymoon suite" comes with its own plunge pool and is high up the hill, with a fab view. The midsize free-form pool is set in the center of the gardens, and almost feels like a natural pond in the jungle. The open-air restaurant has a swell view of the lake and specializes in local cuisine. The friendly owners raise peacocks, and there are always several wandering around the grounds.

El Remate, Petén. ✆ **502/7926-8498,** or 502/5702-9434. 11 units. Q360 double; Q440 deluxe double. No credit cards. **Amenities:** Restaurant; outdoor pool; can arrange tours; Wi-Fi (free).

El Remate After Dark

El Remate is a quiet village. Most visitors head to the small bar at their hotel or hostel to chat with fellow travelers, or they take tours. One popular tour offered at night involves journeying to the lake to see crocodiles. This 2-hour tour involves a ride in a small motor launch with a high-powered flashlight or headlamp. The guide will scan the shore and inlets for the red reflection of the crocodiles' eyes. If you're lucky, they won't submerge as you slowly approach. All of the hotels in town can arrange this tour. The cost is between Q150 and Q240.

FLORES & SANTA ELENA ★

64km (40 miles) SW of Tikal; 135km (84 miles) NW of the Belizean border; 451km (280 miles) NE of Guatemala City

Since accommodations in Tikal are limited, most travelers either choose to (or must) overnight in the sister cities of Flores and Santa Elena. Still, this is not necessarily such a bad thing. Flores itself is a picturesque little town built on an island in the middle of Lake Petén Itzá. A narrow causeway connects Flores to Santa Elena. There's a lot more to do and see in Flores and Santa Elena than there is closer to Tikal, and a far wider range of hotels and restaurants to choose from.

Seen from the air, Flores appears almost perfectly round. This quiet town, with its colonial-style buildings and cobblestone streets, is one of the most fascinating in Guatemala. Though most people spend time here only en route to or from the Tikal ruins, Flores is well worth exploring for a day or two. A walk around the circumference of the island presents a sort of Venetian experience. Buildings come right down to the water's edge. In fact, since the lake's water level has risen over the years, some of the outlying streets and alleys are flooded. Dugout canoes, kayaks, and motor launches sit at makeshift docks all around the circumference of the island.

Santa Elena, Flores's mainland counterpart, on the other hand, is a ramshackle, modern boomtown with little at all to recommend it. However, Santa Elena is where you'll find the airport, the bus stations, a host of hotels, and a good view of Flores. Just to the west of Santa Elena is the town of San Benito, a rough-and-tumble area with little appeal to visitors. The name Flores is often used as a bucket term encompassing the island of Flores itself, along with Santa Elena and San Benito.

Flores is the unofficial capital of the Petén region of Guatemala. El Petén has always been a remote region, and it was here, on the banks of Lake Petén Itzá, that the Itzá people, descendents of the Mayas, resisted Spanish conquest until the end of the 17th century. Hernán Cortés had visited the Itzá city of Tayasal, which once stood on the far side of the lake, in 1525 but had not tried to conquer the Itzás, who had a reputation for being fierce warriors. However, in 1697, the Spanish finally conquered the Itzás, and Tayasal became the last Indian city to fall under Spanish rule. Two years after taking Tayasal, the Spanish

---

Horsing Around

One of the most curious pieces of local history revolves around a sick horse that was left in Tayasal by Hernán Cortés when he passed through the area. The Itzás had never seen horses before, and as soon as Cortés left, they began worshiping it. When the horse died, a stone statue of it was made, and the worship continued until Spanish missionaries arrived in Tayasal 100 years later. The missionaries, appalled by this idolatry, proceeded to pitch the blasphemous statue into the lake. To this day the legendary horse statue has never been discovered, though searches continue to be launched from time to time.

moved to Flores, an island that could easily be defended. They renamed this island Nuestra Señora de los Remedios y San Pablo de los Itzaes and between 1700 and 1701 built a fort here. In 1831, the island was once again renamed, this time being given the name Flores in honor of a Guatemalan patriot.

Essentials

GETTING THERE & DEPARTING

BY PLANE   See "By Plane" under "Essentials" in "Tikal," earlier in this chapter.

BY CAR   To get here from Belize, see "By Car" under "Essentials" on p. 291, earlier in this chapter.

The road between Tikal and Flores is a good, paved road, and the trip takes around an hour by car. To get to either of the sister towns from Tikal, head south out of the ruins and turn right at Ixlú (El Cruce). Continue past the airport. You will come to Santa Elena first. Stay on the main avenue into town and head toward the lake, where you will find the causeway over to Flores.

BY BUS   For information on getting to Flores and Santa Elena by bus from Belize, see "By Bus" under "Essentials" on p. 294, earlier in this chapter. See "Getting Around," below, for details on getting from Santa Elena and Flores to the ruins.

There are several companies operating first-class buses to and from Guatemala City. **Línea Dorada** (www.lineadorada.info; ⒸⒸ **502/2415-8900** in Guatemala City, or 502/7924-8434 in Santa Elena) is a good choice. It operates out of the main bus terminal in Santa Elena, located about 8 blocks south of downtown along 6a Avenida. The trip to Guatemala City takes about 8 to 10 hours, and first-class fares run around Q190 to Q280.

GETTING AROUND

If you're in Santa Elena or Flores, you'll most likely want to go to Tikal or explore the region around Lake Petén.

BY MINIVAN   If you don't have a car, the best way to get around this area is by minivan. Minivans from Flores and Santa Elena to Tikal leave roughly every hour between 5 and 10am, and less frequently thereafter. These minivans leave from Tikal for the return trip roughly every hour from noon to 6pm. Every hotel in Flores and Santa Elena can arrange a minivan pickup for you. The trip usually takes an hour and costs Q50 to Q60 per person each way. You can buy a round-trip fare at a slight savings; however, this commits you to a specific minivan company, and I've found I prefer paying a little extra to have more flexibility in grabbing my return ride when I'm ready to leave.

BY TAXI   Taxis charge between Q350 and Q450 for the one-way trip between Flores or Santa Elena and Tikal. Between Flores or Santa Elena and El Remate, the fare is around Q100 to Q150. The higher rate is for a minivan that can hold anywhere from six to eight passengers. A taxi is your best option if you decide to explore the area around the lake. Be sure to bargain, as the first price you are quoted is almost certainly above the going rate and subject to some negotiation.

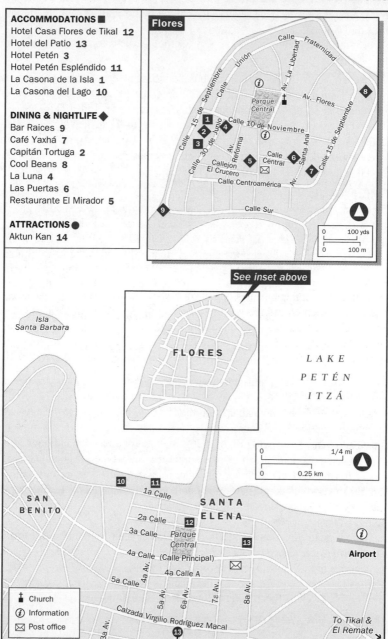

ACCOMMODATIONS ■
Hotel Casa Flores de Tikal **12**
Hotel del Patio **13**
Hotel Petén **3**
Hotel Petén Espléndido **11**
La Casona de la Isla **1**
La Casona del Lago **10**

DINING & NIGHTLIFE ◆
Bar Raices **9**
Café Yaxhá **7**
Capitán Tortuga **2**
Cool Beans **8**
La Luna **4**
Las Puertas **6**
Restaurante El Mirador **5**

ATTRACTIONS ●
Aktun Kan **14**

Flores

Calle Fraternidad
Calle Unión
Av. La Libertad
Calle 15 de Septiembre
Calle
Parque Central
Av. Flores
Calle 10 de Noviembre
Av. Reforma
Calle 30 de Junio
Callejon El Crucero
Calle Central
Santa Ana
Calle 15 de Septiembre
Calle Centroamérica
Calle Sur

0   100 yds
0   100 m

See inset above

Isla Santa Barbara

FLORES

LAKE PETÉN ITZÁ

0   1/4 mi
0   0.25 km

SAN BENITO

SANTA ELENA

1a Calle
2a Calle
3a Calle
Parque Central
4a Calle (Calle Principal)
4a Calle A
5a Calle
4a Av.
5a Av.
6a Av.
7a Av.
8a Av.
3a Av.
Calzada Virgilio Rodríguez Macal

Airport

To Tikal & El Remate

✝ Church
ⓘ Information
✉ Post office

BY CAR   If you have your own car, the road between Santa Elena and Flores and Tikal is paved, well-marked, and heavily traveled. It's about 32km (20 miles) from Flores to Ixlú (El Cruce), and another 32km on to the park and ruins of Tikal.

For information on renting a car, see "Getting Around" on p. 296, earlier in this chapter.

BY BUS   Very inexpensive local bus service connects Flores and Santa Elena to Tikal and several neighboring communities. However, this service is infrequent, slow, and often uncomfortably overcrowded. Línea Dorada (see above) has three daily buses from Santa Elena to Tikal leaving at 5 and 8:30am and at 3:30pm. The return buses leave Tikal at 2 and 5pm. Ask at your hotel or around town for current schedules, as they change periodically. The trip takes 2 hours; the one-way fare is Q50.

ORIENTATION

The town primarily known as Flores actually consists of three smaller towns that have merged. Flores proper sits on a small island out in Lake Petén Itzá, and is connected to the mainland by a long causeway. On the mainland are Santa Elena (nearest the airport) and San Benito (closer to the bus terminal and market). Whether you arrive by air or by bus from Guatemala City or Belize, you will come into town from the east. The road in from the airport leads straight through Santa Elena to the market and bus terminal, while the causeway to Flores is a turn to the right in the middle of Santa Elena. While there are a host of budget lodgings in San Benito, especially around the bus terminal, I strongly advise most travelers to stick to Santa Elena and Flores proper.

FAST FACTS   You'll find numerous banks in downtown Flores and Santa Elena. Most have ATMs, and many of these will work with your debit or credit card. Check with your home bank and the PLUS or Cirrus systems in advance to confirm. All will exchange money. Most of the hotels and restaurants in Flores and Santa Elena will also exchange dollars for quetzales, although they may give you a slightly less favorable rate than you would get at a bank.

The **Flores post office** is on 1a Calle, 3 blocks from Parque Central, or Central Park, which is in front of the church. **Santa Elena's post office** is on Calle 4 and Avenida 7. Both are open Monday through Friday from 8am to 5pm. To contact the **local police,** dial ✆ **502/7926-1365.**

There is an information booth run by the Guatemalan Tourist Board, **Inguat** (www.visitguatemala.com; ✆ **502/2290-2800**), at the Flores airport, and another one in downtown Flores (✆ **502/7867-5334**) on Avenida Flores, on the north side of the Central Park. Both can help provide basic maps to the region and ruins, as well as brochures for local hotels and tour agencies.

What to See & Do

Flores is a wonderful town to explore by walking. The whole island is only about 5 blocks wide in any direction. At the center is a small central park or plaza, anchored by the town's Catholic church. Be sure to take a peek inside to check out the beautiful stained-glass windows. After first exploring the island on foot, you should have a look at the island from the perspective of a boat.

One of the most popular things to do in Flores is take a **tour of the lake ★**. You will be inundated with offers for boat tours. Ask at your hotel or one of the local tour agencies, or talk to the numerous freelancers approaching you on the street. Be sure to inspect the craft beforehand, if possible, and make sure you feel comfortable with its lake-worthiness. Also, make sure your guide is bilingual if you don't speak Spanish. These tours last anywhere from 1 to 3 hours, and usually include stops at La Guitarra Island (Guitar Island), which features a picnic and swimming area, as well as at the mostly unexcavated ruins of Tayasal. Here, be sure to climb **El Mirador ★**, a lakeside pyramid that offers a fabulous view of Flores. Many of these tours also stop at the small **Petencito Zoo** and **ARCAS** (www.arcasguatemala.com), a conservation organization and animal rehabilitation center that has some interpretive trails and displays of rescued animals either in recuperation or unable to be released. These tours cost between Q80 and Q160 per person, depending on the length of the tour and the size of your group. Don't be afraid to bargain. Entrance to the zoo is an extra Q20.

You can also explore the lake on your own in a kayak or canoe. These are also rented all around Flores. Again, ask at your hotel or at one of the local tour agencies. Rates for kayaks and canoes run around Q20 per hour. Be careful paddling around the lake: When the winds pick up, especially in the afternoons, it can get quite choppy and challenging.

If you're a spelunker, you might want to explore **Aktun Kan (Cave of the Serpent),** a large cavern just outside of Santa Elena. The cave takes its name from a legend about a giant snake living there. But don't worry, it's only a legend. Yet another legend has it that this cave is connected to a cave beneath the church on Flores. To reach the cave, either walk south out of Santa Elena on the road that crosses the causeway from Flores, or ask a taxi to take you out there. The fare should be around Q15 round-trip. Although there are lights in the cave (admission Q15), be sure to bring a flashlight for a little extra illumination.

A host of local tour operators here can arrange any of the tours listed above, as well as guided tours to Tikal and the ruins listed below. The best of these is **Martsam Travel ★★** (www.martsam.com; ℭ **305/395-3935** in the U.S. and Canada, or 502/7832-2742 in Guatemala).

YAXHÁ, EL CEIBAL & OTHER NEARBY RUINS

If your life's passion is Mayan ruins or you simply crave more adventure than you have had so far on your visit to El Petén, you should think about visiting some of the more remote ruins of this region. In addition to exploring seldom-visited Mayan ruins, you'll be traveling through uninhabited jungles where you'll likely encounter a great deal of wildlife, which might include coati-mundi, howler and spider monkeys, anteaters, tapirs, and possibly even jaguars.

Thanks to the publicity and infrastructure bestowed upon this site by the TV show *Survivor: Guatemala,* **Yaxhá ★★** is now one of the prime archaeological sites to visit in Guatemala. In fact, this is the third-largest Mayan ceremonial city in Guatemala—behind Tikal and El Mirador. Be sure to climb **Temple 216 ★★★**, located in the East Acropolis. This is the tallest structure here, and provides excellent views of lakes Yaxhá and Sacnab, as well as the surrounding rainforests. The sunsets here rival those in Tikal. Yaxhá is one of the few Mayan cities to retain its traditional Mayan name, which translates as "green waters." You can combine a visit to Yaxhá with a trip to the ruins of **Topoxté,** which are located on a small island in Lake Yaxhá. This small yet intriguing site is thought to have been a residential city for local elites. However, it was also a fortified city where Mayan warriors put up a valiant defense against Spanish forces. *Note:* You'll probably be warned, and see the signs, but just in case, do not swim in Lake Yaxhá, as it is home to a robust population of crocodiles. Many organized tours here also include a stop at the nearby minor ruins of Nakum, which are currently being excavated. However, this makes for a long day. The turnoff for the 11km (7-mile) dirt road into the site is located about 32km (20 miles) east of Ixlú, or El Cruce. The Q80 admission grants you access to Yaxhá, Topoxté, and Nakum. If you want to stay at Yaxhá, camping is allowed at a well-tended campsite down by the lakeshore.

Another popular site is **El Ceibal ★**, which offers one of the most scenic routes along the way. To reach El Ceibal, you first head the 64km (40 miles) from Flores to Sayaxché, which is a good-size town for El Petén (it even has a few basic hotels). From Sayaxché, you must hire a boat to carry you 18km (11 miles) up the Río de la Pasión. El Ceibal is a Late Classic–era ruin known for having the only circular temple in all of El Petén. There are also several well-preserved steles arranged around one small temple structure on the central plaza, as well as a ball court. Many of the designs at El Ceibal indicate that the city had extensive contact with cities in the Yucatán, but whether this contact was due to trade or to warfare is unclear. Your best bet for visiting El Ceibal is to book the excursion with one of the tour agencies in Flores or Santa Elena. Full-day trips run around Q600 to Q800. Overnight trips can also be arranged, combining a visit to El Ceibal with even more obscure Mayan sites such as Aguateca and Petexbatún. If you get to Sayaxché on your own, look for **Viajes Don Pedro** (*(C)* **502/7928-6109**). These folks run regular boats to El Ceibal and charge around Q500 per person round-trip. However, if you have a group, be sure to try to negotiate a flat rate for the boat, which should carry anywhere from four to eight people.

Uaxactún (pronounced "Wah-shahk-*toon*") is another Mayan ceremonial center located 24km (15 miles) north of Tikal. Though many of the pyramids and temples here have been uncovered, they have not been restored nearly as extensively as those at Tikal. One of the most interesting finds at Uaxactún is what is believed to be the oldest-known astrological observatory yet discovered in the Mayan world. In Group E, on the eastern side of these ruins, you can watch a sunrise from the observatory temple that lines up precisely with other temples on the equinoxes and solstices. Your best bet for visiting Uaxactún is to book the excursion with one of the tour agencies in Flores or Santa

Elena. Full-day trips cost about Q600 to Q800 and can be combined with a stop at Tikal, although I think that's trying to cram too much into a single day. If you have your own four-wheel-drive vehicle, you can drive here yourself. The ruins at Uaxactún are open daily from 6am to 6pm, and no admission is charged. However, you must reach it by passing through Tikal National Park, and so you must pay the Tikal entrance fee of Q150. Moreover, be forewarned that the dirt road between Tikal and Uaxactún is sometimes not passable during the rainy season. Be sure to ask locally about current conditions before heading off.

Finally, truly adventurous travelers can book a multiday jungle trek to **El Mirador ★★**, the largest Mayan ceremonial city in Guatemala. Barely excavated, El Mirador features the tallest pyramidal structure in the known Mayan world, La Danta, which reaches some 79m (260 ft.) in height. The trip here involves at least 5 days of hiking and jungle camping. **Martsam Travel ★★** (p. 313) is the best operator to contact for one of these trips.

STUDYING SPANISH

Check in with the **Dos Mundos Spanish Academy** (www.flores-spanish.com; *©* **502/5830-2060**), which offers a wide range of Spanish language learning, from a 4-hour crash course for US$40 to an intensive 30-hour per week program for US$170. They offer accomodations as well so you can really commit.

Where to Stay

EXPENSIVE

Hotel Villa Maya ★★ Hotel Villa Maya is located about 15 minutes from the airport, on the shores of Lake Petén Itzá, but away from the twin cities and toward Tikal. The setting and surrounding forests are lovely. Peace and quiet, if that's what you're looking for, are an added bonus, on top of the slightly reduced travel time to the ruins. However, if you want access to the restaurants and shops in Flores, you'll need either your own car or a taxi. Most of the rooms are found in a series of two-story buildings, set on the edge of the lake. Local hardwoods are used generously to trim detail and furnish the place. The rooms are simple, spacious, and immaculate, and each comes with a small triangular balcony overlooking the lake. The hotel also has a pool with a cascading waterfall, as well as a wonderful dock and deck area over the lake.

15 min. from Santa Elena Internacional Airport on Lake Petenchel, 4km (2½ miles) north of the well-marked turnoff on the road from Santa Elena to Tikal. www.villasde guatemala.com. *©* **502/2223-5000.** 56 units. Q735 double + 22% tax. **Amenities:** Restaurant; bike rental; Jacuzzi; pool; room service; watersports equipment rental; Wi-Fi (free).

MODERATE

Hotel Del Patio ★ This hotel's central courtyard, with its tall fountain flowing into a cloverleaf pool, is classic colonial Guatemala. The rooms are simple, clean, and comfortable, although the decor is definitely dated, and you can find better deals around town. I'd opt for a second-floor unit, just so you can admire the courtyard from above as you enter and exit your room. A midsize kidney-shaped pool and tiny gym, as well as a good international restaurant, round out the amenities.

Calle 8 and Av. 2, Santa Elena, Petén. www.hoteldelpatio.com.gt. © **502/7926-0104,** or 502/7926-1229. 21 units. Q488 double. **Amenities:** Restaurant; bar; small gym; pool; room service; Wi-Fi (free).

Hotel Petén Espléndido ★ This modern, upscale hotel is located in Santa Elena just off the causeway on the shore of Lake Petén Itzá, with a great view of Flores. The rooms feature contemporary decor and more amenities than you'll find anywhere else in town. The bathrooms are even equipped with telephones, and four rooms are truly fitted out for travelers with disabilities (rare to find in Guatemala). Try and snag one of the second-floor rooms with balconies directly fronting the lake. If you don't get one of these, the hotel's waterfront restaurant has a lovely view and serves good international and local cuisine. There's a relaxing and refreshing pool area with a separate Jacuzzi. The Espléndido offers a free airport shuttle, as well as free paddle boats for use on the lake, and has a helpful tour desk and concierge.

1a Calle 5-01, Zona 1, Santa Elena, Flores, Petén. © **502/7926-0880.** 62 units. Q535– Q1,200 double. **Amenities:** Restaurant; bar; concierge; outdoor pool; room service; Wi-Fi (free).

La Casona del Lago ★★ This is the most luxurious hotel of a group run by a small local chain, although it's also the only one not on the island of Flores proper. (Don't confuse this with La Casona de la Isla, which is part of the same chain and in Flores.) Still, this hotel is located right on the shores of the lake, with excellent views of its waters and picturesque island city. The three-story building is built in an L-shape, around a central pool and Jacuzzi area, and painted a bright primary blue, with sparkling white trim. Rooms are spacious, with two double beds, white-tile floors, a couple of sitting chairs, and a separate desk area, and they feature a host of modern amenities, including large televisions.

Calle Litoral, Zona 1, Santa Elena, Flores, Petén. www.hotelesdepeten.com. © **502/ 7952-8700.** 46 units. Q587–Q815 double. Rates include full breakfast and taxes. **Amenities:** Restaurant; bar; outdoor Jacuzzi and pool; conference center; Wi-Fi (free).

INEXPENSIVE

Hotel Casa Flores de Tikal ★ This neat little hotel in downtown Santa Elena offers well-kept rooms at a fair price. Yes, the rooms are tiny, and so are the TVs, but you may find yourself spending more time lounging in the lovely, palm-tree shaded interior courtyard, which has a pretty, if small, pool (it even has a water slide, which is a hit with children). The hotel is kept immaculate, and there's a friendly air to the whole operation. You'll find a simple restaurant on the grounds, as well as an inviting second-floor bar. For a good view, head up to the unfinished rooftop terrace.

Av. 6 and Calle 2, Santa Elena, Petén. www.hotelcasafloresdetikal.com. © **502/7926-2235.** 28 units. Q360–Q416 double. **Amenities:** Restaurant; small outdoor pool; room service; Wi-Fi (free).

Hotel Petén ★   From the street, this hotel looks very modest. Walk through the doorway, though, and you'll find an attractive small courtyard with tropical plants, a tiny semi-indoor pool, and a nice brick-and-stucco building of several floors. The rooms are all spic-and-span. The best rooms are those on the top two floors with private balconies and an excellent view of the lake. In fact, only five rooms here don't have a lake view, so when you reserve or check in, be sure you get one that does. There's a popular restaurant on the ground floor. These folks also have an in-house tour company, and are owned by the same company as a couple of other nearby hotels, in case this one is full.

Calle 30 de Junio, Flores, Petén. www.hotelesdepeten.com. ℂ **502/7867-5203.** 21 units. Q367–Q516 double. Rates include taxes. **Amenities:** Restaurant; Jacuzzi; pool; Wi-Fi (free).

La Casona de la Isla ★   What makes this hotel recommendable is its service, which is friendly and very diligent. As for the guest rooms, all are small and lack much in the way of style, but they are immaculate and do have ceiling fans, and air-conditioning—although some of these A/C units can be rather old and noisy. Most come with a private balcony, and almost all of these have good views of the lake. The hotel is built in an L-shape around a stone terrace with lush gardens and a small swimming pool featuring a sculpted stone waterfall and separate Jacuzzi. Its restaurant serves good Guatemalan and international fare in a small dining room off the lobby, and there's a back patio bar with an excellent view overlooking the lake.

Calle 30 de Junio, Flores, Petén. www.hotelesdepeten.com. ℂ **502/7867-5200.** 26 units. Q455–Q543 double. Rates include taxes. **Amenities:** Restaurant; bar; outdoor Jacuzzi and pool; Wi-Fi (free).

Where to Dine

There are tons of places to eat around Flores and Santa Elena. Most are simple affairs serving local and Mexican cuisine, and geared toward locals and the backpacker crowd. Most of the hotels listed above have restaurants, and most of these are quite dependable. **El Mirador Restaurant** at the Hotel Petén Espléndido (see above) serves good but far from spectacular international fare; however, the setting is certainly the most elegant you'll find in this neck of the woods.

   In addition to the places listed below, **Il Terrazzo** (ℂ **502/7867-5479;** Calle la Union) doesn't take credit cards, but it does serve excellent, hearty Italian food.

Café Yaxhá ★ GUATEMALAN/MAYAN   This is a relaxed and welcoming spot that serves excellent local fare, including dishes based on pre-Colombian recipes and ingredients. I recommend the Pollo Xni Pec, which is chicken in a spicy tomato sauce served with yucca. The German owner is an archaeologist, and photos of archaeological sites adorn the walls, books on the subject matter are available to browse, and talks, slide shows, and guided tours are often offered. This is also a good place to come for coffee drinks and fresh-fruit smoothies.

Calle 15 de Setiembre, across from El Tucán, Flores. www.cafeyaxha.com. © **502/7867-5055.** Main courses Q30–Q90. Daily 7am–9pm.

Capitán Tortuga ★ INTERNATIONAL   This popular restaurant has a long and wide-ranging menu. You can get everything from pizzas to barbecue ribs to vegetarian shish kebabs. They also have a wide range of coffee and espresso drinks, as well as ice creams and freshly baked desserts. The large main dining room sits under a high thatched roof. However, I prefer the tables on the small outdoor patio that fronts the lake, or those in the second-floor, open-air dining room reached from a stairway out back. Service can be slow at times, but if you're with a group or sharing a drink with fellow travelers, you might not mind.

Calle 30 de Junio, next to La Casona de la Isla, Flores. © **502/7867-5089.** Main courses Q32–Q120. Daily 7am–10pm.

La Luna ★★ INTERNATIONAL   This hip little restaurant is the most creative and refined option in Flores. The menu ranges from steak in pepper sauce to lobster tails, with a host of fish and chicken—and even some vegetarian—options in between. I recommend starting things off with stuffed peppers or a falafel side. There are three separate dining areas, and all are artistically decorated. My favorite room features a faux ceiba tree in the center and a wild sculpture on one wall made of wood and mirrors.

Calle 30 de Junio, across from La Casona de la Isla, Flores. © **502/7867-5443.** Main courses Q40–Q130. Mon–Sat noon–midnight.

Flores & Santa Elena After Dark

There are several bars along Calle Sur fronting the lake just over the bridge as you enter Flores. For a view of the lake and a happening dance, DJ, and party scene, you can head to **Bar Raíces** (© 7867-5743), at the far western end of Calle Sur. Another good option, near the center of the island, is **Las Puertas** ★ (© 7867-5242; corner of Calle Centroamérica and Avenida Santa Ana), which is a popular bar/restaurant that has nightly DVD movie showings and occasionally live music. Finally, for a mellow scene, try **Cool Beans** ★ (© 5571-9240; Calle 15 de Setiembre), a popular place for tourists and itinerant backpackers, with a convivial, laid-back vibe, free Wi-Fi, plenty of board games, and a view of the lake to boot. **Il Terrazzo** and **La Luna** are also worth checking out for a nightcap.

USEFUL TERMS & PHRASES

English is the official language of Belize, but the country is one of the most polyglot places on the planet. In addition to English, many Belizeans speak Spanish, and among some members of the population, this is the primary language. You will find Spanish prevalent in the northern and western regions, near the borders with Mexico and Guatemala, but given Belize's long history of immigration, Spanish speakers can be found throughout the country. In fact, conversations among Belizeans are often a mix of English and Spanish ("Spanglish"), with a fair amount of Creole thrown in for good measure.

Creole, or Kriol, is the local patois, a colorful, rhythmic, and often difficult-to-understand dialect. Although based primarily on English, it takes some getting used to before most Westerners can grasp the pronunciations and sentence structures that distinguish Belizean Kriol. While this was originally the language of former black slaves and their descendants, today most Belizeans understand and speak Kriol, and they will often use it among themselves in the presence of foreigners if they don't want to be understood.

In addition to English, Spanish, and Kriol, Belize's Garífuna (or Garinagu) people have their own distinct language, while the various Maya tribes still speak primarily their native languages.

CREOLE TERMS

Creole, or Kriol, is largely based on English, although it does incorporate words and syntax from various African languages as well. Once you get the hang of certain pronunciations and syntactical phrasings, however, it's actually quite easy to understand. Almost any Kriol speaker will understand you if you speak in English. However, they'll be really impressed if you start inserting various Kriol words and phrases into your conversations.

Basic Words

Agen Again
Aks To ask
An And
Bak Back
Bwai Boy
Chinchi A very small amount
Daata Daughter

Da At, on, in, to
Da Is, am, are
Da It is
Deh/di Am, is, are (located); for instance, "Ih deh pahn di boat" means "He/she is on the boat"

Dehn Them
Di The
Doe Door
Fi To
Fo For
Ih He, she, it
Kunku Small
Nize Noise
Noh Isn't it so?
Shudda Should have

Tideh Today
Uman Woman
Unu You all
Vex/bex Angry
Waata Water
Wudda Would have
Yaiy Eye
Yaiy waata Tears, literally "eye water"
Yerriso Gossip

Menu Items

Bail op Traditional dish made with cassava, cocoa, sweet potatoes, plantains, boil cake, and fish or pig's tail
Bambam Traditional dish made with cassava
Bami Cassava bread
Chimoaleh Traditional dish of blackened chicken soup and rice; *chimole* in Spanish
Dukunu Dish of mashed and steamed corn, wrapped in a leaf, similar to a *tamal*
Eskabaycheh Pickled onion soup with chicken or fish; derived from the Spanish word *escabeche* ("pickled")
Garnache Fried tortilla topped with beans and rice
Janny kake Traditional fried or baked bread, served at breakfast
Konks Conch
Panades Traditional dish of finely chopped fish wrapped in a tortilla
Recado Red *achiote* paste
Reyeno Soup made with chicken, pork, and boiled eggs
Rise and beanz Rice and beans with coconut milk
Rompopo Alcoholic drink similar to eggnog
Strech-mi-gots Traditional taffy
Tablayta Coconut candy

Wildlife

Bilam Small river fish
Chaaly prise Large rat
Gaalin Heron
Gibnut Paca
Gwaana Iguana
Hooyu Owl
Jankro Vulture
Janny fidla Fiddler crab
Kwash Coati, coati-mundi
Taapong Tarpon

Tuba River fish
Waari Wild pig or peccary
Waata daag River otter
Weewi ants Leaf-cutter ant
Wowla Boa constrictor, also used to refer to a type of basket used for processing cassava for bread

Folklore & Traditional Terms

Anansi/Hanaasi   Popular character in local folklore, portrayed as the trickster and hero of local tales

Bram   A dance party held at Christmas; a type of dance at parties

Brokdong/Brukdown   Traditional folk music, from "break down"

Gombeh   Typical hand drum made with goatskin

Punta   Sensual and vigorous dance, also refers to its accompanying music

Sambai   Full-moon fertility dance

Tata Duhendeh   Mythical forest gnome, with no thumbs and backward feet

Wine op   A lively, hip-swinging dance

SPANISH TERMS

Basic Phrases

English	Spanish	Pronunciation
Good morning	**Buenos días**	*Bweh*-nohss *dee*-ahss
Good afternoon/ evening	**Buenas tardes**	*Bweh*-nahss *tahr*-dehs
Good night	**Buenas noches**	*Bweh*-nahss *noh*-chehs
How are you?	**¿Cómo está usted?**	*Koh*-moh eh-*stah* oo-*stehd*
Very well	**Muy bien**	Mwee byehn
Thank you	**Gracias**	*Grah*-syahss
Good-bye	**Adios**	Ad-*dyohss*
Please	**Por favor**	Pohr fah-*vohr*
Yes	**Sí**	See
No	**No**	Noh
Excuse me (to get by someone)	**Perdóneme**	Pehr-*doh*-neh-meh
Excuse me (to begin a question)	**Disculpe**	Dee-*skool*-peh
Give me	**Deme**	*Deh*-meh
Where is . . . ?	**¿Dónde está . . . ?**	*Dohn*-deh eh-*stah*
the station	**la estación**	la eh-*stah*-syohn
the bus stop	**la parada**	la pah-*rah*-dah
a hotel	**un hotel**	oon oh-*tehl*
a restaurant	**un restaurante**	oon reh-stow-*rahn*-teh
the toilet	**el servicio**	el ser-*bee*-syoh
To the right	**A la derecha**	Ah lah deh-*reh*-chah
To the left	**A la izquierda**	Ah lah ee-*skyehr*-dah
Straight ahead	**Adelante**	Ah-deh-*lahn*-teh
I would like . . .	**Quiero . . .**	*Kyeh*-roh
to eat	**comer**	ko-*mehr*
a room	**una habitación**	oo-nah ah-bee-tah-*syohn*
How much is it?	**¿Cuánto?**	*Kwahn*-toh
The check	**La cuenta**	La *kwen*-tah

English	Spanish	Pronunciation
When?	¿Cuándo?	Kwahn-doh
What?	¿Qué?	Keh
What time is it?	¿Qué hora es?	Keh oh-rah ehss
Yesterday	Ayer	Ah-yehr
Today	Hoy	Oy
Tomorrow	Mañana	Mah-nyah-nah
Breakfast	Desayuno	Deh-sah-yoo-noh
Lunch	Almuerzo	Ahl-mwehr-soh
Dinner	Cena	Ceh-nah
Do you speak English?	¿Habla usted inglés?	Ah-blah oo-stehd een-glehss
Is there anyone here who speaks English?	¿Hay alguien aquí que hable inglés?	Eye ahl-gyehn ah-kee keh ah-bleh een-glehss
I speak a little Spanish.	Hablo un poco de español.	Ah-bloh oon poh-koh deh eh-spah-nyohl
I don't understand Spanish very well.	No (lo) entiendo muy bien el español.	Noh (loh) ehn-tyehn-doh mwee byehn el eh-spah-nyohl

Numbers

English	Spanish	Pronunciation
one	uno	oo-noh
two	dos	dohss
three	tres	trehss
four	cuatro	kwah-troh
five	cinco	seen-koh
six	seis	sayss
seven	siete	syeh-teh
eight	ocho	oh-choh
nine	nueve	nweh-beh
ten	diez	dyehss
eleven	once	ohn-seh
twelve	doce	doh-seh
thirteen	trece	treh-seh
fourteen	catorce	kah-tohr-seh
fifteen	quince	keen-seh
sixteen	dieciséis	dyeh-see-sayss
seventeen	diecisiete	dyeh-see-syeh-teh
eighteen	dieciocho	dyeh-syoh-choh
nineteen	diecinueve	dyeh-see-nweh-beh
twenty	veinte	bayn-teh
thirty	treinta	trayn-tah
forty	cuarenta	kwah-rehn-tah
fifty	cincuenta	seen-kwehn-tah
sixty	sesenta	seh-sehn-tah

English	Spanish	Pronunciation
seventy	**setenta**	seh-*tehn*-tah
eighty	**ochenta**	oh-*chehn*-tah
ninety	**noventa**	noh-*behn*-tah
one hundred	**cien**	syehn
one thousand	**mil**	meel

Days of the Week

English	Spanish	Pronunciation
Monday	**lunes**	*loo*-nehss
Tuesday	**martes**	*mahr*-tehss
Wednesday	**miércoles**	*myehr*-koh-lehs
Thursday	**jueves**	*wheh*-behss
Friday	**viernes**	*byehr*-nehss
Saturday	**sábado**	*sah*-bah-doh
Sunday	**domingo**	doh-*meen*-goh

Index

See also Accommodations and Restaurant indexes, below.

General Index

A

Photo Credits

Map List

Frommer's Belize, 2nd Edition

Published by
FROMMER MEDIA LLC

ISBN 978-1-62887-386-3 (paper), 978-1-62887-387-0 (e-book)

Editorial Director: Pauline Frommer
Editor: Pauline Frommer
Production Editor: Cheryl Lenser
Cartographer: Roberta Stockwell
Photo Editor: Meghan Lamb
Indexer: Maro Riofrancos
Cover Design: David Riedy

For information on our other products or services, see www.frommers.com.

Frommer Media LLC also publishes its books in a variety of electronic formats. Some content that
appears in print may not be available in electronic formats.

Manufactured in the United States of America

5   4   3   2   1

ABOUT THE AUTHOR

Ali Wunderman is a travel writer, guidebook author, and wildlife journalist and photographer with her work appearing in more than 25 publications. Ali's writing helps other travelers have memorable experiences in the places she loves most, including by illuminating ethical wildlife tourism practices. Central America holds a special place in Ali's heart for creating the foundation for her travel infatuation, though you might just as easily spot her in Iceland, Colombia, or anywhere interesting animals roam. Ali was born and raised in San Francisco, but now splits her time between northern Montana and Belize, along with her husband Michael and their rescue mutt Sophie. Ali also runs a wildlife blog called The Naturalist, and is certified in forklift operation and cow AI, neither of which has ever helped her writing career (yet).

ABOUT THE FROMMER TRAVEL GUIDES

For most of the past 50 years, Frommer's has been the leading series of travel guides in North America, accounting for as many as 24% of all guidebooks sold. I think I know why.

Though we hope our books are entertaining, we nevertheless deal with travel in a serious fashion. Our guidebooks have never looked on such journeys as a mere recreation, but as a far more important human function, a time of learning and introspection, an essential part of a civilized life. We stress the culture, lifestyle, history, and beliefs of the destinations we cover, and urge our readers to seek out people and new ideas as the chief rewards of travel.

We have never shied from controversy. We have, from the beginning, encouraged our authors to be intensely judgmental, critical—both pro and con—in their comments, and wholly independent. Our only clients are our readers, and we have triggered the ire of countless prominent sorts, from a tourist newspaper we called "practically worthless" (it unsuccessfully sued us) to the many rip-offs we've condemned.

And because we believe that travel should be available to everyone regardless of their incomes, we have always been cost-conscious at every level of expenditure. Though we have broadened our recommendations beyond the budget category, we insist that every lodging we include be sensibly priced. We use every form of media to assist our readers, and are particularly proud of our feisty daily website, the award-winning Frommers.com.

I have high hopes for the future of Frommer's. May these guidebooks, in all the years ahead, continue to reflect the joy of travel and the freedom that travel represents. May they always pursue a cost-conscious path, so that people of all incomes can enjoy the rewards of travel. And may they create, for both the traveler and the persons among whom we travel, a community of friends, where all human beings live in harmony and peace.

Arthur Frommer

Before, During, or After your use of a Frommer's guidebook... you'll want to consult

FROMMERS.COM

FROMMERS.COM IS KEPT UP-TO-DATE, WITH:

NEWS
The latest events (and deals) to affect your next vacation

BLOGS
Opinionated comments by our outspoken staff

FORUMS
Post your travel questions, get answers from other readers

SLIDESHO
On weekly-changing, practical but i

CONTEST
Enabling you to win f

PODCAST
Of our weekly, nationwid

DESTINATI
Hundreds of cities, their hotels, r

TRIP IDEA
Valuable, offbeat suggestions fo

*AND MUCH M

Smart travelers consult Fr

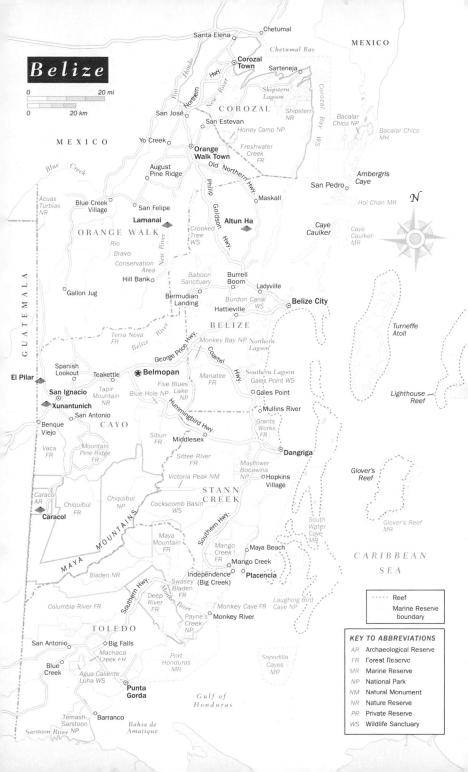

THE WORLD'S MOST TRUSTED TRAVEL AUTHORITY SINCE 195...

Cut through the online clutter! No one wants to click through hundreds of page of Web reviews, wondering which ones to trust. Frommer's experts know ever corner of Belize and they're not afraid to tell the truth about where to eat, stay and play. That's what's made Frommer's America's favorite travel source for nearl 60 years.

- *Detailed maps and a pullout map*
- *Candid, unbiased reviews of the best of Belize*
- *Helpful itineraries*
- *Exact pricing, so there's never any guessing*
- *Smart advice on guided tours, boa rentals, and adventure packages*
- *Picks for every budget, from affordable to luxury*
- *Hidden gems you'll only learn about from Frommer's*

Say hello to the Belize of your dreams—snorkel or scuba dive in the translucen seas surrounding the second longest barrier reef on the planet, climb ancien Mayan pyramids and spelunk through caves filled with archeological artifact from that mighty civilization, hike through dense virgin forests alive with the songs of more than 300 species of birds, fish, swim and kayak in some of the best protected waters in this hemisphere, and rest in quaint B&B's, oceanfron hotels, or plush jungle resorts. Our author has personally visited every hotel, shop restaurant, attraction, and nightspot listed in this book—and hundreds more—t guide you on the trip of a lifetime!

Cover design by David Riedy

Cover image: (front) Keel-billed Toucan © Ondrej Prosicky / Shutterstock.com; (back) Xunantunich ruins, Belize © aindigo / Shutterstock.com

Raincoast/PGC
CDN $29.95

ISBN: 978-1-62887-386-3

51995

9 781628 873863

Frommer's